Library of
Davidson College

Peasants and Governments

Peasants and Governments

An Economic Analysis

David Bevan, Paul Collier, and Jan Willem Gunning
with Arne Bigsten and Paul Horsnell

CLARENDON PRESS · OXFORD
1989

Oxford University Press, Walton Street, Oxford OX2 6DP
Oxford New York Toronto
Delhi Bombay Calcutta Madras Karachi
Petaling Jaya Singapore Hong Kong Tokyo
Nairobi Dar es Salaam Cape Town
Melbourne Auckland
and associated companies in
Berlin Ibadan

Oxford is a trade mark of Oxford University Press

Published in the United States
by Oxford University Press, New York

© D. L. Bevan, P. Collier and J. W. Gunning

All rights reserved. No part of this publication may be reproduced,
stored in a retrieval system, or transmitted, in any form or by any means,
electronic, mechanical, photocopying, recording, or otherwise, without
the prior permission of Oxford University Press

British Library Cataloguing in Publication Data
Bevan, David, 1944–
Peasants and government: an economic analysis
1. Kenya. Tanzania. Kenya & Tanzania.
Peasants. Economic aspects
I. Title II. Collier, Paul III. Gunning,
Jan Willem
305.5'63
ISBN 0–19–828621–X

Library of Congress Cataloging in Publication Data
data available

Printed in Great Britain by
Bookcraft Ltd., Midsomer Norton, Bath

Acknowledgements

Many people and organizations have contributed to this study besides those whose names appear on the cover. In both Tanzania and Kenya the Bureau of Statistics provided assistance without which the surveys in their present form would have been infeasible. We thank the Directors, Mr Mbalilaki and Mr Agunda, and their staffs for their co-operation and efficiency. In both countries academic economists participated in the design of the survey and led the fieldwork. Dr Amani and Dr Ndulu of the Department of Economics, University of Dar es Salaam, and Dr Ruigu and Dr Alila of the Institute for Development Studies, University of Nairobi, made contributions without which the present work would not have existed. The laborious task of data cleaning and programming was undertaken by teams based in Gothenburg, led by Renato Aguilar, and in Oxford, led by Paul Horsnell. Major funding was provided by the World Bank and additional funding was provided by the ILO, by UNICEF, and by the Central Bank of Sweden Tercentenary Foundation. At the World Bank, Shankar Acharya participated in the original design of the research, and our work was monitored helpfully by Robert Liebenthal and David Greene. At UNICEF we were helped by Urban Jonson. The manuscript has been typed by Sally Austin, Nicola Ralph, and Caroline Wise. Often under pressure, they have kept their good humour.

Contents

List of Tables	ix
1. Introduction	1

I. The Peasant Economies of Kenya and Tanzania

2. Peasant Farming in Kenya, 1974–1982	7
3. Peasant Farming in Tanzania, 1969–1983	43

II. Peasants and Price Volatility: Theory and an Application to Kenya

4. Introduction to Part II	71
5. The Response to Price Windfalls: Some Theoretical Considerations	74
6. Responses to Price Changes in Kenya	84
7. A Comparison with Tanzania	140

III. Peasant Supply Response to Shortages: Theory and an Application to Tanzania

8. Introduction to Part III	153
9. The Theory of Peasant Supply Response under Shortages	157
10. Time Series Tests of Aggregate Supply Response	173
11. Cross-section Tests of Household Supply Response	205
12. Conclusion to Part III	214

IV. Peasants and Public Services

13. Introduction to Part IV	223
14. The Distribution of Public Services in Kenya and Tanzania	229
15. An Analysis of the Effects of Public Service Provision	277
16. Peasants and Governments	291
Appendix: The Rural Surveys	299
References	335
Index	339

List of Tables

Table 2.1.	Quantities and prices of crops by marketing channels	13
Table 2.2.	The hiring in and out of labour by farm size, 1974–1975	16
Table 2.3.	The effect of labour transactions on peasant factor proportions	18
Table 2.4.	Endowment ratios (e-ratio) before and after adjustment	19
Table 2.5.	Income structure of resident households by per capita income quintiles	24
Table 2.6.	The subsistence percentage of farm income	25
Table 2.7.	Distribution of households by activity mix	26
Table 2.8.	Mean household per capita income by activity mix	28
Table 2.9.	Per capita income structure of resident households by holding size	30
Table 2.10.	Peasant agricultural production	31
Table 2.11.	Real-producer prices, 1964–1983	32
Table 2.12.	Peasant incomes in Central and Nyanza Provinces, 1974/1975–1982	33
Table 2.13.	Comparison of income quintiles	34
Table 2.14.	Entry into and exit from household activities	35
Table 2.15.	Coffee and tea producer prices	37
Table 2.16.	Use of extra coffee boom money	39
Table 3.1.	Quantities (Q) and prices (P) of crops by marketing channels, 1983	47
Table 3.2.	Endowment ratios (e) before and after adjustment	48
Table 3.3.	Availability of twenty-five foodstuffs in twenty markets	50
Table 3.4.	Availability of goods in the four regions, 1983	51
Table 3.5.	Dispatches of corrugated iron sheets, 1975–1981	52
Table 3.6.	BIT deliveries of Matsushita radios to the regions, 1975–1982	53
Table 3.7.	Participation in black markets	53
Table 3.8.	Income structure of resident households by per capita income quintiles and regions	54
Table 3.9.	The subsistence percentage of farm income	55
Table 3.10.	Distribution of households by activity mix	56
Table 3.11.	Per capita income structure of resident households by holding size	57
Table 3.12.	Production for sale, 1969–1983	57
Table 3.13.	Changes in income composition, 1979/1980–1982/1983	59
Table 3.14.	Changes in income composition, 1976/1977–1982/1983	60

List of Tables

Table 3.15.	The composition of income in 1976–1977; national, four regions, and traced samples	61
Table 3.16.	Changes in income composition, 1969–1982/1983	62
Table 3.17.	Trends in real income, 1969–1982/1983	63
Table 3.18.	A comparison of trends in rural and urban incomes	64
Table 3.19.	Use of extra coffee boom money (Kilimanjaro)	66
Table 5.1.	A taxonomy of price changes	74
Table 5.2.	A taxonomy of income changes	82
Table 6.1.	Coffee production statistics	86
Table 6.2.	Coffee production function: Cobb–Douglas results (unrestricted)	87
Table 6.3.	F-values and significance levels for economies of scale test: Cobb–Douglas results	88
Table 6.4.	Coffee production function: Cobb–Douglas results (restricted)	89
Table 6.5.	Coffee production function: CES results	90
Table 6.5a.	Degrees of freedom (DF) and sum of squares for CES results	90
Table 6.6.	Maize production function: Cobb–Douglas results (unrestricted)	91
Table 6.7.	Maize production function: Cobb–Douglas results (restricted)	92
Table 6.8.	Livestock production function: value of milk production as dependent variable	93
Table 6.9.	Livestock production function: value of improved cattle offtake as dependent variable	93
Table 6.10.	Frequency distributions of the shadow wage in maize	100
Table 6.11.	Difference between provinces in activity mixes	104
Table 6.12.	Fixed costs of 1 hectare of coffee	108
Table 6.13.	Factor proportions in maize and coffee	108
Table 6.14.	Logit of coffee adoption and growing	113
Table 6.15.	Variations in the capital proxy	113
Table 6.16.	Logit of tea adoption and growing	114
Table 6.17.	Two hypothetical sequences of adoption	115
Table 6.18.	Logit of improved livestock adoption	117
Table 6.19.	Determinants of employment in non-shamba activities	119
Table 6.20.	Employment opportunities in the formal sector resulting from the boom	131
Table 7.1.	A comparison of income composition of peasant households around 1975	141
Table 7.2.	A comparison of changes in real income	142
Table 7.3.	Permanent and transient investment compared	145
Table 8.1.	Availability of consumer goods in villages, 1986	155

List of Tables

Table 9.1.	Supply response to changes in crop prices or availability in the case of rationing (for given black-market prices)	169
Table 10.1.	HBS weights for availability indices	176
Table 10.2.	Availability of goods in Tanzania, 1978–1983 (HBS weights)	176
Table 10.3.	Recollection weights for availability indices	178
Table 10.4.	Availability of goods in Tanzania, 1978–1983 (recollection weights)	178
Table 10.5.	Incentive weights for availability indices	179
Table 10.6.	Availability of goods in Tanzania, 1978–1983 (incentive weights)	179
Table 10.7.	Penetration of goods from factory gate to village shops	180
Table 10.8.	HBS weights for distribution indices	181
Table 10.9.	Distribution of goods to RTCs, 1981–1985 (HBS weights)	182
Table 10.10.	Recollection weights for distribution indices	182
Table 10.11.	Distribution of goods to RTCs, 1981–1985 (recollection weights)	183
Table 10.12.	Incentive weights for distribution indices	183
Table 10.13.	Distribution of goods to RTCs, 1981–1985 (incentive weights)	184
Table 10.14.	Output of peasant cash crops by crop, 1975/1976–1985/1986	185
Table 10.15.	Output of peasant cash crops by region and crop, 1975/1976–1985/1986	186
Table 10.16.	Real value of cash crop production by region and crop, 1975/1976–1985/1986	190
Table 10.17.	Real value of cash crop production by region, 1975–1986	193
Table 10.18.	Estimated food crop acreages and yields	194
Table 10.19.	Current period output on current period rationing (availability indices)	195
Table 10.20.	Next period output on current period rationing (availability indices)	195
Table 10.21.	Current period output on current period rationing (distribution indices)	196
Table 10.22.	Next period output on current period rationing (distribution indices)	197
Table 10.23.	A simulation of the government view of incentive goods	198
Table 10.24.	One-way random effects model (logarithmic form)	199
Table 10.25.	The role of price effects	203
Table 11.1.	Supply response to availability on official markets for households making purchases in the black market	212
Table 14.1.	Sample sizes for Kenyan and Tanzanian rural and urban surveys	244

Table 14A.1.	Morbidity: frequency and severity by symptom over the preceding three months, when symptoms are so severe as to curtail activity	246
Table 14A.2.	Morbidity: frequency and severity by age and sex over preceding three months, when symptoms are so severe as to curtail activity	247
Table 14A.3.	Morbidity: incidence of illness by per capita income quintile over preceding three months, all cases	248
Table 14A.4.	Morbidity: action taken by symptom, for most recent illness, % of cases	249
Table 14A.5.	Morbidity: percentage of ill persons getting formal treatment by education of eldest wife and distance to health facility (Kenya only)	249
Table 14A.6.	Morbidity: percentage of population ill by age, sex, and symptom	250
Table 14A.7.	Morbidity: source of water by frequency of illness	251
Table 14B.1.	Outpatient costs over the preceding three months by per capita income quintile	253
Table 14B.2.	Outpatient costs over the preceding three months by type of facility	256
Table 14B.3.	Annual inpatient frequency and costs per stay by per capita income quintile	259
Table 14B.4.	Annual inpatient frequency and costs per stay by type of facility	260
Table 14C.1.	Primary and secondary school attainment by sex and per capita income quintile	261
Table 14C.2.	Adult literacy by per capita income quintiles	262
Table 14C.3.	Annual education costs by per capita income quintile	263
Table 14C.4.	Annual education costs by educational level and per capita income quintiles	265
Table 14D.1.	Government services: most valued improvements	266
Table 14E.1.	Allocation of time by age and sex	268
Table 14E.2.	Allocation of time by relationship to household head	271
Table 14E.3.	Allocation of time by highest education level attained	273
Table 14F.1.	Tanzania: rural–urban comparison	275
Table 15.1.	Time and cash costs per head per year	279
Table 15.2.	Impact of some primary education	282
Table 15.3.	Impact of completing primary education	282
Table 15.4.	Impact of some secondary education	282
Table 15.5.	Impact of extension advice	283
Table 15.6.	Impact of adult days ill on production	284
Table 15.7.	Coefficients of estimated illness equation	285
Table 15.8.	Logit of propensity to use health facility	286

Table 15.9.	Days ill as a function of the propensity to use health facilities	287
Table 15.10.	Labour supply in Kenya	288
Table 15.11.	Time spent fetching water	288
Table A1.	Sample clusters, Kenya	300
Table A2.	Number of cases by region, Tanzania	302
Table A3.	Sample clusters, Tanzania	303

1
Introduction

Peasants form the vast majority of the poor in developing countries. Whether policies can be effective in alleviating poverty is therefore largely a question of the relation between peasants and governments. There are obviously numerous ways in which governments can (and do) affect peasants, either directly or indirectly. An exhaustive treatment is clearly impossible and in this book we are, in fact, highly selective. We focus on two East African countries, Kenya and Tanzania, in a particular period, 1975–83. This implies that we restrict attention to the channels of government influence on peasants which were most important in these countries and at that time. There are four such channels. One of these (the effect of trade, investment, and stabilization policies on the prices paid by peasants for non-agricultural goods) is treated in a companion volume, *Controlled Open Economies* (Bevan *et al.*, 1989). The other three, producer pricing, the availability of non-agricultural consumer goods in rural areas, and the provision of public services, form the subject of the present book. The way the two East African governments affected peasants in these three areas is, we believe, of wider significance.

Both countries benefited from an extraordinarily large terms of trade improvement during the coffee boom of 1976–8 when coffee prices quadrupled following frost damage to coffee crops in Brazil. We will have much to say about the consequences for peasants of this large temporary shock and of the way it was handled by the two governments. This book is, however, intended to be much more than an account of the coffee boom in East Africa. There are two reasons why an analysis of peasant farming in Kenya and Tanzania in the period of the coffee boom has wider significance.

First, commodity price instability is an experience common to many developing countries and the merits of international or national price stabilization have been debated for decades. In this debate it is often implicitly assumed that peasants are unable to handle shocks efficiently and that governments should isolate them from price instability. This argument sees peasants as myopic, unable to recognize a price increase as temporary, and therefore unlikely to attempt to convert it into a permanent income increase through investment. Alternatively, it may be argued that peasants, while willing to save most of the windfall, are unlikely to be able to invest those savings efficiently. For investigating these arguments the East African evidence is particularly relevant.

The most common reaction of governments in developing countries to positive trade shocks has been to adopt a stabilization policy, for example through export taxation. However, Kenya chose to pass the price increase, initially untaxed, on to coffee growers, most of whom are peasants. The Kenyan experience therefore provides a fairly rare opportunity to observe how peasants react to a boom when given the opportunity. The East African evidence indicates that the assumptions often made about that case are wildly off the mark: peasants chose to save a very large proportion of the income, which they recognized as transient, and used these savings wisely. In contrast the Tanzanian government taxed coffee exports very heavily: so heavily that Tanzanian coffee producers hardly experienced a boom. Since pre-boom peasant saving behaviour was very similar in the two countries, comparisons over time for Kenya can be complemented with comparisons between countries for the period of the boom.

Secondly, the boom episode is valuable even if one is not interested in the questions directly related to the boom itself. The boom represented a change so large that the reactions to it are clearly identifiable, providing an opportunity to analyse the economy of peasant farming by highlighting processes which are otherwise extremely difficult to disentangle. We identify a combination of factors in peasant farming which make the process of investment one of large, discrete jumps, instead of consisting of continual, marginal adjustments. One reason is the imperfection of the markets for land, labour, and credit; another the presence of economies of scale (for example, in coffee growing) or indivisibilities (for example, in livestock ownership); and a final one the lack of full information about agricultural activities and the risks associated with them. We show that this defines a hierarchy of activities. Rates of return differ enormously between activities, but there are barriers to entry (for example, credit constraints) into the more profitable activities. As a result peasants follow particular sequences of adjustment to their activity mix, such as starting with the production of food crops only and saving until enough has been accumulated to add livestock, then moving on to cash crops and, finally, to the activity with the highest return: non-agricultural wage employment. The income effect of a boom relaxes credit constraints; as part of the boom-induced investment behaviour we may therefore be able to observe activity switches.

While in Kenya the government exposed peasants to price volatility, in Tanzania peasants were affected by government policies mainly through the effects of these policies on the availability of urban goods in rural areas. Tanzania attempted to control both the retail prices of a wide range of non-agricultural consumer goods and the geographical allocation of these goods (whether domestically produced or imported). As a result peasants were rationed in their demand for urban goods. We study the consequences of this both theoretically and empirically. Some Tanzanian policies towards peasants are so much *sui generis* that they are not of wider interest. Examples are the physical relocation and concentration of the majority of the rural population in 1974 away from the fields they had been working, and acreage

Introduction

restrictions, requiring peasants to allocate particular areas of their plots to designated crops. However, this is not true for the effect of government policies on the rural availability of consumer goods, which, unfortunately, is a problem in many countries besides Tanzania (an extreme example is Mozambique). The questions which we address concern the effect of rationing on the production of cash crops; the effect of uncertain availability on peasants' production and money balances; the extent to which the existence of a black market changes the results; and the extent to which peasants in Tanzania were in fact able to circumvent price control through black-market transactions. These questions are of considerable practical importance: many African countries receive policy advice which ignores the microeconomic consequences of existing rural shortages.

In many parts of this book we rely heavily on evidence from surveys conducted by us in Kenya and Tanzania in co-operation with the Universities of Nairobi and of Dar es Salaam. These surveys provide a wealth of data on peasant households in the two countries. We rely particularly heavily on this data source for the analysis of the third channel of government influence on peasants: the provision of public services, particularly road improvements, extension advice, water supply, schools, and health facilities. The questions which we address in this area concern the peasants' subjective evaluation of the usefulness of these services; their direct productive effects, as measured by production functions; their indirect effects measured by the time spent by household members, for example fetching water or travelling to health facilities; and the effect of the use of piped water or of various health facilities on the morbidity of peasant households. Since health questions were asked of all households in the sample, irrespective of whether they made use of public services when ill, we avoid the usual bias which arises when only those actually using health facilities are studied. This is important since we find that the need for medical attention (as indicated by particular symptoms) is very imperfectly correlated with access to health services. We conclude that much of what governments provide to peasants in the form of public services is in fact extremely useful.

The plan of the book is as follows. In Part I we present a descriptive account of peasant farming in Kenya (Chapter 2) and Tanzania (Chapter 3). The theory of peasant behaviour under price volatility is discussed, extended, and applied to Kenya in Part II. We consider boom-related investment (including coffee planting) in the light of the theory of dynamic resource allocation in the presence of scale economies and market imperfections. Peasant behaviour under shortages is the subject of Part III, which includes tests of the theory developed, using the Tanzanian survey data. Part IV is devoted to the government's influence on peasants through the provision of public services. The final chapter contains our conclusions.

I
The Peasant Economies of Kenya and Tanzania

2
Peasant Farming in Kenya, 1974–1982

2.1. Introduction

The period 1974–82 straddles the largest income shock ever experienced by Kenyan peasants. Between 1976 and 1979 the world prices of coffee and tea were temporarily high as a result of a frost in Brazil. The terms of trade gain during these years was worth one-third of 1975 GDP. Due to President Kenyatta's decision not to impose a windfall coffee tax, this boom was experienced directly in coffee- and tea-growing small farm areas. Some households received income windfalls, and all households faced changed relative crop prices and enhanced opportunities for employment and migration. These shocks induced behavioural responses in the form of investment and changes in the deployment of resources between activities, of which the most obvious was extra planting of coffee. To identify these changes, let alone to understand them, is a demanding undertaking because of the paucity of data on peasant households. For example, extra coffee planting might have been induced by changed price expectations, or by an enhanced capacity to finance the investment involved in tree crops. Our first task was therefore to secure a data set adequate to investigate processes of change.

Fortunately, the first national rural household budget survey, IRS1, had been conducted in 1974/5 by the Bureau of Statistics, and this provided an excellent snapshot of the peasant economy on the eve of the coffee boom. The Bureau made the survey data fully available to the study. In order to provide a similar snapshot of the peasant economy post-boom a survey was mounted in 1982 by the authors in conjunction with the Bureau of Statistics and the Institute for Development Studies at the University of Nairobi. This survey was not national but covered two major regions, Central Province and Nyanza, which between them account for nearly half the rural population. The two provinces were selected on the grounds that Central has the principal coffee-growing region whereas Nyanza has little coffee but a comparable level of household income. The survey is fully described in the Appendix, but two important features deserve mention here. The purpose of the survey was to identify change rather than to portray a non-comparable snapshot. One approach to this was to devote a section of the questionnaire to recall questions about the circumstances of the household in 1975. Clearly such questions are demanding and the eventual form of the questionnaire reflected extensive experimentation during piloting. Our second approach was to use as our sample households which had been included in a previous Bureau of

Statistics survey, IRS3, conducted in 1977/8. Although it would have been preferable to trace the households in IRS1, both because of the date and because it was a considerably better survey, this was not possible. Our third approach was to design the questionnaire in such a way that the concepts of the household, income, and other key variables could be constructed so as to be compatible with IRS1 and IRS4. To our knowledge this is the first large-sample trace of peasant households conducted in Africa. It has generated a set of panel data from which questions of income and activity mobility can be addressed.

Although between them these surveys provide a basis for identifying the changes which took place between 1974 and 1982, to understand the behaviour which brought them about requires more than a statistical analysis of interrelationships between variables. This episode must be placed in the context of the longer-run evolution of the peasant economy and the institutional environment in which peasants operate. Section 2.2 describes the evolution of the peasant economy prior to the coffee boom, the central theme being that during the period 1900–74 there were such powerful shocks and regime changes that the pattern observed in the mid-1970s cannot be regarded as reflecting a fully adjusted steady state. One effect of the coffee boom may therefore be to have accelerated adjustments towards the steady state. Conversely, some of the observed changes between 1974 and 1982 were adjustments which would have happened even without the boom. In addition to slow adjustments towards the steady state, the Kenyan peasant economy is characterized by secular trends such as population growth which are rapidly changing the steady state itself. Kenya combines the fastest population growth rate in the world with little spare land and a low proportion of employment in the non-agricultural sector. Factor proportions in agriculture are thus altering rapidly. This has led some commentators[1] to predict a crisis. Whether or not such forecasts (or more accurately prophecies) are fulfilled will largely depend upon the capacity of the peasant economy to exploit new opportunities. Thus, the Kenyan peasant economy is radically different from areas such as South Asia and Java where settlement patterns have been subject to only gradual change, and can be regarded as closely tracking a slowly evolving steady state.

Section 2.3 provides an overview of the structure of product and factor markets in which peasants operate. Product markets, although subject to extensive regulation and government-sustained monopoly, do not generate the type of problems encountered in Tanzania. Factor markets in contrast are very underdeveloped. Few land transactions occur and only around 6 per cent of labour input on peasant holdings goes through the market. Informal credit channels are miniscule, there being no specialist money-lenders, and insurance is unobtainable despite pervasive risks. The implication of this

[1] e.g. Hunt (1984).

bifurcation between product and factor markets is that either the former bear much of the burden normally undertaken by the latter in achieving allocative efficiency across holdings, or else the shadow prices of factors are holding-specific. This has powerful corollaries for the effects of the coffee boom which are drawn out in our theoretical discussion in Chapter 5.

In measuring changes in the peasant economy between the eve of the boom (1974/5) and its aftermath (1982), it is useful to start from a bench-mark description. Although for narrative purposes it is desirable to start from the beginning of our episode, describing the situation in 1974/5 and then investigating changes, analytically prospective and retrospective accounts are equivalent. Because our 1982 snapshot is generated through our purpose-designed survey we are able to provide a somewhat fuller account of the aftermath. Hence, Section 2.4 describes the peasant economy in 1982 and Section 2.5 describes the income changes between that time and the eve of the boom. Finally, Section 2.6 describes how peasants recall having reacted to the coffee boom and what they thought about these reactions by 1982.

2.2. The Evolution of the Peasant Economy before the Coffee Boom

Until the nineteenth century the interior of Kenya had remarkably limited external contacts. Agriculture was subsistence orientated although there was local trading in food and some long-distance trade in iron and salt. Some tribes depended upon nomadic pastoralism, but even those which cultivated crops practised shifting cultivation since land was abundant.

At the turn of the century white settlement took place. Large areas of land were alienated, the White Highlands were created, and the settlers embarked upon export crop agriculture. Coffee and sisal were introduced on these farms, followed by wheat, maize, and tea. Prior to 1914 African farmers were quite successful in exploiting the new markets, supplying 65 per cent of grain exports and 20 per cent of cotton (Mosley, 1983, p. 74). In contrast, many of the settler enterprises were financially precarious. While the settlers were never in full control of policy, they succeeded in introducing an array of interventions designed to reduce the supply price of African labour. African settlement was restricted to the reserves, causing land pressure; hut and poll taxes were introduced, generating a need for cash income; and the Kipande system of registration for labourers was used to enforce contracts. By the 1920s at least a fifth of the African male labour force was working on settler farms (Collier and Lal, 1986, Table 1).

These cheap-labour policies were reinforced by restrictions on the agricultural activities permitted to Africans. Crucially for our story, Africans were not permitted to grow coffee in competition with settlers. Africans wished to grow coffee: in the 1920s Kikuyu farmers had attempted to get permission but were refused after settler pressure. Despite a pilot scheme in 1937, the ban on coffee production, in Central Province, now accounting for 70 per cent of output, was not lifted until 1951 (Heyer, 1981, p. 103). The ostensible rationale, that is, poor husbandry, disease risk, and the erosion of a reputation for quality, was undermined by the success of African coffee production in Tanganyika and Uganda. Similarly, the authorities restricted African production of livestock, African areas being almost constantly in quarantine. These overt restrictions were further supplemented by the settlers' control of the marketing boards and the orientation of the transport and extension services.

During the 1930s this system started to unwind as a result of the Depression, which bankrupted many settlers, and a shift in agricultural policy which devoted some attention to African agriculture. However, the latter was focused primarily upon soil conservation (a colonial obsession) and food supply. Africans were still excluded from coffee, tea, and pyrethrum production. A further factor undermining the settler monopoly was that while working on settler farms Africans were learning new techniques and acquiring incomes which could be invested. African agriculture became more productive and the area under cultivation increased.

After 1945 agricultural policy gradually shifted further towards a pro-peasant stance as resources were devoted towards roads, marketing, processing, and extension. However, the world commodity boom revived the settler economy which in turn augmented migration and wage labour. The Mau Mau revolt (1952) triggered a major acceleration in the trend on policy (the Swynnerton Plan). This launched the authorities upon the path of encouraging the development of a prosperous commercial peasantry, growing cash crops, with access to credit and extension services, and with the security of tenure conferred by land registration.

When restrictions on coffee growing were lifted, coffee production was rapidly adopted by African farmers. Although the programme was strictly controlled and high standards of husbandry were required, by 1960 there were 105,000 growers and by 1964 236,000 out of a population of around 1.5 million peasant households. Planting was mainly concentrated in Central Province and in Kisii in Nyanza. Tea production was also adopted following the policy change and the establishment of the Kenya Tea Development Authority: by 1964 there were some 22,000 growers. Similarly, in 1955 the Veterinary Department agreed to a controlled introduction of grade cattle into African areas and by the 1960s milk and beef production represented a considerable component of peasant income.

The relaxation of controls ushered in a phase of remarkable growth in peasant marketed output. Between 1954 and 1964 growth averaged 7.3 per cent per annum, and this accelerated in the next decade to 12.6 per cent. Although the removal of controls coincided with some positive interventions it seems likely that the former were decisive. To quote a knowledgeable commentator:

With hindsight, it seems likely that the initial success of the Swynnerton Plan was not due to the process of consolidation and registration per se, but rather to the final removal of restrictions on certain cash crops. (Smith, 1976, pp. 128–9)

The removal of controls was an economic success but a political failure for the authorities, since it did not check the movement towards Independence, the most crucial obstacle to which was the land claims of the settlers. This was accommodated in a way which had important consequences for the subsequent tenure system. The settler farms were bought out (financed by British aid) and some 40 per cent of the area was devoted to settlement schemes, the remainder being sold intact. One constraint upon further settlement was the fear that peasant farmers would not generate a marketable surplus on the land. Even, so, some 500,000 Africans were settled on the former White Highlands.

Paradoxically, the phase of decontrol of crop choice came to an end upon Independence. In 1962 the leading coffee-producing nations had come to an agreement on output restrictions to support the price. From 1964 the Kenyan government co-operated with this policy by banning further coffee planting, and formally acceded to the agreement in 1966. By then peasant coffee acreage and production exceeded that of the estates.

The renewal of restrictions upon planting was followed shortly by a further discouragement to adoption, namely the outbreak of coffee berry disease in 1967. This was compounded by a phase of low prices. Farmers neglected coffee and even uprooted it in a few cases. Policy makers responded in two ways to this stagnation. First, in 1972 the export tax on coffee which had been in force throughout the 1960s was abolished. Secondly, in 1973 a coffee rehabilitation programme was initiated. This was designed to stimulate production on already gazetted areas. Increases in acreage were encouraged but in such a way that coffee was to be grown on units of 'economic size'. The subject of scale economies in peasant coffee production, important for our analysis of coffee adoption, is rigorously investigated in Chapter 6. The consequence of these policy responses to stagnation was that by the onset of the coffee boom there were neither official restrictions on planting nor the apparatus of a coffee tax, which would not have been the case had the boom occurred four years earlier. This change in the policy environment was clearly of major importance in determining the peasant response to the boom.

2.3. The Structure of Product and Factor Markets

Peasants are price takers in all commodity markets, although in aggregate Kenya is a price taker in neither the world coffee nor the pyrethrum markets. Market institutions are an amalgam of private traders, co-operatives, and state agencies, some of which have legal monopolies. Market prices are regulated for many crops at all points in the marketing chain and at times this generates quantity rationing, although never to the extent experienced in Tanzania.

The food-marketing system is dominated by maize. Maize trading across district boundaries or in large volumes is the monopoly of the National Cereal and Produce Board (NCPB), but intra-district trade is undertaken by competitive private traders. The NCPB operates at regulated prices, designed to provide a secure market environment for peasants. The inflexibilities of price regulation have at times created the opposite effect, with peasants willing to sell finding themselves rationed. In some seasons the price has been pitched so high that NCPB grain stores have been filled to capacity and purchases unofficially suspended. Similarly, since the price is undifferentiated through the course of the year there is a powerful incentive to sell upon harvest which again creates rationing due to congestion. However, peasants always have the alternative of the intra-district free market.

The export crop marketing system is dominated by coffee, which is marketed through co-operative societies and the Coffee Board. Although the latter has an extensive apparatus of licensing and a monopoly of all trading, in pricing it operates merely as an auctioneer, charging commission on the price achieved in world markets. It also collects a 3 per cent tax levied by local councils. The Coffee Board transacts with peasants through the coffee co-operative societies, which by 1977 had a membership of 349,000. The societies have developed a range of functions from operating savings and credit schemes to the collection of income tax. The latter is arranged in a way which yields scale economies of coffee income at the level of the individual household, for the applicable rate of income tax is calculated from average coffee payments in the society and then used for all households. Thus low-income households, who would otherwise be below the income tax threshold, pay tax if they grow coffee in an area in which large growers predominate. The societies deduct a percentage of receipts to cover costs. This margin has generally been in the neighbourhood of 20 per cent but fell during the boom.

Tea is marketed through a somewhat different system. All functions, from extension, to collection, processing, and sales are undertaken by the Kenya Tea Development Authority (KTDA), which is a highly efficient organization. To some extent discipline is imposed by the technical requirements of tea, which are demanding. We will see in Chapter 6 that the KTDA appears to have been differentially effective in its extension efforts.

The pattern of marketing for each of the major crops as found in our 1982 survey is reported in Table 2.1. This confirms that whereas the cash crops are sold almost exclusively to marketing boards, food crops are sold predominantly through private traders. For example, only 7 per cent of maize sales are made to the Board, 60 per cent going to traders and the remaining 33 per cent being sold directly in markets by the producer.

TABLE 2.1. Quantities (Q) and prices (P) of crops by marketing channels

	Mean Production	Not Sold Q	Board Q	Board P	Middle man Q	Middle man P	Direct Q	Direct P	Multiple Q	Multiple P	Not stated Q	Not stated P	Cases
Central Province													
Local maize	116.6	97.1	1.4	1.8	12.2	1.2	5.9	1.8	0.0	—	0.0	—	173
Hybrid maize	363.0	298.9	4.5	1.6	37.5	1.2	19.4	1.1	2.0	1.5	0.8	3.7	314
Beans	150.8	121.0	2.3	2.7	18.6	3.3	6.3	4.7	2.4	4.2	0.1	3.4	404
Millet	0.3	0.3	0.0	—	0.0	—	0.0	—	0.0	—	0.0	—	3
Sorghum	0.6	0.6	0.0	—	0.0	—	0.0	—	0.0	—	0.0	—	1
Cassava	0.0	0.0	0.0	—	0.0	—	0.0	—	0.0	—	0.0	—	0
Ground nuts	0.0	0.0	0.0	—	0.0	—	0.0	—	0.0	—	0.0	—	0
Wheat	17.5	0.4	17.2	1.3	0.0	—	0.0	—	0.0	—	0.0	—	1
Yams	0.1	0.1	0.0	—	0.0	—	0.0	—	0.0	—	0.0	—	2
Sweet potatoes	14.8	10.1	0.0	—	4.7	1.5	0.0	—	0.0	—	0.0	—	19
Peas	11.8	7.7	0.0	—	2.1	2.2	1.9	1.8	0.0	—	0.0	—	43
Sukuma wiki	8.9	5.6	0.0	—	1.1	2.0	2.0	1.7	0.2	1.0	0.0	—	18
Other vegetables	103.5	31.3	0.0	—	66.5	0.5	2.1	2.4	0.2	5.0	3.4	0.3	42
Coffee	535.8	1.6	534.2	2.4	0.0	—	0.0	—	0.0	—	0.0	—	118
Bananas	87.2	57.8	0.0	—	20.0	1.6	7.4	1.9	1.9	1.5	0.0	—	49
Tea	636.6	2.8	625.1	1.7	0.0	—	0.0	—	0.0	—	8.6	1.0	85
Tobacco	0.0	0.0	0.0	—	0.0	—	0.0	—	0.0	—	0.0	—	0
Cotton	0.0	0.0	0.0	—	0.0	—	0.0	—	0.0	—	0.0	—	0
Pyrethrum	8.5	0.0	7.5	12.9	0.0	—	0.0	—	0.0	—	1.0	15.0	27
Sunflower	1.5	0.1	0.0	—	1.4	6.4	0.0	—	0.0	—	0.0	—	5
Sugar cane	1.4	0.8	0.0	—	0.6	0.5	0.0	—	0.0	—	0.0	—	2
Other	1018.5	741.0	101.2	1.6	123.8	0.9	31.2	1.8	8.4	1.9	12.9	1.9	303
All crops	3077.5	1377.3	1293.3	2.1	288.6	1.1	76.3	1.9	15.0	2.2	26.9	1.9	1609

TABLE 2.1. (cont.)

	Mean Production	Not Sold	Board		Middle man		Direct		Multiple		Not stated		Cases
		Q	Q	P	Q	P	Q	P	Q	P	Q	P	
Nyanza													
Local maize	513.2	445.0	5.8	1.1	31.0	1.8	30.7	1.4	0.4	1.4	0.2	1.0	259
Hybrid maize	714.8	469.6	48.6	1.1	158.0	1.1	36.8	1.3	0.1	0.6	1.7	3.0	343
Beans	122.0	97.6	2.1	4.6	15.1	3.4	6.9	3.2	0.2	1.8	0.1	3.0	236
Millet	137.9	116.6	3.4	1.7	6.9	0.9	10.6	2.7	0.0	—	0.4	2.8	148
Sorghum	96.4	94.1	0.0	—	1.3	3.1	1.0	1.7	0.0	—	0.0	—	53
Cassava	129.2	102.5	0.0	—	13.0	0.5	13.7	.0	0.0	—	0.0	—	90
Ground nuts	2.2	1.4	0.1	2.4	0.0	—	0.5	3.5	0.0	—	0.2	0.4	8
Wheat	0.0	0.0	0.0	—	0.0	—	0.0	—	0.0	—	0.0	—	0
Yams	0.0	0.0	0.0	—	0.0	—	0.0	—	0.0	—	0.0	—	0
Sweet potatoes	51.7	39.8	0.2	6.0	6.7	0.9	5.1	0.7	0.0	—	0.0	—	81
Peas	1.8	1.3	0.0	—	0.0	—	0.5	0.8	0.0	—	0.0	—	5
Sukuma wiki	16.1	9.8	0.0	—	0.2	0.4	6.1	0.4	0.0	—	0.0	—	24
Other vegetables	8.0	1.6	0.0	—	0.0	—	0.2	0.3	6.1	1.0	0.0	—	10
Coffee	98.8	0.0	98.3	1.0	0.3	1.5	0.0	—	0.0	—	0.2	1.0	86
Bananas	189.3	103.5	0.0	—	47.4	1.1	37.4	0.8	1.0	0.0	0.0	—	61
Tea	72.8	1.5	72.3	0.9	0.0	—	0.0	—	0.0	—	0.0	—	52
Tobacco	6.0	0.2	3.2	5.6	0.2	18.3	2.4	10.0	0.0	—	0.0	4.0	16
Cotton	21.3	0.6	20.0	3.2	0.7	2.0	0.0	—	0.0	—	0.0	—	21
Pyrethrum	18.0	0.7	14.3	10.4	2.9	10.0	0.0	11.4	0.0	—	0.0	—	51
Sunflower	0.0	0.0	0.0	—	0.0	—	0.0	—	0.0	—	0.0	—	0
Sugar cane	1100.6	1.5	670.2	1.4	372.6	0.1	4.4	2.0	0.0	—	51.8	1.0	14
Other	239.1	118.5	10.0	1.0	52.3	1.1	54.8	1.6	2.0	1.5	1.5	2.0	106
All crops	3539.1	1605.0	948.5	1.5	708.5	0.7	211.0	1.5	9.9	1.1	56.2	1.1	1664

While the participation of peasants in product markets is straightforward, their lack of participation in factor markets is puzzling.

In the traditional peasant economy of rural Kenya factor markets had not developed. This is not to imply that no process of resource reallocation existed, for the traditional social conventions which defined and enforced the concept of property probably operated as such a mechanism. Traditional land law afforded private rights to land which entitled a particular household to exclude others from its plot. Although such rights could be inherited, they were of usage rather than of ownership, so that households could not be excluded from permanently idle land by means of ownership claims made by other households. Since the prevailing hoe technology limited the quantity of land which a household could use, as demographic processes increased the size of some households and reduced that of others, land was reallocated between households.

In the period since Independence there have been three major changes in the nature and extent of trade in rural factor markets. Firstly, there has been substantial urbanization, most notably the growth as a result of rural-to-urban migration of the city of Nairobi. This migration was predominantly male. Urban workers commonly retained or acquired wives on rural holdings, visiting the holding occasionally and returning to it on retirement from wage employment. One consequence of this temporary male migration was extensive absenteeism from holdings: by the mid-1970s around 30 per cent of the smallholdings in Central Province were farmed by an absentee holder.

Secondly, there has been an important government programme aimed at privatizing land holdings. Substantial resources were devoted to the registration of plots and to conferring legal ownership titles upon those who made successful claims. This change provided the legal framework for land sales and tenancy, though the latter did not in fact develop. This was probably because, although the legal framework enabled tenancy, the social framework did not. Land sales were not extensive due to continued social and legal restrictions, but appear to have increased land concentration, probably as a result of the new urban middle class accumulating land as a speculative asset.

Thirdly, employment on the estates became less significant. Employment in formal sector agriculture grew slowly in absolute terms and declined as a proportion of the rural labour force. There was therefore a reduction in the opportunity for peasants to sell a proportion of their labour to estates, a process which provided one means of reducing disparities in land/labour ratios between larger and smaller holdings (which are shown below to have been large).

Hired labour still forms only a small component of total labour input on peasant holdings. Our 1982 survey found that 6 per cent of total labour input was hired, less than the 10 per cent found in the IRS1 of 1974 and similar to the 5 per cent found in a survey of Central Province in 1963. Further, much of this hired labour was used to meet seasonal labour requirements as opposed to offsetting permanent differences in land/labour ratios between households. Hired labour in the slackest four-week cycle contributed only 6 per cent of total labour input in 1974.

Of the hired labour used during the year on smallholdings, two-thirds had contracts as casual day-labour and one-third as regular (monthly based) labour. However, even the regular labour force was largely seasonal, only 30 per cent of the regular hired labour force being employed in the slackest cycle. The 1982 survey explicitly asked whether hired labourers had credit or land dealings with their employers, and found the incidence of such arrangements to be negligible: there are no inter-linked factor markets.

Table 2.2 analyses the contribution that hiring of labour by smallholders makes towards reducing *ex ante* differences in factor proportions among smallholdings, the data base being IRS1 which provides the closest approximation to national coverage currently available. *Ex ante* differences in factor endowments are large; for example, land per household member on holdings above 5 hectares is nineteen times greater than that on holdings of less than 0.5 hectares. The rows of the table show the percentages of the population, land, and hired labour distributed over holdings divided into four size classes. Thus, 13.5 per cent of the total peasant population is resident on holdings of below 0.5 hectares. The same holding size group accounts for 1.5 per cent of the total peasant land area and for 5 per cent of the total amount of labour

TABLE 2.2. *The hiring in and out of labour by farm size, 1974–1975*

	Farm size (ha)				All
	<0.5	0.5–1.9	2–4.9	5+	
% population	13.5	42.0	27.4	17.1	100
% land:					
by area	1.5	21.0	41.2	36.3	100
by value	1.5	16.4	41.8	40.3	100
% hired-in labour	5.0	35.0	37.0	22.0	100
Hired-in labour per hectare[a, b]	5.50	2.75	1.48	1.00	
% hired-out labour[c]	14.0	45.0	29.0	12.0	100
Hired-out labour per hectare[b]	28.23	6.48	2.13	1.00	
Hired-out labour per household member[b]	1.48	1.53	1.51	1.00	

[a] In IRS1 the farm wage bill is reported. We assume here that the mean wage rate paid does not differ between size classes in order to convert the data into labour quantities.

[b] 5+class=1.

[c] The data in IRS1 are for earnings from casual and regular employment. We assume here that the mean wage rate earned does not differ between size clssses in order to convert the data into labour quantities. In support of this assumption there are no significant differences between size classes in the ratio of casual to regular earnings.

hired by peasants. The paradoxical finding of Table 2.2 is that there is a clear inverse relationship between farm size class and labour hiring per hectare. Normalized on hired labour per hectare on holdings of 5 hectares and over, holdings in the size class 2.0–4.9 hectares use 48 per cent more hired labour per hectare, holdings in the size class 0.5–1.9 hectares use 175 per cent more hired labour per hectare, and holdings in the smallest size class use 450 per cent more hired labour per hectare.

This implies that the effect of the hiring of labour on differences between small and large farms in the marginal productivity of labour is ambiguous. Suppose that the amount of labour hired per hectare was the same for all size classes. Then, assuming that the marginal product of labour is a monotonically decreasing function of total labour use, the differences between marginal productivities would be reduced since the marginal product on large farms would fall more than the marginal product on small farms. However, since small farms actually hire more per hectare, the effect of labour hiring on the differential is ambiguous.

One possible explanation for this result is that the national data on land area used in Table 2.2 make no allowance for differences in land quality. It might be that the larger holdings are tracts of inferior land which can only sustain low labour/land ratios. Whilst a priori this has some plausibility it is not confirmed by other data. First, IRS1 also collected estimates of land market values. To the extent that market value is a proxy for land quality we can check to see whether there is a discrepancy between land shares by area and shares by value. In fact, as Table 2.2 reveals, there is a close correspondence between shares by value and shares by area with a tendency for the larger holdings to have a *higher* value per hectare. Secondly, as we will show, land is rented out from larger holdings to smaller, suggesting that allowing for quality differences the former remain land-abundant.

We conclude that labour hiring by peasants does not make any substantial contribution towards equalizing the marginal productivity of factors and may well be disequalizing. We next consider whether labour sales are an effective alternative. Sales of labour can be divided into that labour which is sold to other peasants and that which is sold on the non-peasant labour market. Since only some 5–10 per cent of labour input on peasant holdings is hired and some of this is supplied by the landless, sales to other peasants are clearly inadequate to even out the large differences in factor proportions between farms.

The non-peasant labour market provides more important opportunities to sell labour. Our estimate of the allocation of labour resulting from labour transactions is set out in Tables 2.3 and 2.4, the former using IRS1 data (1974/5), the latter our 1982 survey. In 1974 nationally some 18 per cent of the peasant labour endowment was hired out and in 1982 between 13 per cent (Nyanza) and 26 per cent (Central). The distribution of these labour sales by farm size category is presented in the last three rows of Table 2.2. In each size

TABLE 2.3. *The effect of labour transactions on peasant factor proportions*

	Farm size (ha)				All
	<0.5	0.5–1.9	2–4.9	5+	
1. % of household labour which is hired out	18.7	19.3	19.1	12.6	18
2. % of household labour remaining for use on holding	81.3	80.7	80.9	87.4	82
3. Labour hired in as % of household labour	3.0	6.7	10.8	10.3	8
4. Net market effect (%) on labour used on holding ((3)–(1))	−15.7	−12.6	−8.3	−2.3	−10
5. Labour used on holding as % of household labour (100–(4))	84.3	87.4	91.7	97.7	90
6. Hectares per family member before labour market transactions	0.037	0.183	0.502	0.703	0.334
7. Hectares per worker on the holding after labour market transactions	0.044	0.209	0.548	0.719	0.371
8. Change in hectares per worker on the holding due to labour market transactions	+0.007	+0.026	+0.046	+0.016	+0.037

Sources: Table 2.2, IRS1, and text.

class under 5 hectares some 50 per cent more labour per household member is hired out than on holdings over 5 hectares. Naturally, this fairly uniform selling of labour per person represents radically different labour sales per hectare. Labour sales therefore narrow the absolute differences in labour input per hectare but only modestly reduce differences in labour/land ratios, leaving the differences among the first three size categories unchanged.

Unlike labour-hiring transactions, labour sales do unambiguously tend towards equalizing marginal products of factors on farms of differing sizes. It is noteworthy that over 80 per cent of peasant labour sales are in the non-peasant labour market. The pressure of enormous differences in factor proportions appears to be insufficient to enable mutually profitable transactions to be contracted in the peasant labour market. Rather the pressure leads to differential sales of labour on other markets.

Table 2.3 shows the net change in farm factor proportions in different holding size classes resulting from labour transactions. Each size category is a net seller of labour, but the net sales of the largest holdings are close to zero whilst those of the smallest are around 16 per cent of the total labour endowment. However, the contribution which labour markets make towards

TABLE 2.4. *Endowment ratios (e-ratio) before and after adjustment*

Type of factor	Quintiles (by initial endowment ratio)					
	1	2	3	4	5	Total
Central Province						
Initial e-ratio	0.06	0.24	0.40	0.54	0.66	0.40
Potential labour force	4.34	5.62	6.42	5.96	5.32	5.53
Not on holding	1.49	1.97	2.01	1.88	1.38	1.75
Not in labour force	0.76	0.79	1.23	1.06	0.87	0.94
Hired labour	0.00	0.06	0.14	0.22	0.12	0.11
Labour market participation	0.85	0.38	0.14	0.19	0.19	0.35
Labour available	1.25	2.54	3.17	3.04	3.01	2.60
Labour used	0.76	1.94	2.08	2.04	2.15	1.80
Residual leisure	0.49	0.59	1.08	1.00	0.86	0.80
Holding area (acres)	0.24	1.37	2.59	3.23	3.52	2.20
Rented, etc. in	0.11	0.32	0.11	0.15	0.05	0.15
Rented, etc. out	0.04	0.19	0.00	0.07	0.13	0.09
Net holding area	0.31	1.49	2.70	3.32	3.45	2.26
Final e-ratio	0.25	0.59	0.85	1.09	1.15	0.87
Nyanza						
Initial e-ratio	0.09	0.31	0.51	0.67	0.84	0.49
Potential labour force	4.50	6.03	6.38	5.44	4.72	5.41
Not on holding	1.50	2.08	1.92	1.55	1.31	1.67
Not in labour force	0.74	0.94	1.24	0.84	0.75	0.90
Hired labour	0.00	0.14	0.16	0.15	0.10	0.11
Labour market participation	0.77	0.25	0.17	0.18	0.12	0.30
Labour available	1.49	2.90	3.21	3.02	2.63	2.65
Labour used	0.95	1.83	2.43	2.03	2.19	1.89
Residual leisure	0.54	1.06	0.77	0.99	0.44	0.76
Holding area (acres)	0.40	1.89	3.23	3.63	3.96	2.63
Rented, etc. in	0.22	0.13	0.18	0.04	0.15	0.15
Rented, etc. out	0.05	0.13	0.05	0.12	0.10	0.09
Net holding area	0.57	1.89	3.36	3.55	4.02	2.68
Final e-ratio	0.38	0.65	1.05	1.18	1.53	1.01

Source: Our survey.

an equalization of factor proportions is small and their contribution towards the equalization of the marginal product of labour is ambiguous. From row 8 of Table 2.3 we find that the absolute differences in land per worker between size classes are generally increased. For example, holdings in the smallest farm size class experience an increase in land per worker of only 0.007 hectares compared with a mean increase for all holdings of 0.037 hectares. The difference in factor proportions between the smallest and the largest size class is reduced from 19:1 to 16:1, but the absolute difference in land per unit of labour input actually widens.

Whilst the figures used in Table 2.3 represent only orders of magnitude, the central conclusion which we draw from the analysis is quite robust. This is that participation in rural labour markets by peasants has failed to be of a magnitude or of a direction such that it could be regarded as making a substantial contribution towards reducing the poverty and inefficiency consequences of inequalities in entitlements. It is indeed striking that such equalizing tendencies as the labour market provides come predominantly through the indirect effect of differential sales of labour to non-peasant labour markets rather than through the direct exchange of labour among peasants.

Land exchange may occur in a variety of contractual modes, ranging from seasonal rental to the permanent transfer of ownership. Payments can precede or lag the flow of use of land, thus forming an interlinked land and credit contract. Payments can be fixed in advance or be dependent upon the output from the land, thus forming an interlinked land, labour, and insurance contract. In none of these forms is there an extensive land market in Kenya: most holdings are acquired through inheritance.

The 1982 survey, which recorded land changes for the period 1975–82, found that land purchases accounted for only 0.5 per cent of the land area per annum. Both in Central Province and Nyanza some 4 per cent of the land area was cultivated under some form of tenancy: rental, borrowing, or shareploughing (sharecropping being non-existent). Of these, rental accounted for around 60 per cent of all tenancy. The tenancy market was not very active, with only 20 per cent of the area under tenancy in 1982 being accounted for by contracts entered into since 1975. Tenancy appears to be increasing in that the net change in tenancies has increased the area under tenancy by a tenth over the seven years. Further, whereas 80 per cent of new tenancies (by area) were rental contracts, only 50 per cent of lapsed tenancies were so, indicating that not only is tenancy increasing, but that it is also becoming more of a commercial contract and less of a traditional borrowing agreement. However, these trends start from a very modest base. The mean rental per acre was around 450 shillings per annum. This compares with a valuation of land by the owner of 18,000 shillings (though this valuation probably exaggerates the market value of land, since the mean value of land bought during the reference period was only around 5,000 shillings). The implied real interest rate is thus in the range 3 per cent to 9 per cent.

The process of inheritance is gradually reducing the mean holding size; however this process appears to be much slower than is generally thought to be the case. Over the reference period the mean holding shed through subdivision only 0.5 per cent of its area per annum. Since nationally population growth is considerably more rapid than this (4 per cent per annum), either mean household size is increasing or rapid net out-migration is occurring.

The land rental market tends to equalize factor proportions but its effect is slight because the extent of tenancy is limited. The failure of the land rental market to equalize factor proportions can be deduced from Tables 2.3 and 2.4. The land distributions shown in Table 2.3 already allow for land rentals. Table 2.4 stratifies households according to their *ex ante* endowment ratio quintiles and shows the effects of transactions on factor proportions. The top row shows the land per adult household member prior to any transactions. The second row shows the number of adults (aged 15 and above) in the household including non-resident sons, daughters, and spouses, the numbers of whom are shown in the third row. Man years of labour available for the holding (row 7) is defined as row 2 minus this out-migration (row 3), minus sales of labour (row 6), minus non-participation in the labour force (row 4), plus hired labour (row 5). Dividing by six hours per day converts labour hours actually used on the holding into days (row 8) and this is deducted from labour availability to yield residual leisure. It should be emphasized that the number of hours chosen to represent a working day is of no significance. The intention is not to quantify aggregate labour surplus but rather to investigate systematic differences between households in the proportion of labour time devoted to leisure rather than the holding. From the owned holding area (row 9) is subtracted land lent out (row 11), and land held as tenancy (row 10) is added in to yield net holding area (row 12). The final row shows the ratio of this area to labour available for the holding.

In Nyanza a pre-transaction differential between the extreme endowment quintiles of 9.3:1 is reduced by land and labour transactions to 4.0:1. In Central Province the differential is reduced from 11.0:1 to 4.6:1. Labour hiring per hectare again tends not to narrow the endowment ratio: in Nyanza the second most land-scarce quintile uses the most hired labour, hiring three times as much labour per hectare as the most land-abundant quintile. Such land rental and borrowing as occurs (which, as noted, is very limited) is allocatively efficient. Finally, in Nyanza, land-scarce households tend to take more leisure, presumably because of the more limited opportunities for its productive use.

Thus, rural factor markets do not accommodate differences in endowment ratios. A household with a relatively high labour/land ratio can hire labour to other (larger) holdings or can rent in more land. In either case differences between households in endowment ratios would be reduced. But the extent of labour hiring by peasants is very limited despite large differences in factor proportions. Further, an inverse relationship is sometimes found between hired labour per hectare and farm size. Indeed, the net effect of rural labour transactions by smallholders may well be to amplify rather than to reduce initial differences in land per cultivator.

Despite the registration of holdings, peasant-owned land does not appear to be widely used as collateral in the informal credit market. It is probable that a common factor explains both this and the limited extent of tenancy, namely that the contractual mode of the transaction involves the parties to the contract in enforcement problems. Probably the most important constraint upon using land as collateral and upon tenancy is that in the absence of any such traditions there is no social value system enforcing the contract. As a consequence, the creditor or landlord sees himself as risking failure to acquire, or a loss of, property rights because of the difficulty of ensuring physical (re-) possession of the land.

Even on registered holdings there must be considerable uncertainty for a potential landlord. Clearly it is perceived in rural Kenya that land law and land policy remain in a state of flux. In particular, there are many thousands of 'squatters' on large farms, and also large farms which have been unofficially subdivided by their multiple owners. At some stage the position of these groups will be regularized and at such a time usage may again become the criterion by which property rights are assigned.

In the formal credit market two characteristics have tended to be favoured as indicating a low default risk. David and Wyeth (1978) have shown that the commercial banks favour applicants with collateral or those with secure wage employment in the formal sector. The most common form of collateral is land presently owned which clearly works to the disadvantage of those with little land. This leaves as a means of access to the commercial banks for the near landless the possession of secure formal sector wage employment. This pushes the problem for the land scarce one stage further back, namely, to the acquisition of appropriate wage employment.

The commercial banks are not the main channel of peasant finance (though they may be a major source of funding for land purchases). Marketing co-operatives are the most common method by which peasants gain access to finance, the co-operatives themselves generally being funded by the aid agencies. There is commonly excess demand for loans and so the co-operative societies also ration loans. In their case the collateral used is not land but a direct deduction from future crops marketed through the co-operatives. Future crop marketings are typically estimated on the basis of the sales over the previous three years. This system clearly favours those already growing cash crops. The main loan programme, the Integrated Agricultural Development Programme, concentrates on loans with a duration of twelve months only. Whilst the marketing co-operatives do provide a mechanism for financing the expansion of cash crop production, the rules of fund allocation appear likely to preserve rather than to remove differences in income. Thus, in Central Province, where loan financing is most developed, IRS1 found that the value of loans outstanding differed markedly between income classes. Those earning below 2,000 shillings per annum on average had loans of only 200 shillings compared to loans of over 1,000 shillings for those with income above 4,000 shillings.

Between them, the commercial banks, the marketing co-operatives, and the extended family account for nearly all rural credit. Money-lenders are almost entirely absent. This is presumably related to fears of a very high default rate because informal debts other than within the extended family would lack the enforcement of social sanction.

The 1982 survey found only 5 per cent of the sample had current borrowing from co-operatives or banks. Even within the family, credit is very limited. During the previous year only 7 per cent of households had lent to relatives and 9 per cent had borrowed, and in only about a fifth of these cases was interest charged. The average loan was around 400 shillings (around 4 per cent of annual income) and the average duration only three months. Credit in all forms is thus fairly rare.

The thinness of the credit market has been proposed by one of us as part of the explanation for the limited extent and perverse direction of peasant labour hiring combined with the limited extent but normal direction of land rental (Collier, 1985). The argument is that if households are cash constrained then, per hectare, land-scarce households will be least constrained and land-abundant households most constrained. The former would therefore be in a better position to augment both their land and their labour endowments per hectare by market transactions. A corollary of the cash constraint hypothesis is that wage employment, by providing a reliable cash flow, eases the constraint. Whether or not this hypothesis is correct, the lack of active factor markets implies that shadow prices of factors will differ considerably between households unless offset by patterns of specialization in production.

2.4. The Structure of Peasant Income in 1982

This section does not aim to provide either a comprehensive account of the peasant economy or a full presentation of our survey results. Rather we will be focusing upon the structure of incomes and its antecedent, the structure of endowments.

The measurement of household income is critically dependent upon the definitions of its two component concepts. Although a full discussion of our definitions is provided in the Appendix, certain key concepts are set out here. Four concepts of the household are used, the *resident household*, the *non-resident household*, the *extended household*, and the *extended family*. The resident household consists of those living on the shamba at the time of the interview. The non-resident household includes spouses living elsewhere plus those children who are students or making remittances to the resident household. The extended household is the sum of these two. Finally, the extended family adds all other non-resident children of resident members. The purpose of this somewhat cumbersome classification is to provide a framework suitable for the analysis of migration, urban wage employment, and remittances, which play an important part in peasant income-generating strategies. The mean non-resident household is only small, 0.4 persons in both provinces, compared to the mean resident household size of 6.2 (Central) and 7.0 (Nyanza), but it accounts for a disproportionate share of income and provides a diversification of income. We will find in Chapter 6 that the extended family plays a critical role in access to some key components of income.

Income (including the value of own-produced items which are not marketed) is disaggregated in a variety of ways, but that which we will most commonly deploy distinguishes six sources: food crops, cash crops (i.e. non-food crops), livestock, own business, wages, and remittances. The structure of income by per capita income quintile is shown in Table 2.5. Mean per capita income was some 25 per cent higher in Central Province than in Nyanza, and its composition had two pronounced differences. Although income from crops formed a similar share in each region its composition owed much more to cash crops in Central (over 40 per cent against under 25 per cent). Similarly, although wage plus remittance income formed a similar share, within this the composition was more heavily skewed towards wages in Central (75 per cent against 60 per cent). Recall that Central Province is the predominant coffee area and is close to Nairobi. It is therefore to be expected that peasants there earn more from cash crops and are better able to combine wage employment

TABLE 2.5. *Income structure of resident households by per capita income quintiles*

Income categories	Quintile					
	1	2	3	4	5	Total
Central Province						
Food crops	296.6	24.5	21.1	14.5	21.6	20.6
Cash crops	−181.3	8.4	12.5	10.1	20.0	14.7
Livestock	−321.7	8.1	7.9	11.7	9.7	9.0
Own business	9.4	3.4	5.7	8.3	9.4	8.0
Wages	172.9	34.1	44.1	39.5	33.0	37.0
Remittances	124.1	21.5	8.6	15.9	6.2	10.8
Per capita income	13	654	1234	2049	5483	1663
Relative income level	1	40	75	126	336	100
Nyanza Province						
Food crops	83.7	46.3	39.1	32.9	2.2	29.5
Cash crops	−11.6	7.9	7.1	7.7	11.9	9.7
Liverstock	−71.8	12.8	14.3	11.6	9.3	10.1
Own business	6.9	9.5	8.9	8.2	8.8	8.7
Wages	3.3	8.5	12.8	24.2	32.6	25.7
Remittances	89.4	14.9	17.8	15.5	15.2	16.2
Per capita income	45	406	832	1501	4494	1256
Relative income level	4	33	68	122	364	100

with resident household membership, so that earnings appear as wage income as opposed to remittances.

The bottom quintile suffers negative livestock and cash crop income, arising for example from the death of livestock. This is presumably a transitory phenomenon. Comparing across quintiles there is some tendency for income from food crops and remittances to decline relatively as income rises, and for cash crop income to increase. In Nyanza wage income is strongly differentiating, perhaps reflecting the more limited access to such opportunities in that province.

Disaggregating wage income further, we distinguish between agricultural and non-agricultural wage employment, and within the latter by whether the job required education or skills and so could be regarded as being subject to entry barriers. As expected, the poor are more dependent upon wages from agriculture while the high-income quintiles rely upon barrier wage earnings.

Disaggregating crop and livestock income into subsistence and marketed output, there is a pronounced tendency in both provinces for the subsistence share to decline as income increases, as shown in Table 2.6. This can be interpreted either as a manifestation of a risk-minimizing strategy on the part of the poor, or as an indication that those households unable to overcome entry barriers into more remunerative activities are locked into subsistence and are therefore poor, a subject we investigate later.

Most households have diversified income structures. Only a negligible number of households are confined entirely to income from food crops, and many households receive income from each of our six aggregates. Table 2.7 arranges the 64 possible combinations of participation in these six activities in a matrix for each province. The principal inferences to be drawn from Table 2.7 are the diversification and the diversity of income structures. Households differ to an astonishing extent in their income composition: the notion of a representative household appears untenable. We will argue later in

TABLE 2.6. *The subsistence percentage of farm income*

Quintile	Total income		Crop income		Livestock income	
	Central	Nyanza	Central	Nyanza	Central	Nyanza
1	(625.4)	(168.0)	(229.0)	(98.6)	(−43.4)	(−99.1)
2	31.7	56.4	62.6	67.6	143.8	216.9
3	17.4	35.5	44.2	61.9	32.3	80.6
4	13.5	29.7	39.6	52.3	25.3	62.9
5	18.5	21.5	40.9	52.0	18.6	50.2
TOTAL	19.2	29.0	44.6	56.2	38.6	85.9

Note: The subsistence percentage is measured by the ratio of the value of subsistence production and total income.

TABLE 2.7. *Distribution of households by activity mix (incomes greater than 0)*

Farm	Non-farm								
	None	Own business only	Wage only	Remittances only	Own business and wages	Own business and remittances	Remittances and wages	All types non-farm	Total
Central Province									
None	0.9	0.0	10.8	0.3	0.0	0.0	1.2	0.0	13.2
Food crops only	1.8	0.4	8.2	0.9	1.4	0.0	1.1	0.0	13.7
Cash crops only	0.6	0.1	0.0	0.1	0.0	0.0	0.0	0.0	0.9
Livestock only	0.2	0.2	0.1	0.0	0.0	0.0	0.0	0.0	0.5
Food and cash crops	2.6	0.0	1.2	1.0	0.6	0.0	0.4	0.0	5.9
Food crops and livestock	4.9	1.6	5.8	3.2	1.0	0.0	2.9	0.1	19.5
Cash crops and livestock	0.7	0.0	0.0	0.0	0.0	0.0	0.0	0.0	0.7
All types farm income	16.9	1.4	9.5	9.2	0.7	1.7	6.0	0.3	45.7
TOTAL	28.6	3.8	35.6	14.8	3.6	1.7	11.6	0.4	100.0
Nyanza									
None	2.3	0.0	1.9	0.0	0.0	0.0	0.0	4.2	14.3
Food crops only	4.6	2.5	3.3	2.4	0.0	0.5	0.9	0.2	14.3
Cash crops only	0.0	0.0	0.0	0.0	0.0	0.0	0.0	0.0	0.0
Livestock only	0.0	0.0	0.4	0.5	0.0	0.0	0.0	0.0	0.8
Food and cash crops	1.2	0.7	0.4	0.4	0.6	0.0	0.0	0.0	3.3
Food crops and livestock	16.9	4.6	5.3	14.3	1.2	2.1	4.0	2.0	50.4
Cash crops and livestock	0.6	0.0	0.2	0.4	0.0	0.0	0.0	0.0	1.2
All types farm income	13.2	1.4	2.4	5.3	0.5	0.5	2.0	0.4	25.7
TOTAL	38.8	9.2	13.9	23.2	2.3	3.1	6.8	2.6	100.0

this chapter that in a dynamic sense the notion of the representative household may survive this dispersion: our cross-section observations may be of households at different stages in a sequence of accumulation which takes the form of a progression of entry into higher return activities. That there are pronounced differences in the per capita income generated by the different combinations of activities is demonstrated in Table 2.8, but at this level of diversity it is difficult to discern systematic relationships.

Finally, we take a first look at the relationship between the level and structure of per capita income and the principal non-labour endowment of the peasant household, namely land. Table 2.9 reveals an important difference between Central Province, the coffee-growing area, and Nyanza. Whereas in Nyanza there is a pronounced positive association between land area and per capita income, in Central Province such a relationship is far weaker. This appears to be related to the composition of income, for, with the exception of the smallest holding size group, farmers in Central Province with little land have a considerably higher share of their income made up by cash crops. Apparently, land-scarce households in Central Province are far better able to divert their other resources into income-maintaining agricultural activities which require little land.

2.5. Changes in Income, 1974–1982

Agricultural value added at constant prices in the small farm sector increased between 1974 and 1983 at an average annual rate of 3.1 per cent, this being approximately in line with the increasing size of the peasant population (see Table 2.10). Thus, despite a considerable increase in the rural labour force there was no discernible decline in the average physical product of labour in peasant agriculture. The average revenue product probably declined because most producer prices declined in real terms. Table 2.11 shows producer price series for the major crops deflated by the low-income wage earner cost of living index (there being no peasant cost of living index). This shows the real prices of most peasant crops to have declined over the period. However, as we have seen, agricultural income is only a part of total peasant income.

To estimate changes in peasant income through the comparison of surveys is fraught with difficulties. Table 2.12 aligns IRS1 (1974/5) and our own survey using common income concepts, but differences may reflect non-random differences in sampling frames. The changes in real per capita incomes implied by the comparison are, however, credible. In Central Province there is an increase of 6 per cent against a decline of 18 per cent in Nyanza. Since the prices reported in Table 2.11 declined rather more for those crops in which Nyanza specializes (pyrethrum and cotton) than for those in which Central Province specializes (coffee and tea), we would have expected such a pronounced divergence in fortunes. This is supported by the apparent changes in

TABLE 2.8. *Mean household per capita income by activity mix (incomes greater than 0) (shillings)*

Farm	Non-farm								
	None	Own business only	Wage only	Remittance only	Own business and wages	Own business remittance	Remittances and wages	All types non-farm	Total
Central Province									
None	0.0	—	1634.5	240.0	—	—	2343.5	—	1506.4
Food crops only	340.9	824.5	1772.7	792.1	4318.0	—	1252.9	—	1923.0
Cash crips only	−106.8	9799.4	—	732.9	—	—	—	—	2135.3
Livestock only	40.0	970.0	1171.0	—	—	—	—	—	945.5
Food and cash crops	484.6	—	655.9	1170.8	4034.5	—	2763.4	—	1247.7
Food crops and livestock	1024.1	1479.5	1657.9	1894.1	3838.8	—	3318.4	1889.2	1913.3
Cash crops and livestock	163.1	—	—	—	—	—	—	—	163.1
All types farm income	1301.2	2257.5	1675.8	1623.1	1683.3	2526.7	1825.6	1696.7	1599.9
TOTAL	1106.2	1926.8	1627.3	1615.6	3681.7	2526.7	2132.6	1725.6	1662.6

Nyanza								
None	0.0	—	1888.0	—	—	—	—	406.6
Food crops only	326.9	3513.3	1466.0	723.5	—	1324.5	1412.6	1177.0
Cash crops only	—	—	—	—	—	—	—	—
Livestock only	—	—	6500.0	730.6	—	—	—	1279.8
Food and cash crops	752.8	1747.6	151.9	471.3	2622.1	—	—	1032.3
Food crops and livestock	676.8	884.3	1621.0	1031.0	784.9	1064.4	3834.8	4582.0	1341.8
Cash crops and livestock	870.2	—	381.4	239.0	—	—	—	608.4
All types farm income	773.1	2349.8	2506.2	1168.7	1620.6	2624.4	1407.5	766.6	1243.5
TOTAL	664.0	1505.8	1754.0	996.2	1259.6	1499.0	2866.9	3571.5	1255.9

TABLE 2.9. *Per capita income structure of resident households by holding size*

Income categories	Form size (ha)								
	<0.5	0.5–0.9	1–1.9	2–2.9	3–3.9	4–4.9	5–7.9	8+	Total
Central Province									
Food crops	6.0	37.4	17.1	17.4	33.6	41.3	18.0	38.9	20.6
Cash crops	1.6	7.1	7.4	37.6	24.1	27.3	17.1	6.1	14.7
Livestock	5.9	4.2	4.2	19.9	8.2	0.1	28.4	15.1	9.0
Own business	10.2	2.9	17.7	3.2	5.2	1.6	4.4	1.1	8.0
Wages	69.5	36.2	42.4	11.9	11.3	16.8	8.1	27.7	37.0
Remittances	6.8	12.3	11.1	9.9	17.6	12.9	24.0	11.1	10.8
Per capita income (sh.)	1514	1475	1721	2168	1063	2249	1234	2036	1663
Relative income level	91	89	104	130	64	135	74	122	100
Nyanza Province									
Food crops	5.2	29.3	27.3	34.3	27.5	40.6	26.9	15.5	29.5
Cash crops	1.5	0.9	5.4	6.6	15.5	21.1	33.6	5.8	·9.7
Livestock	5.5	–6.1	6.8	8.6	8.5	13.0	25.1	49.5	10.1
Own business	2.4	10.4	5.9	14.7	6.4	6.5	7.9	10.1	8.7
Wages	73.8	53.9	32.9	21.3	23.9	10.3	5.5	5.9	25.7
Remittances	11.6	11.6	22.1	14.5	18.2	8.4	0.9	13.2	16.2
Per capita income (sh.)	770	512	1300	1136	1592	1796	1271	1810	1256
Relative income level	62	41	104	90	127	143	101	144	100

Source: Our survey.

TABLE 2.10. *Peasant agricultural production (at constant prices)*

Year	Agricultural value added (at constant prices)	Peasant share in marketed agricultural output	Index of total peasant agricultural output
1964	100.0	41.0	100.0
1966	111.3	47.5	114.7
1967	113.0	51.0	119.8
1968	118.9	51.0	125.4
1969	126.8	50.3	131.6
1970	132.2	51.7	137.8
1971	134.8	51.4	140.7
1972	147.1	52.5	151.7
1973	148.3	51.4	151.3
1974	150.3	50.6	153.4
1975	150.7	55.6	158.5
1976	150.7	51.2	152.6
1977	166.0	50.3	161.7
1978	172.4	54.8	173.7
1979	171.0	52.7	171.5
1980	168.7	52.2	168.7
1981	179.2	53.8	181.0
1982	187.4	51.7	194.1
1983	195.4	51.2	201.7

Note: The estimate of peasant production up to 1977 is equal to the sum of subsistence agricultural output as given in the national accounts, plus marketed agricultural output multiplied by the share of gross marketed output due to peasants given in the left-hand column. For the remaining years the statistics do not report separately subsistence production, but only aggregate agricultural production. We therefore have derived the share of peasants from this by assuming that the marketed share in the years 1978–83 is 9/19, which is an extrapolation from the period up to 1975. For 1976 and 1977 the share is somewhat higher, but these years are considered to be atypical in this respect. Thus, by first allocating 10/19 of total agricultural output to peasants and then applying the percentage in the left-hand column to the remaining 9/19 we get the estimate presented in the right-hand column.

Sources: Constant price estimates in national accounts of agricultural production at factor cost from *Economic Survey* (1974, p. 55), *Statistical Abstract* (1977, p. 108; 1979, p. 104; 1983, p. 99), Hazlewood (1979, p. 38).

income composition. The decline in income in Nyanza is fully accounted for by farm income alone, whereas in Central Province the real value of per capita farm income is almost constant. In both regions the most dynamic component of income is wage income, and in Nyanza its counterpart, remittances. This is consistent with the general equilibrium effects of the boom over the period analysed in *Controlled Open Economies* in which the expansion of urban employment opportunities is modelled as having powerful income-enhancing effects for peasants. With wages and remittances forming nearly half of

TABLE 2.11. *Real producer prices, 1964–1983*

	Maize	Rice	Pyrethrum	Sugar	Cotton	Coffee	Sisal	Tea
1964	100.0	—	100.0	—	100.0	100.0	100.0	100.0
1965	92.6	—	112.1	—	90.9	89.9	58.2	96.9
1966	101.5	—	119.4	—	80.7	85.8	49.9	99.2
1967	87.8	—	111.9	—	79.2	75.0	48.9	97.8
1968	76.0	100.0	96.3	100.0	81.1	81.6	41.7	72.4
1969	68.0	119.9	91.0	98.3	80.6	80.4	40.5	76.7
1970	67.2	110.0	86.0	87.4	81.3	94.6	34.9	82.7
1971	76.7	98.6	93.1	91.7	80.9	75.8	28.5	75.2
1972	85.9	99.6	99.3	97.4	85.5	89.1	36.5	66.7
1973	75.1	85.9	91.0	88.2	78.7	92.0	67.4	57.5
1974	76.8	86.0	80.6	90.1	86.1	86.1	133.7	59.8
1975	97.5	129.4	70.7	110.1	90.0	77.2	87.6	56.7
1976	98.1	155.4	71.5	117.9	89.5	167.1	61.4	87.8
1977	94.1	127.6	67.0	118.6	102.2	217.5	59.2	114.2
1978	72.1	119.5	76.0	109.1	98.4	135.7	48.0	74.0
1979	75.8	114.1	97.3	100.0	93.9	125.1	58.0	58.1
1980	72.0	100.6	102.7	88.4	94.7	102.8	58.3	60.3
1981	75.4	83.0	86.0	80.9	72.3	73.9	47.6	56.3
1982	68.1	74.2	72.7	83.6	65.9	80.3	51.2	54.4
1983	78.1	80.1	66.1	101.5	64.8	91.6	57.9	55.7

Sources: *Statistical Abstract* (1973, p. 101; 1977, p. 109; 1982, p. 100; 1983, p. 100). Prices are deflated by the lower income consumer price index.

peasant income in both regions by the end of our period, it is easy to see why this particular general equilibrium effect is important.

Our second approach to the measurement of changes in peasant incomes over time is to use the trace feature of our survey, and compare the data obtained with the data of IRS3. IRS3 was conducted as a thirteen-cycle survey with the first observation on each household in the survey being taken in May 1977. It therefore provides a complete annual picture of the agricultural activities of the peasant household. We have combined this information with the cycles of the labour force survey, which was conducted at the same time on the same households, and which provides a description of the off-farm activities of the household. Hereafter we refer to this combined survey as IRS3.

For the purpose of this exercise we wish to focus on changes in peasant household income that are attributable to switches between activities, changes in the proportion of household endowments expended on activities, and changes in ability or in the decision-making process of the household. The other major cause of income mobility is demographic change, and to abstract from the effects of a changing labour endowment we have confined our trace

TABLE 2.12. *Peasant incomes in Central and Nyanza Provinces, 1974/1975–1982*

	Central			Nyanza		
	1974/5	1982	Change	1974/5	1982	Change
Farm income	50.0	44.3	−5.7	71.3	49.4	−21.9
Own business income	7.7	8.0	+0.3	9.3	8.7	−0.6
Wage income	30.3	37.0	+6.7	13.4	25.7	+12.3
Remittances	12.0	10.8	−1.2	6.0	16.2	+10.2
TOTAL %	100.0	100.0	100.0	100.0	100.0	100.0
Total household income						
(current prices)	4241	10234		3911	8787	
(constant prices)	2202	2068		2031	1775	
Per capita income[a]	316.8	335.9		308.7	253.7	
(74/75 = 100)	100	106.0		100	82.2	
Household size	6.95	6.16		6.58	6.99	
Sample size	—	342		—	441	

[a] 1974/75 = 100

Sources: Integrated Rural Survey 1974/5, and our survey.

sample to households who did not relocate and who had a constant pool of family labour over the period between IRS3 in 1977 and our own survey in 1982. Therefore we exclude all households who have experienced any of the following during this period: the death of any member over the age of 15, either in or out migration of adult household members (including migration for the purpose of marriage), and finally households where members have moved into the 15 or older age cohort. This process leads to a final sample of 103 households with a constant labour endowment. For this trace sample we constructed net income measures for both IRS3 and our survey, for food crop, cash crop, livestock, and off-farm earnings (i.e. wage earnings and own-business earnings).

Since the income measures used are equivalent they not only provide a guide to changes in the level of income for a representative household, but also by the use of the trace feature of our data we are able to measure income mobility. We group adults into quintiles of the population. Adults are ranked on the basis of household income per adult. For example, the top quintile of IRS3 is composed of that 20 per cent of the adult population with the highest income per adult in 1977–8. The cross-tabulation of these measures of income rank is reported in Table 2.13, where the cell figures are the total percentages.

Table 2.13 demonstrates that there is considerable income mobility among households, even over a period of only four and half years, and even though our sample is limited to households with a constant labour endowment. Indeed the pattern shown is not significantly different from that which would

TABLE 2.13. *Comparison of income quintiles (percentages of adults)*

1982 income quintiles	1977–8 income quintiles				
	1	2	3	4	5
1	3.23	4.61	6.45	4.15	1.84
2	5.53	2.30	5.07	2.76	4.15
3	2.76	3.69	2.76	6.45	4.61
4	4.15	3.69	3.23	1.38	7.37
5	4.61	5.53	2.76	5.07	1.84

be generated if the two rankings were statistically independent; this would imply that 20 per cent of adults would be expected to remain in the same quintile and 48 per cent would move into a non-neighbouring quintile, i.e. experience a change in income rank of at least 20 per cent, whereas Table 2.13 shows figures of 12 per cent and 47 per cent respectively.

In the following analysis we seek to decompose changes in income into that part due to entry or exit from an activity and that part due to changes in earnings in an activity in which the household remains. It is important to distinguish between these possibilities because they reflect two types of investment, intra-activity and activity-switching, which will be taken up in Chapter 5. The magnitude of activity switches is shown in Table 2.14. There was considerable movement into high-return activities, the processes behind the adoption of these activities being examined further in Chapter 6.

We now separate the effects of activity adoption or exit from those of differential earnings in existing activities, the former being a portfolio adjustment effect and the latter a portfolio composition effect. We construct two counterfactual measures of 1982 income as follows. We disaggregate income into four activities indicated by j (where j equals 1 to 4), namely, food cropping, cash cropping, livestock, and off-shamba earnings (wages and business income) respectively. Consider for each activity the subset of households participating in the activity in both IRS3 and our survey. The growth factor for the mean income from activity j for these households, g_j, is then computed. An estimate of the 1982 income for household i in the case of no switching of activities or differential changes in effort across activities, $\hat{Y}_i$, is then given by:

$$\hat{Y}_i = \sum_j^4 Y_{ij} \cdot g_j,$$

where Y_{ij} is the observed income from activity j for the household in IRS3. This yields the pure portfolio composition effect. To construct the counterfactual measure of income to isolate the portfolio adjustment effect, $\tilde{Y}_i$, we

TABLE 2.14. *Entry into and exit from household activities (percentages of households)*

	1982	
	Not in activity	In activity
Food crops		
Not in activity, IRS3	0.9	2.9
In activity, IRS3	2.9	93.2
Cash crops		
Not in activity, IRS3	39.8	43.7
In activity, IRS3	1.9	14.6
Livestock		
Not in activity, IRS3	9.7	24.3
In activity, IRS3	11.6	54.4
Off-shamba earnings		
Not in activity, IRS3	47.6	35.0
In activity, IRS3	6.8	10.6

adopt the following procedure. Let p_{ij} denote the proportion of the IRS3 income of household i accounted for by activity j. Then were the household to undertake no activity switches and were its income from each of its activities to increase by the factor, g_j, the income shares found in our survey would be:

$$\hat{p}_{ij} = \frac{p_{ij} \cdot g_j}{\sum_{j}^{4} p_{ij} \cdot g_j}.$$

We now define Δp_{ij} as $p'_{ij} - \hat{p}_{ij}$ where p'_{ij} is the actual share in the income of household i of activity j in our survey. We run the regression

$$Y_{ij} = \beta_1 + \beta_2 p_{i2} + \beta_3 p_{i3} + \beta_4 p_{i4} + u_i$$

normalizing on $j = 1$, that is, food cropping. $\tilde{Y}_i$ is then given by:

$$\tilde{Y}_i = g_1 \cdot Y_i + \sum_{j=2}^{4} \Delta p_{ij} \cdot g_j \cdot \hat{\beta}_j.$$

This measure abstracts from the portfolio composition effect by setting the portfolio of each household at the start of the period to food only. Income changes then differ only because of the differential changes in activities, thus identifying the pure portfolio adjustment effect. The combined portfolio composition and adjustment effect is therefore given by:

$$\tilde{\tilde{Y}}_i = \tilde{Y}_i + \sum_{j=2}^{4} \Delta p_{ij} \cdot g_j \cdot \hat{\beta}_j.$$

To investigate the relative importance of the pure portfolio composition effect and the pure portfolio adjustment effect in explaining the variance of the observed household incomes in our survey we run the regression of this income on Y_i, $\hat{Y}_i$, and $\tilde{Y}_i$. From this regression we compute the total sum of squares, the model sum of squares, and also the partial sum of squares for each variable (i.e. the increase of the model sum of squares when that variable is added last to the regression). This enables us to calculate the variance of income that is solely due to the influence of each of the variables, as well as that component that is accounted for by the covariances. The model explains 28.3 per cent of the variance of income in our survey, of which 13.0 per cent is explained by covariance terms. The actual IRS3 income explains a further 2.6 per cent, and the portfolio composition and adjustment effects 0.9 and 11.8 per cent respectively. Thus the most important explanatory factor of the change in peasants' incomes is the portfolio adjustment effect.

The above picture of changes in income between the eve of the boom and its aftermath suggests that behind the veneer of the constant average physical product of labour in peasant agriculture estimated at the start of the section, there was a highly fluid process of income generation. To what extent was this related to the coffee boom?

2.6. Peasants' Behaviour during the Coffee Boom

At the time of the boom there were no restrictions upon coffee planting in existing areas. Around 40 per cent of the farmers in Central Province and 20 per cent of those in Nyanza were growing coffee. Both existing growers and non-growers responded to the price boom by planting. One manifestation of this was that licensed nurseries rapidly exhausted their stocks of seedlings and illegal nurseries sprang up.

Coffee planting is a substantial investment, and so it represented in part a use of the coffee boom windfall for asset formation. This can either be interpreted as a decision to save out of income perceived as transient, or as the irrational response to a temporary change in relative prices which peasants were informed (by the extension service) would be eroded by the time of the first harvest. One way of discriminating between these two hypotheses is from peasants' own reflections on their decisions during the coffee boom. In our interviews those peasants who had planted coffee during the boom were invited to describe their motivations at the time, which generates information of doubtful validity, but more importantly were asked whether they currently regretted their decision. Since this question was asked at a time (late 1982) when the real producer price of coffee had reverted almost precisely to its pre-boom level, households not then regretting having planted coffee can hardly have been induced into the decision entirely by over-optimistic price expectations projected from the boom. Among those with regrets a subset will regret their decision for reasons unrelated to the decline in the price. Households which regretted planting were asked why they did so. We should note that although the questionnaire was pre-coded, respondents were not presented with the list of codable responses. Rather, the range of possible answers was always left open, the enumerator selecting the code which most closely corresponded to the response. The question on regret was, however, a leading question, and as such we must expect responses to overstate the true extent of regret. It is therefore particularly noteworthy that the proportion of planters who appear to have been misled by their inflated expectations is rather small.

Among those households already growing coffee prior to the boom, around half (49 per cent) planted extra coffee during the period 1975–82. Among households not initially growing coffee, 9 per cent switched into the activity during this period. However, not all of these planting decisions are attributable to relative price changes, being caused either by windfall income or by underlying dynamic processes. Respondents were asked whether their planting had been motivated by the price increase. Responses to such questions on motivation are, of course, suspect; however, they do in this instance display a certain coherence. Overall, among those who had planted coffee during the period, whether as an expansion of an existing plot or as a new activity, 51 per cent attributed their decision to the increase in the coffee price during the boom. By contrast, among tea planters only 25 per cent attributed their decision to the temporary price increase, which is consistent with the fact that the increase was considerably less marked. Table 2.15 indicates coffee and tea producer prices for the period 1975–83.

If both existing coffee growers and potential growers on average had common frequency distributions of price expectations, an upwards revision of

TABLE 2.15. *Coffee and tea producer prices (indices, in domestic currency, 1975 = 100)*

	Coffee	Tea
1975	100	100
1976	236	131
1977	372	266
1978	264	196
1979	265	168
1980	246	197
1981	211	219
1982	260	240
1983	326	270

Source: Statistical Abstracts.

those expectations would be a more important cause of planting among the former. The reason for this is that existing growers already have overcome the threshold problems which we will suggest in Chapter 5 constrain entry so that any increase in the expected price of output should induce marginal substitution into the activity. In contrast, non-growers are initially below the threshold of viable entry. Both the income windfall associated with the boom and exogenous dynamic processes will cause some households to cross this threshold irrespective of price expectations, while for others even large revisions in price expectations will not cause the threshold to be crossed. Offsetting this, existing growers presumably do not have the same price expectations as non-growers, because *ceteris paribus*, those with more optimistic expectations are more likely to have adopted coffee already. Hence non-growers should be more surprised by the boom than existing growers and so have a larger revision of expectations. Thus whereas the former effect based on entry barriers should tend to make a price increase relatively less important for new adopters, the latter tends to make it more important. If entry barriers are in fact negligible, a higher proportion of planters should therefore attribute their decision to the price increase. In fact the survey found the reverse to be the case. For whereas 54 per cent of planters who were existing growers attributed their decision to the price increase only 45 per cent of new entrants did so.

An indication of the extent to which the revision of price expectations was unreasonably optimistic is provided by the proportion of respondents who by the end of 1982 were regretting their decision to plant. Overall 22 per cent of coffee planters and 4 per cent of tea planters regretted their decision. In all cases these households had planted because of the price increase. However, not all of these regrets were due to the behaviour of prices; only 79 per cent of those regretting planting attributed their regret to the subsequent decline in the price. Distinguishing between existing growers and new entrants, 26 per cent of the former, but only 14 per cent of the latter regretted this (extra) planting. Further, the price decline was a less important cause of regret among new entrants: planting regret attributed to the price decline was suggested by 22 per cent of planters who were existing growers but only by 8 per cent of new entrants. This again suggests that relative to the incremental planting decision of existing growers new entry is predominantly influenced by considerations other than price.

Households deciding to enter coffee growing or increase their planting of coffee could finance this either by asset substitution or by additional savings. Two direct substitutions are disposals of either land or livestock. A more ambiguous substitution is the use of credit. If the household is credit rationed, as most are likely to be, then the use of credit for one activity has the opportunity cost that it precludes the use of that credit for other activities. In such circumstances the use of credit to finance coffee planting should be regarded as a diversion rather than an augmentation of endowments. Even with this broad definition of asset substitution coffee planting during the period 1975–82 was overwhelmingly financed by an augmentation of assets. No planting households financed their investment by land sales, only 2 per cent by livestock sales, and a further 2 per cent by credit. This again suggests that the primary impetus to coffee planting was not a price-induced substitution among activities but an income-induced expansion in savings.

If coffee and tea planting can therefore be viewed as one major component of peasant asset formation induced by a decision to save out of windfall income, what were the other uses to which the windfall was put? Table 2.16 reports the recollections of coffee-growing peasants as to how they spent the money. Though these data are imprecise, the frequency of responses is some guide. There are clear signs of asset formation. In Central Province over 80 per cent of respondents claimed to have used part of the money to acquire financial assets (probably cash or a savings deposit at the co-operative or Post Office). Over 40 per cent increased their expenditure upon school fees, nearly 70 per cent improved their housing, 40 per cent bought livestock, and 13 per cent bought farm machinery.

In addition to the trace survey we undertook fieldwork among the coffee co-operative societies. Here we describe recollections of the boom period gathered at the Muranga Co-operative Union. On the eve of the boom this union had a membership of 45,000, that is around 15 per cent of all peasant coffee growers, Muranga being among the most important coffee-growing districts in Kenya.

TABLE 2.16. *Use of extra coffee boom money*

Expenditure categories	Percentage who spent on the activity	
	Central	Nyanza
Bigger Harambee contribution	25	15
Bought matatu	2	1
Bought house	2	3
Married more wives	1	9
Spent it on daily needs	98	80
Spent more on school fees	42	47
Spent it on house improvements	68	32
Bought land	8	5
Bought livestock	38	24
Bought farm machinery	13	15
Saved some of it	82	12
Other	12	2

Source: Our survey, coffee growers only, unweighted.

The coffee price increases which started in 1976 came as a shock to peasants in the area, who had never experienced anything like it. Some of them even went back to the co-operative banking section after receiving the payout note to point out that there must have been a clerical error and that they should not be getting anything like the amount they had been credited with.

At first the large coffee payout resulted in drinking and rather careless expenditures. The co-operative union called meetings to explain that the boom was going to be temporary (although they then believed that it would last for around three years), and advised farmers to invest their money. As will be shown in Chapter 6, this is indeed what farmers did. One investment expenditure was land purchases, both within the district and in the Rift Valley. Within the district land was mainly purchased from European-owned coffee estates by groups organized by the union. For example, a group of 1,217 farmers bought a foreign-owned Muranga estate with 300 acres of coffee. Altogether there were some fifteen deals of this nature within Muranga.

There were also some purchases of land from peasants who were not using all their land, though it was unheard of for a farmer to sell land with coffee trees on it. Some land was also bought by people from Nairobi, but it was more common for somebody who had earlier moved to Nairobi to come back to start working his shamba. Land prices tripled during the boom from 10,000 shillings to some 30,000 shillings per acre.

Housing was a major investment. Iron sheets were put on the roofs and many peasants built solid, permanent stone houses. A further investment was in vehicles. Some farmers used their newly obtained loan capacity to get loans for this purpose. Although ostensibly for use in agricultural activities, many instead ran their vehicles as matatus with a hired driver. Some money was also invested in small local shops and in a few cases partnerships were formed to start small industries. Some money was invested in Nairobi and Mombasa. For example, houses were bought in Nairobi. Coffee growers living in Nairobi usually bought new houses for their own use.

Private incomes also went into public investments such as dispensaries, clinics, and churches, the money being raised at Harambee meetings. It was easy to get people to contribute during the boom. On one occasion 750,000 shillings was raised for an investment in a local college of technology.

Investments were also made in coffee factories. The total number was increased from 86 to 95 and existing facilities were upgraded. Some money also went into the expansion of the union. Some 15 million shillings was used to build new buildings and new branch offices were opened.

One of the major investment outlets was, of course, the planting of more coffee trees. The union membership increased from 45,000 before the boom to about 68,000 in 1982. The union had a coffee nursery, but had up to then not been willing to sell any seedlings. The stock had grown to 3 million coffee seedlings, which were sold out within a week. People also brought in seedlings from other areas or started nurseries of their own. By 1982 the market for seedlings had again declined, and seemed to be wholly confined to replacements.

Money was also used to upgrade coffee. Many farmers brought in manure from as far away as Masailand. There were cases of up to twenty car loads, and often two to three buckets per plant were applied. Natural manure has the advantage that it has a long-term effect on output and in that respect this was a worthwhile long-term investment. The quality of the coffee in the area went up as a result of the boom and the accompanying increase in attention to coffee trees. Yields also went up. Since the boom, coffee quality has in some cases come down, but it is still much higher than before the boom.

The boom had a dramatic effect in the local casual labour market. The wage, which had been about 5 shillings per day, rose to 15 shillings. Similarly, the piece rate for coffee picking tripled from 1 to 3 shillings per debe (a quantity measure).

Deposits held with the unions funding section trebled during 1977. The Co-operative Bank in Nairobi, normally the recipient of all deposits from the unions, was flooded with money, and was unable to lend it all. A circular went out to unions that they were only allowed to put their money into a current account at zero per cent interest. Since the union banking section had to pay 5 per cent to its depositors and was not supposed to refuse deposits, this alternative was not viable. Therefore the money was lent to a financial intermediary, Continental Credit and Finance.

Our results are in accordance with those obtained in a survey of the impact of the coffee boom on 52 coffee farmers in Meru in Eastern province by Williams and Kabagambe (1982). They found that the four major uses of the coffee money were house improvements, farm investments, land purchases, and school fees. The major difference from our survey is that land purchases seem to have been more important in Meru, though even in Meru land sales are far from common. During the period 1964–81 only 5.8 per cent of the plots in the area were sold. However, a consequence of the increasing demand for land was a very abrupt increase in land prices in Meru. In real terms they increased by 87 per cent between 1975 and 1977, whereafter they fell by 40 per cent during the next four years (Williams and Kabagambe, 1982, p. 29).

Finally, we discuss the recollections of coffee-growing peasants concerning the short-run supply responses to higher prices during the boom. Households appear to have been responsive to relative prices in their deployment of variable inputs. Over 90 per cent of coffee growers claimed to have increased their use of fertilizer during the boom, and one-third increased their use of hired labour. Both of these are consistent with the increase in the marginal revenue product of initial quantities of these inputs brought about by the boom. Respondents were also asked about changes in their deployment of own labour during the boom. The replies to these questions are probably not very reliable, but they indicate a large (47 per cent) increase in the deployment of own labour on coffee during the boom, of which 60 per cent was achieved by substitution from leisure and 40 per cent by substitution from other crops. While all the above figures must be treated only as broad orders of magnitude they do tend to suggest that households made appropriate substitutions at the margin in response to price signals.

This descriptive chapter has accumulated questions to be answered rather than identify patterns of peasant behaviour in responses to the boom. The probable developments over the period were an increase in per capita income in Central Province and a decrease in Nyanza, considerable asset formation on the part of peasant households, especially in Central Province, and considerable income fluidity. We have now reached the limits of description, not in the sense that we now have all the facts which it would be useful to know, nor in the sense that we have fully reported on our survey data, but rather in the sense that we have exhausted the observed features of direct relevance to our subject. In order to develop a more analytical approach it is necessary to consider theories of peasant behaviour. For the Kenyan case this will be done in Chapter 5.

3
Peasant Farming in Tanzania, 1969–1983

3.1. Introduction

In 1976 Tanzanian coffee farmers were receiving 44 per cent of the world price, as compared with 76 per cent in Kenya. The imposition of a windfall coffee tax combined with the changes in relative prices against exports brought about by macroeconomic policies meant that little of the windfall directly accrued to peasants. There were, however, profound changes in the peasant economy during the period of our analysis, which we will argue, in Part III, were attributable to macroeconomic performance, and hence indirectly to the coffee boom.

The structure of this chapter follows that of Chapter 2. Section 3.2 provides an account of the evolution of peasant farming up to the coffee boom. Two aspects of that evolution are of particular importance. First, unlike in Kenya, Tanzanian peasants had exposure to cash crops for several decades prior to the coffee boom, and so the adoption of coffee probably occurred nearer to a steady state. Secondly, the boom was immediately preceded by institutional transformations of an extraordinary magnitude, which probably shifted the steady state and set many households in disequilibrium at the start of the period.

Section 3.3 reviews product and factor markets. The central feature is the onset of rationing in the consumer goods market in the late 1970s, which had powerful implications for agricultural supply. We also see that because of greater land abundance, the allocation of land to labour is more uniform in Tanzania than in Kenya.

The structure of income in 1983 is described in Section 3.4, which draws upon our survey of some 500 households in Kilimanjaro, Dodoma, Iringa, and Ruvuma. As in Kenya, this was a trace on a previous survey conducted by the Bureau of Statistics in 1976/7. In Section 3.5 we attempt to piece together an account of income changes. Because these changes turn out to be dramatic, we thought it best to consider a rather longer period, namely 1969–83, than in Kenya. This enables us to embrace five household budget surveys spanning the period, including the comparison of our traced sample. Using the 1976/7 survey we are able to demonstrate that our own survey, although it is regionally selective, is in most respects adequately representative of the national peasant economy. Finally, Section 3.6 provides a brief account of the behaviour of coffee farmers during the boom.

3.2. The Evolution of the Peasant Economy Prior to the Coffee Boom

Rural Tanzania in the early nineteenth century had clear similarities to rural Kenya: shifting cultivation was common because of land abundance in most areas and there was little trade other than over short distances. During the century the rural economy experienced profound shocks as long-distance trading developed, introducing slavery, specialization in ivory, and new crops.[1] For example, coffee was being grown in Bukoba before the arrival of the Germans.

German colonization never quite matched the British pattern. Although settler agriculture was encouraged, and included coffee, peasants were permitted and even encouraged to produce cash crops. Indeed, in 1906 the German authorities decided that agricultural policy was to be based on peasant production. Arabica was introduced around Kilimanjaro in 1907, and in the years before the First World War peasants supplied the bulk of national coffee production. The coercive devices of the colonial economy such as the hut tax therefore tended to encourage peasant commercialization rather more than was the case in Kenya. The peasant economy was, however, cruelly debilitated by wars, disease, famine, and rinderpest, and large areas were depopulated.

Between 1920 and 1961 the country was administered by the British under a trusteeship. Under the terms of their mandate the British were obliged to determine policy in the interests of the majority. Pressure from Kenyan settlers nevertheless induced a partial reversal of the German policy, but the opportunities open to Tanzanian peasants remained wider than those of their Kenyan counterparts. An attempt by settlers in the early 1920s to stop African coffee production failed, and by the early 1930s around one-third of the households in Kilimanjaro (the most ecologically suited area) were growing coffee, and had formed their own cooperative marketing organization. More than half the national coffee output continued to be produced by peasants.

From the mid-1930s the authorities based agricultural policy increasingly upon coercion, with an emphasis upon soil conservation and cultivation practices. Although there was an active extension service for peasants, its characteristic stance of confidence, repression, and ignorance was markedly ineffective. In the mid-1950s policy was revised and coercion gave way to the encouragement of progressive farmers. Price incentives were used and marketing co-operatives were encouraged. This policy shift had dramatic effects: between 1955 and 1960 coffee production increased by 40 per cent, and that of cotton and cashew nuts doubled. Thus, by Independence (1961) there was something of a bifurcation in Tanzanian peasant agriculture, with some regions already thoroughly commercialized and growing rapidly while others remained in traditional shifting food cultivation.

[1] An excellent account is given in Iliffe (1979).

With the encouragement of the World Bank, the new government embarked upon a twin strategy of improvement and transformation. The latter, a centre-piece of which was irrigated settlement schemes, proved a costly failure, but the former, focused on infrastructure and institutions, was rather successful. Between Independence and the policy change of the Arusha Declaration (1967), coffee and cotton production grew by 13 per cent per annum and production of tobacco, cashew nuts, and tea by around 9 per cent per annum.

The Arusha Declaration marked the start of a massive policy change away from commercialized peasant production. Villages were created, at first voluntarily and later, in 1974, by compulsion, and this involved the physical relocation of some 60 per cent of the population. Within these villages collective agriculture was strongly encouraged, and the peasant co-operatives were disbanded in 1976. The environment again became heavily regulated: labour hiring was restricted, two days per week on the collective farm were normally required, minimum acreages for particular crops were imposed, inter-cropping was at times banned, weeding became compulsory, and there were restrictions on the freedom of movement out of the village. The window of commercial opportunity which had briefly opened up in the peasant economy, and which had been seized on with alacrity, was rapidly closing. The sudden increase in the world price of coffee intruded into this breathtaking political programme by threatening to exacerbate precisely those supposed distributional aspects of a commercialized peasantry which it was designed to avert and reverse. Senior policy makers and advisers therefore felt no compunction about imposing a windfall coffee tax.

3.3. The Structure of Product and Factor Markets

During the course of the period the government intervened in the markets for agricultural inputs and outputs. It also did so in the market for consumer goods, so that peasants came to be rationed and a black market emerged. These interventions are considered in turn.

3.3.1. *Agricultural Inputs and Outputs*

Until the 1970s crop prices reflected a combination of world prices and transport costs, but during our period they were ostensibly calculated on the basis of costs of production estimated nationally. The same official price prevailed in all regions. For food crops this generated incentives to overproduce in remote areas with high potential for grains, such as Ruvuma. Surpluses cannot be transported, stores fill up, and official purchases are rationed. Following a sembe subsidy introduced in 1980 it became profitable for peasants to sell maize at the official producer price and buy it back at the official consumer price, but of course this was curtailed by shortages of sembe at the official price. One deviation from cost-plus pricing was in the case of drought-resistant crops, whose price was increased to stimulate production as an insurance. This yielded massive surpluses as peasants switched among food crops, and since these could not be stored, they were exported at a large loss.

According to the Central Bank,[2] export crops continued to be priced broadly at export parity (with the exception of coffee). However, as Ellis (1982) has shown, there was a decline in real producer prices for export crops of astonishing proportions during the 1970s. The reconciliation of these positions is that whereas the Central Bank is correct when exchange rate policy is taken as given, the totality of pricing policies, including the effects of macroeconomic policies, powerfully turned domestic relative prices against export crops, which is the outcome Ellis observes.

Marketing of all crops, other than for inter-district food trade, was the monopoly of crop authorities, which also had the responsibility for extension and input distribution. There is some indication that marketing costs, and hence margins, rose over time. Guerreiro[3] shows that at constant prices maize marketing costs per ton rose by around 35 per cent between the late 1960s and the early 1980s. By the end of our period marketing policy was beginning to change again: co-operatives were reintroduced and some regional variations in food prices were permitted, but these changes occurred too late to affect our story.

The extent to which parallel markets for food crops have developed is shown in Table 3.1 which is based on our survey of 1983. Most food production is consumed on the holding, but there is considerable marketing through unofficial channels, though this is not the case for the export crops.

Factor markets are even more truncated than in Kenya. Following villagization, land became the property of the state and its sale, purchase, and rental became illegal. Although to some extent peasants were able to evade these regulations by notionally selling only crops in the ground, the possibilities of enforcement by the village-level party and local government organizations must have introduced substantial risks into such transactions. We were, however, able to identify the contribution of land rental to factor proportions through our survey (see Table 3.2). Overall, 5 per cent of the land area is reallocated through rental. Despite the difficulties of getting these data, they appear reasonably reliable since the area rented in corresponds precisely to that rented out. Ostensibly villagization was in part a land reform; however, although most households were relocated there appears to have been no marked change in the ranking of holding size.[4] Rather there was a slight reduction in mean holding size. The stability in the land distribution probably reflected land abundance: in most areas holding size is closely related to the labour endowment.

[2] Bank of Tanzania (1984, p. 99).   [3] Guerreiro (1984, p. 100).
[4] Collier et al. (1986, Table 3.13).

TABLE 3.1. *Quantities (Q) and price (P) of crops by marketing channels, 1983*

	Mean production (kg)	Not sold Q (kg)	Official sales Q (kg)	Official sales P (sh)	Unofficial sales Q (kg)	Unofficial sales P (sh)	Cases
Local maize	504.0	295.7	143.4	2.0	64.9	4.4	102
Hybrid maize	234.3	150.9	57.4	1.7	26.0	2.3	45
Beans	73.3	30.1	19.8	2.8	23.5	12.4	49
Millet	24.0	12.5	4.6	1.3	6.9	4.8	16
Cassava	54.1	13.7	40.4	0.9	0.0	—	21
Ground nuts	37.5	22.0	2.4	5.7	13.0	10.9	32
Wheat	26.3	8.0	1.5	3.3	16.8	13.6	19
Rice	107.5	32.6	70.4	3.3	4.5	7.7	38
Yams	0.3	0.0	0.3	1.2	0.0	—	1
Peas	3.3	0.2	0.8	2.2	2.3	6.7	10
Other vegetables	0.2	0.0	0.0	—	0.3	2.0	1
Coffee	47.1	9.9	37.1	13.1	0.0	—	86
Bananas	19.7	0.7	4.8	4.2	15.5	2.2	10
Tobacco	14.7	0.4	13.9	13.5	0.4	24.7	28
Cotton	2.1	0.4	1.6	5.3	0.0	—	3
Pyrethrum	3.4	0.4	2.9	11.2	0.0	—	22
Cashew nuts	15.1	0.9	14.2	7.1	0.0	—	1
Sunflower	13.7	4.6	5.7	2.8	3.4	2.1	12
Castor seed	0.2	0.0	0.2	3.1	0.0	—	2
Sugar cane	38.7	21.1	0.0	—	17.6	1.7	7
Onions	9.2	0.0	0.0	—	9.2	3.8	7
Other	41.5	1.1	40.0	2.6	0.4	13.8	10
All crops	1270.5	603.8	462.1	3.7	204.6	5.9	547

Note: Some crops can be grown on several different plots by the same household.

As noted above, the use of hired labour on peasant holdings was strongly discouraged officially. However, in most areas of Tanzania very little labour was hired even prior to this policy. During our period the use of hired labour was negligible. An unpublished FAO survey of Ruvuma in 1975 found hired labour to make up 2 per cent of labour input. An ILO survey of eight regions in 1980[5] found around 1 per cent, and our own survey of 1983 found 2 per cent.

The virtual absence of land and labour markets in peasant agriculture, other than in the most commercialized areas, is probably a further reflection of land abundance. Unlike in Kenya, we should not regard the land and labour endowments as being exogenously determined (except in the long run),

[5] Collier *et al.* (1986).

TABLE 3.2. *Endowment ratios (e-ratios) before and after adjustment*

Type of factor	Quintiles by initial endowment ratio					
	1	2	3	4	5	Total
(1) Initial e-ratio (10)/(2)	0.46	0.53	0.80	1.24	2.87	1.11
(2) Potential labour force	3.51	3.73	3.00	2.81	2.77	3.16
(3) Not on holding	0.25	0.20	0.11	0.13	0.08	0,15
(4) Not in labour force	0.68	0.82	0.35	0.38	0.45	0.54
(5) Labour hired in	0.01	0.01	0.06	0.01	0.02	0.02
(6) Labour market participation	0.23	0.48	0.52	0.22	0.40	0.37
(7) Labour available (2)–(3)–(4)+(5)–(6)	2.36	2.23	2.09	2.09	1.86	2.12
(8) Labour used	0.95	1.04	0.96	1.21	1.42	1.12
(9) Residual leisure (7)–(8)	1.40	1.19	1.13	0.88	0.44	1.00
(10) Holding area	1.60	1.97	2.42	3.49	7.95	3.52
(11) Rented, etc. in	0.61	0.09	0.02	0.13	0.00	0.17
(12) Rented, etc. out	0.00	0.03	0.04	0.09	0.63	0.16
(13) Net holding area (10)+(11)–(12)	2.20	2.03	2.40	3.53	7.32	3.52
(14) Final e-ratio (13)/(7)	0.93	0.91	1.15	1.69	3.93	1.66

Note: Units are number of people for rows (2)–(9); acres for rows (10)–(13).

for the former is a function of the latter. The absence of markets is therefore of much less consequence since land/labour ratios will not differ so markedly across holdings. This is confirmed in Table 3.2 which shows the contribution of factor market transactions to the narrowing of *ex ante* differences in factor proportions. The *ex ante* dispersion of endowments is much narrower than in Kenya.

For most of the period, the formal credit market was the monopoly of the Tanzania Rural Development Bank (TRDB) which lent only to Village Councils and not to individual households. The informal credit market is somewhat more active than in Kenya. Nearly a quarter of households in our sample had lent money in the preceding year, the average amount being 700 shillings and the average duration being twenty months. However, most of this was to relatives and interest was almost never charged.

3.3.2. *The Consumer Goods Market*

Prior to 1975 price control applied in rural areas in theory, but probably was not effectively enforced. That year' saw the start of Operation Maduka which extended state control to the retail level by replacing private, typically Asian-owned, shops (dukas) by village or state-owned co-operatives. Transitional problems (for example private shops being closed before collectively owned replacements could be organized) plagued this system for several years, but in the early 1980s the vast majority of villages had at least one shop. By then a village-level national rationing system had been introduced. The rules which govern this system are interesting because they imply that access to goods at the village level is a matter of luck, even if supplies are available and have been allocated to the village. As Shepherd (1982, p. 138) found for Mbeya Region, after a village had been allocated a supply of a particular commodity it was given only five days in which to send a representative to purchase the goods at a regional centre. If it failed to do so (because it did not hear the news in time, did not have the ready cash needed, or could not organize transport) the supply was reassigned to another village. The activities of private traders in parallel markets provided an inadequate substitute, partly because they were illegal, and partly because of transport difficulties. A study by the Marketing Development Bureau found enormous inter-regional variations in food prices, which suggests that the network of traders is insufficiently dense to produce a well-integrated national market. In addition their evidence indicates that the network had deteriorated: the coefficient of variation of food prices in regional urban centres rose from 0.14 in 1964 to 0.24 in 1970, 0.35 in 1977, and 0.30 in 1980.

Thus, consumers wishing to make purchases in parallel markets faced unreliable supply, a particular good only being infrequently available at a particular location (or, even if continuously available, only at widely fluctuating prices).

The Bureau of Statistics makes regular (incognito) attempts to purchase a range of twenty-five foodstuffs at twenty largely unregulated urban food markets. Between four and five thousand attempts to purchase foodstuffs are thus recorded annually. While the Bureau uses these data for the computation of consumer price indices only to the extent that the attempts were successful, it has allowed us to use the data to construct indices of availability.[6] As shown in Table 3.3, the proportion of attempted purchases of foodstuffs which were unsuccessful (these being instances of frustrated excess demand) has risen strongly over the period for which we have data (1978–82).

While this confirms our thesis that availability deteriorated in the post-boom period, the data are for foodstuffs only, are restricted to urban centres, give no indication of variability, and do not allow a comparison between official purchases and parallel market transactions.

In our own survey we asked households about their purchases of twenty-one commodities, both at official prices and in parallel markets. (These purchases were not illegal, so respondents were not reluctant to divulge this information.) The results are shown in Table 3.4. As may be seen from the first column, most households experienced rationing at official prices for most goods, the percentage of households reporting that they were sometimes

---

[6] Chapter 10 contains detailed discussion of these data, and uses them to study supply response in the presence of rationing.

TABLE 3.3. *Availability of twenty-five foodstuffs in twenty markets*

Year	Attempted purchase of foodstuffs	
	no. of attempts	probability of frustration
1978	4,650	0.154
1979	3,975	0.201
1980	4,425	0.216
1981	4,725	0.242
1982	5,025	0.283

unable to make purchases ranging from between 40 and 50 per cent for agricultural implements such as rakes, axes, and bags to over 90 per cent for consumer goods such as sugar, soap, and cooking oil. In some cases, commodities are available at official prices only a few times per year (e.g. 2.4 times per year on average for cooking oil) and even then so little was available that the typical quantity bought was very small (2.3 bottles in the case of cooking oil). Most importantly, the results in the table's fourth column (which gives the coefficient of variation of the quantity bought) indicate wide variation across households around the average quantity bought, confirming the probabilistic nature of an individual household's access to goods. The data for parallel market purchases are very similar. While some commodities, such as batteries, are more often available in the parallel market, the data on access differ little between markets (for example, 93.5 per cent of households reported unavailability of sugar in the official market, versus 96.1 per cent for the parallel market). Also the variability of quantities in the parallel market is large.

The declining availability of goods in rural areas is also confirmed by the Board of Internal Trade (BIT) data on the deliveries of goods to rural areas.[7] Data on dispatches of corrugated iron sheets, for example, show an increase in deliveries to coffee-growing areas (Kilimanjaro, Arusha, Bukoba, Iringa, and Mbeya) during the boom period[8] and a very sharp contraction thereafter (Table 3.5). In 1981 total BIT dispatches of corrugated iron sheets were only 40 per cent of what they were in 1975. Significantly, when in 1982 total deliveries increased from 10.0 to 15.8 thousand tons, 54 per cent of the increase

---

[7] These data are also described in more detail and used in the econometric analysis of Chapter 10.

[8] When coffee prices started to rise in 1976, the Prime Minister stated in a speech that coffee growers should use the extra money for home improvements. The BIT reacted to this speech by allocating building materials such as cement and roofing sheets on a priority basis to coffee-growing areas. This is reflected in the data.

TABLE 3.4. *Availability of goods in the four regions, 1983*

Goods	Official purchases				Unofficial purchases			
	Access failure[a]	Frequency[b]	Typical quantity[c]	Quantity variability[d]	Access failure[a]	Frequency[b]	Typical quantity[c]	Quantity variability[d]
Maize flour (kg)	52.4	10.4	4.8	0.6	47.9	11.0	4.7	0.6
Rice (kg)	75.2	12.2	3.7	0.7	72.4	10.5	3.2	0.7
Paraffin (bottle)	92.3	12.5	2.4	1.0	87.3	11.1	2.3	1.1
Cooking oil (bottle)	80.9	2.4	2.3	0.9	88.4	6.8	2.6	1.0
Soap (bar)	93.3	8.4	2.3	1.0	81.9	12.1	3.1	1.0
Sugar (kg)	93.5	7.0	2.3	1.0	96.1	8.1	2.8	1.0
Salt (cup)	78.4	3.0	3.3	0.7	74.1	12.0	3.0	0.9
Matches (box)	76.7	17.7	3.3	0.9	71.9	6.7	2.7	0.9
Cigarettes (pkt)	61.1	4.1	1.8	0.9	80.9	5.6	2.3	1.1
Roofing sheet (no.)	69.0	0.5	6.7	0.4	90.4	1.0	8.2	0.2
Bicycles (no.)	60.3	0.3	1.0	0.5	82.9	0.1	1.4	1.3
Bicycle tubes (no.)	57.7	0.3	1.9	0.6	98.0	0.2	2.1	0.4
Battery (no.)	77.3	2.8	4.2	0.5	88.2	4.9	4.4	0.5
Hoes-Jembe (no.)	61.8	2.0	1.9	0.7	63.5	0.3	1.7	0.7
Panga (no.)	43.1	0.6	1.4	0.6	58.3	0.2	1.3	0.4
Rake (no.)	41.6	0.1	1.1	0.5	67.5	0.0	2.5	0.3
Axe (no.)	48.1	0.4	1.3	0.5	62.4	0.1	1.1	0.2
Base (no.)	46.4	0.4	3.7	0.8	61.6	0.1	2.6	0.5
School uniforms	70.0	0.7	1.9	0.5	70.5	0.6	2.1	0.8
Khansa/vitense (no.)	91.7	1.9	1.8	0.7	90.9	1.4	1.5	0.8
Radios (no.)	61.5	0.2	1.0	0.5	88.4	0.2	2.2	1.2

[a] Access failure: percentage of households which reported that (in the past year) they sometimes wanted to buy the commodity, but that it was not available.
[b] Frequency: the number of times (in the past year) the household succeeded in buying the good.
[c] The quantity typically bought if the good was available.
[d] Quantity variability: coefficient of variation for the quantity bought.

TABLE 3.5. *Dispatches of corrugated iron sheets, 1975–1981 (tons)*

	1975	1977	1978	1981
Arusha	815	1,501	1,767	574
Kilimanjaro	1,447	3,140	2,529	669
Bukoba	721	2,471	285	392
Iringa	1,108	1,568	1,625	604
Mbeya	1,173	2,116	1,902	520
Other rural	7,658	10,331	11,239	4,465
Dar es Salaam	11,836	7,768	9,624	2,801
TOTAL (excluding export)	24,758	28,895	28,971	10,025

went to Dar es Salaam. For non-building materials we use the BIT data on deliveries of radios as an example. As Table 3.6 shows, the supply of Matsushita radios to rural regions fell by 60 per cent over the period 1975–82, while the urban regions (Dar es Salaam and Coast) increased their share of a shrinking pie from 25 per cent to 38 per cent.

In Chapter 11 a central distinction is made between those households which purchased their marginal supplies on the black market and those which were confined to official markets, because black-market prices were too high. We have seen that to a considerable extent even black markets are subject to quantity constraints, so that not all households which make purchases on the black market are unrationed at the margin. However, with this qualification, it is useful to aggregate households according to their market participation. We measured whether households were rationed on official markets by whether or not they had at times during the past year wanted to make a purchase of one or more of nineteen basic non-agricultural goods but been unable to do so. Of our sample of 498 households only 1 per cent described themselves as unrationed on official markets. A household was defined as participating as a purchaser on the black market if it had made a purchase of at least one of these nineteen goods during the past year on the unofficial market.

Since the sale of black-market goods is illegal and transport of goods physically difficult, costly, and hazardous because of its illegality, their supply is likely to be greater in border areas. This may manifest itself either in regional price variations or in a differential incidence of shortages. but in either case it should affect the proportion of households able to purchase on the black market. This is borne out by the data presented in Table 3.7. The table shows that a significant group of households in the interior (31 per cent) were unambiguously rationed at the margin, not making any purchases on black markets. An unknown proportion of the remainder were also rationed at the margin even though they succeeded in making some purchases on the

TABLE 3.6. *BIT deliveries of Matsushita radios to the regions, 1975–1982*

	1975	1977	1982
Dar es Salaam, Coast	30,338	37,290	22,579
Rural regions	90,249	134,098	36,465
TOTAL	120,587	171,388	59,044

TABLE 3.7. *Participation in black markets (%)*

Area	Unrationed on official market	Not purchasing on black market	Purchasing on black market
Border (Kilimanjaro, Ruvuma)	0	6	94
Interior (Dodoma, Iringa)	3	31	66

black market. Hence, it is indeed appropriate to formulate an analysis in which both types of household coexist.

3.4. The Structure of Peasant Income in 1983

We now provide a brief characterization of the structure of peasant income as found by our survey of 1983. The same concepts both of income and of the household are deployed as in our Kenyan survey, accounts being given in Chapter 2 and the Appendix.

The composition of income, disaggregated by per capita income quintile, is reported in Table 3.8. An important result, which differs radically from Kenya, is that the proportion of income derived from cash crops (that is, non-food crops) declines as income increases. Dependence upon cash crop income is concentrated among the poor. This is an extraordinary result, but holds not only at the aggregate level but within each of the four survey regions (Iringa, Dodoma, Kilimanjaro, and Ruvuma). The same result was found also in the 1980 ILO survey.[9] The policy of depressing the producer prices of cash crops had therefore been carried to the point at which it was regressive within the peasant community. The principal differentiating activities were livestock and business. Compared with Kenya income from both wages and remittances formed a markedly smaller share of income.

[9] Collier *et al.* (1986).

TABLE 3.8. *Income structure of resident households by per capita income quintiles and regions (percentage unless otherwise marked)*

Income categories	By quintile						By region				
	Total	1	2	3	4	5	Dodoma	Iringa	Kilimanjaro	Ruvuma
Food crops	41.5	−148.6[a]	60.8	55.1	39.5	33.9	30.5	46.5	47.9	50.4
Cash crops	7.0	−26.1	14.9	10.7	6.4	5.0	0.3	2.6	18.6	12.7
Livestock	13.9	326.3	2.7	14.9	20.5	17.4	16.2	13.0	11.3	13.7
Own business	26.3	−41.0	8.2	7.2	9.9	36.6	37.9	27.7	11.6	18.6
Wages	6.4	−9.0	8.6	4.2	14.2	2.9	10.1	6.4	3.0	2.6
Remittances	4.8	−1.5	4.8	7.9	9.4	2.1	4.9	3.8	7.5	2.0
Per capita income (sh)	1549	−73	182	917	1,722	6,208	1,805	1,247	1,667	1,472
Relative income level	100	−5	31	59	111	401	100	100	100	100

[a] Income of the bottom quintile is negative because of livestock losses. Hence as a percentage of income the remaining components of income are shown as negative. Clearly, households in this quintile must have had positive permanent income and positive expenditures.

Despite parallel markets, households are more dependent upon subsistence income than in Kenya (see Table 3.9). Overall, 72 per cent of farm income is derived from subsistence, and 45 per cent of total income.

Households have less diversified incomes than in Kenya. Table 3.10 repeats Table 2.7, showing the distribution of households over 64 possible combinations of participation in our six income-generating activities. Whereas in Kenya exclusive reliance upon food crops was confined to only 4 per cent of households in Central Province and 10 per cent in Nyanza, in Tanzania between 9 and 25 per cent of households, rely exclusively on cash crops. The low share of wages and remittances in income is reflected in the smaller proportion of households deriving an income from these sources. Indeed, fewer households have had any history of migration (46 per cent as against 58 per cent), and the non-resident extended household is half the size of that in Kenya (0.2 persons), although the size of the resident household is very similar (6.4 persons). Peasants are therefore less integrated into the predominantly urban wage economy.

Finally, the lesser importance of land as a differentiating endowment is suggested by Table 3.11, corresponding to Table 2.9, which reveals little systematic relationship between either per capita income or the composition of income and the size of the holding.

3.5. Changes in Income, 1969–1983

The National Accounts data on trends in value added in agriculture are largely dependent upon guesses as to changes in subsistence income. Changes in the volume of those crops all of whose output is marketed through official channels are somewhat more reliable, and are shown for three important peasant crops in Table 3.12. The broad pattern is one of absolute stagnation or decline. Between 1969 and 1983 the peasant population increased by

TABLE 3.9. *The subsistence percentage of farm income*

Quintiles	Total income	Crop income	Livestock income
1	(−179.1)	72.4	−16.6
2	71.5	73.0	182.8
3	65.7	65.4	72.5
4	62.9	66.8	238.5
5	25.6	56.8	35.3
TOTAL	44.9	62.2	106.2

Source: The subsistence percentage is measured by the ratio between the value of subsistence production and income of the respective categories.

TABLE 3.10. Distribution of households by activity mix (incomes greater than 0)

Farm	Non-farm							
	None	Own business only	Wage only	Remittances only	Own business and wages	Own business and remittances	Remittances and wages	All types non-farm	Total
None		0.0	0.0	0.0	0.0	0.3	0.0	0.6	4.3
Food crops only	13.2	6.9	4.5	1.9	3.1	1.6	1.1	0.4	32.7
Cash crops only	0.6	0.0	0.0	0.0	0.0	0.0	0.0	0.0	0.6
Livestock only	0.2	0.7	0.4	0.0	0.4	0.0	0.4	0.0	2.2
Food and cash crops	6.2	0.9	0.6	0.6	1.9	1.1	0.2	1.6	15.1
Food crops and livestock	11.1	3.6	1.6	1.5	2.8	0.2	0.9	1.4	23.1
Cash crops and livestock	0.1	0.0	0.0	0.1	0.0	0.0	0.0	0.0	0.2
All types farm income	11.7	5.4	0.5	2.8	0.7	0.7	0.0	0.0	21.8
TOTAL	46.5	19.3	7.9	6.9	8.9	3.9	2.6	4.0	100.0

Source: Our survey.

TABLE 3.11. *Per capita income structure of resident households by holding size*

Income categories	Holding size (ha)								Total
	<0.5	0.5–0.9	1–1.9	2–2.9	3–3.9	4–4.9	5–7.9	8+	
Food crops	23.4	43.8	29.2	46.8	44.5	42.3	64.3	44.7	41.5
Cash crops	13.1	5.7	3.0	10.1	8.2	11.3	5.5	7.5	7.0
Livestock	8.2	17.3	12.2	15.3	16.0	21.7	6.9	10.9	13.9
Own business	51.7	8.2	47.3	14.1	21.5	14.6	5.7	27.0	26.3
Wages	0.6	15.3	4.3	5.1	5.7	7.2	12.8	6.1	6.4
Remittances	3.0	9.8	4.0	8.6	4.0	3.0	4.7	3.8	4.8
Per capita income	1404	1053	1793	1096	1955	2356	1069	1656	1548
Relative income level	91	68	116	71	126	152	69	107	100

Source: Own survey.

TABLE 3.12. *Production for sale 1969–1983*
(quantity indices)

	Cashewnuts	Cotton	Coffee
1969	100	100	100
1970	94	107	92
1971	117	96	72
1972	137	113	112
1973	134	106	123
1974	139	86	84
1975	119	69	111
1976	81	97	111
1977	91	71	119
1978	54	83	104
1979	85	55	93
1980	26	81	105
1981	54	80	130
1982	40	76	110
1983	49	—	106

Source: Bank of Tanzania (1984), Budget speeches.

around 50 per cent, so per capita production unambiguously declined by a very considerable amount.

There is no regular programme of data collection at the household level in rural areas, hence it is not possible to construct an annual series of the level and structure of income derived from a common methodology. However, Tanzania is better provided than most African countries with snapshot rural surveys, and by comparing the results of these surveys we can obtain some indication as to what the trends must have been. We compare our own survey with four earlier surveys conducted in 1979/80, 1976/7, 1974/5, and 1969. The 1979/80 survey was conducted jointly by the ILO and the University of Dar es Salaam with the assistance of the Bureau of Statistics. Its sample of 600 households covered eight of the twenty regions of Tanzania and it used a methodology very similar to our own survey for 1982/3. The 1976/7 survey was conducted by the Bureau of Statistics with a nationwide sample of over 5,000 households. However, of particular interest for the discovery of trends is a sub-sample of 480 households who were common to the 1976/7 and 1982/3 surveys. The fact that the 1982/3 survey was able to trace these same households greatly improves the reliability of comparisons by removing a major source of sampling error. Further, the fact that the 1976/7 survey contained a large total sample enables us to test whether the smaller and regionally selective 1982/3 sample is representative of rural Tanzania nationally, by comparing the characteristics of the sub-sample in 1976 with those of the entire sample in the same year.

The third survey was conducted by the FAO and refers to the year 1974/5. It contains usable data on ten regions with a sample of 561 households. This survey is unpublished, and knowing little about it relative to the other surveys we include it only for its estimate of per capita income. The fourth survey we use for comparison was conducted in calendar 1969 by the Bureau of Statistics with a nationwide sample of 2,196 households, and was the first large-sample survey conducted in rural Tanzania.

We begin our analysis of trends with a comparison of the results of the 1982/3 and 1979/80 surveys. 1980 was a difficult year for peasants because of drought in many areas. Nevertheless, the comparison suggests that between 1979/80 and 1982/3 there was some decline in living standards attributable to a decline in cash income from farm sources. Per capita household income was on average 1,549 shilling in 1982/3 at current prices and 734 shillings in 1979/80. To convert the 1979/80 figure to constant 1982/3 prices we initially use the official national consumer price index. With the average price level during 1980 as 100, that in 1979 was 76.8 so that on average during the 1979/80 survey the price level was 88.4. Analogously, the average of the 1982 and 1983 price levels was 183.9. Hence, rebasing so that the price level during the former survey was 100, that for the 1982/3 survey was 208.0. We will suggest that the price level facing peasants rose by more than this, but using the official figures, 1979/80 income at 1982/3 prices was 1,527 shillings, implying an increase in per capita real income of around 1 per cent.

The composition of income does not show dramatic changes but rather a tendency for non-farm sources of income to become relatively more important, and within farm-based income for the subsistence portion to become more important. In Table 3.13 we distinguish four components of income, namely food and livestock produced for subsistence, food and livestock sold for cash, non-farm-earned income from wages and businesses, and finally remittances received from friends and relatives living elsewhere.

We now turn to a study of the longer period 1976/7–1982/3. Whereas 1979/80 was a relatively poor year because of drought, 1976/7 was rather atypically advantageous. There was a conjunction of favourable climatic conditions with the coffee boom, and although much of the price increase was not passed through to peasants, there was some increase in the producer price during the survey year. Recall that the 1982/3 survey is a trace on a subset of the households in the 1976/7 survey. Such a tracing of a large group of peasant households over an interval as long as six years appears to be a unique feature of our data set. The task of relocating the same households was considerably simplified by the Tanzanian administrative structures of villages and ten cell leaders which enabled a high proportion of chosen households to be contacted. Due to resource constraints the 1983 survey covered only four regions, and within those regions included only a sample of the households in the 1976/7 survey. The latter survey can thus be used to test how representative our sample was both of the full sample in the four regions, and of the national sample of rural households. We therefore report the results of the survey, first only for those households common to both surveys; secondly, for all households in the four regions sampled in 1983; and thirdly, for the entire sample of rural households.

Among households common to both surveys, mean per capita income in 1976/7 at current prices was 930 shillings. We convert this into 1982/3 prices initially using the official consumer price index, the inter-survey deflator being 3.198. Applying this, income at 1982/3 prices was 2,974 shillings, implying that between 1976/7 and 1982/3 real per capita incomes of peasant households halved. Despite this massive drop, the structure of income was similar in the two years, the major difference being that remittance income was larger both

TABLE 3.13. *Changes in income composition, 1979/1980–1982/1983 (%)*

Income component	Composition in 1980	Composition in 1983	Change in real value[a] 1980–3
Subsistence	49.0	44.9	−7.0
Farm sales	23.5	17.5	−24.5
Non-farm earnings	23.1	32.7	+43.5
Remittances	4.3	4.8	+13.8
TOTAL	100.0	100.0	+1.4

[a] Deflated with official consumer price index.

Sources: Own survey (1982/3) and 1979/80 Household Survey.

relatively and absolutely in 1983. The full compositional changes are set out in Table 3.14.

How representative are these traced households? Compared with the full sample of households in the four regions they have slightly lower per capita income. However, the shortfall is only 2.4 per cent. Compared with the national sample of rural households there is also a small income shortfall of 3.1 per cent.

These differences are sufficiently small to suggest that the traced households were in 1977 representative both of the four regions in which the survey was conducted and of peasant households nationally. The possibility remains that between 1977 and 1983 the traced households ceased to be a representative sample. There are good reasons for expecting this to be the case; in particular the sample would under-represent newly formed households and so the age of household heads would be biased upwards. Since newly formed, young households are likely to have below-average income, the consequence of this sample bias inherent in tracing is to overstate income in 1983 relative to earlier years. Since we have not quantified this bias we make no allowance for it, but it should be borne in mind as a qualification to our income comparisons.

With this caveat the traced households appear representative concerning per capita income, but this may conceal differences in the composition of income. The comparison of income composition in the three samples is shown in Table 3.15.

The comparison shows that although there is one income component, namely wages, for which traced households are unrepresentative of their regions, as it happens this is the one respect in which these regions are unrepresentative of rural households nationally, so that the sample of traced households closely represents the national structure of rural income.

So far we have used as our income deflator the national consumer price index. This is less than ideal as a guide to the rural cost of living, partly

TABLE 3.14. *Changes in income composition, 1976/1977–1982/1983 (%)*

Income component	Composition in 1977	Composition in 1983	Change in real value[a] 1977–83
Subsistence	53.2	44.9	−56.0
Farm sales	19.4	17.5	−53.0
Business	19.0	26.3	−27.9
Wages	6.4	6.4	−47.8
Remittances	2.0	4.8	+27.3
TOTAL	100.0	100.0	−47.9

[a] Deflated with official consumer price index.
Sources: Own survey (1982/3) and 1976/7 Household Budget Surveys.

TABLE 3.15. *The composition of income in 1976–1977: national, four regions, and traced samples*

Income component	Traced households	Full sample four regions	Rural national
Subsistence	53.2	47.6	49.2
Farm sales	19.4	18.3	20.1
Business	19.0	17.9	20.1
Wages	6.4	14.1	8.4
Remittances	2.0	2.2	2.3
TOTAL	100.0	100.0	100.0

Source: 1976/7 Household Budget Survey.

because the underlying process of information gathering about prices is confined to urban areas, and partly because there is a tendency for official enumerators to under-record black-market prices. This bias away from black-market prices would not affect the deflator if the ratio of these prices to official prices was constant. However, the black market is a phenomenon which has emerged since the mid-1970s in response to an attempt by the authorities to prevent prices from rising as a consequence of a deteriorating availability of foreign exchange. Hence, any tendency to under-enumerate the black market will result in an underestimate of the cost of living deflator. To check this the 1982/3 survey collected rural black-market prices for eighteen basic consumer goods, namely maize flour, rice, paraffin, cooking oil, soap, sugar, salt, matches, cigarettes, roofing sheets, bicycles, bicycle tubes, torch batteries, hoes, pangas, school uniforms, khangas, and radios. Official prices for these items were identified for both 1982/3 and 1976/7 from price reviews published in the *Daily News*. As summarized in Table 3.4, the 1982/3 survey also collected data on the quantities of purchases at both official and black-market prices. The price and quantity data were then combined to produce rural expenditure shares for each of the eighteen goods on each of the two markets, expenditure thus being disaggregated into thirty-six components. Since in 1976/7 black markets were insignificant, official prices can be used as the actual prices at which purchases took place in that period. From this information a price deflator was constructed. Since the weights of the eighteen goods in expenditure were for 1983, the price index 1976/7 to 1982/3 is a Paasche index.

The resulting index indeed suggests that the rural price level rose somewhat more rapidly than implied by the national consumer price index. Recall that between the two surveys the latter indicates that the price level rose by a factor of 3.198. Our own index shows the price leval to have risen by a factor of 3.936 over the same period. This implies that by using the national consumer price index we have overstated real incomes in 1982/3 by nearly a fifth (18.7 per cent) relative to their level in 1976/7. Analogously, since it is likely that the divergence between black-market and official prices increased between 1979/80 and 1982/3, our initial comparison between those two years overstates income in 1982/3 relative to 1979/80.

We next briefly make use of the FAO survey of 1974/5. The reported income categories for this survey do not permit comparison of income composition, nor do we know the extent to which survey methodology differed from the other surveys. Mean per capita income was 724 shillings at current prices. In real terms this is slightly lower than 1976/7 survey, but still very much higher than that in either of the later surveys. It therefore tends to corroborate the 1976/7 survey as being representative of the period.

Our final comparison is with the calendar 1969 survey. Mean per capita income at current prices was 303 shillings. Again we initially use the national consumer price index to convert this to 1982/3 prices, the index standing at 724.0 in 1982/3 with base 100 for calendar 1969. Expressed in 1982/3 prices per capita income is thus 2,194 shillings. This implies a decline in real income of 29.4 per cent between 1969 and 1982/3. If our own index of the rural cost of living is used to replace the national consumer price index between 1976/7 and 1982/3, then by 1982/3 the price level stands at 891.1 and the decline in real income is increased to 42.6 per cent.

Changes in the components of income are shown in Table 3.16.

The results suggest that within farm income there has been a substantial retreat into subsistence activities: farm sales have declined as a proportion of farm-based income from 36.7 per cent to 28.0 per cent. The pronounced decline in wage income probably reflects the political moves since 1969 to discourage the use of hired labour on peasant holdings. Remittances are the only component of income to have increased in absolute terms, perhaps reflecting the growth in the urban wage bill relative to rural income. However,

TABLE 3.16. *Changes in income composition, 1969–1982/1983*

Income component	Composition in 1969	Composition in 1982/3	Change in real value[a] 1969–1982/3
Subsistence	43.9	44.9	−27.7
Farm sales	25.4	17.5	−51.3
Business	15.6	26.3	+19.2
Wages	12.7	6.4	−64.5
Remittances	2.3	4.8	+50.2
TOTAL	100.0	100.0	−29.4

[a] Deflated with official consumer price index.

Sources: Own survey (1982/3) and 1969 Household Budget Survey.

the structures of incomes, despite being fourteen years apart, is a recognizably similar.

So far we have restricted our analysis to pair-wise comparisons with the 1982/3 survey. We now consider whether anything can be made of the surveys as a set. In Table 3.17 we present per capita real income series with 1969 as 100, first using the national consumer price index, and then with our own price index replacing it for the period since 1976/7. Since our index cannot be calculated for 1979/80 we have assumed that the increase in our index over the national consumer price index between 1976/7 and 1979/80 was half of the observed increase for the longer period 1976/7 to 1982/3, though clearly this is arbitrary.

Table 3.17 reveals a spectacular, but not unbelievable, income series. The two surveys conducted during the post-boom period convey a consistent message of a disastrous collapse in real income as compared with any of the three previous surveys. Expressed as a secular trend rate of decline over the entire fourteen years the national CPI deflator yields -2.5 per cent per annum and the adjusted CPI yields -3.9 per cent per annum.

Despite this disturbing decline in real income, all the surveys tell a similar story with regard to the structure of income. To the extent that there have been trends in composition, within farm income, subsistence has tended to replace cash. Within non-farm-earned income business income has tended to replace wage employment, increasing from 55 per cent in 1969 to 75 per cent in 1976/7 and 80 per cent in 1982/3 (the 1979/80 survey not reporting this particular disaggregation). Finally, remittances from non-residents (almost entirely urban-based) have increased very markedly, both relatively and absolutely, from around 2 per cent to around 5 per cent of income. This flow of gifts from urban areas may well suggest that the balance of aggregate income, if not per capita income, has shifted in favour of urban areas.

Since we have emphasized the importance of the urban claim upon resources, it is of some interest to set the change in peasant incomes in the

TABLE 3.17. *Trends in real income, 1969–1982/1983*

	Year				
	1969	1974/5	1976/7	1979/80	1982/3
Nominal per capita income (sh)	303	724	930	734	1490
Official CPI	100.0	179.3	226.4	348.1	724.0
Adjusted CPI	100.0	179.3	226.4	388.3	891.1
Real income (official CPI)	100.0	133.0	135.6	69.6	67.9
Real income (adjusted CPI)	100.0	133.0	135.6	62.4	55.1

Sources: Own survey (1982/3) and 1969, 1974/5, 1976/7, 1979/80 surveys

context of changes in the urban economy. Using the budget surveys of 1969 and 1976/7 and our own small survey conducted in Dar es Salaam in 1984 we are able to build up some idea of the changes in urban real living standards at least for the largest city (Dar es Salaam accounts for nearly half the urban population). The details of this comparison are set out elsewhere;[10] here we report only the comparison with the trend in rural incomes.

The results, which are set out in Table 3.18, utilize as the price deflator the national CPI adjusted for black-market prices as described previously. Urban per capita income declined somewhat more rapidly than rural income at −6.1 per cent per annum between 1969 and 1983/4, hence, on average the ratio of urban to rural incomes declined. However, this decline was by no means uniform over the period.

Between 1969 and 1976/7 urban incomes fell markedly relative to rural incomes, the former falling in absolute terms and the latter rising. In contrast, between 1976/7 and 1983/4, while both groups have experienced severe declines in per capita income, it is the rural population which has suffered most. In making the comparison over this second period we must note that the rural survey data relate to 1982/3 and the urban to 1983/4. Since rural incomes had tended to decline, we have simply extrapolated this for the extra year at the average rate for the previous period (−3.9 per cent). The resulting estimates for 1983/4 and the associated ratios are shown in parentheses in Table 3.18. Were no adjustment made, and rural real income in 1982/3 compared with urban real income in 1983/4, the relative recovery in urban incomes would be diminished but by no means eliminated.

TABLE 3.18. *A comparison of trends in rural and urban incomes*

Year	Per capita incomes (1969 = 100)		
	Urban	Rural	Ratio
1969	100.0	100.0	1.00
1971	90.6	—	—
1974	82.5	—	—
1975	69.6	—	—
1976/7	85.1	135.6	0.63
1979/80	—	62.4	—
1982/3	—	57.4	—
1983/4	39.2	(55.1)	(0.71)

Note: The rural income figure for 1983/4 is extrapolated from 1982/3 at the 1969–83 trend.
Source: Bevan *et al.* (1988, Table 15).

[10] Bevan *et al.* (1988).

To conclude, the previous comparison of survey data has revealed an alarming story of severe deterioration in living standards. While the phasing and magnitude of this decline differs between rural and urban groups, the dominant conclusion is not of redistribution but rather of widely shared hardship.

The urban claim on resources increased dramatically during the 1970s, but this was not transmitted to the living standards of the urban population. The commitment to industrial investment resulted in a larger, but a poorer, workforce. This is perhaps why there was such strong political resistance to policy measures perceived as reducing urban real wages. There was never a binding political constraint against the reduction of urban real wages in Tanzania: Table 3.18 demonstrates that the government implemented, and survived, one of the largest reduction in urban living standards experienced outside the context of warfare. However, that the government chose to reduce wages so as to release resources for its expenditure programme indicates how powerfully committed it was to that programme. Urban households could not be squeezed to divert resources to the productive peasant sector because they had already been squeezed for higher priorities.

3.6. Peasant Behaviour During the Coffee Boom

The somewhat stark message of the previous section is that the peasant economy in Tanzania may scarcely have noticed the coffee boom, set as it was against a backdrop of income decline. There was, however, a modest increase in the real producer price of coffee for a short period.

In Kilimanjaro, the coffee-growing region of our survey, 24 per cent of households reported some coffee planting between 1975 and 1983. This was entirely confined to those households already growing coffee, only a single household in our sample having adopted coffee during the period. Slightly offsetting this planting, 3 per cent of households uprooted coffee. Among those who did plant, one-quarter attributed their decision to the increase in the price of coffee during the boom as compared with a half in Kenya, the difference being consistent with the markedly smaller price increase experienced by Tanzanian peasants. The proportion of planters who by 1983 regretted their decision was low, as in Kenya, only 13 per cent. Further, the reason for regret was related to the fact that coffee-growing required too much work rather than that the price had fallen.

This displeasure with the labour intensity of coffee is borne out by the responses to those questions directed to the use of labour during the boom. Recall that in Kenya most coffee-growing households claimed to have increased their own labour input and to have hired more labour during the boom (the latter being consistent with the tripling of wage rates); in contrast, in Tanzania coffee growers claim to have reduced labour input.

Recall that despite the net increase in planting between 1975 and 1983, the production of coffee was actually lower in 1983 than in 1975. Our survey found that in Tanzania coffee plots were usually inter-cropped with a variety of food crops, which was uncommon in Kenya. One interpretation of the labour, planting, and production data is that Tanzanian peasants were reallocating labour away from coffee to food, even though, because of the high cost of uprooting, there was a net increase in the tree stock. This would be consistent with the fact that those regretting coffee planting did so because of its demands on their labour time, and also with respondents' claims to have reduced labour input during the boom years compared with previous behaviour. Finally, it would be consistent with the aggregate production trend.

As in Kenya, we asked coffee growers how they had used their windfall income. In retrospect, the windfall received by Tanzanian peasants was so small that the question is far less appropriate. The responses, reported in Table 3.19, tend to confirm this. Expenditure for daily needs figured much more prominently: the ratio of this response to all others was 0.52 among Tanzanian coffee growers against 0.39 in Kenya. Financial savings, cited by over half of Kenyans, was cited by only around one in ten Tanzanians. When we come to quantify savings rates in later chapters we will see that this suspicion is borne out.

To conclude, during the period on which we focus, 1969–83, there were indeed profound changes in the Tanzanian peasant economy, most notably a collapse in income. Clearly, this change was not directly due to the impact of the coffee boom, for this must at the worst have been negligible. In Part III (Chapter 9) we develop a theory of the interaction of macroeconomic performance and the peasant economy which predicts that the observed

TABLE 3.19. *Use of extra coffee boom money (Kilimanjaro)*

Expenditure categories	Percentage who spent on the activity
Invested in non-farm business	9
Bought house	—
Married more wives	—
Spent it on daily needs	100
Spent more on school fees	67
Spent it on house improvements	41
Bought crop or land	37
Bought livestock	14
Bought farm machinery	14
Saved some of it	11
Other	6

macroeconomic policy interventions would result in just the sort of income collapse we have described. Whether this conjunction is indeed causal is tested in our analytic chapters on Tanzanian peasant behaviour, Chapters 10 and 11. Indirectly, through its effect upon the design of macroeconomic policies, the coffee boom may well have contributed to the sad outcome we have recorded in this chapter.

II

Peasants and Price Volatility: Theory and an Application to Kenya

4
Introduction to Part II

The descriptive account of farming in Kenya in 1974–82 in Chapter 2 made clear that this was a period in which peasants were exposed to very strong price volatility. Price changes were dominated by the coffee boom, consisting not only of the increase in coffee prices (and the associated rise in tea prices) but also of its indirect effects in the form of changes in prices of goods and factors. This Part does not aim to provide an analysis of the boom; nevertheless, the boom plays a central role. This is so not just because of the intrinsic interest of the impact of a commodity boom on peasant producers, but largely because in analysing the boom we encounter restrictions on both the static and the dynamic efficiency of resource allocation which are critical for the understanding of peasants' behaviour as producers.

In *Controlled Open Economies*, we argue that the macroeconomic and general equilibrium effects of the coffee boom in Kenya depended crucially on the behaviour of private agents being constrained (for example by quantitative restriction on imports and by prohibition of the acquisition of foreign assets). The importance of such deviations from the standard model is highlighted when an economy is exposed to a shock. Similarly, at the microlevel, the boom underlines aspects of the decision environment of Kenyan peasants.

The boom had both static and dynamic effects. If we first think of it as a permanent change then it can be analysed in a static model. The theory, summarized in Section 5.1 of Chapter 5 (on Relative Price Changes and Resource Reallocation), is basically the one familiar to trade theorists from the Dutch Disease literature. The boom is a relative price change which has substitution and income effects on peasants' expectations, both in goods and in factor markets. Some of the resulting relative price changes affect peasants as consumers. This involves transfers between peasants and other groups in the economy as a result of relative price changes for consumption goods: this we analyse in *Controlled Open Economies*. As producers, peasants are presented with two price changes: the coffee price increase itself (which may induce substitution away from food crops) and a rise in rural wages (accompanying the increase in employment in the booming activity, i.e. coffee growing, at the expense of other activities; this is the resource movement effect in Dutch Disease models). These price changes lead to substitutions between activities, between inputs, and between labour and leisure.

In Section 5.2 (on Income Windfalls, Investment, and Activity-Specific Returns) we take into account that the coffee boom was not a permanent, but a temporary terms of trade improvement (and was perceived as such by peasants). This implies that peasants would want to save most of the windfall, so that the return on the investments financed with those savings would provide them with a permanent income increase. This can be analysed with standard saving models as long as activities are characterized by constant returns to scale, there are no barriers to entry, all agents are fully informed about available technologies, and there are no indivisibilities in investment.

These conditions are not satisfied in Kenya. This is reflected in large differences in the return to various activities. First, access to non-agricultural wage employment (a high-income activity) is rationed. Secondly, in one activity, coffee growing, there are economies of scale. In addition, factor markets (those for land, labour, and credit) are so imperfect that a peasant household can best be analysed as a country in the Heckscher–Ohlin model, i.e. with the availability of factors given and without access to a capital market. As is well-known from trade theory, the non-tradability of factors is not in itself problematic. But the combinations of these severe restrictions in factor markets and the presence of economies of scale leads to a very different model. Factor price equalization no longer applies: returns to factors (such as to family labour) will differ between households. In addition rates of return now depend upon the scale of operation. Hence when two households differ only in the *size* (but not in the *composition*) of their endowments—the labour/land ratio being identical but one household being better endowed with both factors—then it may be profitable only for the richer household to invest in coffee growing. The same is true for the adoption of livestock, an activity which has constant returns to scale but is characterized by indivisibilities: for a Kenyan peasant a cow represents a very substantial investment.

The combination of indivisibilities, economies of scale, and imperfections in factor markets defines a hierarchy of activities. Returns differ between activities but entry to the high-return activities is barred by the impossibility of borrowing. Peasants are forced to self-finance the transition from one activity to another, starting with food crops only and gaining access to non-agricultural wage employment via the adoption of livestock and of cash crops.

In this world investment behaviour does not consist of marginal adjustments in the size and composition of a portfolio. Under these conditions windfall income may enable peasants to overcome credit constraints: the transient income of the boom enables some households to cross the threshold to the next activity in the hierarchy (possibly, but not necessarily, coffee growing). Quite possibly a boom has a stronger permanent effect in this situation than it would have in the case of a perfect capital market (or, alternatively, in the absence of indivisibilites and returns to scale).

A final twist is added if we relax the assumption of full information. When peasants are imperfectly informed about the technology and the riskiness of coffee growing, the adoption of coffee by one peasant provides his neighbours with free rider opportunities: by observing him they can acquire the information they need to decide whether to invest in coffee themselves. This may lead to copying. In this case the boom will move some peasants up in the hierarchy of activities for a reason quite distinct from the one discussed above. Those for whom the credit constraint is not binding and for whom coffee growing was already profitable and feasible adopt coffee because the boom affects their information set. As others invest in coffee they perceive the activity as profitable and copy the investment decision. In this sense a boom can have a multiplier effect (which would be absent in the case of full information). We will present evidence that this gearing effect was important in Kenya.

The theory of Chapter 5 is followed in Chapter 6 by an empirical application, largely on the basis of survey evidence including our own survey in rural Kenya. Chapter 7 extends the application to a comparison with peasants in Tanzania.

5
The Response to Price Windfalls: Some Theoretical Considerations

5.1. Relative Price Changes and Resource Reallocation

One consequence of the coffee boom was that the relative prices facing peasants changed. Depending upon their expectations and opportunities peasants will respond to these altered incentives by reallocating their resources. We begin our analysis of this decision process with a simple taxonomy of boom-induced price changes, depicted in Table 5.1.

The taxonomy distinguishes between permanent and temporary and between direct and indirect consequences of the boom. The increases in coffee and tea prices are direct, temporary aspects of the boom. As peasants respond to this incentive, attempting to increase production through greater use of purchased variable inputs, they force up the price of those inputs in relatively inelastic supply, the most important such input probably being hired labour. Such an increase in agricultural wage rates is thus an indirect, temporary price change. Such price changes occur not only in factor markets but also in product markets. It is the central point of the Dutch Disease literature that when the beneficiaries of a boom increase their spending on final goods and services, they may force up the prices of goods which are in relatively inelastic supply (either because they are non-tradable, as in the case of many services, or because they are tradable but behave as non-tradables as a result of import controls). We have shown elsewhere that in Kenya such relative price changes were extremely important: during the boom they offset about 40 per cent of the nominal income gain of peasants, and transferred the major part of the gains to urban households. The coffee boom led to a huge increase in investment. Because of biases in investment allocation the long-run effect of this investment was a substantial reduction in the relative prices of non-tradables and of protected importables. Hence while in the short run these

TABLE 5.1. *A taxonomy of price changes*

	Direct effect	Indirect effect
Temporary	Coffee and tea price increases	Wage of agricultural labour increases, and consumer goods prices are higher
Permanent		Consumer goods prices are lower

relative price changes represent an adverse change for peasants (an increase in the price they have to pay for consumer goods), in the long run peasants benefit from an improvement in the terms of trade.

These direct effects are very important if the focus is on changes in income distribution and the way the boom is transmitted through the economy (the focus of our analysis in *Controlled Open Economies*), but they do not affect our analysis of peasants as producers. This is because, in aggregate, the income and substitution effects of change in the prices paid by peasants for non-food consumer goods will affect their demand for, but not the prices of, food crops, these prices being tied to world prices. We therefore concentrate on the effects of the changes in wages and in coffee and tea prices.

The resource reallocation consequences of these price changes can be grouped into substitution among activities, substitution among purchased inputs, and substitution between labour and leisure. We consider these in turn.

The substitution of resources among existing activities in response to the temporary, direct change in relative prices has three components. The rise in coffee and tea prices may induce the diversion of own labour, purchased inputs, and investment from other activities (such as food crops into tree crops) so as to maintain the equality of marginal revenue products of inputs with their marginal costs. Of these the two former are unproblematic. Coffee yields can be increased, and shifted from the next year to the current year, by increased application of labour and fertilizer. The diversion of investment, however, depends upon whether the windfall alters expectations of future coffee and tea prices. Given the gestation period of tree crop investment, the Brazilian frost did not itself constitute an opportunity for profitable tree crop investment, since its effects on price were likely to be largely or entirely eroded by the time the first yields were being received. Coffee trees require four years prior to the first full harvest. The gestation period for tea trees depends upon the process of frame formation: using the traditional method of formative pruning, plucking cannot commence for two and a half to three years after planting; using the new techniques of pegging, a small harvest is possible in the second year after planting. Hence, planting undertaken at the start of the boom, in 1976, would not secure significant yields until at least 1979. However, even if peasants recognized that by planting coffee they could not benefit from the boom, the increase in the price might have changed their expectations about the frequency distribution of prices. Alternatively, the price increase might either have been consistent with existing expectations, or have been regarded as an outlier to be discounted. Since those with more optimistic expectations of coffee prices are *ceteris paribus* more likely to grow coffee, non-coffee growers are more likely to be in the first and last categories.

The second aspect of substitution of resources among existing activities is in response to temporary, indirect changes in relative prices. The increase in the wage rate for agricultural labour due to the increased demand for coffee pickers reduces the relative profitability of other crops which are intensive in hired labour. For example, tea is hired-labour intensive and so were it not for the increase in the price of tea, the increase in the wage rate would unambiguously have reduced tea output.

Turning from the substitution among activities to substitution among inputs, the increase in the cost of labour should induce changes in techniques in favour of labour substitutes. For example, the use of pesticides is an alternative to the more labour-intensive process of weeding. The scope for such substitutions can be quantified through the estimation of production functions.

The final substitution is between labour and leisure. The increase in coffee and tea prices in the short run, and in all peasant outputs (relative to the prices of consumer goods) in the long run, generates conventional offsetting income and substitution effects. If the labour supply curve is 'normal' leisure will be reduced.

5.2. Income Windfalls, Investment, and Activity-Specific Returns

In the preceding section we discussed the changes in incentives for current production brought about by changes in relative prices. However, the coffee boom was also an income windfall which (as we saw in Chapter 2) had powerful implications for asset formation.

The investment activities of peasants can be analysed in a simple, aggregate model if the average rate of return to each factor is independent of the activity in which it is deployed and of the household by which it is owned, despite the absence of factor markets. The impact of the coffee boom windfall can then be analysed simply in terms of the augmentation of the capital stock, on which there will be a common and constant rate of return. If this condition is not satisfied, the windfall must additionally be analysed in terms of changes in the development of endowments between activities. The windfall income may then enable households to move up the hierarchy from lower to higher return activities, depending upon the causes of differences in returns. Four circumstances must jointly hold for returns to be equal: namely, the absence of entry barriers, constant returns in all activities, full information (encompassing complete certainty and common knowledge of and ability to use techniques), and sufficiently large differences in factor intensities between activities relative to differences in endowment ratios between households that no household specializes in fewer activities than the number of factors.

One activity the entry to which may be subject to overt entry barriers is non-agricultural wage labour. The criteria by which employers ration job opportunities might include skill, education, previous experience, and the social network of existing employees. Recruitment criteria confer value on whichever of these endowments is used. In considering the consequences of rationed access it is useful to distinguish between intensive and extensive rationing. In the former some households gain full access while others get zero access. In the latter all households get some access, but less than they would choose. Optimal resource allocation by unrationed households can be simply characterized:

Let the utility function be:
$$U = U(L, Y).$$
Let the time constraint be:
$$T = F + E + L.$$
Let the budget constraint be:
$$Y = wE + pQ.$$
And let the production function be:
$$Q = Q(F), \quad Q' > 0, \quad Q'' < 0,$$
where
Y = income
T = total time available
L = leisure
F = farm work
E = wage work
w = wage rate
p = price of farm output
Q = quantity of farm output

The first-order conditions for the maximization of utility subject to the time and budget constraints are:
$$-\lambda + \mu Q' = 0$$
$$\gamma p - \mu = 0$$
$$U_l - \lambda = 0$$
$$U_y - \gamma = 0$$
$$\gamma w - \lambda = 0$$
$$T - F - E - L = 0$$
$$Y - wE - pQ = 0$$
$$Q - Q(F) = 0$$

where $\lambda, \mu,$ and γ are Lagrange multipliers and U_l and U_y denote the marginal utilities of leisure and income. Normalizing such that $p = 1$, the first-order conditions imply:
$$w = Q'.$$

If access to wage employment is extensively rationed then no household will be able to attain this so that $w > Q'$ for all households. If access is rationed intensively then unrationed households will achieve the condition and rationed households will make no labour sales. In this case, while ever the constraint binds
$$w = Q'n > Q'r,$$

where n and r denote unrationed and rationed households. Thus labour in unrationed households will enjoy a higher return than in rationed households, and will be diverted from agricultural activities.

The second reason why returns might differ between activities is the conjunction of economies of scale with constraints on endowments. This is important, because we will show below that coffee growing is subject to economies of scale within the relevant range of peasant production. Uniform economies of scale in each activity would tend to induce complete specialization in a single activity, unless offset by differences in factor intensities. However, if in a two-activity world only one has increasing returns, those in the other being constant, there will generally be a threshold size at which the latter activity offers an equivalent return. Such a threshold becomes important if households face constraints upon the quantities of factors which can be deployed. As we have seen in Chapters 2 and 3 there are severe imperfections in land, labour, and credit markets in both countries: in effect, households may only use in production those factors which they own. This gives rise to two different effects. First, because households differ in the total quantity of factors which they own, endowment-scarce households will choose not to enter the economies of scale activity even if that offers the higher return for endowment-abundant households. Secondly, because households differ in the ratio of land-to-labour endowments, the returns to each factor will differ across households. The effect of economies of scale in one activity on activity choices is illustrated in Figure 5.1. The upper diagram shows the case of constant returns in both the labour-intensive activity (X) and the land-intensive activity (Y), with the ratio of factor endowments determining the pattern of specialization. The lower diagram shows how these zones are altered by the presence of economies of scale in X. Households will enter the X activity (cross the activity threshold locus) as a result either of an increase in the scale of their endowments (a movement out along a ray through the origin) or as a result of an increase in their endowment of labour relative to land. X-growing households should therefore be either atypically well endowed or atypically labour abundant.

Now consider a three-activity world (X, Y, Z) in which one of the activities (X) is increasing returns and the other two activities differ in their land–labour intensity. If the economies of scale activity is labour intensive relative to the endowment of the household, in equilibrium it will be constrained from exploiting further economies of scale through expanding the activity by the increasing land/labour ratio which this implies in its other activity. Letting Y be labour intensive relative to Z, the household will specialize in X and Z.

Now compare this household with another with the same ratio of land-to-labour endowments but with too small a total endowment to enter X production. Suppose this second household is incompletely specialized, producing Y and Z. Although both households produce Z they will do so using different factor proportions. Labour is more advantageous to the first

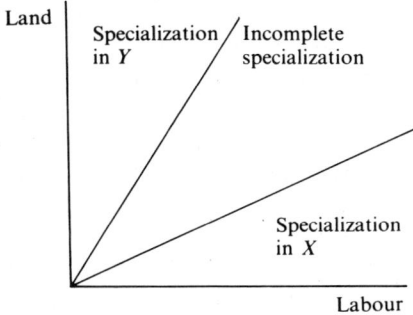

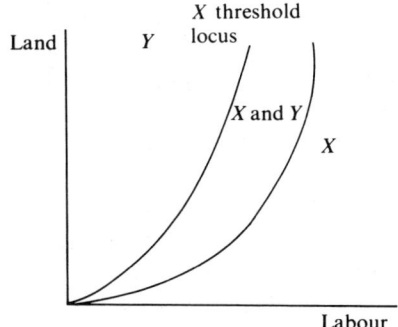

FIG. 5.1 *Factor proportions, scale economies, and specialization*

household (with a perfect labour market the first household would hire labour from the second) and so it will produce Z using a less labour intensive technique. Accordingly, it will have a lower marginal product of land than the less well-endowed household, though it will have a higher average product of both land and labour.

Now consider two households with different factor proportions, neither of which has sufficient endowments to enter X production. If the factor intensities of Y and Z are sufficiently different and the choice of activity is not influenced by considerations of risk, both households will be incompletely specialized and have common marginal products. Where these conditions are not met marginal and average returns will differ according to the ratio of factor endowments: labour-abundant households will have lower returns to labour.

Next, consider two households which differ both by scale and by composition of endowment. Suppose the better endowed household to be relatively land abundant and to have sufficient endowments for X to be profitable. The difference in choice of technique in Z production is now reinforced by the differential endowment. Conversely, if the better endowed household is labour-abundant, the two effects are offsetting.

Finally, consider two households one of which has absolutely more labour and the other more land. If X is labour intensive relative to both Y and Z then the former household is more likely to find X profitable. Hence, abstracting from considerations of risk, the households engaged in X will be both disproportionately well endowed and labour abundant. The latter characteristic will thus tend to offset the tendency of X-producing households to use a less labour intensive technique in Z. Further, because prior to X-production the labour-abundant household has a lower shadow price of labour, even after production of X the household might still have a relatively low average return to labour. In this case the threshold scale at which entry to X is profitable differs by endowment ratio so that those households engaged in X need not enjoy high average rates of return on factors. The entry barrier is breached both by well-endowed and by heavily labour-surplus households.

So far we have considered scale economies only in a two-factor world. However, as will be shown later, coffee not only has a high labour/land ratio but is also intensive in capital. This can be approximated by using a standard trade-theoretic characterization; three factors, two of which are specific, and two goods. Thus, $X = X(K, L)$, $Y = Y(A, L)$. Households may now differ in endowments in three respects; the overall scale of endowment, the ratio of capital to labour, and the ratio of land to labour. As previously, if households differ only in scale, there will be a critical size K^*, L^*, A^*, above which it is profitable for the household to enter X production. All households below this level will earn common return on factors in the constant returns sector (Y), while above it households will earn a higher average return which increases with the size of the endowment.

A corollary of this simple model is that below this critical scale the return to capital is zero. Consequently, if households differ by K/L as well as by scale, then for households with less than K^*, L^*, such differences have no effect upon resource allocation. If both K and L are above these levels an increase in K will reduce Y production as labour is reallocated to X. If initially $K = K^*, L < L^*$, then as K is increased a threshold is reached at which the household enters X production: the lack of labour is offset by sufficient capital. Analogously, if households differ by L/A, those with more A will produce less X.

Each of the models outlined above, two goods–two factors, three goods–two factors, and two goods–three factors, has some insights to offer concerning differences in returns to factors in peasant agriculture caused by economies of scale combined with an absence of factor markets. Each has in common the notion that abstracting from differences in factor ratios there is a threshold to endowments above which average returns increase. Were this the only influence then all households in the economies of scale activity would be enjoying higher returns than those in other activities. Whether or not returns are equalized among these other households depends upon whether the first or second model applies. Between them the models suggest two other influences on entry into the economies of scale activity. Since X is both labour and capital intensive, relative abundance in either factor can make it profitable to enter the activity. However, since entry is motivated by the difficulty in absorbing the abundant factor in other activities, there is no need in these cases for the average return on factors to be higher.

The final reason why returns might differ between activities is due to differences in knowledge or ability between decision takers. Knowledge includes both information about how to undertake particular techniques, and information about the true frequency distribution of consequences. For example, new techniques may carry considerable uncertainty as to their true riskiness, and learning may reduce the dispersion of perceived outcomes, thereby reducing the risk premium in the rate of return to the activity. In the absence of a market for information, knowledge of new techniques, of which all the techniques for activities newly introduced into the peasant economy are an important subset, will differ. Some households, by the good fortune of learning externalities, will have access to a superior production function. Two possible channels of information are neighbours and the extension service. The former is intrinsically differentiated by location, and will generate both static differences between localities and a dynamic process of spatial contagion. The latter will give rise to differentiation if the extension service perceives economies of scale in learning and consequently concentrates its tuition upon a proper subset of households. This happens to be a marked difference in the approaches adopted by the Kenyan and Tanzanian extension services, the former targeting advice on a minority of individual farmers and the latter using only group demonstrations.

If differences in ability are uniform across sectors, they will not give rise to differential rates of return between sectors unless they are correlated with some specialization-inducing characteristic such as risk aversion or factor endowment. For example, if bad farmers accumulate little capital then this will tend to constrain them from entering activity X, so that the returns to X averaged across farmers will, *ceteris paribus*, be higher than in other activities because the farmers engaged in X are on average more able. Sector-specific differences in ability generate the same outcome more directly: if all farmers have a common ability in Y but differential abilities in X, then *ceteris paribus*, there is a threshold level of ability above which households enter X, and all such households other than the marginal entrant enjoy higher average returns than households confined to Y.

The routes by which the boom changed peasant incomes can be distinguished by the same taxonomy as that used for price changes, and are depicted in Table 5.2.

Coffee and tea growers obviously experienced a direct, temporary increase in income with which assets could be acquired. However, the gains from the

TABLE 5.2. *A taxonomy of income changes*

	Direct effect of the boom	Indirect effect of the boom
Temporary	Coffee and tea revenue increases	Wage earnings increases due to higher agricultural wage rates and more urban job opportunities
Permanent	Peasant investment out of transient income increases permanent income	(a) Urban job opportunities are permanently increased by windfall investment (b) Rural incomes increase because of improved rural–urban terms of trade

boom were more widely diffused among peasant households through the labour market. The increase in the demand for hired labour to work on coffee and tea raised both the employment and wage rates of hired labourers, while the urban investment and public sector boom increased opportunities of urban wage employment. Some of the latter opportunities persisted after the boom due to windfall investment in the import substitute and non-tradable sectors.

Each of these three sources of change in peasant incomes potentially induced a permanent increase in income as a result of extra peasant investment. The savings rate for the entire Kenyan economy out of the direct and indirect temporary increases in income was, as we show in *Controlled Open Economies*, considerably higher than that from permanent income and in Chapter 6 we show that this also applied to peasants. However, some of the indirect temporary effects might reasonably be perceived as permanent by the beneficiaries. In particular, the temporary expansion in urban employment opportunities is unlikely to imply that subsequent job losses are borne exclusively, or even primarily, by those gaining jobs due to the temporary expansion. More plausibly the subsequent contraction is accommodated either by a generalized increase in involuntary quits, or by a reduction in recruitment relative to voluntary quits. In contrast, the consequences for casual employment opportunities and wage rates of increased hiring on coffee and tea holdings might reasonably have been perceived as temporary. Although households gaining access to urban wage employment might reasonably have expected their acquisition to be fairly permanent, so that transient income would not be increased, they might nevertheless initially have a high savings rate out of the extra income. This would be the case if the wage job enabled either a liquidity or a risk constraint to a high-return investment to be overcome.

The windfall investment in productive activities may either have been directed solely into existing activities or have supported a discrete switch into high-return activities which the household was previously unable to access. Windfall capital accumulation increases the ownership of assets, changes the relative factor endowment, and increases the total endowments of the household. The first can be expected to increase the ability of the household to bear risk, so that it will wish to adjust the portfolio of its activities. The second may generate a Rybczynski effect, switching resources into the activity which is intensive in the augmented factor. The third will induce different behaviour depending upon whether households are below but close to the threshold endowment for the economies of scale activity. Households which are above the threshold can be expected to allocate a high proportion of incremental productive investment to activity X, both because it is capital intensive and because it offers increasing returns. Households well below the threshold will spread extra capital across the range of existing activities.

However, of particular interest are households sufficiently close to the threshold that the windfall capital induces a discrete switch into activity X. Recall that because of economies of scale, the average return on factors for households able to enter the activity can be higher than that in other households. Hence, for households induced by windfall capital to switch into X, the rate of return on this incremental capital can exceed the average return on existing capital. This of course contrasts with households which do not switch into X as a new activity, for diminishing marginal returns will apply to capital in all existing activities. At best, the marginal return can be kept constant, and then only if the household is able fully to exploit the Rybczynski effect (expanding capital-intensive activities and contracting capital-extensive ones). Considerations of risk bearing, putty-clay characteristics of some capital, and insufficient differences in factor intensities between activities all tend to make this unlikely.

The expansion in opportunities for wage employment raises incomes and also has resource reallocation effects. The former will, as discussed above, be primarily a permanent rather than a transient enhancement for the households involved. However, it will still generate some increase in capital formation. The most straightforward of the resource reallocation effects is the diversion of labour from agriculture. As with the change in the capital stock, this has a Rybczynski effect, this time out of labour-intensive activities. The second effect is the increased ability to bear risk in agricultural activities which induces a portfolio adjustment. Finally, the even cash flow provided by wage employment provides a once-and-for-all release of cash balances which further enhances capital formation.

The above discussion of how peasant households might have responded to the coffee boom windfall suggests that there are few simple a priori conclusions. Rather, we must identify the determinants of the progression from low- to high-return activities, quantifying the characteristics of households in the neighbourhood of activity switches. From this analysis the impact of the boom can be quantified, both as an exogenous augmentation of the capital endowment, and as an increase in the opportunities for wage employment.

6
Responses to Price Changes in Kenya

6.1. Introduction

In this chapter we attempt to quantify the behaviour responses of Kenyan peasants to the coffee boom. In Chapter 5 two types of behavioural response were distinguished, i.e. the resource reallocations triggered by relative price changes and the investment triggered by windfall income.

Our approach is first to establish whether on the eve of the boom different activities were yielding substantially different returns. We indeed find this to be the case. The question is then raised as to why such differences have persisted rather than being eroded by entry and exit. Having identified potential entry barriers preserving inequalities we attempt to identify the determinants of the principal investment-financed activity switches during the coffee boom period. Not all of the changes during this period can be attributed to the boom because some were induced by secular trends. We therefore quantify these trends and compare their magnitude over the period with the boom-induced windfall, so that some attribution of the observed investment behaviour can be attempted.

Section 6.2 provides the tools needed for comparisons of returns in different activities, setting out production functions for three key agricultural activities, coffee, hybrid maize, and improved livestock, and an earnings function for wage labour. Section 6.3 uses these functions as components in the construction and comparison of unit cost functions which provide a means of evaluating relative returns.

Section 6.4 first discusses the barriers which might prevent entry into the higher return activities. Some of these are overt, others are due to differential access to information, or the scale and combination of endowments required for the activity. Section 6.4 then uses logit analysis to identify the characteristics possessed by those who entered the high-return activities during the period 1971–82, as compared to those who remained outside the activity and those already engaged in it. Section 6.5 discusses the secular trends which were themselves changing the characteristics possessed by peasant households and thereby inducing activity switches, and compares them with those changes introduced by the boom. It attempts to attribute the activity switches and other investment of the boom period to these two sources

As revealed in Chapter 2, there are a large number of activities in which peasant households are engaged, and so our analysis must be confined to a few important and representative ones. We take as the base hybrid maize production and wage labour on the holdings of other peasants, activities which are easy to enter. Although hybrid maize is a relatively new crop its characteristics made adoption very swift and it is grown by most households in both Central and Nyanza Provinces. Among the potentially entry-restricted higher return activities the most obvious candidate for investigation is coffee, the major tree crop. At some stages in the analysis we include the other important tree crop, tea. As shown in Chapter 2, there was extensive planting of both crops during the boom period, much of it by new entrants to the activity. Two other potentially high return activities are also investigated, namely non-agricultural wage employment and improved livestock. The former is included because the coffee boom increased the opportunities for wage employment and so it is important to identify the characteristics required for entry. Improved livestock is included because it was potentially an attractive and large asset for households with windfall income. This portfolio of activities of course omits much of the diversity of peasant choices, but it does capture the major potential investment opportunities with the exception of non-farm businesses, which are themselves so diverse as to require a separate study. We are not concerned with choices among the annual food crops, for although these decisions may involve complex considerations of yield and price expectations they are not primarily about investment.

6.2. Production Functions for Major Activities

6.2.1. *Coffee Growing*

Because of the importance of the event of the coffee boom in our study, the activity of coffee growing is of special significance to us. Therefore, considerable attention was devoted to the estimation of a coffee production function. As noted before, a central question in the persistence of entry barriers is whether an activity is subject to increasing returns. To investigate this requires a rather more sophisticated treatment of the production function than is customary.

The sample used for estimation was taken from our 1982 rural survey of Nyanza and Central Provinces (details of the survey being given in the Appendix). The survey provides plot-specific data on crop production and inputs over an entire year. Of the total of 783 households surveyed, 246 were recorded as being coffee growers, all of whom operated a single plot of coffee. Hence there was no need to take into account any management efficiency bias arising from households operating multiple plots. Of these 246 observations, 242 consisted of plots of pure-stand coffee, and four consisted of inter-cropped coffee. To limit the study to pure-stand coffee, these latter four observations were excluded. The sample was further restricted by removing plots with missing values for the area of the plot or for production, and also plots with no recorded total labour input. This produced a final sample of 189 plots of pure-stand coffee, each observation being assigned equal weight in all subsequent calculations.

Descriptive statistics for the sample, as well as a breakdown by province, are provided in Table 6.1, where, and throughout the analysis, the following abbreviations apply:

Q = production of coffee (kg per year).
R = regional dummy (0 = Nyanza Province, 1 = Central Province).
A = area of plot (1/100s of hectares).
F = fertilizer input (shillings per year).
P = pesticide input (shillings per year).
O = family labour input (hours per year).
H = hired labour input (hours per year).

In Table 6.1 the first value in each category is the sample-wide figure, while the second is for Nyanza Province and the third for Central Province. A clear regional difference is shown in Table 6.1 with the average Nyanzan producer

TABLE 6.1. *Coffee production statistics*

	Mean	Standard deviation
Q	1,163.01 (702.68) (1,508.25)	1,604.13 (1,015.34) (1,862.71)
A	80.74 (69.38) (89.26)	68.12 (48.89) (78.71)
F	168.22 (12.72) (284.85)	240.98 (54.44) (260.34)
P	238.28 (18.66) (403.00)	454.76 (31.93) (546.54)
O	867.51 (588.06) (1,077.10)	755.03 (422.40) (874.50)
H	80.31 (38.54) (111.64)	250.57 (93.48) (318.54)

Note: The three values given are for the whole sample and in brackets for Nyanza Province and Central Province. The number of observations is 189, 81, and 108 respectively.

using far lower levels of purchased inputs than producers in Central Province. Part of this difference may be explained by cash constraints, but the difference is so great as to suggest a genuine difference in behaviour towards the use of purchased inputs between the regions and/or systematic differences in availability of fertilizer between regions.

The data were first used to estimate a production function of the form:

$$Q = e^{\beta_0} A^{\beta_1} F^{\beta_2} P^{\beta_3} H^{\beta_4} O^{\beta_5}$$

i.e. $\ln Q = \beta_0 + \beta_1 \ln A + \beta_2 \ln F + \beta_3 \ln P + \beta_4 \ln H + \beta_5 \ln O$.

This Cobb–Douglas function was estimated using ordinary least squares on the complete sample, as well as on each region separately. The results are shown in Table 6.2, where again the first value is for the complete sample, the second for Nyanza Province and the third for Central Province. A standard

TABLE 6.2. *Cobb–Douglas results (unrestricted)*
Model: $\ln Q = \beta_0 + \beta_1 \ln A + \beta_2 \ln F + \beta_3 \ln P + \beta_4 \ln H + \beta_5 \ln O$.

Parameter	Estimate	Standard error	T-statistic
β_0	2.587 (2.203) (3.129)	0.602 (1.341) (0.625)	4.297 (1.643) (5.007)
β_1	0.318 (0.126) (0.463)	0.107 (0.234) (0.110)	2.956 (0.540) (4.190)
β_2	0.111 (0.091) (0.112)	0.035 (0.099) (0.042)	3.178 (0.924) (2.655)
β_3	0.053 (0.078) (0.011)	0.038 (0.074) (0.050)	1.401 (1.050) (0.227)
β_4	0.061 (0.083) (0.036)	0.030 (0.064) (0.032)	2.022 (1.285) (1.164)
β_5	0.310 (0.488) (0.176)	0.076 (0.152) (0.080)	4.062 (3.208) (2.206)
F-value	22.546 (3.644) (12.325)		
Adjusted R-squared	0.364 (0.142) (0.346)		

F-test was carried out against the null hypothesis $\beta_1+\beta_2+\beta_3+\beta_4+\beta_5=1$, i.e. as to whether constant returns to scale can be accepted. The F-values obtained and the associated significance level at which the hypothesis can be rejected are shown in Table 6.3.

Hence constant returns to scale technology is accepted in all cases at the 5 per cent significance level, but must be rejected for Central Province at the 10 per cent level.

The Cobb–Douglas function was therefore re-estimated with the constraint $\beta_1+\beta_2+\beta_3+\beta_4+\beta_5=1$ in operation. The results for the sample as a whole and for the two provinces separately are shown in Table 6.4. The Cobb–Douglas formulation does not show any impressive goodness of fit, with the failure to explain Nyanza Province being particularly marked.

The next production function estimated was a nested constant elasticity of substitution (CES) function of the following form:

$$Q = \alpha_0(1+\beta_0 R)\{\alpha_1 \text{LAND}^{\gamma_1} + (1-\alpha_1)\text{LABOUR}^{\gamma_1}\}^{\gamma_2/\gamma_1}$$

where

$$\text{LAND} = \{\beta_1 A^{\gamma_3} + \beta_2 F^{\gamma_3} + (1-\beta_1-\beta_2)P^{\gamma_3}\}^{\gamma_4/\gamma_3}$$

$$\text{LABOUR} = \{\beta_3 O^{\gamma_5} + (1-\beta_3)H^{\gamma_5}\}^{\gamma_6/\gamma_5}.$$

The model therefore comprises two nests, one of land and the land-augmenting inputs of fertilizer and pesticide, and the other a labour aggregate of hired and houshold labour. Hence within each nest there is a constant elasticity of substitution between inputs, as well as between the land and labour aggregates, while the elasticity of substitution can differ between inputs in different nests. This formulation also provides measures for the economies of scale arising from varying inputs within each nest (γ_4 and γ_6), as well as those arising from varying the scale of the two aggregate measures (γ_2). Regional variations are measured by β_0, which is multiplicative on the aggregates, and hence no account is taken of regional differences between nests.

The estimation of this function is discussed at length in the Appendix to this chapter. The results finally adopted are shown in Tables 6.5 and 6.5a. Within the land nest the specification imposes an elasticity of substitution between

TABLE 6.3. *F-values and significance levels for economies of scale test: Cobb–Douglas results*

	F-value	Significance level
Sample	1.5739	0.2112
Nyanza	0.2193	0.6410
Central	2.9387	0.0895

TABLE 6.4. *Coffee production function: Cobb–Douglas results (restricted)*

Model: $\ln Q = \beta_0 + \beta_1 \ln A + \beta_2 \ln F + \beta_3 \ln P + \beta_4 \ln H + \beta_5 \ln O$
where $\beta_1 + \beta_2 + \beta_3 + \beta_4 + \beta_5 = 1$.

Parameter	Estimate	Standard error	T-statistic
β_0	1.870 (1.622) (2.114)	0.189 (0.504) (0.202)	9.867 (3.220) (10.467)
β_1	0.419 (0.208) (0.585)	0.071 (0.155) (0.085)	5.864 (1.342) (6.858)
β_2	0.108 (0.104) (0.106)	0.035 (0.094) (0.042)	3.090 (1.108) (2.501)
β_3	0.052 (0.073) (0.030)	0.038 (0.073) (0.049)	1.367 (1.002) (0.610)
β_4	0.063 (0.084) (0.038)	0.030 (0.063) (0.031)	2.067 (1.330) (1.194)
β_5	0.359 (0.529) (0.241)	0.066 (0.125) (0.071)	5.425 (4.239) (3.380)
F-value	27.702 (4.547) (14.401)		
Adjusted R-squared	0.362 (0.151) (0.334)		

inputs of $1/(1-\gamma_3)$. The estimate for γ_4 suggests the existence of considerable economies of scale within the land aggregate. This might arise from, for instance, the use of more expensive but more efficient methods of application for pesticides and fertilizers being justified by larger plots, or the use of more specialized pesticides and fertilizers by households devoting a greater area of their shamba, and therefore a greater share in their projected income, to coffee production. Further, smaller border size to area ratios imply less spillage of land-augmenting inputs, and also a smaller proportion of the crop being exposed to damage from weather or from access.

TABLE 6.5. *Coffee production function: CES results*

Model: $\text{LAND} = \{\beta_1 A^{\gamma_3} + \beta_2 F^{\gamma_3} + (1-\beta_1-\beta_2) P^{\gamma_3}\}^{\gamma_4/\gamma_3}$
$\text{LABOUR} = \{\beta_3 O^{\gamma_5} + (1-\beta_3) H^{\gamma_5}\}^{\gamma_6/\gamma_5}$.
$Q = \alpha_0 (1+\beta_0 R) \{\alpha_1 \text{LAND}^{\gamma_1} + (1-\alpha_1) \text{LABOUR}^{\gamma_1}\}^{\gamma_2/\gamma_1}$.

Parameter	Estimate	Asymptotic standard error
α_0	1.961	1.528
α_1	0.580	0.540
β_0	-0.335	0.174
β_1	0.751	0.058
β_2	0.067	0.055
β_3	0.679	0.281
γ_1	0.628	0.329
γ_2	1.100	0.195
γ_3	0.211	0.253
γ_4	1.363	0.377
γ_5	0.219	0.279
γ_6	1.011	0.622

TABLE 6.5a. *Degrees of Freedom (DF) and sum of squares for CES results*

	DF	Sum of squares (millions)
Regression	11	543.78
ESS	178	195.62
Uncorrected total	189	739.40
Corrected total	188	483.76

6.2.2. Maize

The major food crop in terms of value, area under cultivation, and labour input in the our survey is hybrid maize. Of the plots of hybrid maize about 60 per cent are inter-cropped, mainly with beans. The remaining 40 per cent, representing about two-thirds of the value of hybrid maize produced, are pure-stand. As it was not possible to allocate inputs between crops on an inter-cropped plot, the estimation of hybrid maize production functions was confined to the pure-stand sample. Removing observations with missing values for plot area, production, or family labour input gave a total sample size of 159. The use of pesticides or hired labour on these plots proved to be negligible, and therefore subsequent estimation was based on three inputs, land, fertilizer, and family labour hours.

The production function for pure-stand hybrid maize was first estimated as a nested CES function of the form:

$$Q = K\{\alpha N_1^{-\rho} + (1-\alpha)L^{-\rho}\}^{-\frac{\lambda}{\rho}}$$

where

$$N_1 = \{\beta A^{-\lambda} + (1-\beta)F^{-\lambda}\}^{-\frac{\mu}{\lambda}}.$$

A = area under cultivation (1/100s of a hectare).
F = fertilizer input (shillings).
L = family labour (hours per year).
Q = production (kg).

Using non-linear least squares with the Marquardt–Levenberg algorithm (discussed in the Appendix to this chapter) convergence was not achieved. However, the runs of the model fell into two categories. With ρ started at a negative value it tended to zero from below, not becoming positive at any point during the history of iterations. Likewise when started at a positive value, ρ tended to zero from above, not achieving any negative value during the iterations.

Therefore as attempts to estimate a CES function provided no evidence against the Cobb–Douglas form, the model was reformulated as a Cobb–Douglas function in three inputs, i.e. $\ln Q = \ln K + \alpha \ln A + \beta \ln F + \gamma \ln L$. This formulation yields the results shown in Table 6.6.

An F-test was carried out on the null hypothesis $\alpha + \beta + \gamma = 1$. The hypothesis could not be rejected at the 5 per cent level and so the equation was re-estimated with constant returns to scale imposed. The results are presented in Table 6.7. This is the version used in our subsequent analysis.

6.2.3. Improved Livestock

Production functions for improved livestock were estimated from the IRS1 survey of rural Kenya, using only data from Central and Nyanza Provinces.

TABLE 6.6. *Maize production function: Cobb-Doughlas results (unrestricted)*

Parameter	Estimate	Standard error	T-statistic
K	2.052	0.465	4.412
α (land)	0.528	0.092	5.700
β (fertilizer)	0.0502	0.026	1.901
γ (labour)	0.334	0.067	4.969
F-value	24.869		
Adjusted R-squared	0.312		

TABLE 6.7. *Maize production function: Cobb–Douglas results (restricted)*

Parameter	Estimate	Standard error	T-statistic
K	1.678	0.094	17.768
α (land)	0.582	0.064	8.999
β (fertilizer)	0.057	0.025	2.283
γ (labour)	0.361	0.059	6.121
F-value	37.044		
Adjusted R-squared	0.313		

Functions were estimated for both cattle offtake and for milk production. Offtake is defined as the value of cattle either sold, consumed, or given to labour minus net gifts of cattle and cattle purchases, valued in shillings. A major problem faced was that none of the input data for livestock were category specific. Therefore the sample was restricted to those households for whom the value of improved cattle constituted greater than an (arbitrary) 75 per cent of total livestock value (including sheep, goats, pigs, and other cattle). Five inputs were calculated: family labour, hired labour, purchased feeds, the value of own-produced crops (sorghum, potatoes, millet, hybrid maize, local maize, and beans) fed to cattle, and the total area of the shamba. For the offtake equation the value of improved cattle at the beginning of the period was also used, and for the milk production equation the number of cows in milk was used.

The sample size in Nyanza proved to be only nineteen and therefore only observations in Central Province were used. Further there was virtually no hired labour input into either milk or cattle tending, and hence hired labour was removed as a variable. Total farm size was completely insignificant for either milk production or offtake, reflecting the fact that improved livestock is commonly stall-fed, so the variable was removed from the estimation.

For both milk production and the offtake rate the function estimated was a Cobb–Douglas formulation. The results for the two production functions are reported in Tables 6.8 and 6.9.

Although in neither case is the function homogeneous of degree one, the null hypothesis that the coefficients on the inputs sum to unity cannot be rejected at the 5 per cent level. However, improved livestock clearly involves a threshold quantity of investment.

6.2.4. Wage Employment

The 1977/8 Labour Force Survey, 'some of the respondents to which were in our own survey, is an appropriate data set from which to estimate an earnings

TABLE 6.8. *Livestock production function: value of milk production as dependent variable* (sh)

Variable	Coefficient	Standard error	T-statistic
Number of cows in milk	0.732	0.117	6.23
Family labour (hours)	0.119	0.157	0.76
Purchased feed value (sh)	0.317	0.059	5.38
Value of crops	0.0121	0.053	0.40
Intercept	4.179	1.071	3.90

F-Value: 17.265
Adjusted R-squared: 0.438

TABLE 6.9. *Livestock production function: value of improved cattle offtake as dependent variable* (sh)

Variable	Coefficient	Standard error	T-statistic
Opening value of improved cattle (sh)	0.204	0.163	1.25
Family labour (hours)	0.399	0.238	1.68
Value of crops fed	0.039	0.075	0.52
Purchased feed value (sh)	0.238	0.094	2.54
Intercept	0.533	1.671	0.32

F-value: 5.917
Adjusted R-squared: 0.177

function for the wage labour force. The resulting function is reported below, a fuller discussion being provided in Bigsten (1984):

$$W = 4.94 + 0.19E1 + 0.19E2 + 0.37E3 + 0.51E4 + 0.45E5 + 0.28E6 + 0.64T1$$
$$\ (.05)\ \ (.05)\ \ \ (.05)\ \ \ (.05)\ \ \ (.05)\ \ \ (.09)\ \ \ (.13)\ \ \ (.04)$$

$$+ 0.33T2 + 0.04X - 0.0005X^2$$
$$\ (.03)\ \ \ \ (.00)\ \ \ \ (.0001)$$

$\bar{R}^2 = 0.41$
$F = 217.6$
$n = 1473$

where

W = the natural logarithm of the cash wage.
$E1$ = dummy for 1–4 years primary education or more.
$E2$ = dummy for 5–7 years primary education or more.
$E3$ = dummy for 1–2 years secondary education or more.
$E4$ = dummy for 3–4 years secondary education or more.
$E5$ = dummy for 5–6 years secondary education or more.
$E6$ = dummy for tertiary education.
$T1$ = vocational training.
$T2$ = on-the-job training.
X = experience (years in the labour market).

This yields the familiar result that education, training, and experience all raise earnings for those in the labour market. However, the regression of course begs the question of the determinants of access to the market.

6.3. The Comparison of Returns in Activities

The production functions are now used to estimate and compare the returns to factors in the two major agricultural activities, coffee and maize. These returns are then compared with those found in causal agricultural wage labour, urban employment, and improved livestock. To the extent that we identify differences in returns the next question is to account for their persistence in terms of barriers to entry. For the present we restrict our calculation of returns to only two factors, labour and land. The virtual absence of a market in land, as described in Chapter 2, implies that the land endowment of the household can be regarded as an exogenous variable on which it can only earn a shadow rental. The labour endowment of the household is similarly fixed, at least for the extended household. To gain access to some activities, such as coffee and improved livestock, will involve the making of an investment. Since, as we have seen, very few households use credit or land disposals to finance these investments, they require the household to forego consumption, and so there is no explicit opportunity cost in terms of income. In the analysis which follows we show the return upon this foregone consumption or leisure as accruing to land and labour: that is, the effort required to switch activities is not included, merely the consequences. We then estimate the costs of activity switches and the implied return upon the savings required.

We start by combining the production functions for coffee and maize with the vectors of input and output prices to generate profit functions, and from these derive unit cost functions. If factor markets were efficient, and hence factors had market prices which defined shadow prices for endowments retained for use on the holding, differences in the financial rewards between activities would best be expressed as different mark-ups of price over unit cost. However, since factor markets are deficient, the shadow price of factors can be expected to differ across holdings. In view of this, a better way of characterizing differences in financial returns is by means of a comparison of unit cost functions. The unit cost function, a standard tool in duality theory, is defined in factor price space, and denotes the locus of combinations of factor prices which generate a common cost of production when peasants use all inputs optimally. Thus, purchased inputs are deployed up to the point at which their price per unit is equal to their marginal revenue product, and self-employed factors are deployed up to the point of equality between marginal revenue products and shadow prices.

Clearly, the relative prices of the outputs are critical in generating these functions. Our purpose in comparing returns in coffee and maize is not, of course, to demonstrate that under the exceptional circumstances of the boom coffee was the more profitable, but rather to discover whether there were differences in returns at the prices that were expected to prevail on the information set available prior to the boom. For only if there were such differences must activity choices have been constrained by entry barriers of some form.

Since for any pattern of observed behaviour there is some set of expectations which, if held, would fully account for it, we must be wary of attributing changes to unobserved errors in expectations. We are not able to observe expectations of maize and coffee prices on the eve of the boom. However, as it happens, the relative price of these crops was the same in 1974 and 1982, and this lessens the inevitable problems involved in characterizing expectations. In our own survey the reported price of a kilo of coffee berries was 3.0 shillings, and for maize 1.3 shillings, a differential of 2.3:1. Since the conversion from berries to clean coffee is 7:1 the price of 3.0 shillings for berries implies a clean coffee price of 21 shillings. The co-operatives normally operated on a 20 per cent margin, so that their selling price would be 26.3 shillings. This is indeed supported by the wholesale price reported in the *Statistical Abstract* for 1982 of 27.8 shillings. Applying these same margins and working back from the wholesale price in 1974 yields a producer price for berries of 1.08 shillings. The survey price for maize sales of 1.3 shillings per kilo agrees with the *Statistical Abstract* producer price for 1982, and that source reports a maize price in 1974 of 0.464 shillings. Hence, our estimate of the producer prices prevailing in 1974 again yields a differential of 2.3:1. We estimate the unit cost functions using the 1982 price vectors, and because of this coincidence of price structures the procedure is open to two interpretations, under either of which it would be an appropriate characterization of price expectations. First, peasants might have had naïve expectations in 1974 and simply projected prevailing prices into the future. That is, their expectations might have been unit elastic. Alternatively, and at the other extreme of sophistication, they might have had rational expectations about the price that would prevail once coffee planted in 1974/5 had matured. In the former case the relative price in 1974 would be appropriate, in the latter the price prevailing in 1982, a normal non-boom year, would be appropriate since peasants would have anticipated it without systematic error. Hence, whether peasants are naïve or rational the relative prices actually observed in the survey are a sensible proxy for the expectations which motivated peasants in their activity choices on the eve of the boom.

To some extent these expectations were undoubtedly altered by the temporary increase in the coffee price during the boom. However, through the co-operative societies and the extension service peasants were informed about the cause of the change in the world price, and must therefore have regarded it as temporary.

In Chapter 2 we presented evidence on the extent to which changed (and hence over-optimistic) price expectations were the explanation for coffee and tea planting during the boom. Those planters who attributed their decision to the price increase and who by 1982 were regretting this decision because the price had fallen can clearly be characterized as having been misled by erroneous revisions of expectations caused by the boom. However, recall that the proportion of planters with these responses was small: only 17 per cent of those planting coffee during the period and less than 4 per cent of those planting tea. Hence, in seeking explanations for the increase in tree crop planting during the boom we must look beyond the tempting, but probably minor, factor of the over-optimism induced by transient price changes. We might add that some upwards revision in price expectations now appears to have been justified, although in 1982 it did not appear so. In 1982, with the coffee price back down to its 1974 level relative to maize, previous expectations of higher prices would have been judged erroneous. During the subsequent coffee boom of 1985/6 they would have been regarded as shrewd. We were fortunate to be asking our questions about regrets at a time when the price had reverted to its pre-boom level and looked like remaining there.

We begin our comparison of rates of return by constructing a unit cost function for coffee. An important result to come out of the production function analysis is that there appear to be some economies of scale in coffee growing. Recall that this is a potential contributor to (though not by itself a sufficient condition for) the persistence of different rates of return between activities.

Since coffee production is subject to increasing returns to scale, the unit cost function is not uniquely defined, being scale dependent: the scale of operation must therefore be specified either in terms of output or some input. We define the scale of operations in terms of the plot size devoted to coffee, since this is the input least easily varied, and since we are particularly interested in the planting decision. The unit cost curve is then constructed by imposing a shadow wage for own labour, and full employment of the coffee plot size. The household thus optimizes with respect to quantities of all inputs except land, the rate of return on land being computed as the residual profit divided by the land area. Initially we investigate returns at the mean scale of operation, that is the mean plot size devoted to coffee, since this is a guide to actual returns for a representative coffee grower. It may well not be the scale at which entrants are capable of adopting coffee, but that is a subject to which we will return shortly.

With the unit cost function thus defined, the shadow return to land includes all the returns to fixed investment. Figure 6.1 shows the resulting unit cost function.

Next we repeat the analysis for hybrid maize, the most common crop, using the production function to generate its dual, the unit cost function. Unlike coffee, because the activity is subject to constant returns to scale, the unit cost function is uniquely defined. It is superimposed upon the unit cost function for coffee and depicted in Figure 6.1.

We are now able to compare the rate of return to land and labour in coffee and maize by inspecting the unit cost functions. The virtue of this technique is that given that shadow prices differ across households we are able to compare profitability over the range of shadow prices appropriate to the various groups of households. Suppose then that the household faces no ecological constraints upon growing either crop. If it chooses only maize, then, depending upon its factor endowment, it will achieve a vector of shadow average returns on the locus $M-M'$. If it is able to undertake coffee production at the mean size of coffee plot found in the sample it achieves a vector on the locus $C-C'$. The two loci have different slopes which reflect the differing land/labour ratios in the two activities. At all relative factor prices in the relevant range

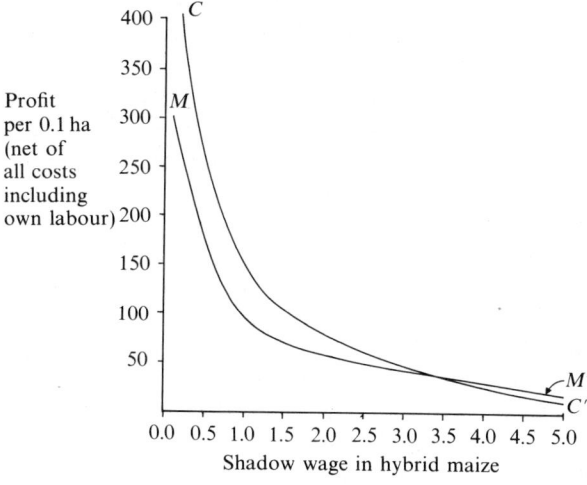

FIG. 6.1. *Unit cost functions for coffee and maize*

coffee is more labour intensive than maize. Hence, at low shadow wages coffee is more profitable than maize (in the sense of affording a higher shadow rental to land), and at high shadow wages the converse is the case. The intersection of the two loci thus defines the critical shadow wage of household labour at which the shadow rental on land is equivalent. This occurs at an hourly wage rate of 3.4 shillings. Hence, below 3.4 shillings per hour as the shadow price for the times of household members coffee is more profitable, whereas above it maize is more profitable.

Clearly, the next critical question is to determine the actual shadow wage rate applicable for most households. One indicator of the relevant range of the shadow wage for household labour is the actual wage for labour hired on peasant holdings. As reported in Section 6.2, this was only 2.03 shillings per hour at the time of the survey. If this is indeed an indicator of the opportunity cost of household labour then coffee was considerably more remunerative than maize. However, because the hired labour market is only the rump of the labour allocation process, accounting for a mere 6 per cent of total labour input on holdings, this wage rate cannot be interpreted as dictating the shadow wage. Even though an individual household may be able to hire as much labour as it chooses at around this wage, hired and family labour cannot be regarded as perfect substitutes. This has indeed established in our coffee production function. More importantly, households can probably not expect to be able to sell as much labour as they might choose on the market at this wage rate. This is partly because the market is both spatially and temporally thin, partly because the problems of adverse selection and moral hazard can only be overcome by the accumulation of reputation within a bounded social network, and partly because the average wage for hired labour reflects a different age and gender composition than does family labour.

We have indeed incorporated this labour market asymmetry implicitly into our estimate of the unit cost function. Hired labour is treated as qualitatively distinct from family labour (from the production function nesting), but there is no limit on its availability so the household hires up to the point of profit maximization. However, there is not necessarily any counterpart in labour sales. The unit cost function is estimated over the full range of possible shadow wage rates because many households can be expected to earn less than the market wage for their labour.

A better guide to the opportunity cost of family labour than the wage in the truncated peasant labour market is the marginal revenue product of family labour in hybrid maize (the most common crop) at the means of the factor inputs observed in the sample, for whereas few households sell their labour to other peasants, most grow hybrid maize. Recall, however, that the returns to labour in the common activity (maize) should be expected to vary according to participation in the pure labour-rationed-entry activity, namely non-agricultural wage labour. We will see shortly that the returns to such employment were somewhat above those to be earned in coffee growing. Since the return to labour in non-agricultural wage employment is therefore likely to be above that in maize (a proposition shortly to be substantiated), *ceteris paribus*, households gaining access to non-agricultural wage employment should deploy their labour away from maize at the margin, thereby having a higher marginal product. Similarly, entry to coffee growing appears to be potentially restricted by the presence of economies of scale (and we must presume that the same is true of the growing). We therefore break the sample down according to whether households are engaged in the non-agricultural wage labour market and in coffee and tea growing.

To get some idea of the shadow price of family labour in those households unable to access any of the three above activities we first estimate the marginal revenue product of own labour in hybrid maize only for these households. So defined, the marginal revenue product was 2.23 shillings per hour. Note that despite the highly truncated nature of the hired labour market, this is not dissimilar to the market wage rate of 2.03 shillings. However, it should be stressed that because of the lack of well-functioning land and labour markets the figure of 2.23 shillings is the mean of a range, for households with differing proportions of factor endowments will cultivate maize using different ratios of land to labour (unless able to arrange compensating differences in the mix of activities as discussed in Chapter 5).

Accordingly, we computed the marginal revenue product of family labour of maize separately for each household within the four groupings defined by participation or non-participation in coffee growing and non-agricultural wage labour. (Households growing tea were excluded since this has many of the same characteristics as coffee, though we have not estimated a tea unit cost function.) The calculation of the marginal product assumed that the *ex ante* returns to inputs were accurately described for each household by the maize production function, so that estimation errors represented only the *ex post* consequences of risk. Thus, the input levels actually chosen by each household were used to generate a marginal product of labour directly from the common production function. The frequency distribution of the marginal revenue product by whether or not the household was growing coffee is set out for each method in Table 6.10.

Recall that coffee-growing households might belong to one of three groups, the atypically labour abundant, the atypically capital abundant, or the atypically well endowed, the two former being factor proportions arguments and the third an economies of scale argument. The table reveals several interesting features. First, participation in the non-agricultural wage labour market indeed appears to raise the opportunity cost of own labour to maize, for no households in this category have a shadow wage below 1 shilling per hour. Second, there is some indication that a group of coffee growers are labour abundant since a higher proportion of non-wage job coffee growers have a shadow wage below 1 shilling per hour (35 per cent) than any other group. Finally, there is a pronounced tendency for those households with

TABLE 6.10. *Frequency distributions of the shadow wage in maize (%)*

Shadow wage	Coffee growers		Non-growers	
	Wage job	No wage job	Wage job	No wage job
<1.0	0	35	0	27
1.0–1.99	11	42	60	40
2.0–2.99	11	4	27	8
3.0–3.99	11	8	0	12
4.0–5.99	55	4	8	7
6.0+	11	8	0	7
All	100	100	100	100
n	(9)	(26)	(15)	(60)

access to both the entry-constrained labour-intensive activities (coffee and wage jobs) to have higher shadow wages than other groups, but this does not extend to the highest shadow wages (above 6 shillings per hour) for at these levels coffee is too labour intensive to be competitive.

To conclude our comparison of returns in coffee and hybrid maize, at the mean size of coffee plot and the mean shadow wage to hybrid maize (2.23 shillings), coffee is considerably more profitable than maize, and this remains true right up to a shadow wage of 3.4 shillings (at which returns are equal). However, because of scale economies in coffee production it is not profitable to engage in coffee production below a threshold scale. At the mean shadow wage the critical minimum size of coffee plot is half the mean size actually operated. Hence, new entrants to the activity must plan to build up to this scale of operation within a reasonable time period, which in turn implies a minimum burden of foregone consumption: households cannot profitably edge into coffee one tree at a time.

We next consider the returns to improved livestock. Although our production functions did not reject the hypothesis of constant returns to scale, there is obviously a minimum entry size for the activity, namely one cow, which is a large investment. The returns to improved livestock cannot be estimated by way of a unit cost function in labour–land space. As shown in Section 6.2, once own-produced inputs fed to livestock are included in the production function, area is insignificant, and this is because most improved livestock is stall-fed. Recall that the hypothesis of constant returns to scale cannot be rejected for improved livestock. Again abstracting from the cost of capital tied up in the activity, all the profits can be ascribed to own labour. At the mean, net profit was 1,150 shillings on milk and 286 shillings on livestock, and mean labour input 1,044 hours. However, since our data base for the improved livestock functions was IRS1, these are at 1974/5 prices as opposed to 1982 prices for our other estimates of returns. The *Statistical Abstract* provides series for the producer price of high-grade beef and of milk and these are used to rescale net profit. Specifically, net profit is increased by the difference between the average of the 1974 and 1975 prices (which precisely agrees with the prices reported in IRS1) and the 1982 prices. Thus rescaled, net profit is 3,824 shillings or 3.66 shillings per hour. Note that this is very considerably higher than the returns in either the casual labour market or hybrid maize production. Indeed, it is in the neighbourhood of the switch-point at which coffee ceases to be more attractive than maize at the prices prevailing in 1982 and 1975. Hence, while improved livestock appears to be an attractive activity for nearly all coffee-growing households, coffee should not be particularly attractive to the average household with improved livestock. In this sense, improved livestock ranks above coffee in the hierarchy of activities.

As an aside, in July 1977 one of the authors was taken to visit farmers considered by the extension service to have been 'progressive'. Several had adopted improved livestock and uprooted their coffee just prior to the boom. The moral of this anecdote is not the gulf between expected and actual returns, but that this switch was commonly perceived as a sequential move up a hierarchy. Finally, we consider the urban wage labour market.

The returns to wage labour were markedly higher in non-agricultural employment than in casual employment in peasant agriculture. Even in 1977/8 the hourly rate of payment for a male aged 30–35 with completed primary education was 3.3 shillings in urban employment. Since mean wage earnings rose in nominal terms by 55 per cent between then and 1982, the hourly return in that year was around 5.1 shillings. In contrast, the hourly wage rate found in our survey for hired labour on peasant holdings was only 2.03 shillings. Some allowance should be made for the higher urban cost of living, but the true returns are probably roughly comparable with those from improved livestock.

So far we have used a combination of unit cost functions and earnings functions to establish differences in returns between activities. Although the near-absence of factor markets means that shadow prices of factors differ substantially between households within each activity combination, there are grounds for suggesting that there is a hierarchy of activities from labouring on other holdings at the bottom, through food production, tree crop production, and improved livestock, to non-agricultural wage labour (at least for those with some education) at the top. If this is indeed correct it should find some correspondence with the per capita income hierarchy of activity mixes portrayed in Table 2.8. From the proportion of households currently in each activity mix (Table 2.7), we might be able to infer something of the sequential movement through this hierarchy.

The key data from these two tables are presented in a form which is easier to assimilate in Figures 6.2 and 6.3. Figure 6.2 displays for Central Province six activity combinations which between them account for the stances of 80 per cent of all households. The vertical axis is the natural logarithm of per capita

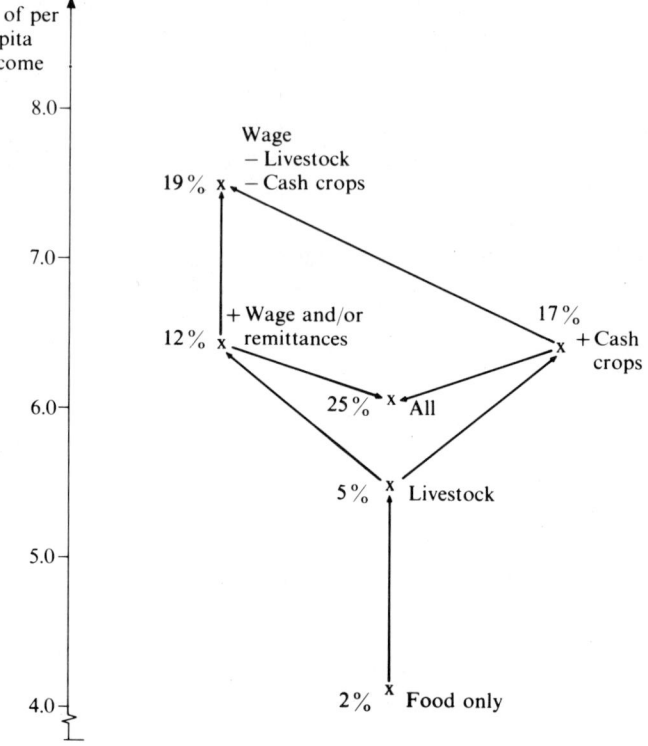

FIG. 6.2   *The accumulation of activities and per capita income: Central Province (80% of households covered by six activity mixes)*

income. Figure 6.3 displays the same six activity combinations for Nyanza, which in this case account for 74 per cent of the stances of all households. Both figures reveal a common sequential hierarchy, though the two provinces appear to be at rather different stages in the process. In both provinces the original activity can be thought of as food growing. Few households are now confined exclusively to this activity, although virtually all households grow food along with participating in other activities.

In each province those households which are engaged exclusively in food production earn drastically lower per capita incomes than do households in any of the other activity combinations. Hence, there is an incentive to access some other activity. The sequence out of specialization in food production which the data suggest has been most common is entry into livestock. We infer this from the fact that there are currently far more households engaged in food and livestock only than in either food and wage labour only or food and cash crops only. We are thus interpreting our snapshot of activity combinations as indicating a stable underlying dynamic process of activity switches, so

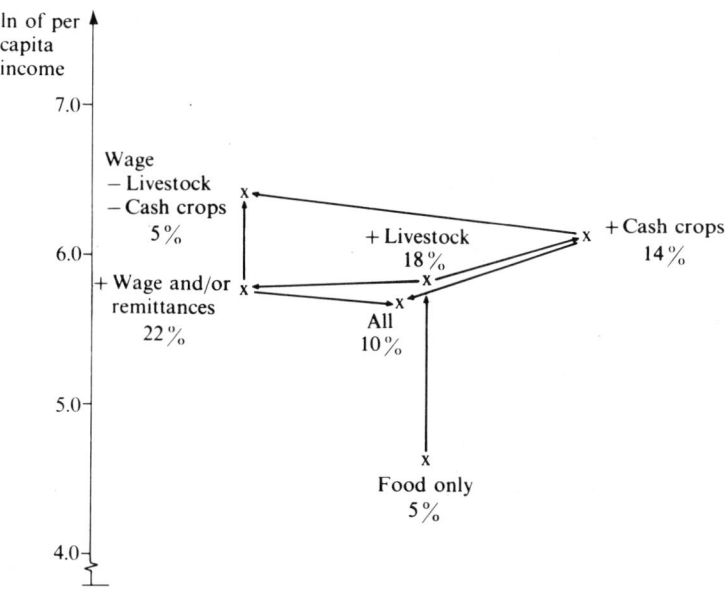

FIG. 6.3. *The accumulation of activities and per capita income: Nyanza (74% of households covered by six activity mixes)*

that the fact that there are currently few households engaged in food and cash crops only suggests that historically few of the households now engaged in multiple activities followed this route. This interpretation of the data is, of course, an assumption. However, it is an assumption which is, as we will suggest, consistent with the differences observed between the two provinces.

Supposing the original activity to be food, and the first switch to be into livestock (not, of course, improved livestock), the second switch seems to be either into the wage labour market or into cash crops. In Central Province 17 per cent of households are in the food–livestock–cash combination against 12 per cent in the food–livestock–wage remittances combination (the figures for Nyanza being 14 per cent and 22 per cent respectively). Either of these moves to adopt an extra activity appears to raise per capita income in both provinces.

In each province a substantial group of households currently engages in all four activities (food–livestock–cash–wage). Presumably most of these households acquired their activity portfolio incrementally and so had made switches from one or other of the activity triples discussed above. In each province the result appears to be a diversification but not an increase in per capita income. This may well be related to the final group of households in each province, namely wage earners who might grow food but who do not engage in either cash crops or livestock. This group is of interest because of its income. In both provinces those with only wage income (or wage–food) have very substantially higher per capita incomes than provided by any other activity combination. Households in this group, which is small in Nyanza (5 per cent) but large in Central (19 per cent), have either divested themselves of these activities having come up through the hierarchy food/livestock/cash crops, or have, as it were, vaulted into the locality. Clearly, this suggests that access to some wage employment is indeed restricted (for example, by skill or education). It may also indicate that activity mobility is dependent upon the type of wage employment. Recall that some households in the sizeable group which engages in all four activities have probably followed the sequence food/livestock/wage/cash (since the food–livestock–wage combination is so common) while others appear to follow the food/livestock/wage/exit-livestock sequence. Of these the latter appear to increase their incomes considerably while the former do not. An interpretation consistent with this is that those who acquire sufficiently good wage jobs thereupon find it unnecessary to engage in other activities, whereas for other households the option of a more diversified income structure is attractive.

To summarize, there appears to be a good basis for ranking activities in the ascending hierarchy food/livestock/cash crops/wages. At the bottom of the household income hierarchy are those engaged only in the two former, and at the top are those engaged only in the last. In between is a large group of households in three-activity combinations between which incomes do not differ substantially. Within this hierarchy, Central Province appears to be more advanced than Nyanza in the progression of activity mobility, the distribution of households being shown in Table 6.11.

The above attempt to infer a dynamic process from a snapshot of activity combinations cannot, of course, bear much weight. However, it is useful as an indicator of which activity switches are likely to be both quantitatively important and to lead to significant augmentations of income. One switch which satisfies the latter but not the former criterion is the move from food into livestock. Although this may well in the past have been a decisive activity

TABLE 6.11. *Difference between provinces in activity mixes (%)*

Activity	Central	Nyanza	Difference
W	19	5	+14
F–L–C–W	25	10	+15
F–L–C or F–L–W	29	36	−7
F or F–L	7	23	−16

Note: W = wage employment; F = food production; C = cash crop income; L = livestock income.

switch it has already been accomplished by all but a small minority of households (although that minority warrants attention on the grounds of its acute poverty). By contrast the switch into the cash crops (which on our restricted definition are largely tree crops) is one which many households have yet to make. In both provinces there is a minority for whom the switch would not be of interest because their existing wage jobs are more remunerative, but in Nyanza 40 per cent of households, and in Central 17 per cent, are currently engaged in either the food–livestock or the food–livestock–wage combinations and could expect to enhance their incomes if they could replicate those households currently in the food–livestock–cash crop combination. Hence, our inference from the distribution over activity combinations supports our previous hypothesis generated from differential rates of return that the adoption of tree crops is a fundamental step in the process of peasant income augmentation.

6.4. Barriers to Entry

Section 6.3 has established reasonable grounds for believing that there are systematic differences in returns between activities. For these to have persisted there must have been some obstacles to entry. Three such obstacles are considered below, namely, ecology, knowledge, and factor proportions. For example, coffee will not grow everywhere, some households may not know how to grow it, or they might not own appropriate quantities of land and labour or have the capacity to generate the savings needed to finance the investment required.

By no means all of the farmers in our sample of Central and Nyanza Provinces had the ecological option of growing coffee, given that the land market is negligible. The survey lacked the resources to assess ecological potential and so the presence of proximate coffee growers was used as an indicator of potential. More precisely, in our subsequent analysis of coffee adoption the sample was restricted to clusters in which some households were growing coffee. A cluster is a small geographical area of 200 contiguous households from which 20 households were included in the IRS4 sample. We deemed non-coffee growers to be ecologically able to grow coffee if at least two households within the cluster sample were currently doing so. Clearly such an indicator has its limitations. First, many households in clusters in which no household (or only one) grows coffee will be falsely characterized as ecologically constrained. However, this is not important for us since, by excluding all such clusters from the analysis of adoption we merely reduce the sample size to a level which remains adequate. More worrying are the ecological variations within coffee-growing clusters. There is no way of knowing how many of the households for which we attempt to explain the failure to adopt coffee in economic terms are in fact ecologically constrained.

Now consider differences in knowledge as an entry barrier to growing coffee. As discussed in Chapter 2, coffee is a relatively recent peasant crop. There are many aspects of planting and cultivation which are still the subject of research and the objective risk of disease has been changing over time. For these reasons we would expect a lack of knowledge to be a significant deterrent to many households, who might be ignorant of techniques and uncertain as to the true nature of risks. Indeed, the extent of risk is highly dependent upon the knowledge of cultivation practices. Although the government extension service provides one channel of information (which we analyse in Part IV), probably the most trusted means of assessing the risks involved is through observation of neighbours, for this provides both direct information on outcomes and a guide to how other decision takers assess the *ex ante* risks.

The hypothesis of knowledge or ability differences between coffee-growing and non-coffee-growing farmers is tested in three ways, each of which rests upon a comparison of performance in activities common to both groups. The major activity common to virtually all households is the cultivation of food crops. The first approach is to compare how farmers acquired their knowledge of the techniques of cultivation in food crops. Farmers were asked 'How did you learn about the method which you are using?', and were grouped by their answers into those using traditional methods, those who had used their own trial and error, those who had imitated other farmers, and those who had learned from demonstrations or extension visits. Arranged in this hierarchy of exposure to information the rank of the response was entered as a variable in a polytomous logit which distinguished between non-growers, adopters in the period 1975–82, and growers prior to 1975. As discussed above, the analysis was confined to those clusters in which all households were deemed to be ecologically able to grow coffee. The specification and results are more fully described in our discussion of the determinants of coffee adoption. Here we report only the result directly concerned with the contribution of knowledge differences between non-growers and growers prior to 1975. The coefficient on the knowledge variable was significant ($t=2.4$) but negative. That is to say, coffee growers were less likely than non-growers to have acted on external sources of information on techniques of food cultivation. Of course, this might reflect that food cultivation was a less important activity for coffee-growing households and so given less attention. It is also compatible with any configuration of information about techniques of coffee cultivation. However, it provides some grounds for doubting the hypothesis that coffee growers are drawn from among the better informed farmers so that any higher returns to coffee than to other activities merely reflect ability differences.

The second approach is to focus not upon the process of information acquisition but rather to infer ability differences from performance in food production. A dummy variable for coffee production was therefore entered into the maize production function of Section 6.2 to test whether coffee growers were more productive. Specifically, the production function was re-estimated as:

$$Q = Ke^{dG} A^a F^b O^c$$

where G is a dummy variable taking the value of unity if the household was growing coffee in 1975.

The coefficient, d, was -0.00000008, with a t-statistic of 0.04. Hence, coffee growers manifestly have no greater ability than non-growers in the common activity of hybrid maize: they are not better farmers *per se*. The third approach is to introduce certain information proxies as explanatory variables in the adoption of coffee. The results of this approach, reported as part of the logit analysis below, indeed suggest that a lack of information may be an important constraint upon coffee adoption. Taken together with the above results it implies that although differences in knowledge are an important component in the entry barriers to coffee, there has not been a pronounced tendency for those households which are generally either more able at farming or better informed to be the ones which gain access to information about coffee cultivation. As far as we are able to discover, information about coffee cultivation is randomly distributed with respect to farmer ability and receptiveness to information.

Now consider the land, labour, and foregone consumption requirements of coffee. The comparison of rates of return through the construction of unit cost functions has already generated as a by-product some information on factor proportions in coffee relative to maize, the former being more labour intensive. However, that analysis abstracted from the loss of consumption necessary for the household to enter each activity. We now estimate this loss, distinguishing between the sunk and irrecoverable costs involved in acquiring specific capital such as trees, and the requirements of working capital.

In order to estimate the sunk investment which a coffee plot constitutes, we switch from our own survey to one conducted by the Ministry of Agriculture (Labour Requirements/Availability, 1979) which observed input requirements for coffee planting in considerable detail.

The flows of costs are detailed in Table 6.12. These flows of costs are then used as a component in the calculation estimating the factor proportions used in producing 100 shillings of output for each of the two crops, presented in Table 6.13. This table uses the data on recurrent inputs (at the mean scale of operation for each crop) and yields from the production function. It shows coffee to have not only a labour/land ratio tenfold that of maize, but also to have a capital/labour ratio double that of maize: in effect coffee uses capital and labour, but very little land relative to maize.

If labour is priced at the shadow wage in maize (2.23 shillings per hour, as deduced above), and land at the shadow rental of 628 shillings per hectare, which from Figure 6.1 is the rate consistent with this wage in maize (which since there is little tenancy is a better guide to the opportunity cost of land

TABLE 6.12. *Fixed costs of 1 ha of coffee*

	Year			
	1	2	3	4
Labour (h)	1,213	639	639	370[a]
Sprays (sh)	0	295	295	295[b]
Seedlings (sh)	800[c]	0	0	0
Land (years)[d]	1	1	1	
Value (sh)	4,133	2,348	2,348	1,120

[a] In year 4 some of the labour input is used to generate output which accrues during the course of the year and is therefore not a long-term investment. We have deducted an estimate of this, based upon a comparison of the labour used for picking in years 4 and 5, from the total input observed in year 4.
[b] Mean expenditure per hectare on pesticides in our survey.
[c] Based on 800 trees per hectare.
[d] Counting the fourth year as generating an income commensurate with food crops (see text).

Source: Ministry of Agriculture (1979, Table 13a).

TABLE 6.13. *Factor proportions in maize and coffee*
(Inputs per 100 sh of output)

	Maize	Coffee
Own labour (h)	13.8	24.9
Land (ha)	0.13	0.023
Purchased inputs (sh)	7.8	15.8
Fixed capital (sh)	81.7	265.0

Source: own survey data.

than is the market rate of rental), then a discounted cash flow calculation on the investment involved in coffee production yields an internal real rate of return of 6 per cent. This is the discount rate at which the investments detailed in Table 6.12 have been aggregated to generate the fixed capital cost in Table 6.13. The data in Table 6.13 should not be regarded as precise, and so this rate of return, being derived from residual profit, is likely to be quite inaccurate. However, on any credible rate of discount we can be confident that coffee indeed has markedly higher capital/labour and labour/land ratios than maize. Indeed, the differences in factor proportions are so pronounced that they approximate to the specific factors model suggested earlier in which coffee is produced by labour and capital and maize by land and labour. They certainly suggest that factor endowments should play an important part in activity choices.

So far we have suggested that there might be a variety of barriers to entering the higher return activities. In coffee (and perhaps tea), economies of scale combined with very high ratios of capital and labour to land may give rise to the threshold problems discussed before. Either non-growing households do not have sufficient family labour, or they cannot make the required savings effort. There might also be informational barriers: either the techniques required for successful coffee growing are not understood by some non-growers, or else they are not well able to assess the objective riskiness of the activity. In the non-wage labour market recruitment processes might impose barriers of skill, experience, personal contacts, or educational attainment. One way of investigating these barriers further is statistically to explain switches into high-return activities in terms of the characteristics of those households (or individuals) who have done so. The technique we deploy, polytomous logit, is used to distinguish between those already participating in the activity before the boom (i.e. in 1975), those entering the activity during the period 1975–82, and those never engaged in the activity.

6.4.1. *The Adoption of Tree Crops*

First we consider the adoption of coffee. The above classification into three groups is not quite a complete account of the decisions which households in our sample took concerning coffee growing. Recall from our above discussion of ecological constraints that we are restricting the sample to those clusters within which at least two out of the twenty households were growing coffee, which reduces the sample to 382 households. Of these, 196 grew coffee both in 1975 and in 1982, 46 adopted coffee during the period and were growing it in 1982, and 130 did not grow it at any time during our period. Among the remaining ten households, eight were growing coffee in 1975 but had abandoned it by 1982, and two households were not growing coffee in 1975, but adopted it only to abandon it prior to 1982. The cell sizes for these two groups are obviously too small for statistical analysis and so they were dropped from the logit sample. It is, however, of interest that only 4 per cent of those entering coffee growing during the coffee boom period should have abandoned it. This is the same rate of exit as that among those households already growing coffee in 1975. That both rates are low may in part reflect a tendency to hysteresis generated by the putty-clay nature of tree crop investment. However, that there is no difference between the rates supports the thesis that the surge into coffee planting by those who had not previously grown it was not principally triggered by false, and rapidly deflated, expectations about future coffee prices.

The determinants of switches into coffee, discussed above and at a more abstract level in Chapter 5, must now be translated into observable proxies.

Other than ecology, from which we are abstracting by sample restriction, two types of determinant have been suggested: information and endowments. The concept of information encompasses differential knowledge of how to grow coffee, of the risks involved, and of more general farming skills which includes the possibility of differential intrinsic abilities. The concept of endowments includes the virtually exogenous land and labour possessed by the household (though fertility and marriage decisions endogenize these in the long term). However, it also includes the access of the households to other high-return activities. Those households which have gained access to non-agricultural wage employment will not only have reduced their labour endowment available for coffee, but probably more importantly, they will have acquired a cash flow from which the initial investment in coffee can be financed. Finally, endowments also include the capacity of the household either to postpone consumption so as to finance the investment in coffee planting, or (a route we have seen in Chapter 2 is far less important), to access financial markets or to dispose of assets.

We use four proxies to capture the effects of differential information. The first two are designed further to explore the hypothesis that coffee growers and adopters (the terms we will use to denote those already growing coffee in 1975 and those who switched into it during 1975–82) had generally better knowledge of farming. Recall that we have already investigated this through the inclusion of a dummy variable for coffee growing in the maize production function and concluded that there was no difference in ability. We apply the same design, that is we look for differential knowledge in the common activity of maize growing. The first proxy, KNOWLEDGE, is a ranking of how farmers acquired their knowledge of the techniques which they are currently using in maize production. The variable takes the values 1 to 4 according to whether the information was traditional, the result of personal experiment, acquired by copying other households, or learned from the extension service. The second proxy, INNOVATION, is a dummy variable recording whether the household has changed its technique of cultivation in food production during the period 1975–82. This proxy may indicate that the decision taker is receptive to new information, though this may be either because of skill in acquiring the information, in deploying it, or of atypically low risk aversion.

The other two information proxies are designed to measure differences in knowledge about coffee. Clearly, this cannot be measured directly because *ex post* those households growing coffee will of course know more about it than those which do not, but this has no bearing upon whether *ex ante* (that is, prior to adoption) households which ended up adopting coffee knew more about it than those that did not. However, the two variables we use overcome this problem by recording the proportion of neighbouring households who have either previously adopted or are currently adopting coffee. GROWER denotes the proportion of other households in our sample of the cluster who were growers (that is, growing coffee in 1975), and ADOPTER denotes the proportion who were adopters (that is, adopted coffee during 1975–82). Recall that a cluster is a contiguous area of 200 households from which we observe a 10 per cent sample, so that our measures based on the latter inevitably contain some sampling error. The two variables both identify the stances of other households in the cluster, but they reflect radically distinct information sets. The former proxies the amount of evidence on the past performance of the activity, its risks, requirements, and rewards, readily observable by the household. The latter is a proxy for events which are of no direct informational value about the returns or risks in the activity, because of the long gestation period involved. Instead it shows the household how other decision takers have evaluated their information sets. Since some of these households will have economic circumstances manifestly similar to those of their neighbours, the imitation of their decisions may provide a cheaper way of reaching a correct decision than the direct acquisition and evaluation of the information. Clearly, were such free-riding as effective as its more costly alternative, ADOPTER would be the only significant variable and behaviour would be lemming-like. This could not be an equilibrium because the returns to acquiring information directly would then be high. If there is an informational equilibrium, both direct information on the activity and the decisions of other households are likely to be given some weight.

The endowments of the household were proxied by eight variables. AREA denoted the cultivatable size of the holding, and the numbers of resident male and female adults were denoted by MALE LABOUR and FEMALE LABOUR. Now consider the endowment represented by access to a non-agricultural wage job. In Chapter 2 it is shown that there is considerable fluidity in the wage labour market, households entering and exiting the activity to a marked extent. This potentially causes a problem because the appropriate characteristic is not whether the household was in the non-agricultural labour market in 1982, by which time coffee adopted during the period would probably be generating a good income, but rather whether it was in the market at the time when it was making the investment in coffee. Fortunately, the trace feature of our survey can be harnessed to overcome this difficulty.

The Labour Force Survey records whether any household members held non-agricultural wage jobs during 1977/8. Planting conducted at any time during our period could not have generated an income by 1977/8, so that this observation measures quite accurately the access to wage income during the phase in which the investment is incurred. It is denoted by the dummy variable WAGE 78.

The capacity of the household to finance investment, other than by its participation in the non-agricultural wage labour market, is proxied by five variables not all of which are entered together. There might be life cycle effects on savings preferences, and this was incorporated by the age of the household head (AGE), entered as a quadratic (AGE 2). The ability of the household to finance cash expenditure on inputs was proxied by expenditure in some common activity. Since maize uses so few purchased inputs, livestock was used as this activity, INPUT VALUE recording the expenditure on purchased inputs per shilling of livestock value. Since many households had no cash expenditure of this form the dummy INPUTS identified whether such expenditure was non-zero. These variables do, however, encounter the problem that causality might run from participation in coffee growing to the ability to purchase inputs for livestock rather than proxying an exogenous ability to finance inputs. Participation in financial markets was proxied by the dummy variables LENDER and BORROWER which denoted whether, during the course of 1982, the household had entered the informal credit market and in which capacity. Since the amount and duration of informal loans is, as we have seen, far too small actually to finance coffee investment, and our observation is not for the period when most of the investments were being made, these variables are probably best regarded as weak indicators of how constrained was the financial position of the household. Those needing to borrow small sums were probably more constrained than those able to lend them. That is, small borrowings in the informal credit market should not be interpreted as indicating that the household has access to financial markets to the extent needed to avoid the need to postpone consumption if investment is undertaken. Finally, the value of livestock, LIVESTOCK, is included as a proxy for liquid assets, although we have seen that few households actually claim to have financed coffee planting through asset disposals.

The logit controlled for two other characteristics of the household. First, the environment in which decision takers operate appears in some respects to be biased against women. Extension advice, credit, and membership of the coffee co-operatives are probably all more difficult for women. We therefore include as a test of such discrimination the gender of the household head, GENDER taking the value of unity if the head is female. Second, households growing or adopting tea will obviously be less inclined to grow or adopt coffee since if they are both ecologically feasible they are closely equivalent and therefore substitute decisions. We therefore include TEA as a dummy variable denoting that the household was either a grower or an adopter of the other tree crop.

The results of the core logit are reported in Tables 6.14 and 6.14a.

The overall performance of the logit is respectable, with 79 per cent of outcomes correctly explained. Although by no means all of the variables are significant, both the endowment and the information variables as a group are consistent with our story, and a few are quite powerful. Focusing upon the propensity to adopt, over the whole sample some 26 per cent households not growing coffee in 1975 adopted it during 1975–82 (note that our sample is confined to coffee-growing clusters). Before discussing the results in detail we report in Table 6.15 the coefficients on the credit and asset proxies (which were entered in the same logit in place of INPUT VALUE and INPUTS), and in Tables 6.16 and 6.16a the results of the core logit run on tea adoption (with

Responses to Price Changes in Kenya

TABLE 6.14. *Logit of coffee adoption and growing*

Explanatory Variables	Coffee adoption 1975–82		Coffee growing pre-1975	
	coefficient	t-ratio	coefficient	t-ratio
Endowments				
WAGE 78	1.29	1.46	0.31	0.38
FEMALE LABOUR	−0.30	1.06	0.10	0.48
MALE LABOUR	0.20	0.78	0.35	1.72
INPUT VALUE	2.88	1.20	−0.49	0.19
INPUTS	0.02	0.04	0.61	1.36
AGE	−0.04	0.74	−0.06	1.60
AGE SQUARED	0.00	0.06	0.00	0.89
Information				
ADOPTER per cent	14.14	5.11	7.37	3.11
GROWER per cent	3.62	3.49	6.07	7.82
KNOWLEDGE	−1.84	2.99	−1.15	2.36
INNOVATION	1.40	1.92	1.55	2.84
Discrimination				
GENDER	−0.78	1.28	−0.45	0.97
Other tree crop				
TEA	−2.14	1.46	−1.85	4.26

Note: The dependent variable in a logit is the natural logarithm of $p/(1-p)$, where p is the propensity to adopt.

TABLE 6.14a.

Model predicted outcome	Actual outcome		
	Non-grower	Adopter	Grower pre-1975
Non-grower	109	3	18
Adopter	0	13	7
Grower pre-1975	21	30	171

TABLE 6.15. *Variations in the capital proxy*

Explanatory variables	Coffee adoption		Coffee growing pre-1975	
	coefficient	t-ratio	coefficient	t-ratio
LENDER	0.68	0.95	0.34	0.63
BORROWER	−0.33	0.53	−0.59	1.26
LIVESTOCK	0.73	1.16	0.86	1.79

TABLE 6.16. *Logit of tea adoption and growing*

Explanatory variables	Tea adoption 1975–82		Tea growing pre-1975	
	coefficient	t-ratio	coefficient	t-ratio
Endowments				
WAGE 78	−0.42	0.63	−0.77	1.00
FEMALE LABOUR	0.42	2.05	0.22	1.00
MALE LABOUR	0.10	0.57	−0.01	0.04
INPUT VALUE	−0.67	0.36	1.60	3.88
INPUTS	0.80	1.99	1.60	3.88
AGE	−0.05	1.47	0.02	0.55
AGE SQUARED	0.0004	1.06	−0.0002	0.52
Information				
ADOPTER per cent	4.20	4.55	−0.92	0.90
GROWER per cent	0.64	0.55	1.58	1.48
KNOWLEDGE	0.95	2.32	0.35	2.37
Discrimination				
GENDER	−1.03	2.34	−1.10	2.37
Other tree crop				
COFFEE	−0.88	2.15	−1.70	3.93

Note: Chi-squared = 105.81.

TABLE 6.16a.

Model predicted outcome	Actual outcome		
	Non-grower	Adopter	Grower pre-1975
Non-grower	60	17	17
Adopter	12	53	22
Grower pre-1975	15	8	27

COFFEE obviously controlling for coffee growing or adoption). Although the tea logit performs less well than that for coffee, it still explains 61 per cent of outcomes, and is particularly good at predicting the adoption decision.

Consider first the information proxies. In both logits the behaviour of other households in the cluster is highly important. In the coffee logit an increase of one percentage point in the percentage of other households in the cluster adopting coffee during the period increases the propensity of a household with mean characteristics to adopt coffee from 0.261 to 0.290. Since the *t*-statistic is high this is solid evidence for the existence of an informational externality. Similarly, in the tea logit the ADOPTER variable is highly significant and powerful. Recall that this suggests an informational free-rider effect. The coefficients are very substantially larger than for the GROWER variable. This may have important implications for the impact of the coffee boom, for it suggests that there may be something akin to informational economies of scale. Compare the two-period sequences of adoption shown in Table 6.17, abstracting from any influences of informational externalities.

The second case involves the bunching of adoption decisions in period 1 compared with a continuous rate of adoption in case 1. The second case might be associated with more informationally induced adoption. This is because households with characteristics insufficient to induce adoption in either period in case 1 are carried over the threshold by the contagion effect of the first period. To the extent that it changed the objective circumstances of some non-growers such that they became adopters, the boom caused just such a bunching of adoption, and therefore through the gearing of informational externalities it caused a long-term increase in the proportion of households growing coffee. The two other information proxies tell a less coherent story. KNOWLEDGE is significant in both logits but of opposite sign; coffee adopters are less likely than non-adopters to have learned their farm practices from the extension service, tea adopters are more likely. This may possibly reflect the differential effectiveness of the Kenya Tea Development Authority (KTDA) extension service, noted in Chapter 2, but this is only a speculation. INNOVATION is significant and positive for coffee adopters but is insignificant for tea. Taken with the previously reported regression result this tends to suggest that coffee adopters are not simply more able farmers.

Now consider the endowment proxies. For coffee adoption, the coefficient on the possession of non-agricultural wage employment in 1978 is so large that it implies that the otherwise representative household would increase its propensity to adopt from 0.24 without a job to around unity with a job. This must obviously overstate the effect of such employment, and indeed, although significant, the standard error on the coefficient is quite large. For tea the variable is not significant. Surprisingly, the only cases in which a labour endowment is significant are female labour for tea adopters and male labour for coffee growers, in both cases the coefficient being positive. This gender

TABLE 6.17. *Two hypothetical sequences of adoption*

		Period 1	Period 2
CASE 1	ADOPTERS	1	1
	GROWERS	1	2
CASE 2	ADOPTERS	2	0
	GROWERS	1	3

difference is consistent with the differing work profiles on the two crops, and since tea is more labour intensive than coffee it should be expected that the labour endowment is more important as a determinant of tea adoption. The land endowment was not significant for coffee, confirming the impression that coffee uses other factors so much more intensively that land is not the important constraint. However, for tea the land endowment was significantly positive. Since we have not developed a production function for tea we are not able to interpret this difference.

The proxy for the ability to finance purchased inputs, INPUT VALUE (and INPUTS), is reasonably significant in five of the eight cases, and in all five it is positive. The life cycle proxy, AGE (and AGE 2), is not significant. However, when the other endowment variables are dropped there appears to be a significant life cycle effect, so it is possible that our other variables are already capturing characteristics which vary through the life cycle. The credit and asset market variables reported in Table 6.15 all have the correct signs but are not significant. This is not surprising since the variables are not closely related to what we are trying to measure. Taken together they tend to support the thesis that the adoption of coffee is constrained by the ability to finance the investment, one important means of which is through access to non-agricultural wage employment. Tea adoption appears to be additionally constrained by the endowment of female labour. In the neighbourhood of mean characteristics, one extra female adult in the household increases the propensity to adopt tea during the period by nearly a quarter (p rising from .47 to .58).

This concludes our discussion of the barriers to the adoption of tree crops and the characteristics required to overcome them. Both information and endowments indeed appear to have operated as important differentiating influences. However, the former appears to reflect a reliance upon localized social networks rather than differences in ability. That is, households with otherwise the same characteristics have powerfully different propensities to adopt tree crops depending upon what they see around them. We are about to find that closed and bounded social networks also appear to be highly significant in the determination of access to the other high-return activities, improved livestock and non-agricultural wage employment.

6.4.2. The Adoption of Improved Livestock

We now consider the determinants of the adoption process in a rather more exclusive high-return activity, namely improved livestock. Overall, only some 20 per cent of households owned improved livestock, which is expensive and rather risky, prior to 1975. During the period 1975–82 a further 10 per cent of households switched into the activity. Potentially some of this was related to the coffee boom windfall. We analyse the adoption of improved livestock using precisely the same methodology applied to coffee and tea adoption.

However, whereas previously the two principle beneficiaries of the boom, coffee and tea growers, were definitionally largely excluded from the adoption process, we can now directly observe the difference in the adoption of improved livestock made by being in receipt of coffee and tea windfalls.

To maintain a comparable methodology, we again restrict ourselves to those clusters in which by 1982 at least two households in our sample had improved livestock, the same type of restriction imposed for tree crop adoption. This excludes 245 households, leaving a sample size of 538. As previously, ADOPTER denotes the proportion of other households in the cluster adopting the activity during the period, and OWNER denotes the proportion engaged in the activity in 1975. The only new variables are INCOME 78, which is household income as observed in IRS4; EDUCATION, a dummy variable which is unity if the head of household has any education; and REGION, which is unity for Central Province. The results are reported in Table 6.18.

The information variables reveal the same pattern as for the two tree crops. Again the most powerful and significant is ADOPTER. A 1 per cent increase in the adoption rate, which means two more households in the cluster adopting improved livestock, induces a further 1.08 households to copy them. EDUCATION, which was found to be insignificant in tree crop adoption, has a powerful effect in the more informationally demanding activity of rearing improved livestock, raising the propensity to adopt by around one half (from 0.147 to 0.218).

TABLE 6.18. *Logit of improved livestock adoption*

Explanatory variables	Adoption 1975–82		Owning pre-1975	
	coefficient	t-ratio	coefficient	t-ratio
Endowments				
AGE	−0.17	(7.0)	−0.16	(8.6)
AGE 2	0.001	(5.0)	0.001	(6.6)
FEMALE LABOUR	0.12	(0.8)	0.32	(2.6)
MALE LABOUR	0.13	(0.9)	0.22	(2.0)
COFFEE	0.48	(1.6)	0.28	(1.1)
TEA	0.57	(1.6)	1.00	(3.7)
INCOME 78	0.000002	(0.1)	0.00027	(2.5)
Information				
ADOPTER	4.22	(3.7)	2.30	(2.2)
OWNER	2.00	(2.4)	4.32	(6.1)
EDUCATION	0.51	(1.5)	−0.14	(0.5)
Discrimination				
REGION	1.29	(2.9)	0.68	(1.8)

Note: Chi-squared = 230.65.

The endowment variables tell a mixed story. The labour endowment clearly distinguishes owners from non-adopters, but does not appear to have influenced adoption significantly. The same is true of income in 1978, which may simply indicate that improved livestock is a good investment which raises income. However, of most direct interest are the coffee and tea grower dummies. Both are powerful and significant (though only at the 10 per cent level). Being a tree crop grower during the boom increased the propensity to adopt improved livestock during the period by around as much as did education. Since we are already controlling for current income (as of 1978/9), the tree crop variables are most probably reflecting the atypically large transient income component of current income for growers of tree crops.

The other variables used in the tree crop logits were also investigated. INNOVATION and KNOWLEDGE failed to discriminate between adopters and non-adopters, but were both powerful and significant in distinguishing between owners and non-adopters. Since those owning improved livestock were only a small minority of the peasant population, it is possible that this reflects a pioneering openness to new information, which becomes less important as an influence upon adoption as the activity spreads more widely across the population. Similarly, there was a pronounced difference in the use of purchased inputs in activities common to both owners and non-adopters. This might reflect either the fact that pioneers tend to be cash-abundant, or that improved livestock generates so much cash that more inputs can be afforded.

6.4.3. *Access to the Labour Market*

The earnings function reported in Section 6.2 and our associated survey data showed earnings in the non-agricultural labour market to be considerably above the shadow wage of household labour in maize (2.23 shillings per hour). Among those in the market, earnings depended upon education, experience, and training. However, this cast no light on what was needed in order to gain access to the market in the first place. For this, a survey of wage earners is clearly of no use because of its truncation. Conversely, a sample of the resident labour force in peasant households is truncated in the opposite direction: many of those who have gained access to wage employment have left the household. However, the concept of the extended family, as defined in Chapter 2, which was one of the definitions of the respondent population used in our survey, precisely captures the appropriate sample. The extended family includes in addition to the resident household all sons, daughters, and spouses of the head who are now non-resident. Data were gathered on their migration histories, employment status, age, gender, and education. Confining the sample to those in the age range 15–60 leaves a sample size of 3,562. We now repeat the technique of polytomous logit in an attempt to explain what determined the assignment of this labour into agricultural wage labour, business (other than the shamba), rural non-agricultural wage labour, and finally urban wage labour, with working on the shamba, leisure, or full-time education as the default.

Eight variables were used in the logit, the results of which are reported in Table 6.19. Three education dummies, PRIMARY 1–4, PRIMARY 5–8, and SECONDARY, denoted the possession of each of three levels of attainment. The dummies were cumulative, so that for those with secondary education all three variables took the value unity. REGION took the value of unity if the resident household belonged to Central Province. GENDER took the value of unity if the person was male, and AGE (entered as a quadratic) was measured in years. Finally, two indicators of the employment of other members of the extended family were included. RURAL KIN denotes the number of other members of the extended family who are in rural non-agricultural wage employment, and URBAN KIN similarly denotes those in urban wage employment.

Most of these variables have powerful and highly significant effects. Being female drastically reduces the probability of participation in any non-shamba activity. For example, with otherwise mean characteristics the probability of access to urban wage employment is reduced by around 80 per cent from .096 to .021. Our labour force is defined on the age range 15 to 60 years. Within that range age has highly significant effects as might be expected. Interestingly, whereas the regional dummy is significant for agricultural wage employment (there being more of such work in Central Province), it is not significant for non-agricultural wage employment once the other variables are included.

Although education plays some part in determining access it is generally not significant and the coefficients are not large. The variables which are both

TABLE 6.19. *Determinants of employment in non-shamba activities*

Variable	Agricultural wage labour		Own business		Rural non-agricultural wage employment		Urban wage employment	
GENDER	1.35	(6.6)	1.13	(5.4)	1.34	(8.6)	1.63	(12.0)
AGE	−0.15	(13.4)	−0.16	(14.4)	−0.16	(16.5)	−0.15	(17.3)
AGE2	0.001	(7.1)	0.001	(8.9)	0.001	(10.8)	0.001	(10.5)
REGION	1.10	(5.6)	0.45	(2.3)	0.08	(0.6)	0.05	(0.4)
PRIMARY 1–4	−0.29	(1.1)	−0.37	(1.3)	−0.20	(0.8)	−0.11	(0.5)
PRIMARY 5–8	−1.07	(5.6)	−0.44	(3.4)	−0.07	(1.3)	0.03	(0.5)
SECONDARY	−1.23	(5.7)	−0.91	(4.4)	0.64	(2.0)	0.21	(0.7)
RURAL KIN	−0.64	(2.7)	−0.25	(1.3)	0.34	(3.5)	−0.14	(1.3)
URBAN KIN	−0.28	(5.6)	−0.02	(0.0)	−0.18	(2.1)	0.37	(9.1)

Notes: Chi-squared = 215.8.
( ) = *t*-statistic.

powerful and highly significant are the two measures of the wage employment of kin. With mean characteristics, having one member of the extended family in urban wage employment increases the probability of such employment for all its other members by nearly 40 per cent (the probability increasing from .096 to .13). Similarly, having kin with rural non-agricultural wage employment increases the probability of all other members of the family having such employment by nearly 40 per cent (the probability increasing from .059 to .085). There are three routes by which the employment of kin might affect the employment of other family members. First, there might be an income effect reducing the need for other members of the household to seek employment off the shamba. This is quite probably the interpretation of the large negative coefficients on both the kin variables in the agricultural wage labour logit. We have seen that wage labouring on shambas is badly paid (at 2.03 shillings per hour it is below the mean shadow wage on maize) and it inevitably carries some social stigma. An income in the household from non-agricultural wage employment makes it less necessary for other members to augment household income in this way. If so, this suggests a general equilibrium labour supply mechanism tightening the shamba wage labour market in response to enhanced non-agricultural employment in addition to the more obvious direct effect. Whatever its explanation the effect is powerful, for example, one extra rural non-agricultural job halves the propensity of each remaining family member to work as an agricultural labourer. Since the typical extended family has around four members in the labour force, the indirect effects of one member gaining non-agricultural wage employment reduce the labour supply to agricultural wage labour by 1.5 times the direct effect: the propensity of the worker gaining the job drops to zero but that of his three relatives halves.

The second route by which the employment of kin might be associated with that of other family members is one which denies a causal inter-connection. If the circumstances of the family are exogenously such that its members need to seek wage work to a greater or lesser degree, then there will be some common pattern to behaviour.

The third route, which we will argue the data support over the second, is if the extended family is itself a source of patronage and information, so that each member in employment is able to assist other members to acquire employment. This is what we referred to as a closed and bounded social network similar to the spatially bounded network which so powerfully influences the adoption of tree crops. The reason why this explanation is to be preferred to the second is that the two variables have radically different effects, each powerfully augmenting employment prospects in its own market but significantly reducing them in the other non-agricultural wage market. For example, if any member of the extended family has an urban wage job this substantially reduces the chances of other members of the family holding a rural non-agricultural wage job. It is not obvious how an explanation based on differential household needs could bring this about, but it is precisely what would be predicted by the first and third explanations: the income effect reduces labour supply to rural wage employment whereas the social network effect increases access to urban employment. Similarly, possession of a rural wage job by one member of the family reduces labour supply to wage employment but in the rural market this is outweighed by the improved access afforded by the social network. Thus, and hardly surprisingly, social networks are also spatially bounded within wage employment (having a job in the town does not enable someone else to get a job in the country).

To put the importance of family social networks in perspective, having one other member of the family in urban wage employment increases the chance of access to an urban job by more than the move from partial primary to secondary education, yet while the latter has received enormous attention the former appears to have gone unnoticed.

The logit analysis of the determinants of access to non-agricultural wage employment thus implies that the family social network plays an important role in access to jobs. However, this is an inference from our analysis rather than a direct observation of the recruitment process. It is therefore encouraging that the inference tallies with an important finding from the migration component of our survey. Respondents were asked an open-ended question on the reason for migration for each member of the extended family who had a migration history, whether or not the person was currently resident. Among males, well over 80 per cent cited employment or the search for employment as the motivation for migration, which is unsurprising. However, in Central Province over half claimed not to have migrated in order to look for work but rather to take up a prior job offer. The same was true in Central Province within the smaller proportion of female migration which was work related (most was related to marriage). For a majority of migrants speculative migration was unnecessary because their social network had already secured them a job. In Nyanza the picture is different. Recall that Nyanza is much further from the principal urban labour market and so a smaller proportion of the labour force has out-migrated into wage employment. On average, therefore, each extended family has fewer members in non-agricultural wage employment. The thesis of bounded social-network-based recruitment would therefore predict that a smaller proportion of other members of the extended family would be helped into jobs. This is indeed what the survey found: only 30 per cent of the male migrants whose motives had been work related had gone to specific jobs as opposed to going to search for a job, and among females it was 40 per cent. Note, however, that even these figures are substantial. In aggregate nearly half of work-related migration occurred in response to access provided by a social network which transcended spatial separation, presumably the family. The importance of this for our story is that it substantiates the previous thesis of the determinants of access to non-agricultural wage employment. We might note in passing, however, that it implies that the migration–unemployment syndrome is to a considerable extent a figment of the data-starved academic imagination (at least for the country in which it was devised).

6.5. The Coffee Boom as an Instrument of Change

We have now established that there are reasonable grounds for thinking that returns differ systematically between activities, with a hierarchy of non-agricultural wage employment/improved livestock/tree crops/food crops. We have further identified informational and endowment-related constraints upon access to the higher return activities based upon the activity choices made during the period of the coffee boom. The question which now arises is to what extent both these changes and the investment which occurred within activities already undertaken (of which extra tree crop planting by existing growers is the most significant), are attributable to the coffee boom, as opposed to underlying long-term processes of change. We begin by briefly reviewing six underlying processes, namely population growth, the diffusion of information, asset accumulation, the life cycle, the growth of non-agricultural wage employment, and random shocks.

6.5.1. Secular Changes

Kenya has one of the highest population growth rates in the world, at around 4 per cent per annum. Since in recent years net urbanization has not been rapid (see Collier and Lal, 1986, Chapter 7) the rural population must have increased at nearly this rate. This increase in the rural population might take the form either of out-migration from existing households to marginal lands, the growth of rural landlessness, an increase in the size of existing households, or sub-division of holdings.

Each of these has rather different implications for the process of peasant accumulation. The first (out-migration) would imply that from the viewpoint of peasant households in our sampled areas (i.e. existing areas of cultivation), population growth is not a dynamic process, for the resident population would stay the same size. This is not to say that households are unaltered by population growth, for the age composition of the representative household is still dependent upon their rate of reproduction, but for a given rate of reproduction the household precisely replicates itself over time.

The demographic data on trends in the size of peasant households during the period are inconsistent and we have not determined a reconciliation. There is some empirical basis for the above interpretation of population growth, that is, that it did not affect household size. First, comparing household size in October 1974 (IRS1) and October 1982 (our survey) for the average of Central and Nyanza Provinces, there is virtually no change (an increase from 6.75 to 6.80). Secondly, this is corroborated by a comparison of the 1969 and 1979 Censi which shows a tendency for household size to fall slightly. Thirdly, our survey found only slow rates of sub-division (see Chapter 2) and land sales so holding size could not have been falling rapidly (this is probably a more accurate way of getting at changes in holding size than the comparison of reported holding sizes across surveys because there are severe difficulties both in measuring the holding area and in determining what counts as part of the holding). Finally, the proportion of labour which is hired, 6 per cent in our survey, shows no tendency to have increased (in an early survey of Central Province in 1963 it was also 6 per cent) so the proportion of rural households which are landless has probably not risen substantially. Thus, there is some empirical basis for regarding the effects of population growth as being off-stage as far as the existing peasant economy is concerned.

However, the above data on household size are contradicted by the comparison of IRS4 (1978) and our own survey. When the sample is confined to traced households or sites the mean household size shows an increase of 5.5 per cent per annum. Partly this may reflect the unavoidable bias involved in a trace, namely that all households in the trace are at a later stage in the life cycle (but see below). Indeed, the mean household size of households in our sample but not part of the IRS4 trace was somewhat smaller than that of the traced households (6.53 against 6.84), implying a growth rate in household size of 4.25 per cent per annum from IRS4. We are therefore left with two incompatible prior surveys, IRS1 and IRS4, which disagree about mean household size. The latter had the larger sample, and by virtue of being the frame on which our own survey was traced has the powerful advantage that comparison of it with our survey is free of sampling error. A further advantage of IRS4 is that its sample frame was much more satisfactory than IRS1. Further, the IRS4 mean household size of 5.5 is very close to that of the 1979 Census for the two provinces (5.4). Although, as discussed in Chapter 2, we regard IRS1 as being the better conducted survey, household size is one of the easier components of survey-based data. To reconcile these differences would require a substantial detour into a demographic analysis of our data which is beyond the scope of our present enquiry.

Tentatively, we suggest that household size increased somewhat while households largely maintained their initial holding size, though this might well be overturned by a fuller analysis of our data. Further, it seems unlikely that rural landlessness increased significantly in view of the constancy of the proportion of hired labour used on peasant holdings. However, the two tenable rival theses of sub-division and increased household size have somewhat different implications for the capacity of peasant households to move up the hierarchy of activities. If household size is increasing (with land area per holding almost constant) then this should gradually enable households to overcome the barriers to tree crops and non-agricultural wage labour. The former should be assisted both by the increase in the labour/land ratio and by the absolute increase in the resources of the household (in terms of Figure 5.1 the endowment of the household is shifting East towards the tree crop adoption zone). Access to non-agricultural wage employment should be better diffused across households by the increased size of the extended family social network. (Clearly, in aggregate there can be no improvement in the probability of gaining non-agricultural wage jobs except through an expansion in employment, but if these jobs are filtered through the social network of the family, changes in household size affect the extent to which part of the labour force is excluded regardless of its desire to generate a cash income through wage employment.) If instead sub-division is occurring (constant household size and reduced holding), then there is no effect on social networks and the rising labour/land ratio is in part offset by the reduction in the scale of the household's endowments (in terms of Figure 5.1 the endowments shift South so that an activity switch into tree crops is only triggered at a higher labour/land ratio). Recall that although for coffee adoption AREA was insignificant, it was significant and positive for tea.

Now consider the second long-term process, learning. The four principal routes for the diffusion of knowledge (or the improvement in farmer ability) are education, the extension service, learning from other farmers, and individual experiment. Of these the two former are considered in Part IV and so will not be discussed here. We have suggested that in view of the large recent changes to which the peasant economy has been subjected, the slow process of trial and error by which a 'poor but efficient' state is reached may not be complete. In particular peasants may be badly informed about the new activities, tree crops and improved livestock. We have found that the process of learning from, or imitating, other farmers is a powerful instrument of change but that the information network is highly localized. Further, the pace at which imitation spreads is a function not merely of the density of past adoption but of the rate of change of the density. This gears up exogenous changes. This is consistent with the history of tree crop adoption in Kenya, as described in Chapter 2: short bursts of widespread adoption interspersed by periods of stagnation.

The third long-term process is asset accumulation. There is some evidence of a long-term trend of rising real per capita peasant incomes. For example, Collier and Lal (1986, pp. 212–13) estimate a growth in per capita peasant income of around 2.5 per cent per annum from the mid-1950s to the mid-1970s. This suggests, though it does not entail, a tendency towards net asset accumulation. The principal assets available for net accumulation are money, livestock, tree crops, and farm equipment, and these must be considered separately since there are no direct data on the permanent savings rate.

Financial asset accumulation, which probably accounts for only a small component of total assets, can be inferred residually from income minus expenditure, but as with all residuals this is precarious. The only survey to have gathered complete data on income and expenditure is IRS1 (1974/5)

Since the transient income of peasant households even in aggregate can be expected to be on average several percentage points of permanent income, the resulting savings rate is probably heavily influenced by this transient component. With this proviso the implied financial savings rate was 5.5 per cent.

Although livestock might appear to be the most adjustable asset, far from being accumulated it appears to have been decumulated. This is suggested both by a comparison of survey snapshots and by national data on milk deliveries. Between 1974/5 (IRS1) and 1982 (our survey) the number of cows per household declined by 0.5 per cent per annum in Central Province and by 3.7 per cent per annum in Nyanza, while nationally milk deliveries grew during the period 1966–83 by only 0.5 per cent per annum, indicating declining production per household. However, within the livestock aggregate there has been a switch from indigenous to improved breeds and from grazing to stall-feeding. The major form of real asset accumulation during the twenty years preceding the boom was almost certainly the switch into tree crops. By the eve of the boom there were nearly 60,000 hectares of mature coffee on peasant holdings, whereas in the mid-1950s there was virtually none.

The fourth long-term process is the life cycle. Most Kenyan peasant households are not at a clearly defined stage in the life cycle, but rather contain overlapping generations. Even so there might be complex life cycle effects. We have experimented with life cycle variables in the logits of the previous section. For example, a change of household head has significant effects upon the adoption of tree crops. However, once we control for endowments and information the most straightforward indicator of the life cycle, the age of the household head, is only significant in the adoption of improved livestock. The intricacies of the life cycle were regarded as beyond the scope of the study.

The fifth process is the expansion of wage employment. We have previously suggested that one class of activity, namely non-agricultural wage employment, was (at least for much of the period) rather better remunerated than other activities and hence had associated with it certain entry barriers such as social networks, skill, and education. Over the period 1970–82 such jobs increased nationally at the rate of 5.3 per cent per annum. Since this was more rapid than the growth of the population it represented a gradual increase in the opportunities of access by peasant households to such jobs. This increase in opportunities can be decomposed into changes in the intensive and extensive margins of job rationing. Families with members already in wage employment have a disproportionately high chance of gaining extra jobs and so their access is disproportionately enhanced by job expansion. Families without representation in the activity stand a lower, but positive, chance of a job. Hence, *ex post* some such households will not only acquire jobs but will improve their subsequent access as a consequence, thus spreading access by widening the social networks with representation in the wage sector. In addition to directly enhancing peasant income, we have shown that this enhances the ability of the household to finance the switch into coffee.

Finally, in the presence of risk, households will continually be experiencing positive and negative income shocks. As we have seen in Chapter 2, income mobility is so considerable that it strongly implies that such shocks are a central feature of the environment. The economy-wide shock of the coffee boom was thus superimposed upon an existing pattern of income shocks, shifting the distribution of unanticipated outcomes away from a zero mean. It is now time to quantify this favourable shock and to assess its effects.

6.5.2. The Impact of the Coffee Boom

The two routes by which peasant households in aggregate benefited from the coffee boom were higher coffee (and tea) prices and an increase in the number of urban wage job opportunities. The major transmission effects to those households which did not benefit directly from either of these routes were through the agricultural hired labour market and through increased public expenditure. Of these, the latter is deferred until Part IV.

The direct beneficiaries of the coffee boom were coffee-growing peasants and the estates. The latter were clearly linked into financial markets and so their part of the windfall became diffused through the national economy. However, around half of coffee production on the eve of the boom was produced by peasants. In 1974/5 peasant coffee production was 35,465 tonnes, the price paid to the co-operative societies being 10,681 shillings per tonne. Allowing for deductions by the co-operatives of 20 per cent this implies payments of 303 million shillings to peasants. On the eve of the boom there were some 300,000 members of coffee co-operatives, so coffee income per coffee-growing peasant was around 1,000 shillings per annum. Had output stayed constant, the pure price effect of the boom over the period 1976–9 would have augmented income by 4,430 shillings at 1975 prices. (Producer prices for coffee were deflated by the consumer price index.)

Although the real price subsequent to 1975 never quite returned to its 1975 level, the boom peaked in 1977 and had largely ended by 1980. Hence, the windfall at the level of the coffee-growing household is similarly defined over the period 1976–9 as for the macroeconomy. The real producer price of coffee over this period was on average 110.8 per cent above its 1975 level. Additionally, the quantity of coffee produced was increased, partly by the application of more purchased material inputs and partly by more labour. In measuring this we must be careful not to include the output generated by extra planting, but if we confine the enhanced output to the years 1976, 1977, and 1978 virtually none can be so attributed. On average in these years marketings of coffee from co-operatives were 30 per cent greater than on the eve of the boom. A small part of this reflected coffee smuggled from Uganda, but most of this did not pass through the co-operatives. Much was sold through the estates (for example, estate marketings in Trans Nzoia, Kipkarren, and Turbo rose fifteenfold in one year), and much was auctioned by the Coffee Board explicitly as non-Kenyan coffee (it being easy to identify since around 95 per cent of Ugandan coffee is Robusta which is little grown in Kenya). Hence, the 30 per cent addition to output was probably due to a genuine increase in peasant production. Further, there were very few new entrants into coffee growing during the early 1970s, so the extra output must have accrued to existing growers. Together with the price interaction effect, this extra quantity augmented mean coffee revenue by 1,900 shillings (although some costs were incurred in the process). Hence, the total revenue enhancement for the mean coffee grower was around 6,330 shillings at 1975 prices.

These were clearly sizeable transient income gains which called for investment decisions. We attempt to measure the assets accumulated by coffee growers during the period, taking money holdings, tree planting, improved livestock, and buildings and equipment in turn.

There are obvious difficulties in identifying the acquisition of financial assets, for households are unlikely to be willing to disclose such information. Our source on financial balances is derived therefore not from our survey but from our fieldwork in a major union of coffee co-operative societies (Muranga), which on the eve of the boom had a membership of 45,000. This 15 per cent sample is our best source of information on financial asset accumulation. In October 1976 the average member household held financial assets with the union banking section as savings deposits of 950 shillings. By the peak of the boom, in October 1977, the average deposit had increased to 2,970 shillings. Recall from Chapter 2 that there was little planting between 1964 and 1974 so that most of these households had accumulated their savings deposits over at least a ten year period, and thus at a rate of less than 100 shillings per year. Hence, an increase of nearly 2,000 shillings per household (i.e. 2,970–950–100) can reasonably be attributed to the boom. In Muranga the average coffee farmer had received during that twelve-month period increased coffee revenue of 4,250 shillings (we have deflated payments made by the union by the Nairobi lower income consumer price index excluding rent, which is the most nearly appropriate index). Comparing the income windfall and the financial savings windfall shows that during this period peasants had a propensity to acquire financial assets out of windfall income of 47 per cent. This was obviously massively higher than the normal rate of financial asset acquisition which we have suggested on the basis of IRS1 data might have been around 5 per cent. This is therefore powerful corroborative evidence for both the theory and for the national accounts and CGE analyses in our book *Controlled Open Economies*, where we estimated a propensity to save out of windfall income across all agents in the market sector of 60 per cent. Further, the trajectory of financial assets is precisely as implied in that analysis: by October 1978 the mean savings deposit had fallen to 1,730 shillings, and by October 1979 to only 1,500 shillings. By the end of our period, October 1982, the mean deposit of the initial members was not more than 1,600 shillings (a figure reached by assigning none of the deposits to those who had joined the union since 1975). This level of savings was no more than might have been expected by 1982 in the absence of the boom. Thus peasants, as other agents, initially acquired domestic financial assets but subsequently ran them down quite swiftly. What did they acquire instead?

On average, during the period 1975–82, those growing coffee on the eve of the boom planted an additional 0.16 hectares of coffee. Recall from Table 6.12 that the investment cost of one hectare of coffee at 1982 prices was around 10,000 shillings (including the opportunity cost of own labour valued in the least remunerative activity, maize). We do not know the average price at which the cost of this investment during the period should be valued, because the consumer price deflator is clearly inappropriate. Indeed, as with other agents peasants were attempting to acquire non-tradable capital (planted coffee) at precisely the time when the relative price of non-tradable capital was high: hired labour was massively more expensive than normal, as were seedlings. It therefore seems not unlikely that the average cost during the period was close to that at 1982 prices. On this basis, the average household acquired around 1,600 shillings worth of these real assets. Not all of this planting by existing coffee growers can be attributed to the boom. Although there had been little new planting in the previous decade, since the costs of uprooting coffee are high there is presumably some tendency for the coffee area of existing growers to increase over time. Unfortunately, we have not been able to determine an attribution of the extra planting between a secular trend and the effects of the windfall. At its lower bound therefore the propensity to invest in coffee trees from the windfall must be judged as zero. At the upper bound, recalling that the income windfall at 1975 prices was 6,330 shillings, the propensity to accumulate real assets in this form was around 25 per cent. Later, however, by comparing the planting behaviour of Kenyan and Tanzanian coffee growers, we will be able to narrow down the likely boom-induced planting effect.

The next asset to be considered is improved livestock. Recall that, overall, the peasant economy was divesting itself of unimproved livestock over the period because of a shortage of grazing land, but improved cattle, often stall-fed, had a high return and this opportunity was being taken up. Our adoption logit on improved livestock found a clear and powerful tendency for coffee growers to switch into improved livestock to a greater extent than implied by their other characteristics. The propensity to adopt was increased at the mean from 0.147 to 0.218 by being a coffee grower during the boom. By 1982, the value per household of improved livestock among those adopting it during the period was some 2,700 shillings. If the differential propensity of coffee growers to invest in improved livestock is taken as attributable to their windfall income (which is reasonable since we are controlling for current income by means of INCOME 78), windfall investment from this source is around 190 shillings, or 3 per cent of windfall income.

The final category of asset formation to be considered is purchases of buildings and equipment and investment in non-farm businesses and land (the last being a pure transfer of the windfall). Not all of these expenditures were directly productive. For example, a common expenditure was on housing improvements, in particular the replacement of thatched roofs with metal. However, this yields a flow of future services and can reasonably be regarded as an investment. In our survey, prior to any mention of the coffee boom all respondents (whether coffee growers or not) were asked about expenditures on the above assets during the period 1975–82. Clearly such a long recall question will generate inaccurate replies but the items being considered were large and purchases of them were rare events: if a household has purchased land this event is unlikely to be forgotten. We are particularly interested in the differential behaviour of those growing coffee at the time of the boom and those neither growing it then nor adopting it during the boom. By comparing these two groups we arrive at an estimate of that extra investment attributable to the windfall. Although coffee adopters are of some interest, since our thesis so far has been to suggest that at least a component of this group will also have experienced a windfall, albeit not directly from coffee revenue, this group does not make a good basis for comparison.

The mean reported expenditure on real assets by households neither growing nor adopting coffee was around 1,080 shillings over the period. By contrast, households growing coffee on the eve of the boom invested 4,450 shillings. The difference implies windfall investment of 3,380 shillings, or some 53 per cent of windfall income. Although this estimate can be refined it is a powerful indicator of a high savings rate out of the windfall. The obvious refinement is to allow for the fact that the two groups had different incomes on the eve of the boom. An upper bound to this difference is that income differential prevailing in 1982. This is an upper bound because although the relative price of coffee had reverted to its 1975 level (as discussed in Section 6.3), the coffee growers were by then enjoying a return on their windfall investment. As an indication of this, the income premium for coffee growers was 22 per cent in 1982 (our survey) against 16 per cent in 1978/9 (IRS4). On the eve of the boom coffee growers perhaps enjoyed around 20 per cent higher permanent incomes and so their absolute savings during 1975–82 in the absence of the boom might have been proportionately higher than the 1,080 shillings of non-growers. Allowing for this would reduce the estimate of the savings rate out of windfall income to 50 per cent.

This investment rate out of windfall income can be compared with that out of permanent income. Taking a simple linear average of the household incomes for non-coffee growers in 1982 (our survey) and 1974/5 (IRS1) suggests an average annual income during the period of around 6,300 shillings, or a six year total of about 38,000 shillings. This sustained the acquisition of 1,080 shillings of real assets, an investment rate of some 3 per cent. Although this calculation is only intended to be approximate, the difference between the investment rates out of permanent and windfall income is so striking as to be robust.

To conclude our discussion of what coffee-growing peasants did with the income windfall, we have determined that they behaved in precisely the same way as private agents in aggregate. In *Controlled Open Economies* we estimated a savings rate of 60 per cent as an average for market sector agents, made up of an initial build-up of monetary assets followed swiftly by monetary decumulation and the purchase of real assets. On our estimate, peasants saved 50 per cent of the windfall in real assets, 3 per cent in improved livestock, and between 0 and 25 per cent in further coffee planting, a total savings rate of 53–78 per cent. In Chapter 7 we use our survey evidence on Tanzanian coffee planting to attribute around half of Kenyan planting to the boom, yielding a 'best-estimate' of the total savings rate of 65 per cent. Monetary assets, as we have seen, were first accumulated, around 50 per cent of receipts going into the banking system, and then rapidly run down.

In the case of the increase in urban wage job opportunities the counterfactual is potentially far more problematic. Fortunately, the CGE model (described in *Controlled Open Economies*) can be used to generate the employment consequences of the boom. Of the various counterfactuals explored in Chapter 7 of that book, we here adopt as the effect of the boom the difference between employment in the absence of both the boom and the oil shocks and in the presence of the boom but still without either the oil shocks or the loss of control of public expenditure. This corresponds to runs 1 and 2 in Chapter 7 of *Controlled Open Economies*. The resulting estimate of the increase in opportunities for wage employment is set out in Table 6.20.

At the height of the boom, in 1978, opportunities for urban wage employment were enhanced by 10.8 per cent, and in 1983, which was probably close to the long-run steady-state effect, by 9.4 per cent. During the boom years, 1976–8, an extra 33,000 urban jobs were created. At the time of the boom there were around 1.5 million peasant households, so that there was the equivalent of one extra job for 2.2 per cent of households.

By 1982 28 per cent of peasant households had some member of the extended family (which includes the resident household) in urban wage employment, which is where most of this expansion took place. Even had all the extra vacancies been acquired by families with no existing representation in the sector, the no-boom counterfactual would therefore have been 25.8 per cent. However, as we have shown, those households already with representation had a greater chance of gaining further job slots. The mean family with representation had around 1.5 members in urban wage employment, giving it a 55 per cent better chance of gaining more jobs than unrepresented families. Solving this recursively, in 1975 some 26.6 per cent of households had family representation in the urban labour market, and these

TABLE 6.20. *Employment opportunities in the formal sector resulting from the boom*

	Employment (000s)			Annual change
	No boom	Boom	Difference	
1975	287	287	0	—
1976	313	322	9	9
1977	303	327	24	15
1978	305	338	33	9
1979	307	338	31	−2
1980	305	328	23	−8
1981	301	322	21	−2
1982	296	318	22	1

Source: Own calculations from a computable general equilibrium model, as described in *Controlled Open Economies*.

households acquired 35 per cent of the boom-induced vacancies, leaving the proportion of unrepresented households to decrease by only 1.4 per cent from 73.4 per cent to 72 per cent.

Clearly, this employment expansion benefited only a very small minority of peasant households. Among the 0.8 per cent of households already with family members in wage employment, but who benefited from the employment expansion, it seems unlikely that gaining one further job would have a powerful impact upon the capacity to grow coffee. Among the 1.4 per cent of households acquiring their first foothold we know from the effect of WAGE 78 in the coffee adoption logit that most who were not already growing coffee would adopt it. According to the coefficient, the adoption propensity would rise from around 0.25 to around unity. Although this is clearly too high, even on this basis boom-induced wage employment can only account for an adoption propensity of around 1.0 per cent within areas ecologically suitable for coffee.

Determination of the adoption rate attributable to the growth of formal sector non-agricultural wage employment other than that induced by the boom is rather more problematic. Actual urban wage employment increased by 43 per cent between 1975 and 1982 (from *Statistical Abstracts*). Of this, Table 6.20 attributes 10 percentage points to the boom ($143 \times (1-296/318)$). Hence, for every boom-induced job there were around three non-boom new jobs. This implies an adoption propensity triple that from boom-induced employment, that is at most 3 per cent. This estimate fails to allow for vacancies arising from labour turnover and the pre-emption of job opportunities by urban school leavers, effects which qualitatively offset each other.

Now consider the second route by which the boom produced windfall benefits to non-coffee growers, namely the wage for labourers on peasant holdings. The transmission of the income windfall to coffee growers through the peasant labour market is difficult to quantify, partly because there is no wage series, and partly because actual wages would in any case incorporate the effects of the oil shock and the public expenditure bonanza. We attempted to build a wage series retrospectively from recall questions in the survey, but not unexpectedly the responses proved unsatisfactory. Anecdotal evidence from our fieldwork in Muranga established that there nominal wages had roughly tripled during the boom, but this was clearly an area in which the boom was particularly pronounced (coffee earnings were considerably higher than the national average for coffee growers). Instead, we again relied upon the CGE model to simulate the peasant labour market in the two counterfactuals already adopted for the urban labour market. Comparing the two runs, the market peaked in 1977 with wages 28.6 per cent higher than without the boom, and with the volume of employment 20.4 per cent higher, implying an increase in the wage bill of 54.8 per cent. Over the period of the boom (1976–9), the wage bill was on average higher by 30 per cent. By 1983, which we again interpret as being the long-run steady state, the wage bill was, however, only 5.5 per cent higher than it would have been in the absence of the boom. In IRS1 the average wage bill was 161 shillings, implying a windfall payment during the boom of 193 shillings per household. However, only a small minority of peasant households, around 10 per cent in our survey, sell labour to other peasants. Hence, for this group the windfall was very substantial at around 1,930 shillings over the period. Few of these households were growing coffee prior to the boom since we have seen from the agricultural wage logit of Section 6.4 that such work appears to be concentrated among the poorer households and is normally slightly less well remunerated than growing maize. For this very reason it is unlikely that the windfall for labourers induced a substantial adoption propensity among the group. A dummy variable for casual wage labour in 1978 was tried on the coffee adoption logit and was found not to be significant. Between the implausible bounds of zero and 10 per cent induced adoption in ecologically suitable areas the true figure probably lies near the bottom of the range.

During the period 1975–82, in those areas ecologically suited to coffee 26 per cent of households not growing coffee on the eve of the boom adopted it. So far it does not appear that we have accounted for much of this switch in terms of the consequences of the coffee boom. The boom-induced expansion of non-agricultural employment we have seen could only have accounted for an adoption rate of at most 1 per cent, and non-boom employment growth for at most 3 per cent. Windfall earnings from casual wage labour perhaps accounted for a further 1 or 2 per cent. Therefore, in total we can account for in the range of 4 to 6 per cent. Yet the upsurge in planting is unlikely to have been coincidental. There are, however, two further effects to be included.

The first of these remaining effects is over-optimistic price expectations engendered by the boom. Recall from Section 6.3 that we concluded that only around 17 per cent of planting had been induced by falsely optimistic price expectations (these households attributed their planting decision to the price increase, regretted having planted, and attributed their regret to the price decline, so that this characterization of their behaviour seems well founded). This therefore accounts for a further 4.4 percentage points of the adoption rate, bringing us in total to a boom-attributed rate of around 8–10 per cent. This is sufficient to account fully for the 26 per cent adoption rate as a boom-induced phenomenon, because of a fourth and very powerful effect, namely the externalities generated by the spatially defined social network. A decision by one household to adopt coffee is very powerfully geared by the free-rider decision process. Recall from Table 6.13 that by far the most significant variable in the coffee adoption logit is ADOPTER, the proportion of other households in the neighbourhood taking the same decision.

In fact the multiplier is so large (and with a t-statistic of 5.11 we can be confident of its size), that the observed rate of adoption of 26.1 per cent will be generated by an underlying adoption rate of only 9.0 per cent. That is, if we can directly account for an adoption rate of 9 per cent, as we have done, the remaining adoption is fully accounted for by the copying or contagion effect. Since this copying of the decisions of neighbours effect may seem doubtful to those agricultural economists more accustomed to measuring fertilizer response, it is worth noting that there is a large literature analysing precisely this effect in stock markets. A recent survey on stock market pricing, Shiller (1984), summarizes the present consensus with the following quotation:

mutual reinforcement through exchange of information among peer groups by word of mouth [is] a major condition for the emergence of a uniform response to new stimuli by very many people. (Katona, 1975, p. 203)

As with their savings rate out of transient income, far from claiming that the behaviour of African peasants is peculiar, we are merely quantifying an effect the potency of which is already acknowledged to be a general feature of human behaviour.

The copying effect gears other changes: for every household adopting coffee as a result of a change in its economic circumstances, around 1.9 other households copy. Thus, the non-boom-attributable adoption rate of up to 3 per cent previously estimated would have generated a total adoption rate of 8.7 per cent, leaving a boom-attributable adoption rate of 17.3 per cent. It should be obvious that these numbers merely indicate orders of magnitude.

To conclude this section, we have suggested first that those peasants who directly benefited from the coffee boom, namely coffee growers, had a high savings rate out of the windfall commensurate with that for the rest of the economy. Second, we have found that the indirect effects of the boom account for a large component (around 70 per cent) of the observed upsurge in the coffee adoption rate, itself a massive investment undertaken by the peasant economy which switched a large group of households into an activity with a significantly higher return. We should note, however, that although there are also very powerful copying effects in improved livestock and tea, a considerable component of tea adoption during the period cannot be explained by the coffee (and tea) boom. Recall from the tea logit that the female labour endowment is a significant determinant of tea adoption, presumably because tea is far more labour intensive than coffee. The adoption of tea might well, therefore, reflect an interaction of the secular trend of a rising labour/land ratio and the copying effect (together with an atypically good development authority), to produce an idea whose time had come.

6.5.3. *Peasant Asset Formation*

The trajectory of peasant asset formation, as opposed to its magnitude, might well have been socially inefficient. For private agents as a whole this is one of our major themes developed in *Controlled Open Economies*: in a regulated environment asset choices will be distorted into less efficient patterns. As did other private agents, peasants clearly suffered from restricted asset choices. During 1977 inflation was 17.5 per cent (on the lower income consumer price index), the rate of interest paid on cooperative savings deposits was 5 per cent, and many peasants were probably unable to access even this rate of interest, which (as we have seen in Chapter 2) was generous in local terms. Nationally, there was a sharp decline in the proportion of savings to demand deposits, as banks often refused to accept money into the former (the interest rate they themselves could earn on rediscounted Treasury Bills averaged only 1.5 per cent during the year).

The heavily negative real interest rate on financial assets presumably accelerated peasant investment in real assets. We noted in Muranga the tendency observed at the aggregate level for such a bunching of investment to drive up the prices of items purchased for investment. We have not been able to quantify the consequences or rephasing peasant investment; however, there are grounds for believing that the net effect of bunching is less detrimental in the peasant sector than in the rest of the economy, and may well be beneficial. This is primarily because of the gearing provided by the copying effect which we will discuss shortly. Additionally, the principal beneficiaries of the rents generated by the bunching of coffee planting were probably households selling casual labour, and these tend to be among the poor.

We have seen that there is a hierarchy of activities according to their returns within peasant agriculture, and that peasants tended to direct windfall investment not just into the activities in which they were already engaged, but into new higher return activities, such as improved livestock.

The only sense in which such investment might have been socially inefficient is if the export quota negotiated through the International Coffee Agreement imposed large differences in social and private returns to marginal coffee production. In the short term, with the onset of a second world coffee boom in 1985, the extra planting had a high social payoff. In the longer term extra coffee output is likely to be valuable because Kenya probably has an interest in gradually increasing its quota by means of stock accumulation, which is feasible under the ICA rules. However the workings of the coffee cartel are beyond the scope of our study, so that we accept as a possibility that the marginal social value of coffee production is considerably below its price. If this were the case, further production could be discouraged either by decentralizing the national production quota (the policy in force until the early 1970s), or imposing a coffee tax to bring the domestic price to that level at which production is equal to the national quota. The former policy is probably the more costly to enforce, but the latter involves a transfer from peasants to the government. However, neither should be confused with a stabilization policy. If production quotas are used to regulate output, a coffee boom calls for a clearly signalled temporary suspension of the production quota (with the information that quotas will revert to their intial household-specific levels after the boom). If virtual prices are used, peasants similarly need to be informed that the domestic price will revert to that level at which only initial production is profitable. There is no more reason to believe that peasants would be myopic about quotas or virtual prices than about world prices. The coffee boom induced planting because it occurred at a time when production was regulated neither by quotas nor by taxation, and we suspect that this was in fact the appropriate policy stance.

Now consider further the second feature of peasant response to the coffee boom, namely, the copying effect which induced peasants who had not benefited from the windfall to emulate the windfall investment behaviour of those who had benefited. For example, we have seen that around 3 per cent of the windfall income of coffee growers was used to acquire improved livestock by households who had not previously had any, and that for every such household a further 0.54 households were induced to copy the behaviour. In this case the effect is to increase the investment response to the windfall by some 1.5 per cent. There was also a pronounced copying effect in tree crop planting. In Kenya around 40 per cent of all coffee planting between 1975 and 1983 was accounted for by new entrants to the activity, in contrast (as we will see in the next chapter) to a negligible percentage in Tanzania.

We have decomposed the adoption rate into that part directly attributable to windfall income, that part due to errors in price expectations, and that part due to copying. Although between them these effects fully accounted for the observed adoption rate of 26 per cent, only a small proportion was attributed directly to windfall income. We have estimated that the planting of coffee by existing growers constituted an investment equal to around 25 per cent of their windfall income (of which by comparison with Tanzania we will deduce that around half would have happened without the boom). The coffee planting by new adopters induced by copying and errors in expectations (85 per cent of all adoption) is thus equivalent to around 14 per cent of windfall coffee income. (Coffee planting by new entrants was two-thirds that of existing growers, so $0.67 \times 0.85 \times 0.25 = 0.14$.)

Between them these two induced investments in improved livestock and coffee by peasants who did not themselves benefit from the boom thus add, on our estimates, a further 17 per cent to the savings rate of the peasant economy out of windfall coffee income. When this is combined with the savings rate of coffee growers (65 per cent), the total windfall savings rate of the peasant economy is 82 per cent. This probably overstates the induced savings effect, since some of the investment copying probably only diverted savings from other uses. However, both coffee planting and improved livestock constituted such large investments by new adopters (there being in each case a threshold scale for the activity), that it is reasonable to regard most of this as reflecting an additional savings effort. Our survey showed that few households admitted to regretting their induced investments. They had gained access to an activity further up the hierarchy of returns, which might in turn afforded a basis from which to make further progress at a later stage.

Thus, the copying effect induces further savings which amplifies the investment effort from the income windfall. Allowing for this effect it may well be that the peasant sector had a higher savings rate out of the windfall than did other private agents. Indeed, this would not be surprising since peasants were best placed to appreciate the transient nature of extra income, being its first-round recipients. This reinforces the argument that there should be no expectation that government taxation of the windfall would raise the aggregate savings rate: the reverse is more likely.

Appendix: Model Estimation for the Coffee Production Function

The model was estimated by the method of non-linear least squares, using the Marquardt–Levenberg iterative algorithm (Marquardt, 1963), and hence the residuals for each iteration were regressed on the partial derivatives of the model with respect to the parameters until a convergence criterion was achieved. The choice of the Marquardt–Levenberg method for the iterative process was made for several reasons. The algorithm is in effect no different from taking sets of ridge regressions, and therefore can be expected to perform well in the presence of high degrees of partial correlation between parameters, which was thought might occur with the functional form of the model. Secondly, as noted by Judge *et al.* (1980), the algorithm seems to perform well even if the initial vector of parameter estimates is greatly different from that vector which minimizes the objective function. Representing the model as a function of the twelve parameters θ_1 to θ_{12} and the explanatory variables Z_1 to Z_6, we have:

$$Q = F(\theta_1, \ldots, \theta_{12}, Z_1, \ldots, Z_6) + \varepsilon$$
$$= F(\theta) + \varepsilon.$$

If $\underline{Z}$ is an 189×12 matrix of the partial derivatives of the model with respect to the parameters, i.e. $\underline{Z} = \partial F / \partial \lambda$, we have the normal equations represented by the following, where $\underline{q} = Q - \hat{Q}$;

$$\underline{Z}' F(\theta) = \underline{Z}' \underline{q}.$$

Hence an algorithm of $\underline{Z}$ and $\underline{q}$ is needed to compute a step-change d to the vector of parameter estimates, such that the error sum of squares (ESS) is reduced.

The Marquardt–Levenberg method uses the algorithm;

$$d = (\underline{Z}'\underline{Z} + \lambda \underline{I})^{-1} (\underline{Z}'\underline{q}).$$

Computationally if the iterations begin with a parameter vector θ_0, λ was started at 10^{-8} and a value for d computed. Then λ was reduced by a factor of ten if ESS $(\theta_0 + d) <$ ESS (θ_0), and increased by a factor of ten in the reverse case. This proves to be more flexible than the other computational methods available; for instance the Gauss–Newton algorithm, $d = (\underline{Z}'\underline{Z})^{-1} \underline{Z}'q$, may have difficulty converging along a direction vector where there is a possibility of ESS $(\theta_0 + d) >$ ESS (θ_0), in which case step-halving is usually employed which could occur far from a minimum of the objective function. This indeed occurred when our model was estimated using Newtonian algorithms, as no initial vector of parameter estimates (other than those close to final estimates obtained using the Marquardt–Levenberg algorithm) could be found which satisfied the convergence criterion before becoming stuck in unsuccessful step-halving procedures.

Specifically the convergence criterion employed was that convergence was assumed to be achieved on iteration i if $(\text{ESS}_i - \text{ESS}_{i-1})/(\text{ESS}_i + 10^{-6}) < 10^{-8}$. Other criteria were tested but it was found that less strict criteria tended to lead to fast convergence with results highly sensitive to the choice of the initial vector of parameter estimates, and tighter criteria led to exponential increases in computer time with little discernible change in the final parameter values. Hence for these practical reasons the above criterion was soon employed for all runs of the model, with the maximum number of iterations set at 100. Further to the choice of objective function, iterative algorithm, and convergence criterion, the model was supplied with the set of first derivatives of the objective function with respect to the parameters, and an initial vector of parameter estimates chosen. As the process will lead to a minimum ESS which can a priori only be assumed to be local, the stability of estimates in response to changes in the initial vector of parameter estimates, and to the choice of iterative algorithm was also explored.

Using different initial estimates and algorithms, and with the choice of convergence criterion specified above, the model was run over 100 times. Presenting such a large volume of results poses problems, but the results of the runs can be presented in two parts, i.e. those runs that converged and those that failed to converge. A set of estimates from a successful run is presented in Table 6.5.

The results in Table 6.5 were produced with the Marquardt–Levenberg algorithm. Three other algorithms were tried, namely the Gauss–Newton, algorithm, the method of steepest descent, and the multivariate secant method. All three alternative algorithms failed to find convergent direction vectors, unless an initial set of estimates close to those in Table 6.5 was used. Using the Marquardt–Levenberg algorithm, the results were found to be sensitive to the initial estimates for some of the parameters. Specifically the estimates for β_0, β_1, β_2, and α_0 proved to be unresponsive to the initial estimates, and all convergent runs produced estimates for these parameters varying by no more than 5 per cent from the estimates presented in Table 6.5. Some combinations of the other six parameters failed to achieve results compatible with Table 6.5, with γ_2, γ_4, and γ_6 being the most disruptive parameters. However, these combinations produced only two outcomes. Firstly iterations would achieve convergence, but only with parameter values inconsistent with theory. The most common results were β_3 to be pushed to unity (i.e. the effect of hired labour to be ignored) or α_1 to be driven to zero (all factors in the land nest ignored). Some of these runs produced a lower ESS than that shown in Table 6.5. Hence the results in Table 6.5 only represent a local minimum of the objective function, but are representative of the only results obtained that are consistent with production theory. The second outcome was for non-convergence within 100 iterations. The path of iterations for these runs was inspected and the vector of parameter estimates was found in all cases to be moving outside the bounds of theory.

7
A Comparison with Tanzania

7.1. Introduction

In the preceding chapters we have produced an account of the peasant economy in each country during the period of the coffee boom and its aftermath, and produced a detailed analysis of responses to the boom in Kenya. This chapter brings out some comparisons with Tanzania. Prior to the boom the two peasant economies had similar structures and had inherited many common features of ecology and culture. Yet these initially similar economies produced radically divergent outcomes during our period. This chapter attempts to draw out some of these divergences and discuss to what extent they are attributable to differences in economic policies.

7.2. The Peasant Economies in 1975

We do not wish to claim that prior to the boom the two peasant economies were identical. Clearly, as set out in the opening sections of Chapters 2 and 3, they had rather distinct evolutions, notably as regards the timing of the introduction of coffee. Tanzanian peasants were free to adopt coffee, and duly did so, decades before their Kenyan counterparts. Nevertheless, by 1975 peasant agriculture in the more populous parts of Tanzania bore a reasonably close resemblance to that in Kenya, in both countries coffee being the major cash crop and maize being the major food crop. Coffee production in the peasant sector per capita of the peasant population was around 3.5 kg in Kenya and 4.3 kg in Tanzania (the peasant sector accounting for around half the total production in Kenya and around 85 per cent in Tanzania). Peasant agriculture was similarly commercialized in both countries (see Table 7.1). Although both economies have only small urban and industrial sectors, the somewhat greater size of those sectors in Kenya contributed to the greater importance of wages and remittances in peasant income. In Kenya, non-agricultural wage activities were an integral part of the peasant economy, with considerable migration both to and from urban areas, and large remittance flows. In Tanzania this was less true: fewer households in our survey had migration histories. The average household had only half as many spouses of the head living away but with economic links), and remittances both as a share of income and per migrant were very much lower. Peasants were more economically isolated in Tanzania.

TABLE 7.1. *A comparison of income composition of peasant households around 1975 (%)*

	Kenya	Tanzania
Subsistence	35.5	49.2
Farm sales	21.5	20.1
Business	9.7	20.1
Wages	22.4	8.4
Remittances	10.9	2.3
TOTAL	100.0	100.0
Mean per capita income (1974/5 prices)	524 Ksh	737 Tsh

Sources: Tanzania, 1976/7 National Household Budget Survey, (national sample); Kenya, IRSI, 1974/5 (national sample).

The land endowment of the average Tanzanian household was larger than that in Kenya. In our 1982 and 1983 surveys the Tanzanian mean was some 50 per cent greater than that in Central Province, reflecting a markedly lower labour/land ratio. However, much of this land was probably of a lower quality. The very approximate income comparison of Table 7.1, in which the Tanzanian data are deflated to the same year as the Kenyan, should not, however, be interpreted as indicating that living standards were higher in that year. Although the two currencies were still officially trading at parity in 1974/5, the Tanzanian price level was already probably somewhat higher than the Kenyan. Rather, the comparison should indicate that there was no substantial difference in the level of development.

In both countries the governments had intervened heavily in crop markets. In food markets inter-district trading was prohibited but this prohibition was widely evaded, while cash crops were the monopoly of marketing boards. Arguably, in neither country were these marketing arrangements ideal, and there is some evidence that in Tanzania they were rather higher cost (see Guerreiro, 1984), and subjected peasants to longer delays in payment (our survey found a 70-week delay in final coffee payments). During our period the cooperative societies were temporarily disbanded in Tanzania, and indeed there was continuous institutional flux, failure provoking change, change causing confusion, and confusion delivering further failure. These are, however, nuances on what were rather similar marketing structures.

In neither country were peasant factor markets well developed. The peasant hired labour market, uncontrolled in Kenya and officially discouraged in Tanzania, allocated only around 6 per cent of the labour input on the holding in Kenya and 2 per cent in Tanzania. Tenancy, which was predominantly the free lending of land rather than a commercial undertaking, allocated only 2 per cent of the land area in Kenya and 5 per cent in Tanzania. Informal credit was, at least by 1983, rather more substantial in Tanzania, but even there it was largely intra-family and entirely non-commercial, no interest being charged. Hence, peasants in both economies were largely confined to their own land, labour, and financial resources.

Despite these similarities in income levels and structures, the crop marketing environment, and resource constraints, outcomes during the ensuing period were unmistakably different.

7.3. Divergences in Outcomes, 1975–1983

We will consider two groups of outcomes, namely, income and accumulation.

We assemble the ten snapshots of mean income, which have been reported previously, in Table 7.2. Each of these figures can be questioned, and some look rather doubtful. Income in Central Province in 1978/9 was probably somewhat higher than in 1974/5, even though by then the boom was largely over. Income in Tanzania was probably lower in 1974/5 than implied by the FAO survey, since that is 33 per cent above the estimate made by the 1969 Household Budget Survey. However, we are probably entitled to make two inferences from these snapshots: income was broadly constant in Central Province, Kenya (presumably with the exception of the unobserved boom period), and declined precipitately in Tanzania. Nyanza appears to be in an intermediate position, but since this conclusion is based on only one pair of surveys and the implied income change is not dramatic, it may well be an artefact.

The first of these inferences, that per capita income in Central Province was broadly unchanged between the end-points of our period, is consistent with the National Accounts estimates of the growth in agricultural value added at constant prices, which at 3.1 per cent per annum (Table 2.10) are in line with the growth of the peasant population. The second inference cannot so readily be matched against national data, simply because there are so many fewer agricultural data for Tanzania. However, two components of peasant income

TABLE 7.2. *A comparison of changes in real income* (real per capita income, 1974/1975 = 100)

	1969	1974/5	1976/7	1978/9	1979/80	1981/2	1982/3
Kenya (Central)		100		97		106	
(Nyanza)		100		*		82	
Tanzania	75	100	102		47		41

* IRS4 income for Nyanza is not reported, see the discussion of Table 2.13.
Sources: Tables 2.12 and 3.17.

can be checked, namely wage income and export crop income. Our investigation of the living standards of urban wage earners (Table 3.18) found a 44 per cent decline in real per capita income between 1975 and 1984. Rural wage earners within peasant households probably mirrored this change in income since wage rates are nationally determined. Per capita earnings from export crops declined steeply. Taking coffee, which is of course the single most important peasant cash crop, between 1975 and 1983 volume declined by 5 per cent, and the real producer price by 58 per cent using the official CPI and by 66 per cent adjusting for black markets (Table 3.12). On top of this the rural population grew by at least 20 per cent. Combining these factors implies a decline in real per capita coffee income of 72 per cent.

Applying these changes to the shares of export crops and wages (including remittances) in income in 1983 (Table 3.3), implies that even if all other sources of income had been constant, real income would have declined by 31 per cent. Further, since these two components account for almost the entire 'export base' of the peasant economy, they presumably precipitated some decline in the non-tradable components of income which were dependent upon the expenditure of this income. Finally, the deterioration in the availability of inputs must have adversely affected all economic activities. This is certainly the implication of the comparison of income structures in 1977 and 1983 reported in Table 3.9, which found little change in the relative composition of income. We should stress that we are not attempting to defend the specific numbers shown for the Tanzanian real income series, but rather to substantiate the broad conclusion that there was a severe decline. It is evident that the surveys and the national data are telling broadly the same story.

Our two inferences from the survey snapshots, of unchanged real per capita income in Central Province and a severe decline in Tanzania, are therefore both substantiated by national data. We defer consideration of their implications and turn to the comparison of accumulation.

In Chapter 6 we investigated four types of asset formation on the part of Kenyan peasants, namely financial assets, improved livestock, tree crop planting, and expenditure on land, buildings, and equipment. Recall that in the coffee-growing area of Muranga, Kenya, where we were able to observe financial asset behaviour through savings deposits, we found that in the first year of the boom peasants saved almost 50 per cent of windfall income.

An investment of some importance in Kenya but negligible in Tanzania was improved livestock. Using a logit analysis of the adoption of improved livestock we were able to isolate that component of adoption by Kenyan coffee growers which was attributable to windfall income. Controlling for other characteristics, coffee growers had a propensity to adopt improved livestock during the period some 50 per cent greater than would otherwise have been expected. Combined with information on the value of improved livestock in 1982 we arrived at a mean value of windfall investment of 190 shillings.

One investment undertaken by some coffee growers in both countries was the further planting of coffee. In Kenya one-half, and in Tanzania one-quarter of all those growing coffee on the eve of the boom had planted additional trees by 1982/3 (49 against 24 per cent in our surveys). As a result the total tree stock of existing growers increased by 22 per cent in Kenya and by 10 per cent in Tanzania. Recall from Chapter 6 that we have valued the extra planting per coffee-growing household in Kenya at around 1,600 shillings. Had Kenyan households instead only increased their tree stock by the Tanzanian proportion, their investment would have been around 730 shillings. If we adopt this as the counterfactual of what would have happened in Kenya without the boom, windfall-attributable planting by existing growers was worth around 870 shillings. We are inclined to treat this as an upper bound since the decline in the real producer price of coffee in Tanzania from 1978 onwards must have reduced the planting rate in the latter part of our period, though this is somewhat offset by the increase in price in 1976 and 1977.

The best opportunity for comparison of investment behaviour is provided by expenditure on land, buildings, and equipment over the period 1975–82(3), information on which was collected by identical survey procedures in both countries. Our concern is in each case to quantify the investment rates out of permanent and temporary incomes. In each case our control group of households without windfalls is made up of all the households not growing coffee, and this provides us with a measure of rate of investment out of permanent income. Our analysis is set out in Table 7.3, and is explained in the notes to the table. We approximate permanent income by the average of the incomes found in the budget surveys at either end of our period, correcting for the somewhat higher incomes of coffee growers. The estimates are clearly nothing more than approximations, but since they are only used as the denominator in the calculation of the permanent investment rate, quite large inaccuracies can be tolerated. Windfall income has already been calculated for Kenyan coffee growers in Chapter 6. Tanzanian coffee growers in effect received no windfall.

Repeating the procedure used to estimate the Kenyan windfall, the real producer price in Tanzania was only above its 1975 level in 1976 and 1977, and even over these two years prices were raised only by the equivalent of a one year increase of 16 per cent. This amounted to a windfall of around 160 shillings compared with 6,330 shillings in Kenya. Obviously, this is too small to produce identifiable behavioural responses, and so our calculation of a windfall investment rate is only meaningful for Kenya. However, we attempt to calculate windfall investment in Tanzania as a control experiment. If, for example, coffee growers happen to have atypically high permanent investment rates, Tanzanian farmers will show up as appearing to have windfall investment with no windfall income and our procedure will be faulted. Such a different behaviour pattern of coffee growers is conceivable: were they a self-selected group of ambitious households with a will to accumulate, a 'peasant bourgeoisie', we would find just such a pattern.

TABLE 7.3. *Permanent and transient investment compared*

	Coffee growers		Non-growers	
	Kenya	Tanzania	Kenya	Tanzania
Total investment (sh.)	4,450	1,490	1,080	1,520
Permanent income (sh.)	46,000	55,000	38,000	50,000
Permanent investment rate (%)			2.8	3.0
Permanent investment (sh.)	1,380	1,650	1,080	1,520
Windfall investment (sh.)	3,070	−160	0	0
Windfall income (sh.)	6,330	160	0	0
Windfall investment rate (%)	49	—	—	—

Note: Total investment is expenditure on land, buildings, and farm and business equipment over the periods 1975–82 (Kenya) and 1975–83 (Tanzania) as recorded in our surveys. Permanent income is the simple average of nominal household incomes in IRS1 and our survey (Kenya), HBS 1976/7 and HBS 1983 (Tanzania), multiplied by six (Kenya) and seven (Tanzania) to arrive at nominal income over the respective periods. This figure is then used for non-coffee-growing households, whereas coffee-growing households are assumed to have permanent incomes above this by 20 per cent (Kenya) and 10 per cent (Tanzania). The former figure is based on IRS4 and our 1982 survey as discussed in Chapter 6; the latter is based on our 1983 survey which found a differential of 7 per cent, and increased to allow for the relative decline in the incomes of coffee growers. Permanent investment rate is estimated only for non-coffee growers, and is total investment/permanent income. Permanent investment is actual investment for non-coffee growers, and for coffee growers is permanent income multiplied by the permanent investment rate of 3 per cent. Windfall income is deviation in real coffee earnings during 1976–9 (Kenya, see Chapter 6 for deviation), and 1976–7 (Tanzania, see text). Windfall investment rate is windfall investment/windfall income.

Our results as set out in Table 7.3 reveal, however, that Tanzanian coffee growers have a virtually identical investment rate to that of Tanzanian non-coffee growers, and so they show up as having neither windfall income nor windfall investment. Equally striking, the Kenyan group of non-coffee growers has precisely the same investment rate out of income, 3 per cent, as the two Tanzanian groups. There thus appears to be some commonality of behaviour both between countries and between coffee and non-coffee growers, as far as investment out of permanent income is concerned.

This commonality of behaviour, together with the lowness of the investment rate, makes the behaviour of Kenyan coffee growers, the one group to receive a substantial windfall income, all the more striking. Their investment expenditure is massively out of line with their permanent income, and yields a windfall investment rate of some 50 per cent. When the windfall investment in improved livestock and coffee trees is added to this total, as calculated above, the overall rate of investment out of windfall income is 65 per cent.[1]

[1] This is close to our estimate of the windfall savings rate of the entire non-government sector, namely 60 per cent. See *Controlled Open Economies*.

Although non-coffee growers in each country had common, and rather low, rates of investment expenditure on land, buildings, and equipment, there is one respect in which their accumulation behaviour differed radically. Within ecologically suitable areas, of those who were non-growers in 1975, by 1982 some 26 per cent had adopted coffee in Kenya and virtually none had done so in Tanzania. Since coffee planting is a major investment, subject to a threshold scale of entry, this divergence in coffee adoption constitutes a further substantial divergence in the rate of investment out of income. In Kenya the coffee boom induced extra investment even among those who were not receiving windfall coffee income.

7.4. Explaining the Divergences

The previous section has identified three major divergences in outcomes: the severe decline in income in Tanzania, the adoption of coffee in Kenya but not Tanzania, and the high investment rate of coffee growers in Kenya. We defer discussion of the first of these until Part III.

A maximizing agent (who would respond to a temporary windfall by first accumulating financial assets and then decumulating them and converting them into real assets), could scarcely be better concretized than in the behaviour patterns of the peasants we have been observing. It would be hard to account for these behaviour patterns except by recourse to the distinction between permanent and transient incomes. But this has the powerful corollary that peasants must have recognized the boom to be temporary in order to have structured their responses accordingly.

The surge in coffee adoption in Kenya but not in Tanzania cannot, however, be attributed to the optimal deployment of a windfall, for the simple reason that only a small minority of those who adopted coffee had a windfall to deploy. In Chapter 6 we attributed less than 3 per cent of the 26 per cent adoption rate to the secular trend growth in opportunities for wage employment. Since only a few per cent of adopters could have been beneficiaries of the boom through either the non-agricultural or the peasant labour markets, the majority financed this large investment without extra income. The two questions which arise as a consequence are why such a response should have been induced by the boom, and whether it was desirable.

One of the central results of our analysis of peasant behaviour has been the importance of social networks. Two networks have a dominant influence upon the opportunities which peasants objectively face or subjectively perceive. The network of the neighbourhood, defined in our Kenya survey as the surrounding 200 households, we have found to be overwhelmingly the most important determinant of the adoption of the high-return activities of coffee, tea, and improved livestock. In each case, the proportion of neighbouring households already undertaking the activity was influential, but far more powerful was the proportion in the process of adopting the activity. As we have stressed, because of the gestation periods involved in these activities a household learns nothing directly about the returns to an activity by watching its neighbours adopt it, whereas of course, it can learn by watching existing growers. We therefore concluded that the two represent distinct inducements to adoption, namely, an information effect and a copying effect. We cited other research showing that such a copying effect is a fundamental aspect of human behaviour.

The second social network shaping opportunities is the family, defined in the precise and narrow sense of the resident household plus all non-resident sons, daughters, and spouses of the household head (the extended family in our terminology). Whereas the neighbourhood network determines agricultural opportunities, the family network determines labour market opportunities. We identified this effect through the influence of the labour market participation of other members of the extended family on the probability of access to non-agricultural wage jobs. In establishing this result we controlled for other determinants of access such as education. In both Kenya and Tanzania such participation by other family members is the single most powerful determinant of access to wage jobs.[2] Further, we narrowed this down according to the location of the job: having kin in the urban labour market powerfully assisted in acquiring an urban job; having kin in the rural non-agricultural labour market similarly helped to get a rural job.

Potentially, this might have been just another manifestation of the copying effect: if an elder brother goes off to town this provides a role model for the younger brother. Presumably this is a component of the effect. However, recall that we found that a substantial proportion of migrants (in Central Province 50 per cent) already had job offers prior to migration. The only credible account of such offers is that they were secured through kin already in employment. Even speculative migration is likely to be made objectively easier by having close kin in urban employment, if only through the easier access to urban hospitality during job search. We may therefore conclude that the influence of the family network upon opportunities goes beyond a copying effect in that it objectively alters those opportunities. The family network is thus an economic asset, the value of which differs between households. Since the private benefits of privileged access have an almost offsetting cost to other households, its principle output is the generation and transmission of inequality.

The family and the neighbourhood constitute the social space inhabited by the peasant household. In Part IV we will investigate to what extent behaviour transcends the boundaries of this space through schooling and extension services, both being attempts to enlarge the information set beyond that generated through social interaction. In Part II we have established the

---

[2] We report our analysis of the Tanzanian data in detail in *Quantitative Studies in the Economies of Rural Africa* (forthcoming).

potency of this social space as a determinant of the activity mix in which the household is engaged: behaviour would simply be unintelligible if characterized purely in the framework of atomistic constrained optimization with full information.

The importance of the social space in determining activity choice is well demonstrated in the explanation of the divergent patterns of coffee adoption in Kenya and Tanzania. Why was there a 26 per cent adoption rate in Kenya and a zero adoption rate in Tanzania, despite a much smaller differential in planting by existing growers? First, consider a widely held hypothesis: Kenyan peasants adopted coffee because they were dazzled by a price increase which they believed was permanent. This hypothesis forms part of the bedrock of the case for agricultural commodity price stabilization: Platonic Guardian governments can protect peasants from themselves. The myopic peasant hypothesis will by now be held only by the myopic reader. First, a 65 per cent savings rate out of the windfall is clearly inconsistent with the notion that coffee growers believed the price increase to be permanent. The hypothesis is at once driven back to being a statement about the differential myopia of coffee-growing and non-coffee-growing peasants: only coffee growers are shrewd. But we have already tested the thesis that coffee growers are superior and rejected it: in Chapter 6 we established that there was no difference in the performance of the two groups in a common activity. Finally, only 17 per cent of planters attributed their decision to the price increase, regretted the decision, and attributed their regret to a fall in the coffee price. We have, in effect, a dynamic counterpart to Schultz's famous hypothesis: peasants are poor but farsighted.

Having rejected the hypothesis of myopia we are left with a 26 per cent adoption rate to explain, of which we attribute not more than 9 per cent to non-boom processes. In Chapter 6 we developed an alternative explanation which started with an analysis of the diffusion of the coffee boom through to non-coffee growers via the transmission mechanisms of the non-agricultural and the peasant labour markets. We estimated that the expansion of non-agricultural employment due to the boom would potentially have enabled an extra 2.2 per cent of peasant households to gain a foothold in this activity. However, because of the informational advantage possessed by those households already in wage jobs, only 1.4 per cent more households entered the activity. Although in ecologically suitable areas probably many of these households thereupon adopted coffee (as suggested by the adoption logit of Chapter 6), this mechanism was clearly only a small component of the overall adoption rate. Similarly, the bonanza in the casual labour market in coffee areas during the boom benefited only a small group of households because the hired labour market is so small, and many of these households would have been too poor to contemplate the adoption of coffee. We concluded that these transmission mechanisms from the boom could account for an adoption rate of only a few per cent. Since the 17 per cent rate of myopia among adopters accounts for an adoption rate of 4.4 per cent, between them general equilibrium effects and myopia yield an adoption rate in the range 5–10 per cent, none of which would apply in Tanzania. (Although there was an expansion in urban wage employment in Tanzania due to the boom, the virtual absence of remittances meant that there was no transmission effect back to resident households.)

A key result in Chapter 6 was that the copying effect would augment a 5–10 per cent adoption rate by a further 9–18 per cent (from the coefficient on ADOPTER in the logit of coffee adoption), so that the 17+ per cent adoption rate not attributable to non-boom growth is fully explained. We should not let this convey a specious degree of precision. Rather, the quantification exercise implies that the general equilibrium effects of the boom on non-coffee growers cannot account for other than a small proportion of the adoption rate, but clearly did generate some additional adoption. Similarly, only a small proportion of adoption can reasonably be attributed to myopic price expectations. Between them these effects leave a large residual which can be accounted for by the copying effect, strong evidence for which was found in each of our three adoption logits. Since none of these influences applied in Tanzania we have therefore accounted for the massive divergence in adoption rates, answering the first of our two questions.

Despite our dismissal of the myopic peasant hypothesis we have explained most adoption in terms of a copying effect. We wish to stress that these two positions, though superficially in contradiction, are entirely compatible and between them afford considerable insight into the peasant world. All behaviour is influenced by the social space which the agent inhabits, the copying effect being a manifestation of this relationship. The peculiarity of the peasant household is the narrowness of its social space: interactions occur only with a small number of other agents with spatial or kinship proximity. The copying effect is therefore not widely diffused across society but occurs only within a subset of the many closed and bounded social networks through which interaction is channelled. Thus it not only gears up the rate of adoption but gives rise to differential behaviour. Although behaviour is influenced by social interaction it is not, of course, uniquely determined by it. As other agents, peasants gather information on the consequences of alternative courses of action and use it in reaching decisions. We have found that to the extent that decisions are based upon forecasts of consequences rather than copying, there is no basis for believing that peasants are myopic. Copying does not constitute an imperfection in intertemporal preferences, but rather an alternative process of decision taking to the private calculus of forecasted consequences. As discussed in Chapter 6, it can be interpreted as free riding on the calculations of other households, or simply as a primitive feature of human behaviour.

Our second question was normative: was this induced adoption desirable? Two levels of answer must be distinguished: private and social. The adoption of coffee may be socially undesirable in Kenya regardless of its consequences for the individual household taking the decision because Kenya is a large country in the world coffee market and a member of a producer cartel. First however consider the question of private consequences.

Kenyan peasants were overcoming entry barriers. That is, as established in Chapter 6, coffee is a high-return activity with an entry barrier generated by economies of scale. Below a threshold size of coffee plot of around half the mean plot size of existing growers, the activity is less remunerative than maize. The copying effect induced households to make the considerable investment effort required to overcome this threshold, and thereby left them *ex post* better off even though *ex ante* it was a course of action they had either rejected or not considered. Our survey snapshots of Central Province before and after the boom do not show any marked increase in per capita income: merely a growth of 1 per cent per annum. We are not claiming that the surge in adoption was enough in itself to transform peasant incomes in Kenya, but it was undoubtedly an accelerated step up the hierarchy of activity mixes discussed in Chapter 6. This is supported by the low rate of regret among adopters.

Whether the adoption of coffee was socially beneficial depends upon the workings of the International Coffee Agreement. An extended discussion of this subject would take us beyond the scope of our study. However, two points are worthy of note. First, the formula determining the distribution of quotas under the agreement enables a country to increase its quota by building up its coffee stock. Coffee-producing countries thus operate under a controlled competition for market share which can over time be won by the least-cost producer. Second, compared with its rivals Kenya has a high labour/land ratio, which is rising rapidly, and does not have the alternative activities of manufacturing (as in Brazil) and drugs (as in Colombia). Nor does it at present have a large market share. It is therefore our impression that it is socially efficient for Kenya to increase its production, even though for bargaining purposes it cannot normally actively encourage production. In reaching this impression we have benefited from sources knowledgeable on both the ICA and Kenyan coffee production which we are not able to acknowledge. We should stress, however, that our comments on this important matter are by way of an impression rather than being a result of our research.

We have now discussed two of the three divergences in outcomes between the two peasant economies, the remaining one being the collapse of per capita income in Tanzania. To some extent this is quite a straightforward story of resource reallocation from peasant income to public expenditure. Since some of this expenditure directly benefited peasants it is logically possible that the decline in income was welfare-improving for peasants in the short term, in addition to being potentially welfare-improving for future generations of urban wage earners. We investigate the consequences of Tanzanian public expenditure in Part IV. However, the fall in peasant incomes is more complex then resource reallocation to the public sector. We provide an analysis of it in Part III.

III

*Peasant Supply Response to Shortages:
Theory and an Application to Tanzania*

8
Introduction to Part III

In many developing countries, governments have engineered a deterioration in the terms of trade faced by peasant farmers, for example by imposing taxes on export crops. Much theoretical and empirical research has been devoted to analysing how peasant supply would respond if this deterioration were reversed, and the consensus is that supply would respond positively. These analyses usually assume, at least implicitly, that peasants trade on markets which clear. In practice, there are often problems of availability, both of imports and of consumer goods. This Part considers the implications of such problems, and extends the usual analysis to cover them. It shows that supply response may well be perverse in these circumstances, even when it is positively related to price in the case where markets clear.

While the sources of market failure in developing countries are manifold, those which stem from policies, and which are in principle reversible, are of particular interest. For example, many governments impose price controls on consumer goods. Often the apparatus of price controls is a façade: the 'control' system merely rubber stamps market-determined prices. Clearly, in this case price controls have no effect. A second variant is for official prices to be set below market prices but for the controls not to be enforced. Without enforcement there are no penalties for trading at market-clearing prices, and so transactions at official prices coexist with normal trading on the uncontrolled market. While consumers are unable to purchase all they wish in the official market, on the unofficial market prices rise to their market-clearing level. In these circumstances, it might appear that the only consequence of price controls is to make income transfers to consumers, and that a market-clearing analysis remains adequate. This would only be true, however, if all peasants traded actively on the unofficial market, and that is unlikely to hold.

The coexistence of official and unofficial markets faces the peasant with a kinked budget line. Individual equilibrium may take place on either facet (or the cusp, of course); there is certainly nothing to guarantee that all peasants will enter the unofficial market. Some will be priced out of the market, given that they can obtain a rationed supply on the official market. They would like to purchase more at official prices but they do not choose to purchase more at unofficial market prices. We may describe these peasants as fully rationed, in contrast to those partially rationed peasants who are rationed on the official market but make purchases on the unofficial market.

A third variant is for official prices to be set below market-clearing prices and for the government to attempt to suppress transactions at prices above these levels. Such transactions become illegal and subject to penalties and are commonly referred to as the black market. The extent of the black market depends upon how far official prices are from market-clearing prices, the penalties for trading, and the probability of detection. Black markets are qualitatively different from unofficial markets because traders have an incentive to conceal rather than to disseminate information. Because of this, black markets are unlikely to provide the sort of easy access to goods at known prices which is meant by the description 'market-clearing'. That is, to some extent shortages persist in the presence of black markets.

In Tanzania price controls were of this third variety, so that peasants faced shortages of both consumer goods and farm inputs over a period of several years. During the 1970s the allocation of many resources ceased to be market-determined. In the market for consumer goods private trading was abolished in rural areas. National controlled prices were set by the Price Commission, which determined the prices of some 2,000 items. Prices were set on a cost-plus basis without any attempt to balance supply and demand. Initially, the apparatus of price controls was something of a façade since prices started at around market-clearing levels. However, from 1978 onwards controlled prices rapidly fell below market-clearing levels. In part, this was because costs were kept artificially low by an over-valued exchange rate. Since this resulted in excess demand for foreign exchange, the latter was allocated by the Cabinet and the Central Bank. Allocations came to be both item- and firm-specific. Many types of consumer goods ceased to be imported, and so the available range of goods progressively narrowed. A second reason for the divergence of controlled prices from market-clearing levels was that since priority was given to capital goods, the supply of consumer goods (both those imported directly and those made from imported inputs) contracted. Prices would have needed to rise considerably in order to clear markets. Instead, the incidence of unsatisfied demands was determined in the first instance by the Board of Internal Trade which was responsible for allocating all goods among the regions. However, there was no formal rationing system at the household level. The rule of pan-territorial pricing created a powerful disincentive to incurring the transport costs necessary to supply rural areas. Hence access to consumer goods in the villages tended to be both limited and sporadic.

Evidence from our survey showing the pervasive nature of shortages on both the official and the black markets in rural areas has already been given in Chapter 3. Further survey evidence for 1986 (Cooksey *et al.*, 1987a, b) confirms that markets were not clearing. The 1986 survey sought to identify which goods were needed as incentives to peasant crop sales. It concluded that the greatest incentive would be provided by additional supplies of basic consumer goods, namely, clothes, sugar, soap, cooking oil, kerosene, salt, and matches. This list of goods was identifed by peasants regardless of income level, which is consistent with quantity constraints. It is important to our subsequent analysis to establish that shortages were to a large extent sporadic: often the desired good would not be available (at any price), occasionally it would be available at the official price or on the black market at a higher price. The 1986 survey asked respondents in villages to classify the availability of items, the answers for the above list of goods being shown in Table 8.1.

The most common description of the availability of these commodities was that they were only sometimes or rarely available (between these two, 'rarely' was more frequent than 'sometimes'). With such severe shortages black markets developed despite draconian penalties. However, these markets were themselves very patchy in rural areas both because of the penalties and because the attempt by the state to control prices was supported by its monopolies of the rural transport system and of consumer goods imports and manufactures. Black markets are no more market-clearing than official markets even though their prices are higher. The 1986 survey did not distinguish between availability on the official and black markets, so that the description of availability as limited and sporadic applies to their combined provision. However, our 1983 survey (as reported in Chapter 3) asked respondents about availability on each market separately. This found that for almost all goods there was excess demand in both markets.

During 1986 and 1987, as part of a Structural Adjustment Programme, this control regime was partially dismantled and the supply of consumer goods to rural areas was substantially increased. This was financed partly by foreign aid and partly by the repatriation of foreign exchange illegally held abroad. Initially, the resulting influx of consumer goods improved availability in the major cities. This gradually spread to rural areas. Cooksey *et al.* (1987b) document through survey evidence the improvement in village-level availability which took place between 1986 and 1987. Ndulu and Hyuha (1986)

TABLE 8.1. *Availability of consumer goods in villages, 1986*

Good	Degree of availability (%)		
	Always	Sometimes/rarely	Never
Clothing	3	44	53
Sugar	0	68	32
Soap	5	68	27
Cooking oil	10	55	35
Kerosene	3	67	30
Salt	33	54	13
Matches	16	67	17
Average	10	60	30

Source: Cooksey *et al.* (1987a, Table 1).

report a survey conducted in June 1986 which found villages becoming supplied with imports but with domestic manufactures still very scarce. Unfortunately, at the time of writing (mid-1987), it is too early to assess the consequences of this regime change. The temporal focus of this study is therefore 1978–86 which may turn out to be the entire duration of the quantity-constrained phase.

In the next chapter we set out the theory of peasant supply response under conditions of shortage, arguing that it is dramatically different from under conditions of market-clearing. We then construct two tests of the theory for Tanzania, using time series (Chapter 10) and cross-section data (Chapter 11). Chapter 12 provides an evaluation of our tests and an assessment of the significance of our results for economies like Tanzania.

9

The Theory of Peasant Supply Response under Shortages

In this chapter we develop a simple theory of peasant supply response under conditions of rationing. The model presented here is simplified in two important respects. First, the stochastic nature of shortages gives rise to extremely complex multi-period dynamics. These are finessed in the present model and it appears unlikely that any model could fully incorporate them and retain analytic tractability. A more complex modelling of stochastic dynamics which generates the same results as the present model is given in *Controlled Open Economies*. Secondly, the aggregative structure of the model is kept extremely simple; the alternatives to the production of cash crops, namely leisure or the production of food, are treated as a single aggregate. We assume that food is produced only for own consumption. In Tanzania during our period this is not such an unrealistic assumption as might first appear. Dar es Salaam, the major urban centre, was largely fed by means of food imports rather than purchases from peasants. Hence, net sales of food by peasants in exchange for urban-supplied consumer goods were probably modest relative to non-food cash crops. In *Controlled Open Economies*, we discuss disaggregation of this model and demonstrate that the results presented here are robust, generalizing to all disaggregations which preserve the key assumption.

9.1. The Basic Model

Consider first the simple case of a barter economy in which the cash crop is exchanged directly for consumer goods. In the absence of price controls consumer goods will be fully available and peasants will optimize by choosing to work on their cash crop up to the point at which the disutility of the last hour of work equals the utility derived from the goods purchased with that work. However, once control-induced shortages are introduced, the peasant cannot purchase all the goods he wishes to buy. He will therefore choose to do only enough work on the cash crop to pay for the goods which he expects to be available since further production would be wasted effort, yielding no additional consumption. In this situation, an increase in the price of the cash crop will reduce cash crop output unless it coincides with an increased availability of consumer goods. With constant availability (and hence expenditure), the peasant will wish to maintain his crop income at a constant level, so an increase in the price of the cash crop will induce a proportionate reduction in supply. Thus, the supply elasticity is minus unity regardless of its value in the absence of shortages. While supply response to price is perverse, an increase in the availability of consumer goods at a given cash crop price will induce a corresponding increase in cash crop production, since peasants wish to buy more goods in exchange for crops than is possible at prevailing prices.

This simple analysis of perverse response to price and positive response to increased availability is complicated once we move from a barter economy to one in which goods can only be purchased for money.

To simplify, suppose that peasants receive cash from their crop sales at the close of the harvest, consume goods evenly throughout the year, and hold money balances only to finance this consumption. Hence, when goods are fully available, the maximum money stock held by the peasant (which he has upon being paid for his crop) is equal to his planned annual expenditure. When the availability of goods is limited the money stock which the peasant chooses to hold depends critically upon the form of the rationing regime. When there is a known ration, future expenditure is also known so the desired maximum money stock is equal to this (reduced) annual expenditure.

However, in rural Tanzania rationing has been a matter of chance: although shortage has been the norm, a household may sometimes strike lucky, in which event its ability to purchase goods is determined by the money stock held. This has important consequences for the relation between goods availability and the money stock held. If the household knew the amount available for certain this relation would be proportional. Since the household cannot buy as much as it wants it will always want to hold just enough money to buy the maximum amount available, hence money stocks will decline if rationing becomes more severe. If, however, availability is uncertain (and the household has limited access to credit) there is a second effect working in the opposite direction. If the household were to hold a money stock sufficient to buy the mean quantity available it would for lack of money not be able to profit from above-average availability. Hence it may want to hold a larger money stock to reduce the probability of being constrained. The strength of this effect depends on the utility of leisure (since money can be accumulated only by working more), on the riskiness of availability, and on the household's aversion to risk.

We now present a simple model of the peasant household which formalizes the previous discussion. To keep the model as simple as possible, the peasant household is assumed to produce the cash crop as a function of labour input subject to constant returns. One unit of the crop is produced by one unit of labour, and is paid for one period in arrears. The price of a unit of the crop is the same as the price of a unit of the purchased commodity. We suppose that utility is inter-temporally additive, with instantaneous utility at time t given by:

$$U = U(L_t, G_t) \quad (9.1)$$
$$- \ \ + $$

where G_t = the purchased commodity and L_t = labour on the cash crop.

The allocation of remaining labour between subsistence crop production and leisure is not studied in the model since it has no monetary implications.

If the commodity market is unrationed then in equilibrium the household optimizes by choosing G^* such that

$$\frac{\partial U}{\partial G_t^*} = -(1+r)\frac{\partial U}{L_t} \quad (9.2)$$

where r is the rate of interest, and enters equation (9.2) because of the delay in payment. The demand for money in this unrationed equilibrium will be set equal to expenditure, the simplest possible form:

$$M^* = G^* \quad (9.3)$$

(where * denotes unrationed equilibrium values).

In equation (9.3) and subsequently, time subscripts are omitted since we restrict attention to stationary values. The budget constraint requires that income should equal expenditure, so

$$G^* = L = L^*. \quad (9.4)$$

With prices unchanged, the quantity of the consumer good is now reduced and informally rationed so that the expected level of purchases is less than the desired level:

$$E(G^R) < G^* \quad (9.5)$$

where G^R = the quantity of consumer goods purchased under the rationing regime and $E(\ )$ = the conditional mathematical expectation of the term in brackets.

In any particular period the actual purchases of goods may differ from the long-run average $E(G^R)$. However, we will assume that the good is storable and that should the household have a run of bad luck such that its stocks fall to zero, it is able to borrow from other households (as long as its consumption does not exceed the sustainable level $E(G^R)$), an amount which it returns once its stocks are positive. With this assumption, consumption in each period equals $E(G^R)$. This has implications for labour input and the marginal utilities of goods and leisure as depicted in Figure 9.1.

Since the budget constraint will still bind, income will equal expected expenditure, so that:

$$E(G^R) = L = L^R \quad (9.6)$$

where L^R = optimal labour input under the rationing regime.

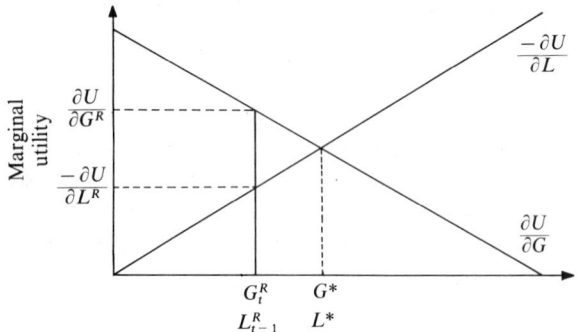

FIG. 9.1. *The effect of shortages on the marginal utilities of leisure and consumption*

Hence, the marginal utility of goods is greater, and the marginal disutility of labour is smaller than in the unrationed equilibrium. That is:

$$\frac{\partial U}{\partial G^R} > \frac{\partial U}{\partial G^*} \quad \text{and} \quad \frac{-\partial U}{\partial L^R} < \frac{-\partial U}{\partial L^*}. \tag{9.7}$$

The net benefit of a permanent one-unit increase in the ration, $E(G^R)$, is therefore the discounted sum of the extra utility from one more unit of the good per period minus the extra labour needed to pay for it:

$$\frac{\partial W}{\partial G^R} = \int_{t=0}^{\infty} \left(\frac{\partial U}{\partial G^R} + \frac{\partial U}{\partial L^R}\right) \bigg/ (1+r)^t dt = \frac{1}{r}\left(\frac{\partial U}{\partial G^R} + \frac{\partial U}{\partial L^R}\right) \tag{9.8}$$

where W = the discounted sum of utility.

The utility of money in such a regime derives from the unpredictable access to goods. The access to goods depends upon the type of rationing regime encountered. When there is no formal rationing system at the household level availability is likely to be uncertain.

The household cannot purchase more than is available and cannot purchase more than it can pay for. Purchases are therefore subject to the double constraint:

$$G \leqslant M \text{ (the money stock constraint)} \tag{9.9}$$

and

$$G \leqslant G^A \text{ (the availability constraint)} \tag{9.10}$$

where G^A denotes the quantity of goods available. In the barter case considered above, the ration G^R was identical to G^A, but because of the double constraint it is now possible for G^R to be less than G^A. Which constraint is encountered depends on the level of the money stock and the distribution of availability $F(G^A)$.

Since goods consumption is below its desired level it is never rational to choose not to make a purchase of available goods if money is available. Thus, one of the constraints (9.9) and (9.10) must always bind, so that either

$$G = G^A \tag{9.11}$$

or

$$G = M. \tag{9.12}$$

This creates a critical connection between the money stock held and the average value of goods consumption.

$$E(G^R) = \int_0^M G^A \cdot F(G^A) dG^A + M \cdot \int_M^\infty F(G^A) dG^A. \tag{9.13}$$

Equation (9.13) states that expected purchases are the sum of two terms. The second term is the probability that the individual will be subject to the money stock constraint multiplied by the average purchase when this constraint binds, which is of course the money stock itself. The first term is most easily thought of, analogously, as the probability that the individual will be subject to the availability constraint multiplied by the average purchase when this constraint binds. Since the availability constraint can only bind when purchases are less than the money stock, average purchases must be less in this case. Hence, goods consumption is either equal to the money stock (if the money stock is the constraint) or less than the money stock (if goods availability is the constraint) so that expected goods consumption, $E(G^R)$ is less than M. For all types of distribution, $F(G^A)$, the first-order derivative of $E(G^R)$ with respect to the money stock is positive and the second-order derivative is negative. Unfortunately, the right-hand side of equation (9.13) includes a censored distribution which is likely to lack analytically tractable properties.

Recall that since all prices are normalized, $\partial M/\partial L =$ unity and from equation (9.6) $\partial L^R/\partial E(G^R) =$ unity. The cost of an increment in the money stock is therefore the marginal disutility of labour, and for the money stock to be in a long-run equilibrium, this marginal cost must equal the marginal benefit. The latter is equal to the change in goods purchases multiplied by the benefit from an increment in goods purchases, previously derived in equation (9.8). Hence, the equilibrium money stock, M^R, will satisfy:

$$\frac{-\partial W}{\partial L^R} = \frac{1}{r}\left[\frac{\partial E(G^R)}{\partial M}\left\{\frac{\partial U}{\partial E(G^R)} + \frac{\partial U}{\partial L^R}\right\}\right]. \tag{9.14}$$

Now consider how the optimal money stock changes in the long run if there is a change from a permanently unrationed to a permanently rationed commodity market. From equations (9.3), (9.5), and (9.13):

$$M^* = G^* > E(G^R) < M^R. \tag{9.15}$$

This indicates that a priori $M^R \lessgtr M^*$ depending upon the utility function and $F(G^A)$. We will specify a simple instantaneous utility function, additively separable in L and G, in which both third-order derivatives are set to zero. Thus:

$$\frac{\partial U}{\partial L} = \alpha L \tag{9.16}$$

and

$$\frac{\partial U}{\partial G} = \beta - \gamma G. \tag{9.17}$$

From equation (9.2), in unrationed equilibrium,

$$M^* = G^* = \frac{\beta}{\alpha + \gamma + \alpha r}. \tag{9.18}$$

From equation (9.14)

$$\frac{\partial E(G^R)}{\partial M} = \frac{\alpha r}{\beta/E(G^R) - \gamma - \alpha} \tag{9.19}$$

and from equation (9.13)

$$\frac{\partial E(G^R)}{\partial M} = \int_M^\infty F(G^A) dG^A \tag{9.20}$$

so in rationed equilibrium

$$\frac{\alpha r}{\beta/E(G^R) - \gamma - \alpha} = \int_M^\infty F(G^A) dG^A. \tag{9.21}$$

Finally,

$$\frac{\partial(\alpha E)(G^R)/M}{\partial M} = -F(M). \tag{9.22}$$

The geometric representation of the solution of equations (9.19), (9.20), and (9.13) is shown in Figure 9.2. When $E(G^R) = G^* = M^* \partial E(G^R)/\partial M = 1$, and the solution is traced out by the broken line. By contrast, a rationed equilibrium is traced out by the dotted line. Equation (9.19) defines the curve in the north-east quadrant; inspection of the equation shows that the curve is convex. The south-east quadrant simply contains a 45° line, rotating the $E(G^R)$ axis. The curve in the south-west quadrant is defined by equation (9.13) relating expected purchases in the rationed regime to the money holding: evidently expected purchases in the rationed regime always fall short of G^*. Finally, the curve in the north-west quadrant is defined by equation (9.20), i.e. by the cumulative distribution of purchasing possibilities.

As drawn in Figure 9.2, the rationed money stock is greater than the unrationed money stock, but clearly a different distribution of purchasing possibilities could yield the converse case. Indeed, for a sufficiently severe ration (when schedule (9.20) is twisted far enough anti-clockwise around the

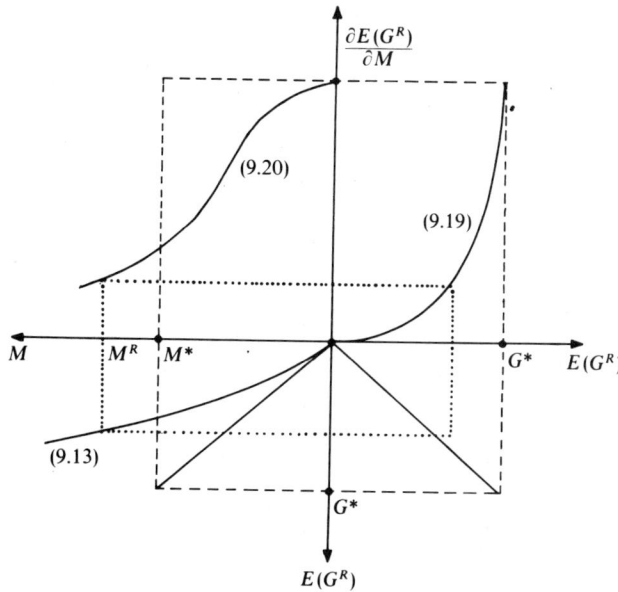

FIG. 9.2. *The effect of shortages on optimal money balances*

vertical intercept) the money stock will be lower than when goods are unrationed. However, computations using credible values and distributions suggest that the onset of rationing may well be characterized by an increase in the desired money stock.

These changes in the money stock matter because they imply changes in cash crop output. If the peasant chooses to increase his money stock then he is choosing to sell more crops than is required to finance his expected expenditure on goods. Conversely, a reduction in money stocks can only be effected by selling fewer crops than would be required to cover expenditure. The effects of a change in goods availability on crop sales must therefore be separated into two time periods: the short-run response during which peasants are adjusting their money stocks to the new desired level, and the long-run response which remains once money holdings are fully adjusted. The short- and long-run responses may either reinforce or offset each other. If availability deteriorates so that in the long-run crop sales are reduced, in the short run this is partly offset by peasants selling crops in order to accumulate money balances. However, further deterioration induces a reduction in money stocks so that the short run reduction in cash crop production is then more pronounced than the long-run reduction.

From the present model it might appear possible that during the onset of shortages peasant supply response might even increase. However, this is not the case. In *Controlled Open Economies* we show that any accumulation in money stocks only partially offsets the reduction in labour supply.

Hence, we are left with two predictions as to the consequences of the emergence of shortages in a peasant economy such as Tanzania. First, there may be an accumulation of real money balances, and secondly, there may be a reduction in marketed supply. In fact, both predictions concern the coefficient on goods availability as an explanatory variable of marketed supply. The second prediction is simply that it will be significant and positive: a decline in goods availability will reduce future crop marketings as peasants adaptively revise downwards their expectations of the quantities of consumer goods they are likely to be able to purchase. The first prediction is that, if peasants indeed accumulate money balances in response to stochastic rationing, then expressed in elasticity form the coefficient should be less than unity. For example, a 1 per cent decline in the availability of goods would reduce subsequent crop marketings by less than 1 per cent.

9.2. The Specification of Expectations

The elasticity of crop marketings with respect to goods availability in previous periods is determined by two elements, namely, the elasticity of expectations and planned changes in money balances. The former describes how expectations of availability adapt to current experience. Potentially, such expectations could be extrapolative (a deterioration in availability generating the expectation of a further deterioration in the next period), or regressive (a deterioration generating the expectation that in the next period availability will improve so as to partially offset the current deterioration). Between these is the case of unit elastic expectations: peasants expect in the next period what they are currently experiencing, hence a current deterioration is forecast to persist. Expectations formation during the period was likely to be adaptive rather than rational because the experience of the regime was too recent for its macroeconomic properties to be understood: peasants did not 'know the model'. A similar argument can be used to suggest that unit elastic expectations are perhaps more likely than powerfully regressive or extrapolative expectations.

Flemming (1976) suggests that expectations can be characterized as having various 'gears' through which economic agents move. In the lowest gear agents forecast variables based only and directly on their past values. Only if such a forecasting procedure systematically mis-predicts do agents move up a gear to base their forecast also on past rates of change of the variable. Again if this mis-predicts they move to a yet more complex formulation which includes rates of change of rates of change. This principle that agents start with simple formulations which are made more complex only in the face of systematic error would suggest that in their brief experience of shortages peasants simply projected their current experience.

If peasants indeed had approximately unit elastic expectations then a 1 per cent deterioration in availability would reduce subsequent crop marketings by 1 per cent only if peasants choose to maintain constant money balances. If instead, as we have suggested, they choose to accumulate money·balances, then crop marketings decline by less than goods availability; some crops are sold in order to acquire the extra money. Hence, our model predicts that in elasticity form the coefficient on availability should be significant, positive, and less than unity.

9.3. Rent-Seeking Introduced

In the above model the peasant facing shortages was acquiring rents upon both intra-marginal and marginal purchases of consumer goods: that is, even at the margin, the peasant would have been willing to pay more for the good than was actually paid. In general, such rents can be expected to attract rent-seeking behaviour; that is, the peasant will expend resources in an attempt to increase the quantity of goods available. Barring discontinuities, the expenditure on rent-seeking will be such that at the margin costs equal benefits, so that the marginal utility of consumption is again equated to the costs of consumption. So far the only rent-seeking mechanism which we have considered has been the accumulation of money balances. As embodied in equation (9.21), in equilibrium, the household indeed equates the value of consumption at the margin with the cost of achieving that consumption.

However, the household may additionally have other strategies which increase access to goods by the expenditure of resources. The most obvious of these is by means of search, incurring time costs. The expected value of G^A, $E(G^A)$, becomes endogenous for the individual household, being a function of labour devoted to search, L^s. In equilibrium, again barring discontinuities,

$$dU/dG \cdot dE(G^A)/dL^s = -dU/dL. \qquad (9.23)$$

In rural Tanzania discontinuities in the search process are quite likely. Search involves the expenditure of time on travel to widely dispersed locations at which goods might be available. Search expenditures are thus intrinsically discrete, so that equation (9.23) is likely to be an inequality.

The costs of rent-seeking through search are L^s. Whereas the accumulation of money balances is a socially costless form of rent-seeking (costly for the peasant economy but merely a transfer as far as the national economy is concerned), L^s is a real resource cost both to the peasant society and to the whole economy.

If some households specialize in search and trade the value added by the activity, we have a black market. The value added in search is the acquisition of rents, some, all, or none of which may be offset by the costs incurred in search. A black market can therefore be thought of as a market in search activities.

In the presence of a black market the peasant's problem is:

$$\text{maximize } U(G_1 + G_2, L)$$
$$G_1, G_2, L$$
$$\text{subject to } p_1 \bar{G}_1 + p_2 G_2 \leq L$$

where cash crop output is (as before) proportional to labour input (L); G_1 and G_2 are the amounts bought officially and in the black market respectively; and the maximum amount available at the official price (p_1) is $\bar{G}$.

This problem is illustrated in Figure 9.3. Since the black-market price must be higher than the official price ($p_2 > p_1$), the budget line is kinked. If, for example, availability (G_1) is equal to HE then the budget line consists of two segments, CE and EF. In the diagram prices are taken as given while availability varies. Three cases are possible:

1. $0 \leq \bar{G} < A_3 B_3$. In this case the peasant will buy in the black market. For example, for $\bar{G}$ equal to HE, he will choose point B_2, consuming $A_2 B_2$ of which EH is acquired officially and the rest in the black market. Note that as availability decreases from $A_3 B_3$ to zero, the optimum shifts along the income expansion line i_2 from B_3 to B_2 to B_1. Going down the income expansion line leisure decreases and hence cash crop production increases. Therefore, for peasants participating in the black market, for a given black-market price, cash crop production is *negatively* related to availability.

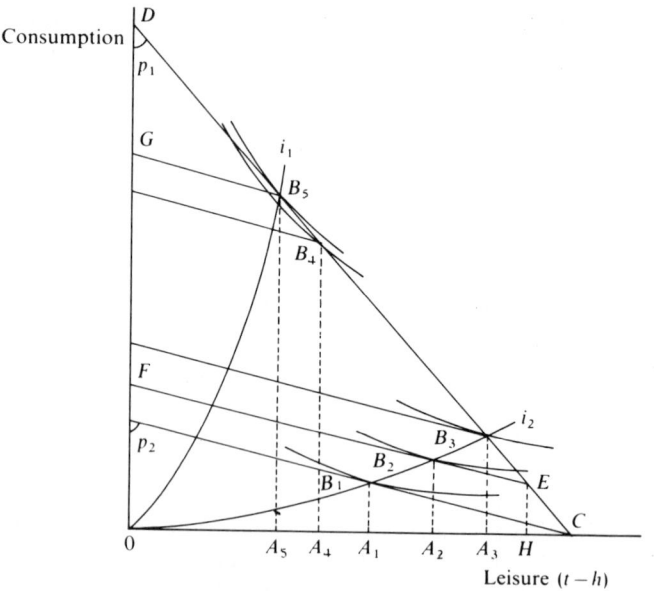

FIG. 9.3. *Determinants of black-market participation*

2. $A_3B_3 \leq \bar{G} < A_5B_5$. This is the case we considered previously. An unrationed equilibrium is not possible and the existence of a black market makes no difference: it is optimal for the peasant not to buy in it. Rationing is reflected in increased leisure. If, for example, $\bar{G}$ equals A_4B_4 then cash crop output is A_4C. As availability decreases from A_5B_5 to A_3B_3, the optimum shifts along the line CD from B_5 to B_3, and this implies an increase in leisure and a decrease in cash crop output. Hence, in this case, cash crop production is *positively* related to availability.

3. $\bar{G} \geq A_5B_5$. In this case the peasant will choose point B where he is in unrationed equilibrium.

Although case (3) is uninteresting, both the other cases are pertinent. Some households will participate in black markets and be characterized by case (1), others will be priced out of black markets and be characterized by case (2). For given black-market prices the supply responses of these households to a change in goods availability at official prices will therefore differ. Viewed in cross-section terms, with all households facing the same black-market prices but with differential access to goods at official prices, the supply response function is not monotonic. As availability improves, the optimum first moves along the income expansion line i_2 from B_1 to B_3, and then along the budget line CD, from B_3 to B_5. The resulting supply response function is depicted in Figure 9.4.

Next consider the effect of an increase in the producer price of the cash crop for the two types of household. If the initial equilibrium is at a point such as B_4 in Figure 9.5 then, as we have already noted, supply response is unambiguously perverse: the peasant who is rationed and who does not participate in the black market will reduce his cash crop production if the producer price is raised. Suppose, however, that the peasant does buy consumer goods in the black market. Treating the black-market price as given, an increase in the producer price of coffee will then have a substitution effect (implying an

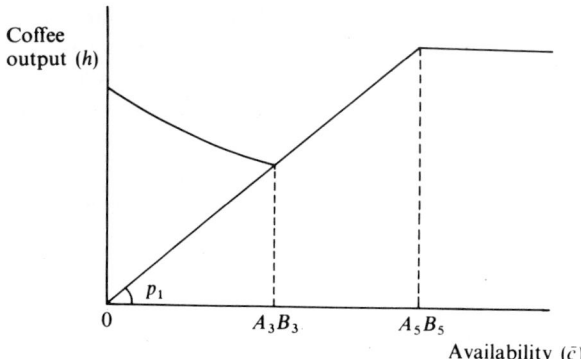

FIG. 9.4. *The supply–response function*

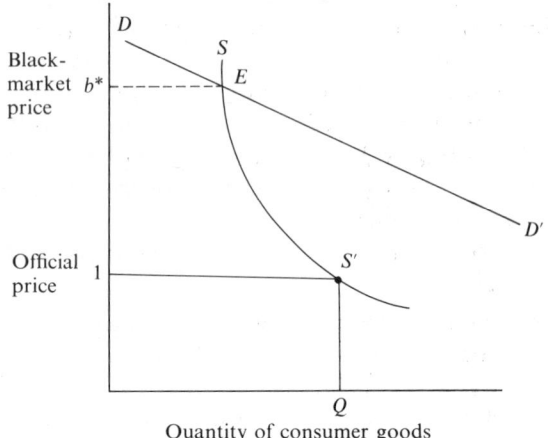

FIG. 9.5. *The black-market equilibrium*

increase in coffee output) and an income effect (which works in the opposite direction). On the reasonable assumption that supply response is normal in the unrationed case then the substitution effect must dominate. We summarize our results for the two groups of farmers, those who do participate in the black market and those who do not, in Table 9.1.

Since supply responses to both crop prices and availability are qualitatively different for peasants in and out of the black market (given black-market prices), it might appear that peasant supply response in aggregate is a priori ambiguous, depending upon the weighted sum of these responses. This however, would be to commit a fallacy of composition. In aggregate, search (whether conducted by each household or marketed via the black market) does not increase the supply of consumer goods to the peasant economy. Thus, although $E(G^A)$ is endogenous for each individual household, for the quasi-representative household appropriate for the analysis of aggregate supply response, $E(G^A)$ remains exogenous. That is, the supply response of the peasant economy in aggregate is captured by a model in which the aggregate constraint is incorporated as applying to the representative household (as in the basic model). Peasant labour devoted to search does not alter the value of official goods sales (a fixed quantity multiplied by the official price), and so does not change the income which the peasant sector needs to generate from crop sales. This continues to hold even when the value added from search is itself marketed through the black market, and the peasant sector is a net purchaser of search services from other parts of the economy.

Consider the case in which search services are provided by a class of urban-based black marketeers. Imagine, first, a pure barter economy: black marketeers devote resources to search which enables them to acquire goods in

TABLE 9.1. *Supply response to changes in crop prices or availability in the case of rationing (for given black-market prices)*

	Supply response (increase in cash crop production) to an increase in:	
	The producer price of the cash crop	Availability of consumer goods at official price
Peasants who only buy officially	Perverse (−)	Normal (+)
Peasants who also buy in the black market	normal (+)	Perverse (−)

exchange for coffee at official prices. They then trade with peasants, exchanging these goods (other than those which they consume themselves) for coffee, the rate of exchange being the black-market price. Black marketeers are, however, constrained in aggregate by the fixed total supply from the public sector of consumer goods at official prices. The value of this supply, at official prices, thus constitutes the ceiling to the coffee which black marketeers need to sell to the government in exchange for the consumer goods. Hence, from the viewpoint of the government, the volume of coffee which it receives is the same whether or not a black market exists (that is, the official price of goods in units of coffee multiplied by the quantity of goods). Similarly, the volume of coffee sales by peasants is the same whether the direct purchaser is the government or the black marketeers. Since black marketeers do not consume coffee, they only purchase the amount they need to sell to the government. The only difference is that with a black market peasants receive fewer consumer goods. Since the returns to search accrue to the black marketeers, the peasant sector receives the same value of goods, but made up of a higher price and a lower quantity than if search were undertaken only by peasants themselves.

This analysis is essentially unaltered if barter relationships are replaced by monetary ones. There are now two official prices, for coffee and goods (both of which we set to unity), and additionally a black-market price, b, for goods. Black marketeers purchase goods at the official price in exchange for money, the total value of their expenditure being constrained by the fixed supply of goods, Q. The income of black marketeers, Yb, is therefore:

$$Yb = (b-1)Q. \qquad (9.24)$$

Black marketeers equate their income with their expenditure on goods, Cb:

$$(b-1)Q = Cb. \qquad (9.25)$$

Peasants sell a quantity of coffee, F, directly to the government at the official price in exchange for money. Cash income, Yp, equals their expenditure, Cp, namely that part of goods supply not consumed by black marketeers multiplied by the black-market price:

$$Yp = F = (Q - Cb)b. \qquad (9.26)$$

But, from equation (9.25):

$$Q - Cb = Q/b. \qquad (9.27)$$

So, substituting (9.27) into (9.26):

$$F = Q. \qquad (9.28)$$

That is, the volume of coffee sales is identical to that which occurs when peasants are directly quantity rationed (namely that which equates the values of coffee sales and goods purchases at official prices).

The argument is depicted in Figure 9.5. S–S' is the supply curve of goods to peasants (that is, $Q - Cb$), and from (9.27) it is unit elastic. D–D' is the demand curve of peasants for goods. This may have any slope subject to the normal property of being negatively related to price. However, for an equilibrium, E, to exist, the arc elasticity between E and S' must be greater than (minus) unity. Market stability is ensured despite the perverse supply curve because at the official price (unity) there is by assumption excess demand. The market clears at b^*.

There are two qualifications to the identity of peasant supply with or without black markets. First, the demand for cash balances will not be the same. With clearing black markets there is no need for peasants to build up money holdings in excess of expected expenditure. The latter, $b(Q - Cb)$, is identical to Q, expected expenditure in the rationed economy case in which black markets are absent. Hence, peasant money demand is unambiguously less with black markets than without them. Nationally, therefore, money demand is also lower unless there is a large money demand on the part of black marketeers. The second qualification is that the invariance of peasant crop supply does not hold in the presence of smuggling. Smuggling augments the supply of consumer goods and so can achieve a positive supply response.

With these qualifications, supply responses in the presence of black markets are identical to our previous analysis of responses under rationing. An increase in either goods availability at given official prices or the official prices of goods at given availability, will increase aggregate supply. Black marketeers purchase a greater value of goods at official prices and must therefore sell to the marketing authorities an equally greater volume of crops. Since this greater volume of crops must be purchased from the peasant sector, black marketeers must therefore increase the value of their sales to the peasant sector by an equal amount. The only difference introduced by the black market is the decomposition of this extra value of sales into prices and quantities.

Monetary accumulation, as analysed in the basic model, is the only exception to the unimportance of rent-seeking for supply response, because it constitutes a chosen divergence of peasant income requirements in excess of expected expenditure. If all the rents are absorbed by search (directly, or indirectly through the black market), then this monetary accumulation story is eliminated. Taking search into account, no rents remain on purchases and so there is no incentive to build up money balances as a device to increase availability. However, this is most unlikely. Some goods do reach consumers for the expenditure of sub-marginal search costs, and the rents which these goods represent can only be acquired through the possession of cash balances. There are two reasons for the persistence of randomly available rents. First, some goods reach consumers at official prices, but in the absence of a household-level official rationing system, these supplies are unpredictable. That is, luck is present in the distribution system, so that there is the chance of acquiring the rents implied by official prices without the need for rent-seeking search.

Secondly, the essence of black markets is that they are illegal. That is, there are penalties for detection. Such penalties are normally modelled in economics as a component of the cost of transactions. However, this is a thoroughly inadequate characterization of the structure of the risks involved in black-market operations, the central feature of which is that because of penalties, sellers alter their behaviour so as to minimize the risks associated with each transaction. The risks of detection per transaction increase with the duration of the attempt to make the transaction and with the dispersion of knowledge about the opportunity to buyers. Thus, relative to legal transactions, sellers will hold stocks for a shorter period and advertise less widely. The opportunity cost to the seller of these responses is that, since both temporally and spatially they reduce the set of potential purchasers, a lower price will be achieved. Black marketeers must sell at a price which ensures an immediate sale after only a few approaches to potential consumers. The price must therefore be set at a level at which on average some rents are passed on to consumers. The counterpart to this is that not all the search costs are marketed: consumers remain rationed even at black-market prices unless they themselves incur search costs. But, just as with official supplies, because the availability of goods to an individual peasant on the black market is partly random, there remains an element of luck: rents may be acquired from time to time by the consumer as long as cash balances are sufficient to take up opportunities.

The above discussion arrives at four important conclusions. First, search by the household and black markets are equivalent in being rent-seeking activities which use resources. Secondly, changes in either the official prices or the quantities of goods sold at official prices give rise to supply responses which are in aggregate unaffected by whether the resulting changes in rents are wholly or partly offset by rent-seeking (in either its household search or black-market forms), as long as there is no regime switch. Thirdly, whereas this holds in aggregate, it does not always hold at the level of the individual household. The supply response to increased availability of goods at official prices will be qualitatively different depending upon whether the household is at the margin satisfying its demands on the black market. Fourthly, the introduction of search and black markets does not eliminate the key monetary feature of non-market-clearing, namely that there is an incentive to hold money balances in excess of expected expenditure in order to take advantage of opportunities for the acquisition of rents.

9.4. Conclusion

In the three previous sections we have developed a theory of peasant supply response to shortages, starting with a barter model, then introducing monetary accumulation and search. Each of these steps has significant macroeconomic implications. The barter case was sufficient to establish the presumption of a spiral of decline: shortages reduce crop marketings and the latter, via their implications for foreign exchange, worsen shortages. The analysis of the demand for money under conditions of stochastic shortages introduced the possibility that this spiral is likely initially to be disguised by monetary accumulation, which provides the government with a temporary windfall. Finally, the introduction of search suggests that there will be a diversion of peasant resources into socially costly rent-seeking activities. These macroeconomic ramifications lie beyond our scope in this book, but are considered in *Controlled Open Economies*. One test of the theory is indeed whether economies characterized by binding price controls encounter such macroeconomic problems. In the case of Tanzania there is no doubt that the theory meets this test. However, macroeconomic decline constitutes rather indirect evidence and here we are concerned to apply direct microeconomic tests of hypotheses. The theory set out above contains two classes of such hypotheses, namely, those which appertain to aggregate supply response of the peasant sector, and those which appertain to differences in supply response between households. These are explored in turn in the next two chapters.

10
Time Series Tests of Aggregate Supply Response

10.1. Introduction

This chapter uses time series data to estimate the elasticity of aggregate supply response to changes in availability. The theory developed in Chapter 9 predicts that the coefficient on availability should be significant, positive, and less than unity. The test of this hypothesis is complicated by the unusual and specific data required. Indeed, the central innovative feature of the analysis is the construction of two data sets each of which permits the elasticity to be estimated. Since the data sets are independent, the results constitute a check on each other. Section 10.2 discusses the measurement problems and their resolution and Section 10.3 presents the results.

10.2. The Measurement of Rationing and Peasant Response

10.2.1. *The Problem*

We use two distinct notions of the measurement of rationing. The first is essentially probabilistic. We measure the probability of making a successful purchase for a group of key commodities, and then derive an index showing what proportion of the desired basket of commodities under the operative official prices an agent can expect to purchase. This measure of availability provides a measure of excess demand, and hence we are able to quantify rationing which, by its very nature, is a directly unobservable phenomenon. The derivation of this measure is explained in Section 10.2.2.

The alternative measure, namely trying to gauge the absolute level of supply, is derived by observing all factory-gate departures of a set of goods. In a country with less central control of the market and distribution of key goods than Tanzania, the collection of such data might pose insuperable problems. By the use of such data we are able to construct indices of relative changes in supply over time. We describe the data characteristics and associated transformations needed for this process in Section 10.2.3.

Rationing in Tanzania has only prevailed over relatively few years producing very short time series, a problem compounded by the difficulties of obtaining comparable data over any non-trivial time period. Indeed the post-1986 situation in Tanzania suggests that the period of deep rationing is at least temporarily over, and hence no more information is being added to extend the series. We overcome this problem by increasing the breadth of the existing time series by regionalizing the data. This provides panel data of sufficient depth for useful analysis, and also describes the previously unrecorded regional incidence of rationing.

A further problem is the observation of rural areas, where there is virtually no data collection on the operation of goods markets. Our approach leads to observation at one remove, i.e. at the level of regional towns. This level provides the direct observations that constitute the basis for our probabilistic approach. It also provides an indication of the combined size of the official and the black markets (the location of which are heavily biased to urban areas). The omission of black-market supplies would otherwise have distorted our supply-based measures. The penetration of supplies to rural areas is quantified in our discussion of the supply-based indices.

Another problem is how to produce a measure of incentives consistent with rationing theory. We are analysing a situation where peasants possess a large overhang of money stocks. In the longer run expected purchases will be made from a combination of money stocks and current cash flows. The problem is therefore to model the willingness of peasants to generate future cash flows.

We address this problem by using the only satisfactory data on this process, i.e. the production of cash crops by peasants. These data have been obtained on a regional basis and are described in Section 10.2.4. The lack of any satisfactory data on the production and marketability of food crops, or on rural non-farm activities means that the contribution of these to the generation of cash flows is unmeasurable. Further it means that we cannot address quantitatively some of the effects of incentive changes induced by goods market rationing. Hence, the extent to which peasants unable to achieve desired purchases in the goods market are driven into a more subsistence-based mode of production can only be inferred rather than directly analysed. In Section 10.2.4 we present some of the unsatisfactory and inconclusive data to demonstrate this point.

10.2.2. *Availability of Goods*

To obtain quantitative measures of the degree of goods market rationing in each region of Tanzania, we have utilized data collected in the construction of the Tanzanian National Consumer Price Index (CPI). Price series are constructed for the main town of each region on a quarterly basis, the prices being obtained from actual purchases made by statistical officers. On average this entails some twenty-four attempts to purchase each listed good per year per region.

We have chosen nine key goods, toilet soap, laundry soap, matches, cooking oil, margarine, butter, khanga, cigarettes, and paraffin. By referring to the original coding sheets used by the regional statistical officers, we are able to construct series for each good for both the number of attempts to purchase and also the number of successful purchases. For both types of soap and also for cooking oil we have aggregated across brand varieties, and the number of attempts to purchase these goods is on average 120 per region per year. In total across regions and years the data set therefore represents the outcomes of some 10,000 attempts to purchase goods. Hence the data produced as a by-product in the construction of the CPI allow us to make up in breadth of regional coverage for the shortness of the time series. These series are available for the period 1978–83. The series are too short to enter the availability of each of the nine goods as separate determinants of agricultural output, and therefore it is necessary to construct an aggregate series of goods availability for each of the regions.

The critical choice in the construction of an aggregate availability index is that of a weighting scheme. The ideal weighting scheme would involve the shares out of actual expenditure in the rationed situation facing official prices. We have used two methods to construct three such schemes, one using the only available information on budget shares in Tanzania, the other utilizing the results of a more recent survey.

The only usable information on budget shares is provided by the 1969 Household Budget Survey (HBS). Unfortunately this survey was carried out during a relatively unrationed period and hence we would expect the expenditure shares derived from it to differ considerably from those in the rationed situation we analyse. The survey provides information on a zonal basis (a zone representing three or four regions, plus a separate zone for Dar es Salaam). The weights on this zonal basis are shown in Table 10.1 as weights out of total expenditure on the nine selected goods.

Two points need to be stressed about the weights in Table 10.1. The relatively high weights for khanga (women's clothing) are derived solely from the expenditure share of standardized khanga, no other times of clothing having been included. Secondly, there is considerable variation in the weight for cigarettes, from 2.2 per cent of expenditure on the goods subset in zone 4, to 25.9 per cent in Dar es Salaam.

Combining the weights in Table 10.1 with the percentage availability series for each good and then aggregating, we obtain regional series for a measure of total goods availability. This is shown for all twenty regions in Table 10.2, which portrays a general tightening of goods market rationing over the period. In all but three regions availability is lower in 1983 than in 1978. It should be noted that as data were unavailable for seven regions for 1978 we have imputed the 1979 value for these regions.

Our second and third weighting schemes are both derived from the results of Cooksey *et al.* (1987a). In a rural survey of Tanga and Mwanza they asked respondents to recall their pre-rationing purchasing patterns. For our subset of goods we have derived a weighting scheme following that employed by Cooksey *et al.* For each good a score of 3 is assigned if the good was the first

TABLE 10.1. *HBS weights for availability indices*

	HBS zones						
	1	2	3	4	5	6	7
Cooking oil	0.149	0.057	0.047	0.143	0.087	0.052	0.044
Butter	0.164	0.072	0.062	0.122	0.011	0.015	0.133
Margarine	0.036	0.006	0.003	0.003	0.011	0.004	0.022
Paraffin	0.142	0.153	0.266	0.197	0.211	0.161	0.136
Khanga	0.106	0.277	0.090	0.224	0.244	0.356	0.097
Toilet soap	0.073	0.111	0.196	0.094	0.175	0.109	0.121
Laundry soap	0.199	0.133	0.198	0.149	0.191	0.149	0.141
Matches	0.037	0.043	0.055	0.046	0.043	0.028	0.046
Cigarettes	0.173	0.150	0.083	0.022	0.028	0.126	0.259

Notes:
Zone 1: Arusha, Kilimanjaro, Tanga.
Zone 2: Coast, Dodoma, Morogoro.
Zone 3: Kagera, Mara, Mwanza, Shinyanga.
Zone 4: Kigoma, Singida, Tabora.
Zone 5: Iringa, Mbeya, Rukwa.
Zone 6: Lindi, Mtwara, Ruvuma.
Zone 7: Dar es Salaam.

TABLE 10.2. *Availability of goods in Tanzania, 1978–1983 (HBS weights)*

	1978	1979	1980	1981	1982	1983
Arusha	82.703	61.850	46.587	56.892	44.371	64.721
Coast	90.384	72.241	52.442	53.954	54.670	26.349
Dar es Salaam	57.298	57.298	54.903	50.049	50.957	48.755
Dodoma	55.800	60.322	52.768	66.391	48.990	58.343
Iringa	89.449	69.547	59.471	31.866	26.075	45.244
Kagera	80.646	80.646	56.364	57.968	63.787	57.241
Kigoma	65.966	62.742	59.517	36.192	42.996	32.747
Kilimanjaro	89.989	78.254	59.715	62.018	47.666	43.205
Lindi	61.101	61.101	74.466	77.562	72.022	53.614
Mara	95.044	86.511	69.245	64.978	81.438	64.042
Mbeya	60.006	60.006	67.011	57.487	28.963	52.599
Morogoro	75.445	53.630	37.175	40.255	68.020	58.369
Mtwara	76.931	76.931	62.558	78.374	76.643	70.149
Mwanza	50.729	50.729	0.936	40.017	45.163	50.537
Rukwa	73.618	70.506	63.891	61.752	39.064	54.494
Ruvuma	82.989	54.741	65.596	49.014	52.856	58.502
Shinyanga	64.372	64.372	55.013	48.495	41.415	37.547
Singida	36.085	16.269	21.294	31.903	20.771	17.134
Tabora	22.862	22.862	35.392	56.699	67.545	68.183
Tanga	52.235	47.225	48.407	49.589	55.027	61.406

mentioned by the respondent, 2 if the second, and 1 if the third. The aggregate score as a proportion of the total score across the subset of goods is then the weight.

This weighting scheme has the advantage over the 1969 HBS weighting in that the perception held of the pre-rationing situation may be different from the actuality, and it is this perception that will be a better guide to the interpretation by individual agents of the degree of rationing they face and their response to it. However, we can no longer assign regional weights, and the derived weights apply to a smaller basket of goods. The latter point is made less serious by the fact that the two goods we are unable to assign weights to, butter and margarine, were the least rationed goods in the basket over the period. We can only assign a weight for all types of soap combined, and apply half this weight to both toilet and laundry soap. The derived weights, together with the number of first, second, and third responses per good, are shown in Table 10.3. The availability indices derived from the use of these weights, denoted as recollection weights, are shown in Table 10.4. This confirms the general tightening of goods market rationing over the period 1978–83.

The third weighting scheme is derived from another question from the Cooksey survey. Respondents were asked which goods they believed would motivate farmers to produce more if those goods were in greater supply. These weights, denoted as incentive weights, are shown in Table 10.5.

The availability indices derived from these weights (Table 10.6) therefore have a rather different interpretation to the other two measures. The weights are distorted by the state of rationing and are marginal weights. Therefore if perceptions about what really motivates are correct, this measure would be expected to out-perform that based on past purchasing patterns.

It should be noted that the three sets of availability indices are based on data collected in towns, and will overestimate availability in rural areas.

10.2.3. Distribution of Goods

The availability indices described above represent measures of excess demand. In this section we derive measures of supply using distribution data collected by the Board of Internal Trade. All data on the distribution of controlled goods within Tanzania are collated by the Central Monitoring Unit (CMU) of the BIT. The CMU was set up in 1981, and data for earlier years are incomplete and of lesser quality. We therefore construct supply measures only for the period 1981 to 1985. The BIT allocates controlled goods in advance to Rural Trading Co-operatives (RTCs), and this allocation is given to the factories concerned. In the case of goods produced by more than one company, the total allocation is made up of separate allocations from different factories. However, the allocation figures themselves provide a very poor measure of actual supplies. Allocations are based on expected output, and, especially for industries such as soap and textiles which are particularly prone

TABLE 10.3. Recollection weights for availability indices

	Mentioned first	Mentioned second	Mentioned third	Total score	Weight
Cigarettes	2	4	3	17	0.0131
Khanga	1	5	0	13	0.0100
Cooking oil	25	44	69	232	0.1786
Paraffin	18	36	51	177	0.1363
Matches	6	17	35	87	0.0670
Soap (all types)	118	141	137	773	0.5951

TABLE 10.4. Availability of goods in Tanzania, 1978–1983 (recollection weights)

	1978	1979	1980	1981	1982	1983
Arusha	76.798	48.140	35.827	53.642	34.897	51.283
Coast	90.013	62.469	48.237	43.414	35.388	33.954
Dar es Salaam	48.859	48.859	43.431	31.119	33.384	25.146
Dodoma	54.491	49.167	31.222	68.390	42.438	39.226
Iringa	84.088	65.626	62.551	24.254	18.283	35.063
Kagera	74.454	74.454	38.306	39.664	45.679	39.534
Kigoma	52.625	50.026	47.427	27.247	30.885	26.930
Kilimanjaro	78.653	76.062	57.396	42.055	46.753	34.177
Lindi	41.770	41.770	40.037	50.027	33.614	32.087
Mara	92.562	85.123	62.255	54.276	81.404	50.704
Mbeya	49.754	49.754	52.672	51.078	26.284	35.016
Morogoro	62.705	47.525	24.953	33.379	46.435	48.117
Mtwara	49.026	49.026	41.352	51.961	47.432	38.000
Mwanza	48.068	48.068	3.572	30.218	30.062	33.390
Rukwa	58.351	51.991	42.632	38.108	41.379	29.895
Ruvuma	78.813	65.754	31.935	42.208	36.056	33.152
Shinyanga	57.467	57.467	54.015	42.225	25.031	19.009
Singida	39.721	15.636	14.233	21.822	23.435	15.058
Tabora	18.585	18.585	33.128	35.899	57.647	55.169
Tanga	56.210	51.302	48.075	44.848	40.809	41.833

to production problems, the actual distribution may bear little resemblance to the allocation. Also the separate allocations made from each factory mean that the shortfall of actual distribution from allocation may vary considerably between regions. A region predominantly served by a factory that incurs serious technical constraints is unlikely to receive any considerable reallocation from other factories. In some years some regions have received

TABLE 10.5. *Incentive weights for availability indices*

	Mentioned first	Mentioned second	Mentioned third	Total score	Weight
Cigarettes	1	0	1	4	0.0057
Khanga	9	15	5	62	0.0888
Cooking oil	15	28	32	133	0.1905
Paraffin	6	11	24	64	0.0917
Matches	3	4	15	32	0.0458
Soap (all types)	48	96	67	403	0.5774

TABLE 10.6. *Availability of goods in Tanzania, 1978–1983 (incentive weights)*

	1978	1979	1980	1981	1982	1983
Arusha	79.894	46.631	29.649	49.643	30.775	52.195
Coast	89.600	60.787	42.485	41.485	32.527	30.106
Dar es Salaam	41.845	41.845	36.362	24.485	27.490	18.744
Dodoma	49.214	45.823	29.219	64.506	37.371	36.439
Iringa	84.561	66.192	57.008	21.255	12.034	32.420
Kagera	73.863	73.863	36.769	37.929	46.220	37.989
Kigoma	53.199	50.232	47.265	22.767	28.009	23.961
Kilimanjaro	78.903	76.598	55.379	37.350	39.391	28.658
Lindi	42.260	42.260	40.891	50.479	34.278	29.250
Mara	92.783	85.566	63.378	55.292	81.957	51.481
Mbeya	48.806	48.806	56.123	49.457	25.291	38.160
Morogoro	62.281	42.740	17.954	26.457	46.267	44.461
Mtwara	49.910	49.910	41.192	52.553	48.565	40.167
Mwanza	45.899	45.899	3.811	27.337	22.869	28.345
Rukwa	58.900	52.614	45.562	39.001	34.550	31.147
Ruvuma	79.715	59.604	35.004	37.334	32.242	32.635
Shinyanga	54.871	54.871	47.472	37.453	19.034	13.627
Singida	34.868	11.314	10.552	17.584	18.469	14.623
Tabora	12.779	12.779	29.228	36.440	58.955	56.244
Tanga	51.804	43.861	44.036	44.211	35.713	40.033

virtually no supplies of key goods, while other regions obtained their entire allocation. This has been particularly true for the distribution of soap.

Our supply measures are therefore based on the factory-gate distribution figures submitted by companies to the BIT. We have only considered distribution to the RTCs in each region, excluding all distribution to government, armed forces, diplomatic and cultural missions, and the tourism industry. A potential weakness of this approach is that the distribution from factory gates may not be a good measure of goods actually arriving at the RTCs. Evidence on this issue is provided by a report of the Tanzanian Industrial Studies and Consulting Organisation (TISCO, 1985). This report traced the distribution of soap from factory gate to village shops. The estimated demand in rural areas for soap for 1984 was 28,795 tons, of which village shops received only 5,770 tons. The breakdown of the dispersal of a typical 100 cartons of soap in six regions is given in Table 10.7, which shows the distribution at regional and district level, and the leakage, presumably into parallel markets, between factory, region, district, and village.

Table 10.7 shows that on average only 25.5 per cent of soap distributed actually arrived in village shops. Further, 40 per cent of the distribution cannot be accounted for by consumption at either regional, district, or village level.

This suggests that official marketing channels are an important source of goods supply for the parallel unofficial market. Hence the factory-gate distribution figures may be a more satisfactory estimate of goods supply than estimates enumerated at the village shop level since they give a better view of combined official and black-market supplies. The TISCO findings suggest that the lack of penetration to the village level may cause a serious data problem if the extent of this lack of penetration is variable over the period of analysis.

We use distribution figures for eight goods, galvanized corrugated iron (GCI) sheeting, hoes, ploughs, matches, salt, toilet soap, laundry soap, and sugar, aggregating across factories where necessary. To make the figures commensurate across goods we express distribution for each good in each region in terms of the percentage of the level of distribution in 1983. To

TABLE 10.7. *Penetration of goods from factory gate to village shops*

Region	Distributed (cartons)	Region		District		Village shops receive
		Received	Distributed to district	Received	Distributed to village	
Arusha	100	95	81	70	45	39
Mara	100	98	71	53	47	23
Mbeya	100	95	73	72	29	20
Morogoro	100	65	60	57	35	30
Mwanza	100	87	78	66	26	20
Tanga	100	60	53	48	39	21
TOTAL	600	500	416	366	221	153
%	100	83.3	69.3	61.0	36.8	25.5

Source: TISCO.

aggregate to a single measure of supply we then employ the weighting schemes described in the previous section.

The zonal weightings derived from the 1968/9 HBS are shown in Table 10.8. Expenditure on GCI sheeting, hoes, and ploughs was not recorded in the survey, and hence these goods are dropped from the aggregate series. The indices of distribution to regions obtained by the use of these weights are shown in Table 10.9. The weighting schemes derived from the Cooksey survey utilize all eight goods. The weighting scheme and the resultant supply indices are shown in Tables 10.10 and 10.11 respectively, for weights based on the recollection of purchases in the pre-rationing period, and in Tables 10.12 and 10.13 for weights based on the perception of what act as incentive goods for farmers.

10.2.4. Crop Production

As our focus is on the effect of goods market rationing on peasant agriculture, we exclude plantation production. We consider the seven major peasant cash crops, i.e. cashew nuts, cotton seed, tobacco, pyrethrum, and three types of coffee, mild arabica, hard arabica, and robusta. Thus sisal is excluded since it is solely a plantation crop, and so are sugar and tea for which output figures cannot be separated into the plantation and the (relatively insignificant) peasant components.

Although food crop production is also marketable, we have not included it because of the lack of any reliable data. While cash crop production can be

TABLE 10.8. *HBS weights for distribution indices*

	HBS zones						
	1	2	3	4	5	6	7
Sugar	0.510	0.384	0.292	0.324	0.357	0.355	0.467
Salt	0.095	0.166	0.122	0.306	0.201	0.190	0.040
Laundry soap	0.127	0.174	0.255	0.120	0.189	0.173	0.194
Toilet soap	0.205	0.208	0.259	0.191	0.207	0.237	0.226
Matches	0.064	0.067	0.071	0.059	0.046	0.045	0.074

Notes:
Zone 1: Arusha, Kilimanjaro, Tanga.
Zone 2: Coast, Dodoma, Morogoro.
Zone 3: Kagera, Mara, Mwanza, Shinyanga.
Zone 4: Kigoma, Singida, Tabora.
Zone 5: Iringa, Mbeya, Rukwa.
Zone 6: Lindi, Mtwara, Ruvuma.
Zone 7: Dar es Salaam.

TABLE 10.9. *Distribution of goods to RTCs, 1981–1985 (HBS weights)*

	1981	1982	1983	1984	1985
Arusha	118.611	106.865	100.000	118.999	63.060
Coast	97.607	121.033	100.000	74.100	57.735
Dar es Salaam	117.734	104.357	100.000	107.320	70.199
Dodoma	117.138	106.373	100.000	120.792	68.785
Iringa	112.699	106.460	100.000	90.940	59.220
Kagera	93.347	130.595	100.000	127.382	103.720
Kigoma	93.257	118.540	100.000	80.561	134.904
Kilimanjaro	122.991	123.079	100.000	131.937	84.258
Lindi	114.296	94.482	100.000	103.481	44.061
Mara	90.779	86.911	100.000	119.616	90.378
Mbeya	79.245	110.881	100.000	137.116	82.974
Morogoro	80.717	142.032	100.000	95.894	45.761
Mtwara	76.197	76.042	100.000	122.787	36.688
Mwanza	92.392	95.653	100.000	99.227	70.179
Rukwa	80.840	152.192	100.000	110.659	82.773
Ruvuma	70.773	123.630	100.000	139.143	108.512
Shinyanga	62.686	132.888	100.000	104.002	62.055
Singida	76.748	100.178	100.000	106.705	100.512
Tabora	85.359	100.081	100.000	135.102	80.978
Tanga	151.683	119.223	100.000	123.387	100.622

TABLE 10.10. *Recollection weights for distribution indices*

	Mentioned first	Mentioned second	Mentioned third	Total score	Weight
GCI sheeting	16	19	12	98	0.0360
Hoes	12	13	14	76	0.0279
Matches	6	17	35	87	0.0320
Ploughs	2	2	2	12	0.0044
Salt	66	88	93	467	0.1717
Sugar	236	195	109	1,207	0.4438
Soap (all types)	118	141	137	773	0.2842

observed from what is marketed through official channels, food crop production figures are based on estimates made by district agricultural officers. These estimates are often incomplete and based on no underlying quantitative data. While the system of food crop accounting has recently been changed to a survey-based method, there remain no reliable estimates of food crop production over the period of interest.

TABLE 10.11. *Distribution of goods to RTCs, 1981–1985 (recollection weights)*

	1981	1982	1983	1984	1985
Arusha	108.211	98.053	100.000	107.305	56.107
Coast	110.558	125.683	100.000	82.833	58.995
Dar es Salaam	98.134	96.403	100.000	115.542	77.782
Dodoma	115.599	103.345	100.000	121.127	70.175
Iringa	122.579	107.398	100.000	96.471	63.061
Kagera	113.138	159.327	100.000	163.106	118.928
Kigoma	100.536	111.982	100.000	99.075	109.454
Kilimanjaro	123.910	128.001	100.000	122.902	78.948
Lindi	117.922	97.684	100.000	98.472	49.548
Mara	87.649	85.229	100.000	128.704	84.949
Mbeya	89.250	111.552	100.000	149.516	99.299
Morogoro	87.336	149.006	100.000	103.341	46.339
Mtwara	84.943	78.769	100.000	127.767	39.540
Mwanza	83.868	100.006	100.000	109.236	72.944
Rukwa	80.868	144.394	100.000	113.998	79.849
Ruvuma	77.206	123.672	100.000	136.586	109.106
Shinyanga	59.685	115.975	100.000	107.371	59.800
Singida	86.303	105.812	100.000	114.176	99.380
Tabora	95.681	99.559	100.000	129.293	86.367
Tanga	144.203	102.591	100.000	115.352	101.435

TABLE 10.12. *Incentive weights for distribution indices*

	Mentioned first	Mentioned second	Mentioned third	Total score	Weight
GCI sheeting	59	41	30	284	0.1528
Hoes	86	25	25	333	0.1761
Matches	3	4	15	32	0.0169
Ploughs	23	23	10	125	0.0661
Salt	17	32	51	166	0.0878
Sugar	106	82	61	543	0.2871
Soap (all types)	48	96	67	403	0.2131

By collating data from the Ministry of Agriculture and the various marketing boards, we have obtained output series for these crops for the period 1975/6 to 1985/6. Crop accounting years typically run from October to October; for example, the 1975/6 figures represent output marketed in 1976. These raw output series are shown by crop in Table 10.14, and by region and crop in Table 10.15. For the three types of coffee and also for tobacco, output

TABLE 10.13. *Distribution of goods to RTCs, 1981–1985 (incentive weights)*

	1981	1982	1983	1984	1985
Arusha	84.836	82.308	100.000	107.508	48.170
Coast	90.048	119.407	100.000	99.716	56.689
Dar es Salaam	107.624	150.961	100.000	133.825	70.397
Dodoma	94.216	86.843	100.000	128.770	62.476
Iringa	92.719	94.895	100.000	116.176	52.052
Kagera	104.279	138.407	100.000	303.415	110.072
Kigoma	82.575	98.718	100.000	124.785	103.879
Kilimanjaro	91.188	102.230	100.000	120.724	78.509
Lindi	87.338	85.863	100.000	81.578	40.029
Mara	73.973	77.370	100.000	111.335	95.791
Mbeya	81.804	112.741	100.000	193.302	114.137
Morogoro	162.574	146.047	100.000	135.995	38.712
Mtwara	66.400	72.135	100.000	149.456	33.164
Mwanza	71.572	91.684	100.000	122.703	59.962
Rukwa	71.595	125.415	100.000	106.740	68.960
Ruvuma	58.077	114.635	100.000	138.864	94.537
Shinyanga	48.751	104.826	100.000	98.287	50.971
Singida	74.170	93.996	100.000	104.411	90.758
Tabora	81.851	90.462	100.000	122.809	78.542
Tanga	107.325	97.588	100.000	100.355	88.186

has remained fairly constant, although with considerable shifts in the regional composition of output. Over a period of rapid population growth this represents a considerable fall in per capita output. Output has collapsed for cashew nuts and pyrethrum, falling by two-thirds, with a more modest 25 per cent fall over the period in cotton seed production (but a 50 per cent fall from its 1976/7 peak). For these three goods the fall in per capita output has therefore been particularly dramatic.

To move from absolute output series to value series, we have constructed price series for each crop over the period from data furnished by the Marketing Development Bureau. These are official prices applicable to all crop sales made on official markets, and were known in advance by farmers. Hence if farmers wished to attain a set cash income based on their expectations of next period rationing, they could seek to achieve a set output with no price uncertainty. The one exception to this is coffee, where typically payment consists of an advance payment and a final payment which is announced after output is marketed. We have added the advance and final prices together, thus assuming that farmers were on average correct in their expectations of the final payments.

We deflate the value series of output by the CPI with 1978 as the base year, thus arriving at series for the real value of output. These series are shown by

TABLE 10.14. *Output of peasant cash crops by crop, 1975/1976–1985/1986*

	1975/6	1976/7	1977/8	1978/9	1979/80	1980/1	1981/2	1982/3	1983/4	1984/5	1985/6
Mild arabica	33.396	27.321	31.450	25.313	25.997	44.357	31.956	35.359	32.396	34.261	35.835
Hard arabica	3.220	3.224	3.751	3.151	3.287	4.092	4.447	3.232	2.630	2.391	3.058
Robusta	10.792	10.995	12.023	12.946	14.216	11.237	10.947	12.624	11.448	10.827	11.780
Cashew nuts	83.719	97.626	69.199	57.029	41.539	56.559	44.391	32.946	47.086	37.786	25.773
Pyrethrum	3.945	3.251	2.546	1.641	1.621	2.002	1.899	1.602	1.438	1.532	1.351
Cotton seed	123.750	193.900	147.750	161.700	175.100	150.050	125.000	124.700	136.100	144.900	96.600
Tobacco	13.932	18.822	18.079	17.879	16.445	15.539	13.097	10.467	13.430	12.488	15.040

Note: Units are millions of tonnes for cotton seed, thousands of tonnes for other crops.

TABLE 10.15. Output of peasant cash crops by region and crop, 1975/1976–1985/1986

	1975/6	1976/7	1977/8	1978/9	1979/80	1980/1	1981/2	1982/3	1983/4	1984/5	1985/6
Arusha											
Mild arabica	4.396	5.327	4.312	4.127	3.731	6.867	4.561	4.488	4.402	4.207	6.073
Pyrethrum	0.506	0.355	0.173	0.046	0.023	0.059	0.069	0.031	0.020	0.021	0.012
Coast											
Cashew nuts	19.585	23.897	12.999	15.606	11.366	7.790	9.629	6.791	16.161	9.975	4.230
Cotton seed	2.000	0.300	0.750	1.200	2.300	1.300	0.300	0.200	0.200	0.100	0.100
Iringa											
Mild arabica	0.106	0.036	0.057	0.027	0.031	0.042	0.038	0.045	0.056	0.093	0.050
Pyrethrum	2.189	1.916	1.730	1.154	0.961	1.213	1.108	1.036	0.949	0.081	0.848
Tobacco	3.438	4.148	4.266	3.721	3.005	1.766	2.133	1.757	2.400	2.341	1.323
Kagera											
Hard arabica	2.042	2.082	2.386	2.097	2.445	2.755	3.207	2.026	1.472	1.524	2.020
Robusta	10.543	10.829	11.818	12.776	13.956	11.019	10.744	12.548	11.337	10.733	11.615
Cotton seed	8.800	13.200	10.000	11.400	9.000	8.550	8.100	5.500	4.900	5.700	2.800
Tobacco	0.000	0.019	0.039	0.000	0.038	0.055	0.063	0.019	0.010	0.004	0.004
Kigoma											
Mild arabica	0.018	0.017	0.035	0.060	0.041	0.033	0.036	0.015	0.099	0.098	0.050
Cotton seed	1.050	2.500	2.400	2.300	2.400	1.850	1.300	1.100	1.400	1.100	0.500
Tobacco	0.038	0.074	0.000	0.000	0.065	0.027	0.015	0.039	0.000	0.000	0.000
Kilimanjaro											
Mild arabica	20.081	16.058	18.030	11.382	13.364	23.253	16.352	16.872	13.023	15.361	14.471
Cotton seed	0.700	0.900	0.850	0.800	0.500	0.350	0.200	0.000	0.100	0.200	0.400

Lindi										
Cashew nuts	16.491	24.443	11.231	10.333	10.412	15.158	7.566	6.892	7.392	6.406	3.784
Tobacco	0.003	0.005	0.005	0.012	0.008	0.004	0.005	0.005	0.000	0.000	0.000
Mara										
Hard arabica	0.427	0.171	0.230	0.315	0.280	0.300	0.421	0.248	0.220	0.290	0.405
Cotton seed	12.700	18.400	17.800	16.900	17.800	12.800	7.800	7.200	7.900	12.900	6.300
Mbeya										
Mild arabica	5.091	2.823	3.981	4.558	4.297	6.570	6.172	6.652	8.899	6.746	8.568
Cashew nuts	0.927	1.050	0.376	0.253	0.000	0.001	0.230	0.130	0.045	0.008	0.007
Pyrethrum	1.250	0.980	0.643	0.441	0.637	0.730	0.722	0.535	0.469	0.530	0.491
Cotton seed	1.700	2.300	2.850	3.400	2.700	1.450	0.200	1.900	2.800	3.900	4.100
Tobacco	0.500	0.838	1.222	1.303	1.513	1.675	1.569	1.021	1.650	1.517	1.609
Morogoro										
Hard arabica	0.251	0.171	0.235	0.139	0.243	0.168	0.125	0.103	0.038	0.144	0.100
Robusta	0.237	0.161	0.195	0.160	0.248	0.186	0.197	0.066	0.101	0.091	0.155
Caheew nuts	0.508	0.460	0.334	0.149	0.234	0.111	0.099	0.158	0.146	0.119	0.005
Cotton seed	3.400	6.900	5.200	6.900	2.600	4.200	5.800	4.800	5.900	3.900	5.400
Tobacco	0.021	0.009	0.000	0.000	0.005	0.011	0.004	0.001	0.000	0.000	0.000
Mtwara										
Cashew nuts	35.194	37.763	34.279	22.417	15.137	27.870	21.038	15.667	18.256	19.500	15.455
Mwanza										
Cotton seed	41.000	78.000	46.200	52.400	68.600	58.900	49.200	43.800	49.200	52.500	32.800
Ruvuma										
Mild arabica	3.250	2.297	4.155	4.660	4.231	6.578	4.197	6.427	5.210	7.320	6.100
Cashew nuts	4.741	4.750	7.615	5.459	2.035	3.408	3.984	2.148	1.700	0.906	1.319
Tobacco	2.259	4.522	3.700	3.958	3.457	3.986	4.055	1.946	3.000	0.354	1.034

TABLE 10.15. (cont.)

	1975/6	1976/7	1977/8	1978/9	1979/80	1980/1	1981/2	1982/3	1983/4	1984/5	1985/6
Shinyanga											
Cotton seed	41.600	63.000	54.600	57.800	59.800	51.900	44.000	52.400	56.300	57.300	38.800
Tobacco	0.397	0.475	0.456	0.458	0.437	0.341	0.219	0.237	0.460	0.291	0.753
Singida											
Cottom seed	1.100	1.100	0.800	0.500	0.600	0.550	0.500	1.700	1.500	1.700	0.500
Tobacco	0.413	0.493	0.474	0.476	0.456	0.391	0.444	0.248	0.320	0.408	0.557
Tabora											
Cotton seed	9.700	7.300	6.300	8.100	8.800	8.200	7.600	6.100	5.900	5.600	4.900
Tobacco	6.863	8.200	7.882	7.918	7.433	7.253	4.556	5.156	5.550	7.573	9.758
Tanga											
Mild arabica	0.454	0.763	0.880	0.499	0.302	1.014	0.600	0.860	0.707	0.436	0.523
Hard arabica	0.500	0.800	0.900	0.600	0.319	0.869	0.694	0.855	0.900	0.433	0.523
Robusta	0.012	0.005	0.010	0.010	0.012	0.032	0.006	0.010	0.010	0.003	0.010
Cashew nuts	2.553	3.224	0.844	1.565	1.026	1.577	1.033	0.652	2.474	0.494	0.721
Tobacco	0.000	0.039	0.035	0.033	0.028	0.030	0.034	0.038	0.040	0.000	0.002

region and crop in Table 10.16 and aggregated by region in Table 10.17. The values in both tables are expressed in thousands of real 1978 Tanzanian shillings. The real product price for all crops has fallen dramatically over the period and hence Tables 10.16 and 10.17 show an even more drastic slide than Tables 10.14 and 10.15. The rural population of Tanzania increased by 33 per cent between 1976 and 1985. Aggregating Table 10.15 across regions for 1975/6 and 1985/6, and expressing the results in per capita terms reveals how severe the collapse in cash crop incomes was. Over this period real per capita cash crop income in Tanzania fell by some 70.2 per cent. There were no recorded purchases by marketing boards of the seven crops in Rukwa and Dodoma over this period. Also, we have excluded Dar es Sslaam, which does however produce a small amount of cashew nuts. This makes the final size of our panel data set seventeen regions.

We noted above that there are no reliable data on food crop production from which to analyse whether the collapse in cash crop production led to a shift towards food crop production. For completeness in Table 10.18 we present collected FAO data on food crop production. The table shows an increase in food crop acreage between 1974/6 and 1982, with a drift back after 1982. However, the combined effect of acreage and yield changes is not enough to increase per capita production over the period.

10.3. The Results

In the previous section we constructed panel data sets with which to test whether changes in measures of goods market rationing affect the production of peasant cash crops. We now explore this relationship using two econometric models. The final size of the panel was seventeen regions, Dodoma, Dar es Salaam, and Rukwa having been dropped. Analysis is carried out using the two derived measures of rationing, namely the probabilistic availability series for 1978 to 1983 and the distribution indices for 1981 to 1985. We also use the three variants of each measure derived from the use of the 1969 Household Budget Survey, recollection, and incentive weights described in Section 10.2. First, we use a one-way fixed effects model, that is, we estimate models of the following form:

$$q_{it} = \alpha_i + \beta X_{it} + \varepsilon_{it}$$

where q is the real value of cash crop production, X is some measure of goods market rationing, the subscript i indexes regions, and the subscript t indexes time. Thus we assume that the intercept term varies across regions but not time, while the parameter of greatest interest, the slope coefficient of X, is constant across both regions and time.

We also estimate a variant of this model using the method of generalized least squares on a one-way random effects model. Let Ψ_i be a random shock

TABLE 10.16. *Real value of cash crop production by region and crop, 1975/1976–1985/1986*

	1975/6	1976/7	1977/8	1978/9	1979/80	1980/1	1981/2	1982/3	1983/4	1984/5	1985/6
Arusha											
Mild arabica	95.727	108.621	78.780	32.442	33.629	51.440	32.767	25.461	30.124	30.225	36.667
Pyrethrum	2.539	2.575	1.125	0.266	0.109	0.268	0.333	0.116	0.084	0.092	0.044
Coast											
Cashew nuts	24.510	29.338	14.949	23.645	16.147	14.164	23.214	12.698	33.850	21.948	7.815
Cotton seed	4.768	0.670	1.725	2.567	5.446	2.521	0.535	0.352	0.359	0.189	0.204
Iringa											
Mild arabica	2.308	0.734	1.041	0.212	0.279	0.315	0.273	0.255	0.383	0.668	0.302
Pyrethrum	10.984	13.900	11.245	6.685	4.551	5.514	5.342	3.874	3.975	4.317	3.133
Tobacco	28.684	34.258	31.568	24.541	20.871	11.238	12.958	11.827	12.926	13.245	7.884
Kagera											
Hard arabica	44.466	42.453	43.592	29.642	10.710	7.514	9.169	7.993	7.201	8.212	9.497
Robusta	229.584	220.810	215.925	180.595	61.133	30.052	30.719	49.507	55.464	57.834	54.605
Cotton seed	20.977	29.464	23.000	24.385	21.310	16.582	14.450	9.667	8.797	10.750	5.723
Tobacco	0.000	0.157	0.289	0.000	0.264	0.350	0.383	0.128	0.054	0.023	0.024
Kigoma											
Mild arabica	0.392	0.347	0.639	0.472	0.370	0.247	0.259	0.085	0.677	0.704	0.302
Cotton seed	2.503	5.580	5.520	4.920	5.683	3.588	2.319	1.933	2.513	2.075	1.022
Tobacco	0.317	0.611	0.000	0.000	0.451	0.172	0.091	0.263	0.000	0.000	0.000
Kilimanjaro											
Mild arabica	437.282	327.433	329.408	89.473	120.455	174.186	117.476	95.717	89.119	110.362	87.372
Cotton seed	1.669	2.009	1.955	1.711	1.184	0.679	0.357	0.000	0.180	0.377	0.818

Lindi											
Cashew nuts	20.638	30.008	12.916	15.656	14.792	27.560	18.240	12.887	15.483	14.095	6.991
Tobacco	0.025	0.041	0.037	0.079	0.056	0.025	0.030	0.034	0.000	0.000	0.000
Mara											
Hard arabica	9.298	3.487	4.202	4.453	1.227	0.818	1.204	0.978	1.076	1.563	1.904
Cotton seed	30.274	41.071	40.940	36.150	42.147	24.824	13.915	12.655	14.183	24.329	12.877
Mbeya											
Mild arabica	110.861	57.563	72.733	35.830	38.731	49.215	44.341	37.738	60.898	48.467	51.731
Cashew nuts	1.160	1.289	0.432	0.383	0.000	0.002	0.554	0.243	0.094	0.018	0.013
Pyrethrum	6.272	7.109	4.180	2.555	3.017	3.318	3.481	2.001	1.965	2.332	1.814
Cotton seed	4.052	5.134	6.555	7.273	6.393	2.812	0.357	3.340	5.027	7.355	8.381
Tobacco	4.172	6.921	9.043	8.594	10.509	10.659	9.532	6.873	8.887	8.583	9.588
Morogoro											
Hard arabica	5.466	3.487	4.293	1.965	1.064	0.458	0.357	0.406	0.186	0.776	0.517
Robusta	5.161	3.282	3.563	2.262	1.086	0.507	0.563	0.260	0.494	0.490	0.729
Cashew nuts	0.636	0.565	0.084	0.226	0.332	0.202	0.239	0.295	0.306	0.262	0.009
Cotton seed	8.105	15.402	11.960	14.759	6.156	8.145	10.347	8.437	10.592	7.355	11.038
Tobacco	0.175	0.074	0.000	0.000	0.035	0.070	0.024	0.007	0.000	0.000	0.000
Mtwara											
Cashew nuts	44.045	46.361	39.421	33.965	21.505	50.673	50.718	29.295	38.238	42.905	28.553
Mwanza											
Cotton seed	97.735	174.107	106.260	112.086	162.431	114.230	87.772	76.986	88.330	99.112	67.044
Ruvuma											
Mild arabica	70.772	46.837	75.912	36.632	38.136	49.275	30.152	36.461	35.653	52.591	36.830
Cashew nuts	5.933	5.831	8.757	8.271	2.891	6.196	9.605	4.016	3.561	1.993	2.437
Tobacco	18.847	37.347	27.380	26.104	24.011	25.365	24.635	14.099	16.158	2.003	6.162

TABLE 10.16. (cont.)

	1975/6	1976/7	1977/8	1978/9	1979/80	1980/1	1981/2	1982/3	1983/4	1984/5	1985/6
Shinyanga											
Cotton seed	99.166	140.625	125.580	123.636	141.594	100.655	78.496	92.102	101.077	108.065	79.308
Tobacco	3.312	3.923	3.374	3.021	3.035	2.170	1.330	1.595	2.478	1.646	4.487
Singida											
Cotton seed	2.622	2.455	1.840	1.070	1.421	1.067	0.892	2.988	2.693	3.206	1.022
Tobacco	3.446	4.072	3.508	3.139	3.167	2.488	2.697	1.669	1.724	2.308	3.319
Tabora											
Cotton seed	23.123	16.295	14.490	17.326	20.837	15.903	13.558	10.722	10.592	10.561	10.016
Tobacco	57.260	67.723	58.327	52.222	51.626	46.155	27.679	34.708	29.892	42.847	58.149
Tanga											
Mild arabica	9.886	15.558	16.078	3.923	2.722	7.596	4.311	4.879	4.838	3.132	3.158
Hard arabica	10.888	16.313	16.443	8.481	1.397	2.370	1.984	3.373	4.403	2.333	2.459
Robusta	0.261	0.102	0.183	0.141	0.053	0.087	0.017	0.039	0.049	0.016	0.047
Cashew nuts	3.195	3.958	0.971	2.371	1.458	2.867	2.490	1.219	5.182	1.087	1.332
Tobacco	0.000	0.322	0.259	0.218	0.194	0.191	0.207	0.256	0.215	0.000	0.012

TABLE 10.17. *Real value of cash crop production by region, 1975–1986* (thousands of 1978 Tanzanian shillings)

	1975/6	1976/7	1977/8	1978/9	1979/80	1980/1	1981/2	1982/3	1983/4	1984/5	1985/6
Arusha	98.226	111.196	79.905	32.709	33.738	51.708	33.100	25.577	30.208	30.318	36.712
Coast	29.278	30.007	16.674	26.212	21.593	16.685	23.749	13.050	34.209	22.136	8.019
Iringa	41.977	48.892	43.855	31.439	25.702	17.066	18.574	15.957	17.285	18.230	11.319
Kagera	295.027	292.885	282.976	234.622	93.417	54.497	54.722	67.295	71.516	76.818	69.849
Kigoma	3.212	6.538	6.159	5.391	6.504	4.007	2.669	2.281	3.191	2.779	1.324
Kilimanjaro	438.951	329.442	331.363	91.185	121.639	174.865	117.833	95.717	89.299	110.739	88.190
Lindi	20.663	30.049	12.953	15.735	14.848	27.585	18.270	12.921	15.483	14.095	6.991
Mara	39.572	44.558	45.142	40.602	43.373	25.642	15.119	13.634	15.259	25.891	14.781
Mbeya	126.518	78.016	92.943	54.635	58.649	66.006	58.265	50.194	76.870	66.755	71.527
Morogoro	19.543	22.811	20.200	19.212	8.674	9.383	11.531	9.406	11.578	8.883	12.293
Mtwara	44.045	46.361	39.421	33.965	21.505	50.673	50.718	29.295	38.238	42.905	28.553
Mwanza	97.735	174.107	106.260	112.086	162.431	114.230	87.772	76.986	88.330	99.012	67.044
Ruvuma	95.552	90.016	112.049	71.008	65.038	80.837	64.392	53.577	55.372	56.587	45.429
Shinyanga	102.478	144.548	128.954	126.657	144.630	102.825	79.826	93.697	103.555	109.711	83.795
Singida	6.068	6.527	5.348	4.209	4.588	3.555	3.589	4.657	4.417	5.515	4.341
Tabora	80.383	84.018	72.817	69.548	72.463	62.058	41.237	45.429	40.485	53.408	68.165
Tanga	24.231	36.253	33.933	15.134	5.824	13.111	9.009	9.767	14.687	6.569	7.007

which hits region i for all years of the period of estimation. The model can then be formulated as:

$$q_{it} = \beta X_{it} + \Psi_i + \varepsilon_{it}.$$

We apply generalized least squares as follows. An estimate of the variance of Ψ_i, $\sigma^2_{\Psi i}$, is the mean squared residual of $\beta(X_{it} - \bar{X}_i) - (q_{it} - \bar{q})$. We obtain the mean squared error of the regression of the means of the real value of production per region on a constant term and the means per region of the measure of goods market rationing, and multiply this mean squared error by the number of time periods in the estimation. Let this be λ. Efficient estimates of β are now obtained by running the regression:

$$\left[q_{it} - \left\{ 1 - \left(\frac{\sigma^2_{\Psi i}}{\lambda} \right)^{1/2} \right\} \bar{q}_i \right] = \sigma_i + \beta \left[X_{it} - \left\{ 1 - \left(\frac{\sigma^2_{\Psi i}}{\lambda} \right)^{1/2} \right\} \bar{X}_i \right] + U_{it}.$$

Note that the random effects model leads to a classical regression with only two parameters, while the fixed effects model includes seventeen regional intercepts plus β. Thus in comparing results we would expect the F-statistic to be more significant for the fixed effects model. Indeed the significance level of all the F-tests preserved in the results below for the fixed effects model is below 1 per cent.

We consider the effect of goods market rationing on both current period and next period cash crop production. Higher order and mixed lag structures

TABLE 10.18. *Estimated food crop acreages and yields*

	Area harvested (000s ha)			
	1974–6	1982	1983	1984
Maize	1,167	1,350	1,350	1,250
Rice, paddy	211	270	270	270
Wheat	437	680	660	650
Millet	200	450	400	350
Sorghum	437	680	660	650
Total cereals	2,452	3,430	3,340	3,170
	Yield (kg/ha)			
Maize	1,037	1,147	1,010	905
Rice, paddy	1,399	1,404	1,481	1,481
Wheat	710	706	697	692
Millet	645	829	838	814
Sorghum	710	706	697	692

Source: FAO *Monthly Bulletin of Statistics* (various issues).

were tested but provided no further significant results. We consider first the measure of availability. Table 10.19 presents results for the regression of current period cash crop production on the current period indices, and Table 10.20 for the regression of next period cash crop production on the current period indices. Results are presented for both the fixed and the random effects models, with t-statistics shown in parentheses.

Comparing tables, it is clear that goods market rationing operates on cash crop production with a one-period lag. This suggests that current rationing

TABLE 10.19. *Current period output on current period rationing (availability indices)*

	HBS weights	Recollection weights	Incentive weights
Fixed effects model			
β	−0.00941	−0.11429	−0.13383
	(−0.111)	(−0.712)	(−0.441)
F-statistic	70.975	96.998	97.454
Chi-squared	248.10	306.93	307.34
Random effects model			
Constant	0.91064	0.84363	0.84487
	(0.579)	(0.420)	(0.424)
β	−0.00939	−0.11417	−0.13374
	(−0.123)	(−0.776)	(−1.025)
F-statistic	0.015	0.602	1.050
Chi-squared	0.015	0.597	1.051

TABLE 10.20. *Next period output on current period rationing (availability indices)*

	HBS weights	Recollection weights	Incentive weights
Fixed effects model			
β	0.23213	0.37319	0.34996
	(1.456)	(2.515)	(2.532)
F-statistic	17.719	18.825	18.847
Chi-squared	153.55	158.41	158.50
Random effects model			
Constant	1.708871	1.44571	1.52310
	(0.835)	(0.731)	(0.772)
β	0.23212	0.37314	0.34981
	(1.583)	(2.734)	(2.751)
F-statistic	2.507	7.475	7.568
Chi-squared	2.511	7.338	7.427

affects expectations of next-period rationing and hence generates expected effective demands (and thus expected cash requirements) one period in advance. For all three models the unlagged relationship (Table 10.19) shows not only statistically insignificant coefficients on the rationing measure, but also statistically insignificant equations (from the F-statistics of the random effects). The fixed effects model produces seventeen constant terms, one per region, which are significantly different from zero and thus increase the F-statistic for this model. However, the lagged relationship (Table 10.20) shows significant coefficients for β, as well as significant equations even in the fixed effects form of the model, for the recollection and incentive weighting schemes, and better results (though not quite significant at a 10 per cent level) for the HBS scheme than using the unlagged version of the model.

This pattern is repeated in Tables 10.21 (unlagged) and 10.22 (lagged) using the distribution measures constructed for the period 1981 to 1985. There is again a clear indication that goods market rationing affects output following a one-year lag.

Comparing the three weighting schemes, a clear ranking emerges. Weights based on peasant perceptions of what motivates agricultural production perform best, then those based on recollections of the pre-rationing period, and the least effective scheme is that using the 1969 Household Budget Survey expenditure shares. This ranking is true of both the distribution-based and the availability-based data sets. For the former alone this might be explicable in terms of the dual role of farm implements: they are in excess demand just as basic consumer goods and hence their supply raises expenditure, but additionally they increase directly agricultural production. Farm inputs are included in the distribution-based basket of goods, the weight on them being

TABLE 10.21. *Current period output on current period rationing (distribution indices)*

	HBS weights	Recollection weights	Incentive weights
Fixed effects model			
β	−.05438	−0.03169	−0.03429
	(−0.908)	(−0.552)	(−0.828)
F-statistic	44.819	44.423	44.720
Chi-squared	211.59	210.90	211.42
Random effects model			
Constant	0.96741	0.93286	0.91864
	(0.859)	(0.825)	(0.817)
β	−0.05434	−0.03165	−0.03426
	(−1.008)	(−0.579)	(−0.919)
F-statistic	1.015	0.335	0.844
Chi-squared	1.015	0.324	0.842

TABLE 10.22. *Next period output on current period rationing (distribution indices)*

	HBS weights	Recollection weights	Incentive weights
Fixed effects model			
β	0.06669	0.09404	0.11043
	(1.421)	(2.290)	(2.702)
F-statistic	94.192	80.844	83.257
Chi-squared	271.04	257.61	261.00
Random effects model			
Constant	0.34093	0.31554	0.36146
	(0.444)	(0.416)	(0.475)
β	0.06669	0.09406	0.11045
	(1.580)	(2.546)	(3.004)
F-statistic	2.495	6.483	9.024
Chi-squared	2.499	6.375	8.755

largest in the incentive scheme which, as we have noted, performs best. However, the superiority of this scheme holds equally for the availability-based data set. Since this set contains no agricultural inputs, the ranking cannot be due to their production effect. Recall that the ideal, but unobserved, weight would be the share of each good in expenditure during rationing. The ranking of models is probably best explained in terms of their relative proximity to this ideal, the poor performance of the 1969 budget survey weights indicating how substantially shortages have changed the composition of expenditure.

Further evidence on this point is provided by the performance of an index intended to proxy the government view of incentive goods, using a basket comprising only GCI sheeting, hoes, and ploughs. These are the goods officially designated as incentive goods which also appear in the Cooksey survey. The results from this index are even less significant than those from the HBS weights, again implying that we are picking up more than a direct capital stock to output link.

Assume that the government believes all goods unimportant for incentives other than GCI sheeting, ploughs, and hoes, but correctly perceives peasant preferences between these three goods as shown in Table 10.12. To model this we give all other goods zero weight, and, from Table 10.12, give GCI sheeting, ploughs, and hoes the weights 88/186, 76/186, and 12/186 respectively to derive a measure of the degree of rationing of incentive goods as seen from the government's view. The results of running both the fixed and random effects models on this scheme are shown in Table 10.23: no significant explanatory power is achieved. Clearly the results of the incentive model in Table 10.22 are not well explained by any direct capital stock to output link.

TABLE 10.23. *A simulation of the government view of incentive goods*

Fixed effects model	
β	0.045933
	(1.133)
F-statistic	76.195
Chi-squared	253.82
Random effects model	
Constant	0.47812
	(0.605)
β	0.045967
	(1.260)
F-statistic	1.5873
Chi-squared	1.592

This substantiates the argument of Cooksey *et al.* that incentive goods for farmers are really basic consumer goods, especially sugar, cooking oil, soap, and combined varieties of clothing, rather than the official view that incentive goods are cement, radios, bicycles, hoes, ploughs, and GCI sheeting.

The performance of the recollection model relative to that of the HBS scheme is unsurprising. The latter uses weights derived from an unrationed situation. Hence even if notional demand vectors had remained constant over the period, we would not expect this model to perform well. In the rationed situation we would expect the actual, but unobserved, budget shares to differ markedly from those in a relatively unrationed situation, especially given that there is considerable variation between the degree of rationing across goods.

The above analysis has demonstrated that there is a clear relationship between current-period rationing and next-period agricultural output. To gauge the strength of this relationship we have re-estimated the one-way random effects model in order to derive the elasticity of cash crop production with respect to changes in the rationing indices. We estimate the model in logarithmic form as follows;

$$\log q_i = \beta \log X_{it} + \psi_i + U_{it}$$

and hence the slope coefficient on X_{it} provides an estimate of the elasticity. We apply generalized least squares in the manner described above, and run the transformed equation for the three weighting schemes for both the availability and the distribution measures. The results for all six regressions are shown in Table 10.24.

For the availability indices the logarithmic form of the model reproduces the ranking of models shown in Table 10.20. All three models fit less well in the logarithmic than the linear form, but only the HBS version loses all

TABLE 10.24. *One-way random effects model (logarithmic form)*

	HBS weights	Recollection weights	Incentive weights
Availability indices			
Constant	0.04479	0.03769	0.03840
	(1.545)	(1.330)	(1.361)
β	0.05486	0.27297	0.26167
	(0.836)	(2.338)	(2.460)
F-statistic	0.698	5.466	6.052
Chi-squared	0.695	5.414	5.979
Distribution indices			
Constant	0.01872	0.01543	0.01912
	(0.776)	(0.651)	(0.808)
β	0.25688	0.32127	0.23767
	(2.569)	(3.153)	(2.979)
F-statistic	6.600	9.944	8.875
Chi-squared	6.486	9.600	8.617

significance on a standard *F*-test. The recollection and incentive weighting schemes produce estimates of the elasticity of cash crop production with respect to changes in the rationing indices of 0.27 and 0.26 respectively. The significance of these estimates is discussed further in Chapter 12.

The results of the distribution indices show greater variation from the linear form shown in Table 10.22. The use of the HBS weights remains the least effective scheme, though it produces much better results in the logarithmic form. However, the relative order of the other schemes switches. Taking the results of the random effects model across Tables 10.20, 10.22, and 10.24 and ranking weighting schemes on the basis of *F*-tests, we find that the incentive scheme outranks the recollection scheme in all three other estimations, and the HBS scheme performs least well in all four.

The above analysis has abstracted from the potential role of price effects which we now incorporate. Running the model separately for each crop with the addition of a real price term cuts down the size and reliability of the panel data set considerably, especially when it is considered that some crops are only grown in very small quantities in some regions. We therefore adopt the following procedure. For each region we take the major crop in value terms and run the panel regression of output of that crop on its real price and the rationing indices. As Table 10.16 shows, the major crop for all regions but two constitutes at least 80 per cent of the total value of cash crops in 1985/6, a pattern that remains consistent over the time series. The remaining two regions, Singida and Tanga, are dropped from the panel and hence the inbuilt bias implicit in constructing any aggregate weighted real price series is avoided.

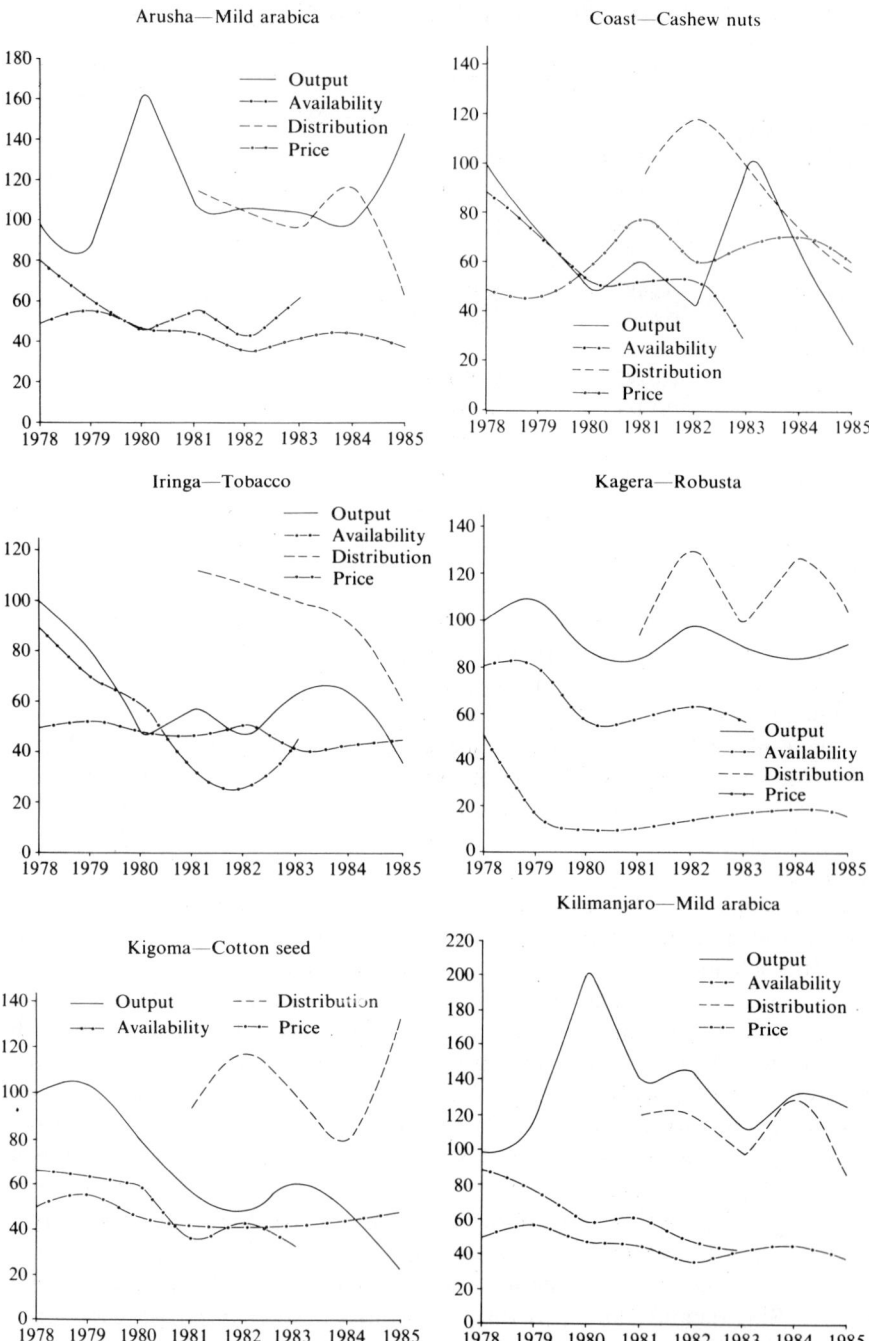

FIG. 10.1 Output, price, and shortages in fifteen regions, 1978–1985

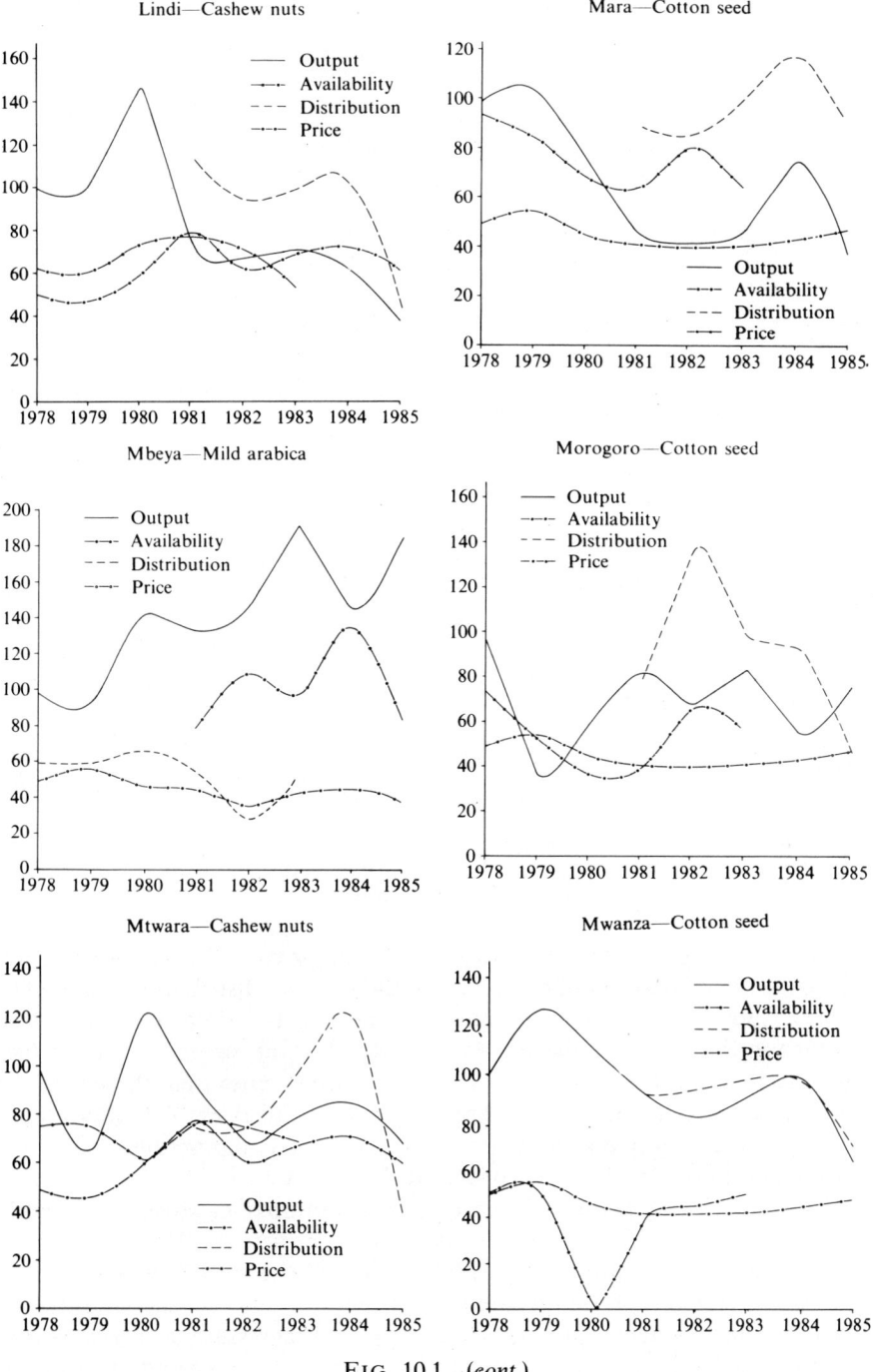

FIG. 10.1 (cont.)

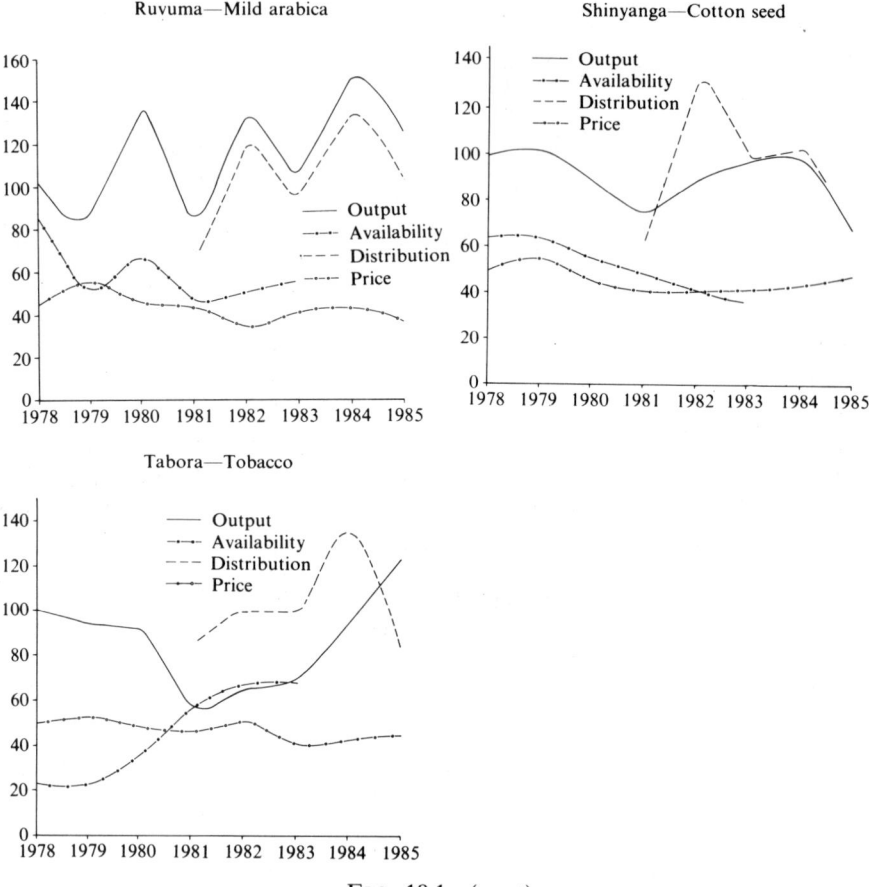

FIG. 10.1 (cont.)

Figure 10.1 is a graph of the output of the major crop, the real price of that crop, the regional availability index, and the regional distribution index. (The indices shown are those using recollection weights for each of the fifteen regions in the panel for the period 1978–85.) For all regions it is clear that there is considerably more volatility in the output series than there is in the price series. Also the price series appears to track the availability index fairly closely, suggesting that it might prove difficult to decompose their individual effects upon output, as indeed proves to be the case.

As the producer price for each crop is announced in advance, the only element of surprise for the peasant household in the real price series comes from incorrect expectations of the real consumer price level. If we assume that on average these expectations are correct then the correct regression to test the preceding results for price effects becomes the regression of current period output of the main cash crop upon current period real price and the previous period's measure of rationing. The results are shown in Table 10.25, noting that as above the time period for the regressions on the availability and the distribution indices is different. We present the results of the fixed effects model, there being no significant differences between these results and those generated by the random effects model. The coefficient on the rationing index is reported as β_1 and that on the price series as β_2.

The introduction of price effects does nothing to diminish the significance of the rationing indices based on the regional distribution of controlled goods. For all three weighting schemes the price effect is negative, as we would expect, but never gains significance. Indeed, while the two sets of results are not strictly comparable as the dependent variable has been changed, the rationing indices prove to be more significant than those shown in Table 10.22. For the simulations based on the distributional measures of rationing the relationship between current-period cash crop output and previous-period degree of rationing is not affected by consideration of price effects.

This strong result is not replicated using the availability-based indices, neither price nor rationing variables being significant. However, except in the case of the index based on the HBS weights, the rationing index performs better than the price. The failure of these models might perhaps be due to the high level of multicollinearity observed between price and the availability indices. Any relationship between the two while spurious would tend to reduce the significance of the rationing term. One reason why this problem affects the availability series more severely than the distribution series is the somewhat different time periods involved.

TABLE 10.25. *The role of price effects*

	HBS weights	Recollection weights	Incentive weights
Distribution indices			
β_1	54.580	57.185	28.567
	(3.162)	(3.329)	(2.526)
β_2	−659.97	−668.07	−813.36
	(−0.786)	(0.826)	(−0.918)
F-statistic	94.62	96.19	88.05
Chi-squared	240.2	246.39	240.01
Availability indices			
β_1	−0.3587	26.507	27.817
	(−0.012)	(0.945)	(1.075)
β_2	104.07	−7.224	−17.677
	(0.297)	(−0.020)	(−0.050)
F-statistic	100.61	101.90	102.27
Chi-squared	280.56	281.66	281.98

The main results of this analysis are as follows. First, budget shares from an unrationed state provide a poorer proxy for those in the rationed state than schemes based on peasant perceptions. Second, these perceptions of how goods market constraints affect agricultural output appear to be rather accurate. Third, it is clear from the analysis of price effects that the supply responses are indeed a function of the severity of rationing, rather than merely of movements in real producer prices. Fourth, in the circumstances then prevailing in Tanzania, the major incentive goods appear to have been basic consumer goods, rather than the types of consumer durables and agricultural capital perceived in that role by the government. In this respect we have been able to substantiate the hypothesis put forward by Cooksey *et al.* Finally, our estimates of the elasticity of agricultural supply with respect to availability do indeed support the hypothesis put forward in Chapter 9, that is, that elasticity should be significant, positive, and less than unity. The implications are considered in detail in Chapter 12.

11
Cross-section Tests of Household Supply Response

11.1. The Design of a Testable Hypothesis

While our panel survey for 1976 and 1983 provides too few data for time series testing, it does permit cross-section tests which cannot be undertaken on the aggregate data deployed in the previous chapter. Recall that the theory being tested is that instead of income and expenditure both being determined endogenously as functions of endowments and prices, planned income is adjusted so as to equal exogenously constrained expenditure plus any desired change in monetary assets. However, cross-section evidence that planned cash incomes are associated with expected expenditure fails to establish the direction of causality. Evidence of a positive association could reflect expectations of exogenously constrained expenditure inducing an income adjustment (our hypothesis) or exogenous changes in income inducing changes in expenditure. We must therefore identify and test those hypotheses of the model which are causally distinguishable from the expenditure-determined income account.

The model indeed has such distinctive hypotheses. It distinguishes between households which choose to make purchases on the black market and those which rely only upon the official market. The two groups of households were shown to behave in radically different ways in response to changes in the availability of goods on official markets for given black-market prices. As shown in Figure 9.4, households which relied only upon official markets would increase their marketed supply in response to greater availability, whereas households also using black markets would actually reduce supply. The reasoning behind the latter, counter-intuitive, result is that if the household is able to purchase a good at official prices which it would otherwise buy on the black market, it benefits from an increase in its real income. But as long as it is able to make extra purchases on the black market (that is, if it is unrationed at the margin in the black market), enhanced availability at official prices does not give rise to a substitution effect, the price vector appropriate for its marginal trade-off between working to produce cash income and other uses of time (leisure and subsistence crops) being that prevailing in the black market. Since part of this pure income effect would be used to increase the consumption of leisure and subsistence crops, the household would plan to reduce its cash income.

We refer to the relationship depicted in Figure 9.4 as the supply response function. It amounts to a pair of hypotheses about the relationship between expenditure and income for the two groups of households. These hypotheses are testable on our data set. However, the construction of an appropriate test is not straightforward. First, consider the independent variable in the model, namely the availability of consumer goods at official prices. The relationship depicted in Figure 9.4 has on the horizontal axis the quantity available for purchase at the official price. More precisely, this is the quantity which the household expects to be available in formulating and achieving its production plans. Assume for the moment that by 1983 households held rational expectations of the amount of goods available for purchase at official prices. Since official prices can be treated as known, this translates into a rational expectation of expenditure at official prices:

$$\hat{G}_i = G_i + \mu_i \tag{11.1}$$

where ^ denotes an expectation.

The assumption of rational expectations is sufficient but not necessary for our purposes. It would not matter were all households to make a common systematic error in addition to varying non-systematic errors, that is:

$$\hat{G}_i = aG_i + \mu_i. \tag{11.2}$$

Our survey collected data on the quantities of eighteen goods purchased at official prices over the course of the preceding year. Multiplied by the vector of official prices this provides an estimate of expenditure on a significant subset of the goods likely to be available on official markets (the array of such goods having become progressively more limited). It should at once be stressed that even for the subset of commodities this estimate is likely to be noisy: household budget surveys usually have considerable difficulty in getting accurate records of consumer expenditure and for a twelve-month recall survey this must be especially so. Against this, however, many of the items in our list were relatively rare purchases and so might have been remembered, while others were sufficiently frequent for repondents to describe typical behaviour rather than to rely upon the recall of specific events. We may expect, therefore, that there should be some positive relation between observed expenditure on this subset and total expenditure at official prices. We will denote these two magnitudes of expenditure by S and G respectively.

In the theory of Chapter 9 the dependent variable was the quantity of the marketed crop. However, although the relationship in Figure 9.4 is depicted in quantity–quantity space, for given crop and official commodity prices it can equally well be expressed in cash income–expenditure space. While the theory could best be presented in terms of a single marketed output and a single purchased commodity, clearly in empirical testing we are dealing with bundles of sales and purchases which need to be aggregated by means of price vectors. Hence, it is appropriate to regard the dependent variable as cash income. Note that whereas the theory referred explicitly only to marketed crop output, it is not about any single source of cash income in isolation. Crop marketing was chosen as the label for the dependent variable only because it is the most important and the most likely component of income which peasants might adjust. Total household cash income in 1983 ($Y83$) is a variable created from the prices and quantities recorded in our survey, as has been described in Chapter 3.

Having measures for income (Y) and expenditures at official prices (S), we return briefly to the identification of expected expenditure at official prices $\hat{G}$. Recall that $\hat{G}$ might differ from actual expenditure, G, due to a forecasting error by the household. Indeed, that households plan on the basis of large unavoidable errors due to the haphazard nature of scarcities has been a major component in our theory of the demand for money. We are able to identify the extreme cases of these forecasting errors, namely those households for whom actual expenditure at official prices on the observed subset of goods (S) exceeds income (Y). The household will not generally plan for total expenditure at official prices to exceed income. Hence, for the observed subset, S, to exceed income, either actual expenditure at official prices substantially exceeds expectations or actual income falls far short of expectations. (That is, since $G > S$ and $\hat{G} \leqslant \hat{Y}$, $S > Y$ entails either $G > \hat{G}$ or $\hat{Y} > Y$.) We defer consideration of cases in which income falls far short of expectations. However, when expenditure at official prices substantially exceeds expectations, our observed expenditure at official prices, S, is *a fortiori* a very poor predictor of expected expenditure at official prices, G. Hence, we discard cases of $S > Y$ from our sample.

Although only a few observations are eliminated through this procedure, since these tend disproportionately to involve pairings of high values of S with low values of Y, we will see that this shifts the sample against confirmation of our hypothesis.

Figure 9.4 describes the relationship between availability of goods at official prices and cash income for the representative household given black-market prices. That is, it describes how the behaviour of the household will vary according to its expectation of expenditure on the official market. Our test must use not the representative household over time but a dispersion of cross-section observations of households. The dispersion which we will be making use of is that, because of different locations, contacts, influence, expertise, and resources, households will differ as to their rational expectations of opportunities for expenditure at official prices. Were this the only difference between households then the model of Chapter 9 would be readily testable, for the scatter of S,Y observations should conform to the function depicted in Figure 9.4. However, households also differ in terms of endowments and preferences.

Consider first the effect of differences in endowments. Under conditions when expenditure is unconstrained by availability households will have different planned incomes because of differences in circumstances which can be described as endowments. We will denote planned income when expenditure is expected to be unconstrained by availability by Y^*. Those households with higher Y^* will, for common preferences, only enter the zone of non-participation in the black market (cross the switch point in Figure 9.4 at which supply response is positive) at a higher level of S. In terms of Figure 9.3, which is the underlying diagram from which 9.4 is derived, if households differ in their endowments of labour, their budget lines will have corresponding differences and so the length of the income expansion line prior to non-participation in the black market will differ. Figure 11.1 illustrates the resulting supply–response functions for two such differently endowed households. The low endowment household (i) has the supply–response function B_{1i}–B_{3i}–B_{5i} (the labels corresponding to points in Figure 9.3). Point B_{5i} is the position the household would choose were it unrationed, and is therefore on the budget line C–D. The high-endowment household would choose a higher level of unrationed expenditure, B_{5ii}, and has correspondingly displaced positions throughout its supply–response function. If the income expansion lines i_1 and i_2 in Figure 9.3 are linear, the displacement of the function is throughout proportional to the difference in planned cash incomes when expected expenditure is unconstrained (Y_i^*, Y_{ii}^*). For example, if household i represents the mean household, an observation for household ii of x_{ii} (the vector $\hat{Y}$, $\hat{G}_1$) should be scaled down to the mean by the factor Y_i^*/Y_{ii}^*, to x'_{ii}.

Note that the displacement of the supply–response function consequent upon differences in planned cash incomes when expenditure is unconstrained effects the estimation only of the B_1–B_3 portion of the function, that is households in the black market. For this group if differences in planned cash income are large (and we have shown from the 1976/7 survey discussed in Chapter 3 that they were), the failure to correct for them would introduce both

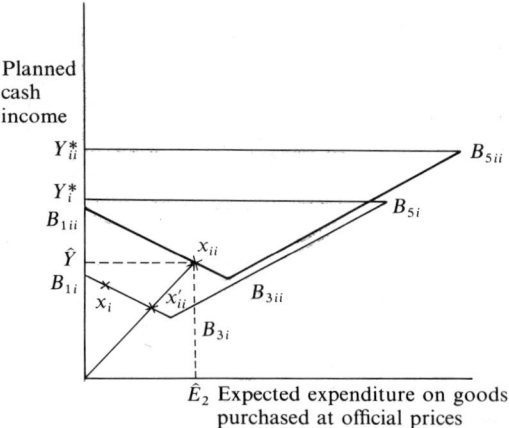

FIG. 11.1. *Supply–response functions for differently endowed households*

much noise and many biases into the estimation of the supply–response function. In contrast, households on the B_3–B_5 portion of the function, that is those not in the black market, will merely be displaced along the line of the function. Thus, in order to test the supply–response function for those in the black market hypothesized in Figure 9.4, the observed dispersion of S, Y pairs must be rescaled to the endowment set of the representative household.

We therefore require an estimation for each household of Y^* relative to the mean Y^* (denoted as Y_m^*), to yield the scaling factor Y^*/Y_m^*. Potentially the chosen cash income of the household in circumstances of unconstrained expenditure could be estimated from the observed vector of productive endowments. However, such an approach would introduce considerable additional noise into the test since the mapping from an endowment into income will differ between households. Fortunately, the panel data aspect of the survey can be used to provide a more compelling indicator of Y^* and Y_m^*, namely actual cash income in 1976/7 ($Y77$ and $Y77_m$). Recall that in 1976/7 households were not subject to serious availability constraints for consumer goods so that $Y77$ should approximate to $Y77^*$. We cannot assume that $Y77^*$ will approximate to $Y83^*$: households in rural Tanzania have experienced very substantial reductions in real cash income between 1976/7 and 1982/3, and only part of this should be attributed to the reduced availability of consumer goods. Thus $Y83^*$ might be considerably lower than $Y77^*$ for all households. However, the planned income of the household were there no availability constraints in 1983 ($Y83^*$), might bear the same relation to the mean, $Y83_m^*$, as it did in 1977. That is, $Y77$ is a good approximation to $Y77^*$ and $Y77^*/Y77_m^*$ is a proxy for $Y83^*/Y83_m^*$. However, our analysis of income mobility in Kenya (Chapter 2) suggests that this relationship might be weak.

Recall that we have dropped from the sample those few households for whom $S > Y$ since this indicated either that $G > \hat{G}$ or $Y < \hat{Y}$ to a pronounced extent, implying that S would be a very poor proxy for $\hat{G}$. We are able, through the trace data, to identify an additional small group of households for whom Y was likely to be very much less than $\hat{Y}$, namely those for whom cash income relative to the mean was drastically lower in 1982/3 than in 1976/7. Households with heavily negative transient income will be over-represented, and indeed are likely to predominate, among those households which have suffered atypically large declines in actual income. That is, because households with atypically large declines in income are likely to be suffering from some unexpected catastrophe (illness, death, crop failure), actual income is liable to be a very poor indicator of planned income, and it is the latter which enters the hypothesized supply–response function. In order to exclude such households, having adjusted the 1982/3 cash income by the divergence of the household's cash income in 1976/7 from the mean in that year as described above, those (few) households whose mean-adjusted income was less than 25 per cent of the 1982/3 mean were dropped from the sample.

We have now made some allowance for differences between households in planned income with expectations of unconstrained expenditure, and for those cases in which there were very large discrepancies between either planned and actual income or planned and actual expenditure at official prices. The remaining important difference between households noted above is in preferences. Figure 11.1 depicted two households with differing planned incomes but they were assumed to have the same preferences, hence the slope of the supply–response function when the households planned not to be in the black market was common. Differences in preferences in either Figure 11.1 or Figure 9.3 refer only to the choice between the set of purchased goods and the leisure–subsistence composite. However, since we observe only the proper subset, S, of puchases, in our test differences in preferences between goods purchased at official prices and other purchased goods will also give rise to differently sloped supply–response functions. However, since we cannot observe differences in preferences (in particular we cannot infer them from differences in purchases since these will reflect differential availabilities) we are unable to make any allowance for them.

Both differences in planned incomes on expectations of unconstrained expenditure and differences in preferences will a priori influence which households rely only upon the official market and which also make purchases in the black market. As depicted in Figure 9.3, the only difference between these two groups was that the former had a rational expectation of greater availability at official prices. However, households may also choose to rely only upon the official market if they have atypically low planned incomes on expectations of unconstrained expenditure. In terms of Figure 9.3 such households have their budget lines closer to the orgin, so that for common access to the official market they are more likely to be on the B_3–B_5 portion of the budget line. Finally, households in which preferences are such that time allocated to the leisure–food composite is more highly valued relative to purchased goods are more likely to rely only upon the official market.

11.2. Results

We first estimate the B_3–B_5 portion of the supply–response function, that is the relationship between differences in expenditure on goods at official prices as proxied by our set of eighteen goods, and cash income for those households relying only upon the official market. The purpose of this estimation is to subject the data to a test which if it fails invalidates subsequent analysis: if there is not a clear positive relationship between expected expenditure on goods purchased at official prices (as proxied by S) and planned cash income (as proxied by $Y83$) then either our hypothesis is wrong or the proxies are unusable. Unfortunately, if the model passes this test nothing is established other than that these two proxies are usable. This is because such a positive relationship is, as discussed above, open to the alternative explanation that households do not face binding constraints on expenditure on official markets and so the causal relationship is from planned income onto expected expenditure on official markets rather than the other way round.

Although causality cannot be inferred from the relationship, there is a good statistical fit between expenditure on goods at official prices (S) and cash income in 1982/3 for those households relying only on official markets:

$$S = 0.077 Y \qquad (11.3)$$

$$(6.516)$$

$$F = 42.46$$
$$R^2 = 0.51$$

where ( ) = t-statistic.

Thus, 7.7 per cent of cash income is spent by such households on these eighteen goods (all at official prices). The regression was re-estimated including a constant term but this was found to be negligible and insignificant. Hence, the non-black-market component of the supply–response function lies on the ray 0–B_3–B_5. Further, the income expansion line is linear through the origin (Figure 9.3), which was an assumption made above. Recall that if the income expansion line is linear then the entire supply–response function B_1–B_3–B_5 is displaced by differences in Y^* (income on the expectation of unconstrained expenditure) in proportion to such differences, and this property has been invoked in rescaling observations on the B_1–B_3 portion of the function. The results are also encouraging because they suggest that our proxy for expenditure at official prices is not so noisy as to be useless.

We now turn to the estimation of the second part of the supply–response function, the portion B_1–B_3, which describes the behaviour of those households in the black market. The hypothesis generated by our model of behaviour under constrained availability is for this group unambiguously distinct from that generated by a conventional analysis. Clearly, if households are in fact not availability constrained then the causal relationship between cash income and expenditure on goods at official prices must run from the former to the latter. In this case we should reproduce the relationship already established in equation (11.3), namely that expenditure on those goods is significantly and positively related to cash income whereas, on our hypothesis, an increase in the rational expectation of expenditure at official prices will reduce planned cash income for households making their marginal purchases unconstrained in the black market. Recall that we have previously suggested in Chapter 9 that the black market is itself subject to availability constraints. Some households which are able to make some purchases on the black market are unable to make as many purchases as they would wish even on that market. For this group which is rationed at the margin in both markets, improved availability on the official market would have the same positive effect on planned cash income as for households relying only upon official markets. Only for those households not rationed at the margin in the black market does our analysis imply a negative relationship between the expected availability on official markets and planned cash income. Unfortunately, our data set is unable to distinguish among those making purchases in the black market from those rationed and those unrationed at the margin.

We have seen that for those households only in the official market, whether or not they are rationed at the margin the relationship between income and expenditure should be positive (only causality being different). For those households in the black market the relationship should be positive for those rationed at the margin and negative for those unrationed. Hence, unless all households in the black market are rationed at the margin, our estaimate of the B_1–B_3 portion of the supply–response function should exhibit either a negative or at least a less positive relationship between income and expenditure on goods purchases at official prices.

Our sample of households in the black market was sufficiently large to permit the B_1–B_3 portion of the supply–response function to be estimated separately for each region. The results are reported in Table 11.1.

These results support the hypothesis developed in Chapter 9. In both the entire sample and in three of the four regions the coefficient on purchases in official markets is negative: the better a household's access to goods at official prices the more it had reduced its cash income since 1976/7. Although in only two of the regions was the coefficient and the entire equation on the edge of being statistically significant, the results for the discrepant region (Kilimanjaro) provide no comfort for the alternative hypothesis, for the equation simply failed to identify any relationship between cash income and expenditure at official prices.

The magnitude of the coefficient on expenditure at official prices can potentially be used to calculate the leisure-enhancing income effect by being

TABLE 11.1. *Supply response to availability on official markets for households making purchases in the black market*[a]

Region	Constant	(t)	Expenditure on official markets	(t)	F-statistic
Iringa	204.5	4.0	−3.4	1.5	2.2
Dodoma	387.5	2.7	−3.8	0.5	0.3
Ruvuma	219.5	4.0	−3.2	1.6	2.4
Kilimanjaro	153.7	3.7	+0.7	0.2	0.0
All	194.6	6.2	−1.3	0.8	0.6

[a] Dependent variable is cash income (adjusted to the mean as described in the text) and purchases on official markets are for eighteen goods (S). Both variables are measured in units of 100 shillings.

combined with the black market–official market price differential. Denote the ratio of the price of the eighteen goods on black markets to the official price by b, so that if the official price is P, the black-market price is bP. The income gain from 100 shillings extra access to the official market would therefore be $(b-1)\,100$. If the household is unrationed at the margin in the black market then this income gain will be spent partly upon black-market purchases (which are therefore reduced by less than $b.\,100$) and partly upon extra leisure, so that planned cash income is reduced.

The actual difference observed in our survey between black-market and official prices weighting each of the eighteen goods by its share in expenditure, was that mean black-market prices were 3.0 times official prices. This implies a full income gain[1] per 100 shillings of extra availability of goods at official prices of 200 shillings. The coefficient on expenditure at official prices for the pooled sample, -1.25, implies a reduction in total expenditure of 125 shillings. It follows that expenditure in the black market falls by 225 shillings $(100 - 225 = -125)$. The full income gain of 200 shillings is therefore divided between a reduction in labour supply on marketed production valued at 125 shillings, and an increase in purchase of goods (valued at black-market prices) of 75 shillings. Although such a division of the real income gain is credible, the high standard error on the pooled data coefficient unfortunately means that the calculation is little more than illustrative.

Referring again to Figure 11.1, we have established that the B_1–B_3 portion of the supply–response function indeed appears to be negative, whereas the B_3–B_5 portion is clearly positive. While these results constitute the core of the cross-section support for the relationship hypothesized in Chapter 9, one further prediction of the model is also testable, namely differences in income on the expectation of unconstrained expenditure between households which rely only upon the official market and those which also purchase on the black market. Recall that the former group should be biased towards those who have lower cash income when expenditure is expected to be unconstrained. This is a pronounced characteristic of our sample. Recall that our proxy for income on the expectation of unconstrained expenditure is the cash income of the household in 1976/7 ($Y77$). The mean for households in the black market is double that for households relying only upon official markets.

This concludes our application of the model developed in Chapter 9 to Tanzanian cross-section data. The results are evaluated in the next chapter.

---

[1] 'Full income' gain is that which would occur were labour supply constant.

12
Conclusion to Part III

The central hypothesis of Part III has been that peasant supply of marketed crops was influenced by the consumer goods shortages that developed in Tanzania in the late 1970s. Investigation of this hypothesis is fraught with difficulties, as will have become clear to the reader. We begin the chapter with a brief review of the problems and the devices adopted to circumvent them, and conclude it with a discussion of the implications of our results.

Ideally, a study of the impact of goods availability on peasant supply would cover the availability of inputs to peasant production (including seed, fertilizer, and pesticides as well as agricultural implements), and the supply of complementary activities (including transport to the market) as well as the supply of consumer goods. In conditions of foreign exchange shortage, price controls, and extensive rationing, all these factors are likely to inhibit production in general, and production for the market in particular. Disentangling the specific incentive effect of consumer goods availability would then require simultaneous modelling of all three. Similarly, an ideal study would cover subsistence production and marketed food production as well as cash crops. It is easier to enforce price controls and single channel marketing for cash crops than for food. In a complex control regime such as Tanzania's, effective relative prices can follow a volatile and idosyncratic path. It would therefore be possible in principle for a decline in cash crop production to represent no more than a transfer of marketed activity in favour of food.

A comprehensive approach of this kind is quite infeasible. Data on the availability of inputs and complementary production are only available in the very partial form of the Board of Internal Trade figures. This makes possible only the tentative inference that our results do indeed reflect the impact of consumer good availability rather than proxying the parallel shortage of inputs. The corrugated iron sheets/ploughs/hoes index is the nearest we can come to an inputs index, and this fails to explain the production data, performing very badly relative to the consumer goods only indices. On the other hand, the composite index which includes both types of good (constructed from peasant's opinions on incentive goods) performs best of all. This may be simply because it picks up a larger weight of expenditure; or it may be because it comes closer to capturing the full range of availability effects. The conclusion is that our equations are indeed picking up a consumer goods availability effect, but that this may be compounded, to an unknown extent, with an input availability effect.

A similar difficulty afflicts the other component in a comprehensive approach. There are data on the output and marketing of food, but by common consent they are so unreliable as to be unusable. However, the infeasibility of a comprehensive analysis of production is probably not too serious. The urban sector of the economy became increasingly dependent on imported food during our period. It is quite clear that the decline in cash crop production was not accompanied by a switch to marketed food production; indeed, the evidence suggests that both sectors declined. This would also be expected on theoretical grounds, as consumer goods availability deteriorated in the normal case.[1]

To summarize this discussion, absence of data made it infeasible to control for other aspects of the general availability problem and for other dimensions of peasant supply. In consequence the analysis had to be restricted to the direct relation between cash crop production and consumer goods availability. However, for the reasons given, this does not appear to compromise the qualitative nature of our conclusions, though it does provide a reason for treating the quantitative implications with caution.

Even in this more restricted form, there are formidable problems to be tackled. First consider the time scale. Apart from relatively minor 'fine tuning', production decisions are at best an annual event, and in some cases (such as tree crops) a change may take many years to work through. The latter problem is likely to be acute in the analysis of a recovery. During the phase of decline covered by this study, it is unlikely to be so serious. Uprooting mature trees can be accomplished quickly enough; it is replanting and waiting for maturity that takes time. In any event the relevant period of analysis is the year, rather than any shorter interval. The period of rationing was relatively short, seven or eight years in all. Since our data do not cover even this short period completely, and since time lags are important, time series econometric analysis would only be possible if some way of further disaggregating the data could be achieved. We were able to obtain regional breakdowns of all our series for seventeen regions, so a regional disaggregation was adopted, enabling us to construct a panel data set.

Apart from the technical problem of obtaining an adequate number of observations, there is another difficulty associated with time: the dynamics of adjustment to rationing are likely to be quite complex and may involve long and unstable lags. There are two reasons for this. The first reflects the central part played in supply response by expectations. The decision to produce next year must be taken, to a large extent, in the light of this year's prices and availability. Next year's availability will be heavily conditioned by the aggregate of this year's supply decisions, since these determine the foreign exchange that will be available. We analyse this macroeconomic aspect of the

---

[1] There could conceivably be an increase in marketed food production even as consumer goods availability declined, if there was a really dramatic increase in the food/cash crop relative price, or if food sales gave privileged access to the black market in consumer goods.

onset of rationing in *Controlled Open Economies*. Here we need note only that the process may well be highly unstable, with a tendency to cumulative contraction or implosion. In these circumstances it would be far fetched to attribute rational expectations to peasant producers. On the other hand, simple adaptive expectations are likely to produce continual underestimates of the severity of the rationing problem. An adequate account of expectation formation would therefore have to allow for revision of the adaptive rule itself and this may itself induce highly volatile behaviour.[2]

We have not attempted to tackle this problem directly, though our results do bear on it, as discussed below. Our main equations utilize a simple one-period lag. These greatly outperformed the unlagged versions, as reported above: they also outperformed unreported equations with longer lags.

The other reason for supposing that the dynamics are complicated is that, even if the average severity of future rationing were both stationary and known in advance, peasant supply would follow an adjustment path while money stocks were altered to their new desired level. Even if rationing were deterministic, this process would take time. In the stochastic rationing case which we believe more descriptive of the Tanzanian experience, it is likely to be protracted and may well have the characteristics of a 'honeymoon' period. In the rationed regime, it pays peasants to hold large money stocks to permit them to capitalize on any stochastic, short-term, and local relaxation of rationing associated with the vagaries of the distribution system. During the onset of rationing, supply is therefore reduced less than a barter model would predict, while money stocks are built up.

We have no direct evidence on the behaviour of peasant holdings of cash. However, the real money supply increased dramatically in this period, and it was certainly believed in official circles that much of the increase was held by peasants.[3]

In any event, there are two distinct mechanisms suggesting that the supply response to the onset of rationing will be initially muted, that of adaptive expectations and that of enhanced optimal money holdings.

The other major category of problem in testing the hypothesis is that it involves unobserved magnitudes, namely the actual supply of goods and the notional demand for them at the village level and hence the associated excess demand. Lacking these measures, we had to devise proxies for them, the availability index being an index of probabilities of completing a purchase, and the distribution index being a measure of supply. The construction of these indices was discussed in detail in Chapter 10. Here we need only stress two points. First, they are at best monotonically related to the underlying phenomenon, and will tend to underestimate its severity. The probabilities relate to regional urban purchases, and while it is very likely that movements

---

[2] See Flemming (1976).
[3] The evidence on the real money supply is discussed in *Controlled Open Economies*.

in these will be associated with parallel movements in village shops, they are bound to be much higher than the rural probabilities, and to track relative movements in a fairly noisy way. Similarly, our distribution data relate to goods leaving the factory gate. As Table 10.7 shows, the bulk of them were siphoned off before reaching their official destination at the village shop. While some of this leakage may still reach the villages, the bulk is likely to be retained within the urban sector. Unless the leakage is a stable proportion of total distributions, we are again reduced to a monotonic relationship between our proxy and the underlying phenomena. It should get the sign of changes right, but again provide a noisy measure of their magnitude.

The second point concerns the weighting schemes. In an unrationed framework, the natural weight to attach to a good is its market price. In a rationed framework, there is in principle a choice to be made between the actual (or supply) price and the virtual (or demand) price at which the available ration would cease to bind. In many applications of rationing theory, the virtual price is the appropriate magnitude since this is a measure of opportunity cost.[4] The present context is rather different. Given the existence of excess demand, supplies will always be purchased. This reduces the money stock of the purchaser by the product of the rationed quantity and the actual price paid. The value of marketed production required to restore his monetary position is therefore measured by the supply price: the official price on official markets, otherwise the parallel market price. Hence the supply response induced by a unit change in availability is a function of the price at which consumer goods are actually purchased, not of their virtual price. It is a function of the price rather than being equal to it because of the various dynamic and monetary complications already noted.

While the appropriate price is clear enough, a price needs to be coupled with a quantity measure to obtain the incremental expenditure associated with an availability change. However, our availability data do not permit us to infer either quantities or values. Hence we experiment with three weighting schemes, as discussed in Chapter 10. The first scheme uses the expenditure weights of the 1969 Household Budget Survey. These weights therefore derive from an unrationed period: it is perhaps unsurprising that they appear to proxy the unobserved rationed expenditure weights rather poorly, and that this weighting scheme is by far the least satisfactory of the three. The other schemes rely on questionnaire evidence, the second scheme concerning pre-scarcity spending and the third scheme concerning opinions on what goods would best motivate farmers. While the second scheme looks back to an unrationed period, goods are ranked from the perspective of currently rationed villagers. Hence both these schemes are likely to reflect, in somewhat different ways, the realities of the rationed equilibrium.

In the light of the difficulties and reservations previously noted, the robustness of our time series results is truly remarkable. As the tabulations of

[4] See, for example, Neary and Roberts (1980).

Chapter 10 show, both the second and third schemes work well in the lagged regressions, with availability and distribution each being significant determinants of supply at the 1 per cent level. On the whole the third scheme works better, suggesting that villagers' perceptions are a reasonably accurate guide to their motivation.

These regressions establish that there is a robust and significant relationship between consumer goods availability and subsequent cash crop supply, with reduced availability inhibiting production. Two potential qualifications may be disposed of quickly. First, it might be argued that our results are consistent with a different version of the availability story. If there were a clearing black market, high availability in one period would imply low consumer goods prices; the resulting high relative prices of the cash crops would then induce an increased supply of cash crops. Hence a lagged relation between peasant supply and consumer goods availability would result even if markets continually cleared. The link would still be established, but the mechanism would not involve rationing, and would not require the theoretical apparatus developed in Chapter 9. This argument is plausible enough a priori, but the evidence is clearly against it. Both our own 1983 survey and the 1986 Cooksey survey establish that peasants were typically unable to obtain goods in any market, not simply in the official market at official prices.

The second potential qualification relates to the identity between a household's purchases and sales in equilibrium. If our lagged regressions were simply picking up an echo of this identity, then the unlagged versions would dominate them. In fact, as we have seen, the unlagged versions perform very poorly.

The cross-section analysis was more problematic than the time series. The thesis tested was that, for given black-market prices, among households purchasing in that market those with better access to goods at official prices would, *ceteris paribus*, market less. This was because a positive income effect would reduce labour supply. By contrast, among households not making black-market purchases those with better access would market more as the quantity constraint upon expenditure was relaxed. The data base did not include a complete account of expenditure, and among households making black-market purchases did not distinguish between those rationed and unrationed at the margin. The results, while not counter to our hypothesis, are also decidedly more fragile. The sign of the coefficient upon supply response to expenditure on official markets was generally as predicted. For households not making black-market purchases the relationship was positive and significant. However, for households in the black market, while it was negative for the pooled sample, and for three of the four regions, it was significant in only two of these cases, and in one region there was an insignificant positive relationship. Thus the cross-section results corroborate, rather than themselves substantiate, the supply–response hypothesis.

While our time series results are statistically significant, it remains to be considered whether the effect is economically significant; that is to say, whether the size of the reduction in cash crop production is large relative to the reduction in the value of consumer goods made available to peasants.

The nature of our empirical work means that we are forced to rely on inference in addressing this question. The indices we have constructed to proxy availability and supply do not measure expenditure. Hence, the coefficients in the linear regressions do not measure the incremental value of cash crop output per shilling of increased availability. We have supplemented these regressions with logarithmic regressions, where the β coefficients provide estimates of the elasticity of peasant supply with respect to the relevant index. There are three points to note about these results. First, their statistical significance is broadly similar to that of the linear regressions, with the exception of the first scheme for the distribution index, which is promoted into a statistical significance by the transformation. Second, and unlike the linear regressions, the magnitude of the (significant) β coefficients is now very similar between availability and distribution regressions. This is encouraging for within a rationed environment availability should be proportionate to distributions. A 1 per cent increase in the quantity of goods distributed should increase the probability of availability upon an attempted purchase by 1 per cent. Given this proportionality, the two measures should indeed generate the same elasticity. Finally, the value of this common elasticity is substantially below unity, ranging in the five significant cases between 0.24 and 0.32.

It remains to interpret these elasticities. While individual peasant farmers may spend a proportion of thier cash crop earnings on goods and services produced within the rural sector, the rural sector as a whole must spend these earnings on goods provided externally to the sector, or accumulate cash balances. In long-run equilibrium (i.e. when there is no need to adjust cash balances), rationed or not, the whole flow of cash earnings by the sector will be spent on these externally provided goods. A 1 per cent increase in equilibrium availability would be associated with a 1 per cent increase in marketed production, until the point at which the ration ceased to bind. This implies an equilibrium elasticity of unity.

Our estimates lie well below this, at around one-quarter to one-third of the equilibrium value. The measured elasticity conflates the two phenomena discussed earlier that would dominate the dynamic adjustment following the onset of rationing, namely the conjunction of expectations about future rationing and the enhancement of optimal money balances relative to purchases. The estimated elasticities are consistent with planned monetary accumulation, unless the elasticity of expectations is well below unity. It seems most unlikely that peasants would have been optimistic of an early improvement in availability, as a low expectations elasticity would imply. Since availability was deteriorating, even unit elastic expectations entail systematic forecasting errors. In any event, the estimates imply that the output reduction during the onset of rationing was much reduced relative to its long-run value.

A more sombre implication of the theory is that these low elasticities are temporary, and that in the absence of corrective action they would rise. If corrective action is taken, the natural question is whether changes in availability are symmetrical in effect. If they are, marginal improvements in availability will induce only small output increases. To solve the rationing problem, it would be necessary to break out of the availability constraint, and induce a discontinuous jump in expectations to those of an unrationed economy. Interestingly, recent events in Tanzania have taken precisely this form, with dramatic increases in official aid accompanying the unlocking of illegally held foreign exchange thus transforming the supply of consumer goods in urban and subsequently, rural areas.[5] At the time of writing it is too early to assess the consequences of this switch, but the hope must be that it will be maintained long enough to induce a self-sustaining supply response. In this connection, we note, finally, that the supply response could be self-sustaining even if the long-run elasticity were below unity. This follows from the existence of heavy taxation of cash crops. Adequate incremental foreign exchange may be generated to finance the increased imports of consumer goods, even if the (shilling) elasticity is below unity. To illustrate: suppose rationed peasants purchase 100 shillings worth of goods, selling cash crops for 100 shillings which are valued at world prices, using the official exchange rate, at 200 shillings. Then a supply elasticity of 0.5 means that an additional ration of 10 shillings worth of consumer goods generates production worth only 5 shillings to the peasant, but generates 10 shillings of foreign exchange. The enhanced availability is self-financing in foreign exchange terms, and has the additional advantage from the perspective of supply, of running down the peasant's cash holdings.

The conclusion can be briefly stated. Theoretical analysis suggests that rationing of consumer goods will severely reduce peasant supply, that the initial effect will be muted relative to the long-run effect, and that it will be a difficult and delicate matter to design policy to reverse the process. Our empirical analysis provides solid support for the first two propositions in the case of Tanzania. Empirical investigation of the third must wait on events.

---

[5] See Ndulu and Hyuha (1986).

IV
Peasants and Public Services

13
Introduction to Part IV

One of the most important ways in which governments influence the lives of peasants is through the provision of public services. A major feature of our survey design was that it collected extensive data on access to and use of public services by rural households, and permitted these data to be related to other economic variables. This part of the book summarizes this information (Chapter 14) and analyses it (Chapter 15). This chapter provides a brief introduction, and discusses the problem of valuing public services.

Survey data on the level and distribution of public services necessarily take a quantitative form, such as numbers of children enrolled, or numbers of visits to a health dispensary. On occasion, these data may be combined with information on the cost of provision to yield an estimate of the distribution of expenditures. However, there is no reason to believe that these calculations provide any sort of estimate of the value that households place on these services. To suppose otherwise would imply that provision was 'right' in the rather narrow sense of being set at the levels that households would choose if faced with charges that accurately reflected costs. There is nothing to suggest that public services are distributed in this way nor indeed that they should be.

In consequence, any attempt to value public services has to be indirect. There are two main possibilities. Where the public service is a productive input, it can be inserted in a production function, and an estimate of its value derived from this. This procedure is familiar and will not be discussed further here: it, and a related technique are deployed in Sections 15.3 and 15.4 of Chapter 15.

The other possibility is to infer valuations from the user costs which households are prepared to incur to obtain access to public services. This procedure is used in Section 15.2 of Chapter 15: since it is less familiar, the underlying rationale is discussed here. The means by which households obtain access is of central importance in determining both incentive and distributional effects of public provision.

13.1. Valuation with Free Access to a Fixed Ration

It is often assumed, for example, that the representative type of public expenditure consists of a pure public consumption good supplied at zero price. It follows that all households consume the same amount, so the problem is one of how different households value this common quantity. The crudest solution to this valuation problem is simply to allocate the costs of provision across households according to some arbitrary criterion. If the allocation is uniform across households, public expenditure emerges as highly egalitarian; if the allocation is proportional to household income, it emerges as distributionally neutral. Both assumptions have been commonly made in incidence studies, but neither has any direct economic rationale.

An elegant, though somewhat special, device is that of Aaron and McGuire (1970). Let the utility function, W, be additive in disposable income, Y, which is all consumed in a one-period model, and in the quantity of the public good, G. That is:

$$W(Y, G) = U(Y) + V(G) \quad \begin{matrix} U', V' > 0 \\ U'', V'' < 0. \end{matrix} \quad (13.1)$$

Then the shadow price placed by the household on the fixed quantity G is:

$$P_G = V'/U' \quad (13.2)$$

and the relative value attached to the public good supply by two different households is:

$$\frac{[P_G G](1)}{[P_G G](2)} = \frac{U'(2)}{U'(1)}. \quad (13.3)$$

In the convenient special case where the sub-utility function U is isoelastic, that is:

$$U = \frac{Y^{1-\eta}}{1-\eta} \quad \eta \neq 1$$
$$= \ln Y \quad \eta = 1. \quad (13.4)$$

then

$$\frac{[P_G G](1)}{[P_G G](2)} = \left[\frac{Y(1)}{Y(2)}\right]^\eta. \quad (13.5)$$

It follows that the public good is distributionally neutral in the logarithmic case ($\eta = 1$), regressive[1] if $\eta < 1$, and progressive if $\eta > 1$. The purpose of this illustration is to show that, lacking considerable information on household preferences, it is impossible to draw any firm conclusions about distributional impact even when a uniform quantity is consumed.

Notice that the same model is applicable in the case of publicly provided private goods, so long as they are supplied in a uniform, free ration, have no costs of access, and cannot be obtained in the market. Uniform consumption is now a consequence of government decision, rather than of the economic characteristics of the good, but that makes no difference to the analysis.

---

[1] The convention is adopted that expenditure is said to be regressive (progressive) when it benefits the poor disproportionately little (much).

13.2. Costly Access

In practice, uniform consumption of public services is very rare, outside of the general overhead category of services like defence. The principal reason is that access to most services is costly.[2] Even public goods like empty roads, radio broadcasts, or national parks require some complementary private expenditure before a household can benefit from them. For predominantly private goods, like curative health services, there may in addition be the costs of waiting for service. Indeed, if the public sector provides a private good at a reduced or zero charge, it must either raise supplies to the point at which all households are saturated (taking into account complementary private costs in the absence of queuing), or some non-price-rationing device must be used. Whatever the device is, there will initially be a gap between the demand or virtual[3] price associated with the ration and the supply price which is the sum of the private costs and official charges. This gap means that there is an economic rent associated with access to the service and it will pay households to engage in rent-seeking activities in an attempt to appropriate this rent by obtaining an enhanced share. If there is free entry into rent-seeking, which appears plausible, the rents will be exactly dissipated[4] by these efforts. In other words, the supply price is driven up to equality with the demand price by the addition of these rent-seeking costs. This equality will not in general hold for each household, but for households on average.

This suggests a valuation procedure in three stages, each ascertaining a group of costs associated with the service. The first stage ascertains those charges officially made for the service; the second ascertains the set of other private costs incurred in using the service; the third stage ascertains any costs incurred in increasing the quantity or probability of access to the service.

It is the third stage which is likely to prove most problematic. For example, if children of party functionaries obtain privileged access to secondary education this enhances the rents associated with achieving such political positions, increasing the energy with which they are pursued. There is no realistic prospect of quantifying this type of cost.

At the other extreme, a rationing scheme which operates on a first-come, first-served basis is much more apt for quantification. The only way of enhancing access is to queue, and queue length will rise until the opportunity cost of queuing time of the marginal queue member is just sufficient to close the gap between his demand and supply prices.

To illustrate the point, let utility (W) be a function of consumption of the private good (Y), leisure (L), and government services (G). Let the household have total time T to be allocated between work producing the private good,

---

[2] This was a major finding of the Meerman (1979) study.
[3] See Neary and Roberts (1980) for a discussion of virtual prices under rationing.
[4] See, e.g. survey by Tollison (1982).

leisure, and queuing time Q. Let government services cost P_G per unit with the private good as numeraire, and let access to government services be an increasing function of queuing time, i.e. $G = G(Q)$, $G' > 0$. If lump-sum income is A, and the household's production is $F = F(T - L - Q)$, then its maximization problem is:

$$L = W(Y, L, G) - \lambda\{Y + P_G G - A - F(T - L - Q)\}$$
$$- \mu\{G - G(Q)\}. \quad (13.6)$$

The first-order conditions are

$$W_1 = \lambda$$
$$W_2 = \lambda F' = \mu G'$$
$$W_3 = P_G \lambda + \mu.$$

Hence:

$$\frac{W_3 G}{W_1} = P_G G + \frac{W_2 G}{W_1 G'}. \quad (13.7)$$

If G', the derivative of access with respect to queuing time, is constant, $G/G' = Q$ and equation (13.7) can be written:

$$\frac{W_3}{W_1} G = P_G G + \frac{W_2}{W_1} Q. \quad (13.8)$$

W_3/W_1 is the household's marginal rate of substitution between public services and the private good; W_2/W_1 is that between leisure and the private good, that is, the shadow wage rate. So equation (13.8) states that the household's valuation of the public services it obtains is equal to the sum of the cash outlay (on charges and complementary private expenditure) plus the queuing time, evaluated at the shadow wage.

Of course, if $G'' \neq 0$, this neat result no longer holds. If $G'' > 0$ (<0) so that queuing is increasingly (decreasingly) productive, then equation (13.8) overvalues (undervalues) the true benefit. In the subsequent analysis, $G'' = 0$ is taken as a bench-mark, but this qualification should be noted.

This discussion has been conducted in terms of queuing costs, but it is clear that a parallel analysis could be carried out for any other class of costs incurred solely for the purpose of enhancing access to underpriced publicly provided goods. Indeed, in the one variable factor model adopted here, Q can be interpreted as labour resources devoted to any such mechanism.

The same valuation procedure can be applied when public expenditure acts via factor inputs as when it generates final output, always provided that households are successful optimizers. This procedure will underestimate the value attached to the expenditure, to the extent that information on the resources devoted to obtaining access is deficient; to the extent that the marginal costs of obtaining access are increasing; and to the extent that no avenues exist for obtaining improved access.

13.3. Distributional Consequences

The distributional implications of the preceding analysis are striking. In one sense, in the bench-mark case, there are none. To the extent that public services are rationed, so that there is an *ex ante* gap between demand price and supply price, then a rent-seeking equilibrium will effectively charge households their demand price.[5] Resources are wasted, and households pay exactly what they are prepared to pay for the ration they eventually obtain. The overall distribution clearly differs from what it would have been in a different expenditure regime, but this difference lies in the realm of general equilibrium effects, rather than being attributable to particular categories of spending. This conclusion is quite independent of whether the public expenditure is 'subsidized', that is charged below production costs, or not. Each household benefits from the public expenditure only to the extent that it obtains producer or consumer surplus from it, and in that sense the expenditure is distributionally neutral.

There are, of course, a number of important qualifications to this stark conclusion. First, the rents associated with rationing may not all be bid away. To the extent that they are not, they represent direct distributional transfers to the affected households. Second, the preceding analysis was confined for transparency to a world of certainty, perfect foresight, and finely divisible quantities of services. In a world of uncertainty and indivisibility, matters are less neat. Resources must be devoted to raising the probability of access, and in the out-turn this may be obtained, or not. Provided households form rational expectations, the earlier conclusions go through on average. However, within the average, particular households will be more fortunate than others, so there is an additional set of random redistributions.

Third, there is a quite separate distributional issue concerned with the relation between what households actually pay (inclusive of access costs) and the costs of providing the service. If it is assumed that these costs are constant over the population of interest, however, this point will be of limited intra-group significance. For example, it would not alter conclusions concerning the redistributive consequences of health provision within the rural sector, though it would probably alter those concerning rural–urban redistribution.

Since detailed cost information is available for neither Kenya nor Tanzania, no attempt is made here to pursue this issue further.

13.4. Conclusion

It may be possible to infer the valuation placed by households on public services from data on shadow wages coupled with information about time

---

[5] Another consequence is that incentive effects may be ignored.

spent obtaining access. This procedure can be used to supplement estimates of direct output effects from production functions and provides a feasible alternative to direct estimation of utility functions, where these functions must have public expenditures added to their arguments. These valuations may be used, in turn, to examine the distribution of public expenditures, for example by income quintile: redistributive inferences are, however, much harder to draw.

14
The Distribution of Public Services in Kenya and Tanzania

14.1. Introduction

This and the following chapter are devoted to analysing the impact of public expenditure. The present chapter reports the results of the public expenditure component of our surveys and provides a descriptive basis for a discussion of public services, how they are distributed, and who has access to them, particularly within the rural sectors. Chapter 15 uses the valuation procedure of Chapter 13 and a variety of statistical techniques to analyse the effects of public expenditure.

This chapter is organized as follows. Section 14.2 outlines briefly the design and scope of the surveys. Section 14.3 discusses the Kenyan data, while Sections 14.4 and 14.5 discuss the Tanzanian data, and draw some comparisons between the two. Detailed tabulations are provided in an annex, where the data for the two countries are presented side by side.

14.2. Survey Design

The design of the surveys is discussed in detail, and the questionnaires reproduced, in the Appendix. (See also the annex to this chapter.) This section is restricted to a brief discussion of that part of the questionnaire devoted to consumption of public services. For the most part, this follows closely on the pioneering work of Meerman on Malaysia,[1] eliciting detailed information on outpatient visits, inpatient stays, and other categories of health care, and similarly for education and other services. Meerman demonstrated the importance of user costs in obtaining access to ostensibly free services; consequently particular attention was paid to constructing a comprehensive list of expenditure categories and to the time required to obtain service.

The innovative aspect of the present study was to add a set of questions designed to throw light on the distribution of ill health in the population. This enables us to relate morbidity to other household and individual characteristics, such as income, source of drinking water, sex, and age, and also to relate access to health care to a measure of need.

[1] Meerman (1979).

Since the survey was to be carried out by enumerators with no medical training, it was necessary to devise a list of symptoms which were sufficiently common, obvious, and distinct to permit accurate self-diagnosis while acting as reliable signals of real ill health. In the end, five were selected: fever; diarrhoea or vomiting; fever and diarrhoea or vomiting; cough with no blood in sputum; cough with blood in sputum.[2]

While the principal focus of the surveys was the rural household, it was desirable to obtain some comparative data on the urban need for and use of public services. In Tanzania, accordingly, we conducted a small urban survey and an urban–rural comparison is reported later in this chapter. In Kenya, the Central Bureau of Statistics had agreed with the ILO to incorporate a public service 'module' into its ongoing household survey. Since this was designed to generate somewhat similar data on the use of health and education facilities to our own, and since it was conducted at much the same time as our Kenyan rural survey, it seemed unnecessary to carry out a parallel urban survey of our own. Unfortunately, the CBS data are not yet available and a rural–urban comparison for Kenya must be deferred until they are.

14.3. Kenya

This section reports the main results obtained for Kenya. No attempt is made to give a comprehensive account here, since the amount of data is vast and the permutations virtually endless. In addition, as is inevitable, some of the answers proved less interesting than the questions. As an illustration, we intended to examine the relation between morbidity and the means of sewage disposal. However, the vast majority of the sample reported a common means for this, namely pit latrines. Hence analysis of this relationship proved neither feasible nor, for our sample at least, very interesting.

We have not merged the Central and Nyanzan data since they are very different in a number of important respects, and a merged set would probably not be a reliable guide to the overall position in Kenya nationally.

Finally, it should be stressed that the intention is to report highlights and draw major inferences with respect to our own data, and not to provide any wider survey of the public service position in Kenya.[3]

14.3.1. Morbidity: Quality of the Data

The morbidity data constitute a major feature of the surveys. However, they rely on self-reporting by the household respondent, rather than on obser-

---

[2] We are very grateful to the late Sir Michael Wood, then Director General of the African Medical and Research Foundation, for providing this list. It is an expanded version of the set used to assess child health in the nutrition module of the Kenyan IRS4. See CBS, Nairobi (1982).

[3] For such a survey, see Vandemoortele (1983).

vation by a qualified outsider. Second, they are restricted to the three months[4] preceding the surveys, which, as a consequence of the survey logistics, occurred in different months in the three cases of Tanzania, and Nyanza and Central Provinces in Kenya.

It is therefore important to gauge how reliable the data are likely to be. It is difficult to do this directly, precisely because of the scarcity of data on morbidity for these areas. However an indirect comparison is possible, using the results of the pilot survey for a new information system carried out in 1975/6 by the Ministry of Health.[5] This pilot survey was restricted to Kitui, Mombasa, and Kwale districts, and showed a vast under-reporting by the previous system. (It appears to have recorded less than 10 per cent of the cases picked up by the pilot.)

The pilot probably remains the best source, despite subsequent attempts to improve the overall system. It suggests that there is no very marked seasonal pattern in incidence of the main diseases, so the restricted period and lack of simultaneity in our data are unlikely to constitute a major problem. The major diseases related to our list of symptoms are malaria, diarrhoea diseases, and chest infections. The number of cases of these per quarter is reported very steadily at around 14 per 100 population. These are cases that actually reach the notice of the health authorities, that is they are presented for treatment at a health facility. Our data have 17.8 per cent of the population ill with these symptoms in Central Province[6] (23.6 per cent in Nyanza). However only 79 per cent of those ill in Central[7] go to a health facility (66 per cent in Nyanza) so that only 14.1 per cent (15.6 per cent in Nyanza) would come to the attention of the authorities.

The conclusion is that our morbidity questionnaire appears to be generating data that are both believable *a priori* and fit closely with what little is known from other sources.

14.3.2. *Results for Morbidity*

Tables 14A.1 and 14A.2 present data for the cases where symptoms are sufficiently severe to curtail activity, for example to prevent children going to school or adults from working. The major impressions from Table 14A.1 are that the population under study does suffer a substantial amount of ill health, and that Nyanza seems to be markedly worse affected than Central. Roughly twice as many individuals are incapacitated there (25 per cent as opposed to 12 per cent), and they suffer somewhat more frequent occurrences per quarter (2.2 as opposed to 1.8). In consequence, Nyanza loses well over twice as many

---

[4] October for Nyanza, December for Central, and September for Tanzania. The three month limit was determined during pilot studies so as to generate a reasonable volume of data without unduly stretching the capacity for recall.

[5] Reported in *Social Perspectives*, CBS, Nairobi (August 1976).

[6] Table 14A.6.   [7] Table 14A.4.

days work per head of population (2.7 as opposed to 1.2). In contrast, the intensity of each occurrence appears to be very similar in each case (4.9 days lost to work as opposed to 5.3). The greater ill health in Nyanza does not reflect a radically different pattern of symptoms so much as increased incidence of all types of symptoms.

Table 14A.2 breaks the same information down by age and sex, for all symptoms aggregated together. The main conclusions are that, overall, male and female patterns are rather similar, with females being somewhat more prone to illness, but that the age structure of sickness is quite different between the sexes. In particular, prime age (16–49) females are markedly more prone to illness than corresponding males, one and a half times as likely to be ill, and twice as likely to lose working days. This presumably reflects the toll taken on this age group by very frequent child-bearing.

Table 14A.3 presents data on the frequency of symptoms by per capita income quintile for all cases, not just the severe ones. The major result of these tabulations is that there appears to be very little variation, with the exception of the two lowest quintiles in Central, where morbidity is unusually low. Whatever weight is attached to this observation, it does seem clear that good health is not positively correlated with current income. However, current income may be a poor estimate of permanent income.

Table 14A.4 gives details of action taken by ill individuals. While fewer than half went to a health facility immediately, a considerable majority (79 per cent in Central, 66 per cent in Nyanza) did so eventually.

Table 14A.5 disaggregates the same data by distance from the nearest health facility and by an educational variable, chosen here to be the educational level of the wife (eldest wife if there are more than one). The table also gives the distribution of the sample by these two variables. It shows that Central Province smallholders have markedly more educated wives, but that the distance pattern is rather similar. As to behaviour, distance from the facility appears to inhibit households from obtaining treatment in Nyanza, but not in Central. The probability of obtaining treatment rises with education in both cases. These relationships are examined further in Chapter 15.

Table 14A.6 provides data on illness by age, sex, and symptom for all cases, not just the more severe ones. The incidence of different symptoms shows much the same age and sex pattern as that of all symptoms together.

Table 14A.7 tabulates illness against the source of drinking water. The results are in part confused: for example streams appear to be safer than springs in Central, though the converse is true in Nyanza. However, there is one consistent result of considerable policy significance; communal piped water (and even, to a lesser extent, private piped water) is a severe health risk. It is associated with a dramatically higher than average incidence of illness in Central (35.7 per cent ill compared to the sample mean of 19.5 per cent; 58.9 per cent occurrences of symptoms compared to 32.3 per cent) and a somewhat higher incidence in Nyanza (34.0 per cent ill against 27.3 per cent; 75.7 per cent occurrences against 60.3 per cent). There are a number of possible explanations for these disappointing results. The pipes may provide a favourable environment for the organisms causing illness. Alternatively, householders may assume that piped water is safe, and so neglect to take such precautions as boiling it. A similarly disturbing result is the very high rate of illness for people using boreholes in Nyanza (54.8 per cent of population ill, 102.2 occurrences per 100 population).

Although not too much weight should be attached to these specific numbers, these pronounced differences do suggest that the benefits of rural water supply programmes may be ambiguous at best, and that more detailed studies of the relation between water supply and health status are a priority.

14.3.3. *Principal Implications of the Morbidity Data*

There are four principal conclusions to be drawn from this part of the survey. First, health status is poor, but access to health facilities relatively good: hence the policy indication is a greater stress on preventive measures. Second, there is a marked difference in health status between Central and Nyanza Provinces, with morbidity in the latter being much higher. Third, there appears to be little correlation between illness and current income. Finally, communal piped water supplies are currently a dubious asset from the perspective of health.

14.3.4. *Health Care*

Tables 14B.1 and 14B.2 analyse outpatient costs over the preceding three months. Cash costs are broken down into fees, travel, and other costs; the other type of user cost is the patient's time, and this is broken down into time spent travelling to and from the health facility, time waiting for treatment, and treatment time itself. Typically a course of treatment requires several visits to the facility; for convenience cash and time spent are displayed both per course and per visit.

In most respects, unit outpatient costs are very similar in the two provinces. The average time spent per visit is nearly the same, 2.7 hours in Central and 2.8 hours in Nyanza, with the breakdown for Central (Nyanza) being 1.1 hours travelling (1.2 hours in Nyanza) 1.4 hours waiting (1.3), and 0.2 hours in treatment (0.3). Cash costs per visit are a little lower in Central at 6.5 shillings (compared to 9.3 in Nyanza). The difference is due principally to lower fees in Central at 2.5 shillings (compared to 5.0 in Nyanza); travel costs at 3.0 shillings in Central and 3.2 shillings in Nyanza and other costs at 1.0 shillings in Central and 1.1 shillings in Nyanza are much the same.

There are more visits per course in Central (3.2 as opposed to 2.3); this has the effect of bringing the cash costs per course closely in line (21 shillings in

Central as opposed to 22 shillings in Nyanza) but making time costs per course diverge somewhat (8.9 hours in Central, as opposed to 6.4 in Nyanza).

Residents of Central make more visits per head of population (0.43 as opposed to 0.29),[8] but the number of courses per head of population is very similar in each case (0.14 in Central, 0.13 in Nyanza). In consequence the pattern of costs per head of population is very similar to the pattern per visit. Cash costs per member of the population are 2.8 shillings in Central and 2.7 shillings in Nyanza; time spent is 1.2 hours in Central, 0.8 hours in Nyanza.

Table 14B.1 tabulates these cost breakdowns against per capita income quintile. The numbers are rather volatile in this disaggregation, so must be interpreted with caution. Nevertheless, they again indicate a systematic difference between provinces. In Nyanza, it appears that there is little relation between current income and either costs or frequency of care. In Central, the number of visits per head of population rises, but the unit cost of a visit falls (unevenly) with income quintile.

Table 14B.2 breaks the outpatient data down by type of health facility. Government facilities are grouped into three tiers; dispensaries and health centres are combined to make the first tier, district hospitals constitute the second, provincial hospitals the third. The other two categories are private mission hospitals and private clinics respectively.

The pattern is much as would be expected: private facilities are a great deal more expensive, primarily because of the high fees they charge. Dispensaries and health centres are cheaper than other government facilities, because it is less expensive to get to them. The number of visits per course rises with tier in the public system, but time per visit shows no obvious pattern; in particular, travel time is not greater with tier, presumably because the greater cost is buying faster transport. Time spent per visit is lower in the private facilities, mainly because waiting time is much less.

Tables 14B.3 and 14B.4 give data on inpatient costs over the preceding twelve months. Here the provincial pattern is very different. Inpatient stays are more frequent in Nyanza (2.6 per cent of the population, as opposed to 1.5 in Central), last longer (15.8 days, as opposed to 12.1), and cost more (193.6 shillings, as opposed to 127.0). In consequence Nyanzan residents spend more time in hospital (0.42 days per head, as opposed to 0.19) at greater expense (5.1 shillings per head, as opposed to 1.9). The greater cost occurs in both fee and travel categories.

Table 14B.3 gives inpatient data by income quintile. These results should be treated with circumspection, since the sample size is small (31 in Central, 84 in Nyanza), but once again fail to reveal any systematic pattern. Neither frequency nor duration of stay appear to depend on income in either province.

---

[8] Both of these are rather low by comparison with the study in Machakos by Van Luijk, whose figures would suggest a quarterly rate of 0.73. Comparison with his morbidity data also suggests that the people in our sample are relatively healthy, or only report relatively serious episodes.

Distribution of Public Services 235

The same holds for cost in Nyanza, but this falls, unevenly, with income in Central.

Table 14B.4 gives inpatient data by type of facility. The same facilities are involved as in Table 14B.2 (though the lowest government tier is missing in the Central data). Once again, costs are dramatically higher in the private facilities; it is also the case that duration of stay is below average in these facilities. Within the public sector, fees fall as patients ascend the tiers; in Nyanza, the effect is strong enough to make total costs fall with tier. Costs are much higher in Nyanza for all facilities other than provincial hospitals.

14.3.5. *Principal Implications of Health Care Data*

The costs of accessing outpatient services are very similar in the two provinces; the costs of inpatient care are much higher in Nyanza. Despite this, residents of Central Province make considerably more use of outpatient facilities than do those of Nyanza, while the latter spend far more inpatient days per head of population. Recalling the much higher morbidity recorded for Nyanza, one interpretation of these results is that (relative to Central residents) Nyanzan residents are getting appropriate amounts of inpatient care, but too little outpatient care. The argument would be that inpatient stays reflect a more acute need for curative services, so are relatively inescapable, whereas outpatient services can more readily be foregone. Putting this in perspective, we can note that, compared to Central residents, Nyanzan residents spend 2.2 times as many inpatient days (0.42/0.19 from Table 14B.3), they report 2.4 times as many days lost from illness (2.74/1.16 from Table 14A.1) and 2.6 times as many severe occurrences of symptoms (56.0/21.9 from Table 14A.1). However, they are only two-thirds as likely to make an outpatient visit (0.29/0.43 from Table 14B.1).

What is not clear is why there should be this large relative discrepancy. If it were a simple consequence of differential supply and demand, we should expect to see signs of excess demand for outpatient care in Nyanza, such as longer waiting times. Since these are not observed, it would appear that the lower relative usage of outpatient care reflects a lower relative valuation of the services provided. If this is so, it may also help to explain why morbidity is higher in Nyanza in the first place.

14.3.6. *Education*

Table 14C.1 gives data on attainment in primary and secondary schools. This is measured by a coverage ratio, the ratio of numbers currently enrolled or completed to numbers in a specified age cohort. In view of the amount of repeating, late entry, and the like, we have set these age cohorts rather high, at 5–15 for primary schooling and 16–21 for secondary. What emerges is that there is little difference between the provinces in primary attainment (75–80 per cent) but a very marked discrepancy in secondary attainment (40 per cent in Central as opposed to 11–12 per cent in Nyanza). Interestingly, there appears to be little difference in attainment by sex.[9] Nor does there appear to be any marked relationship with income.

Table 14C.2 reports adult literacy by per capita income quintile and again fails to uncover any pronounced relationship.

Tables 14C.3 and 14C.4 tabulate student costs. In both provinces, the largest single item is Harambee (self-help) contributions, whose importance was greatly increased by the Presidential directive of 1979.

These contributions account for 39.2 per cent of total out-of-pocket expenses in Central and 35.0 per cent in Nyanza. The other two major cost categories are fees (27.0 per cent in Central, 22.6 per cent in Nyanza) and uniforms (21.9 per cent in Central, 29.0 per cent in Nyanza). Books account for 7.5 per cent and 9.0 per cent respectively. Despite this rather similar breakdown of costs, total unit costs are notably higher in Central (452.9 shillings per student, as opposed to 244.4): this reflects the higher proportion in the much more expensive secondary tier. Since this also means a higher proportion of students in the Central population (36.3 per cent as opposed to 33.4 per cent), total cost per head of population is twice as high in Central (164.3 shillings, as opposed to 81.6). Table 14C.4 provides a decomposition by educational level, and shows that unit costs are higher in Central Province for both primary and secondary pupils. Harambee contributions and uniforms together account for 80 per cent of primary costs, whereas fees account for 70 per cent of secondary costs.

Table 14C.3 provides a breakdown by income quintile. The structure of costs appears to be relatively independent of income, nor is there any obvious relation between income and total cost.

The principal implication of these data, however, is to confirm yet again what a high proportion of income rural households in Kenya devote to educating their children. For Central, it is almost exactly 10 per cent; for Nyanza, 5.4 per cent. Furthermore, these are merely out-of-pocket expenses: if the opportunity cost of lost labour supply was taken into account, the investment in education would be markedly greater yet.

14.3.7. *Ranking of Government Services*

Table 14D.1 investigates subjective valuations of services, cross-tabulating those past improvements which are most valued against those which are most desired for the future.

For both provinces, road improvements were cited overwhelmingly most frequently as the most useful of government's past services (42.5 per cent in Central, 55.1 per cent in Nyanza). Other highly valued improvements were in

---

[9] This tallies with other sources. See e.g. Maas and Criel (1982).

primary schools (14.7 per cent Central, 16.3 per cent Nyanza), and, for Central, in health facilities (14.1 per cent, but only 4.5 per cent in Nyanza) and in water supply (12.4 per cent, but only 3.3 per cent in Nyanza).

The most desired improvements were water supply for both provinces (38.5 per cent Central, 25.1 per cent Nyanza), more roads (25.4 per cent Central, 12.5 per cent Nyanza), and improved health facilities (17.4 per cent Central, 24.6 per cent Nyanza).

In view of the data discussed earlier, it is interesting that Nyanzan residents should be so much less satisified with past health improvements, while attaching more importance to these for the future. The great weight attached to water supply improvements might appear ironic in view of their dubious health benefits, but of course they are also valued for reducing time spent on the onerous business of fetching it.

Another interesting feature of the table is the low occupancy of the main diagonal. The vast majority of households would most appreciate a different type of improvement from the one they most valued in the past. Indeed well under 10 per cent in each province most want 'more of the same thing'.

Overall, it appears that people are satisfied with the provision of primary education (at least, it remains the leading priority for very few); otherwise, there are proponents for increased provision of all the other categories of spending considered, with the sole exception of extension services in Central (a mere 2.3 per cent). Indeed these services appear to be something of a poor relation, with few households being much impressed by past efforts either (2.3 per cent Central, 3.0 per cent Nyanza).

14.3.8. *The Allocation of Time*

The surveys generated a great deal of information on the allocation of time, and some of this is summarized in Tables 14E.1, 14E.2, and 14E.3. The amount of time accounted for varies from individual to individual, and also systematically by the main categories reported, namely age cohort, gender, relationship to the household head, and highest education level attained. This variation in reported activity reflects, in part, the genuinely greater activity of some groups, notably prime-age women; it also doubtless reflects a variable degree of under-reporting.

The components of interest in the present chapter are those related to public policy, namely time spent on health, education, and, indirectly, on fetching water. The data are presented in per cent of reported time, and care is needed in interpretation. For example, education accounted for 43 per cent of the reported time for males in Central Province, and for 28 per cent of that for females (Table 14E.1). This discrepancy reflects the larger reported total active hours of females, rather than any great discrepancy in hours spent per year in education; as already noted, these are rather close (376 hours for males, 345 hours for females).

These tables contain a great deal of very interesting information. Consider first the distribution of activity between the sexes. The differences are very marked, though wholly in line with what is known in general terms already. Women work much harder than men (30–40 per cent longer hours), most particularly in Central Province. They do around 60 per cent of the work on the shamba, and virtually all the fetching of wood and water. The only areas in which men predominate are those involving work off the shamba, and the total extent of these is nowhere near sufficient to compensate for their fewer hours on the shamba.

Both sexes appear to work harder in Central. Otherwise, the pattern is much the same in each province except for time spent on two activities: more time is spent fetching water in Nyanza (a staggering 26 per cent of recorded female hours) than in Central (17 per cent), and on a much smaller scale, accompanying others to outpatient services is almost exclusively a female activity in Central, while shared between the sexes in Nyanza.

As to the broad shape of the allocation, two features stand out. First is the very heavy weight attaching to education, around 25 per cent for females and over 40 per cent for males. This simply confirms what emerged from the earlier data on education, and is a consequence of the extreme demographic structure of the Kenyan population. Second is the tremendous diversion of effort into fetching wood and water at 30 per cent to 40 per cent for females, though only 5 per cent to 10 per cent for males. As a consequence, the proportion of time spent on production is rather low, at 30 per cent to 40 per cent for females, and 40 per cent to 50 per cent for males. Time lost through illness, or attendance at health facilities, is relatively small, 3 per cent in Central and 6 per cent in Nyanza.

Table 14E.1 also gives the allocation by age. The heaviest burden in all cases falls in the prime age band 30–49. Education obviously dominates the younger age cohorts, and off-farm employment is mainly in the age range 20–49. Work on own shamba goes on increasing (relatively) throughout, however, so that it occupies a larger share of active time of the over 50s than of the group aged 30–49.

Table 14E.2 disaggregates by relationship to household head. (The table omits the very small number of non-relatives.) Household heads themselves and their wives are reported as having far more active hours than other family members. The children are reported as working substantially shorter hours: interestingly, there appears to be little difference between hours worked by those aged between 6 and 15 and those aged over 15 (except for daughters in Central Province, where the older girls do work substantially harder). The same is true for other relatives, who also appear to have similar time allocation patterns to the children. Indeed, this disaggregation suggests that there are really two classes, leaving aside very small children (and, possibly, very old men in Central): heads and their wives, on the one hand, and the rest. It is true that these data are based on subjective evaluations, usually by the head of the household or his wife, so this difference may reflect bias. We are not in a position to check for this, and in any case, the difference in hours appears to be a remarkably homogeneous phenomenon, so can perhaps be taken at face value.

Table 14E.3 disaggregates by highest educational level attained, excluding time spent in education. This exclusion dramatically widens the gap between recorded male and female hours; the latter are now nearly double the former, in each province. In Central, time spent in wage employment rises with educational level, while that on own or other shambas falls (except female time on other shambas which rises at the secondary level). This is broadly what we would expect. In Nyanza, time spent in wage employment also rises with the primary education levels, but falls at the secondary level. There is very little pattern in shamba working over the primary levels, but secondary-educated individuals of both sexes spend a very high proportion of time on own shamba working. This curious result may reflect the phenomenon of over-qualification in a very thin labour market or sample truncation due to the migration of many of the educated.

14.4. Tanzania Compared with Kenya

In this section, the Tanzanian data are briefly reviewed; since in many respects the general shape of the results is similar, this is accomplished by comparing and contrasting them with those for Kenya, rather than replicating the earlier discussion.

14.4.1. *Morbidity*

In many respects, the incidence of morbidity in our Tanzanian rural sample is intermediate between the Central and Nyanza cases, but closer to the former. The percentage of severely affected individuals (14.0 per cent, Table 14A.1) is slightly up on the Central figure (12.1 per cent) and well below that for Nyanza (24.9 per cent). The same is the true for the number of severe occurrences at 26.4 per cent. Days lost per occurrence are slightly higher than for Kenya at 6.2, but days lost per head of population lie between the Kenyan figures of 1.16 and 2.74 at 1.65. These broad results hold also for the individual regions: morbidity appears to be relatively uniformly distributed in Tanzania. The sex/age pattern is also very similar to that in Kenya (Tables 14A.2, 14A.3, and 14A.6), as is the lack of any clear relation between morbidity and income (Table 14A.3)

Tanzanians are more likely (91 per cent) to visit a health facility when ill even than Central Province Kenyans, and they are much more likely to do so immediately (76.1 per cent as compared to less than 50 per cent in Kenya, see Table 14A.4).

The relation between morbidity and source of water is also rather different. Most notably, communal piped water appears to be marginally safer than average in Tanzania, in marked contrast to the Kenyan (and particularly Central) data. It is true that the improvement is marginal relative to the mean: 17.5 per cent of population ill compared to the sample mean of 20.0 per cent, 34.8 occurrences per 100 population, compared to the mean of 39.6. However, if the original source was a stream or pond, the improvement would be more dramatic. Ignoring all other factors for purposes of illustration, a switch from stream to piped water would lower the percentage of population ill from 26 per cent to 17.5 per cent in Tanzania: and *raise* it from 14.7 per cent to 35.7 per cent in Central Province, Kenya. (In Nyanza there would be little effect, a change from 30.0 per cent to 34.0 per cent.) To repeat, these numbers must be treated with great caution, but there is clearly a need for further investigation here.

14.4.2. Health Care

The similarity between Tanzania and Kenya, particularly Central, carries through to outpatient care. In Tanzania there are 3.2 visits per course of treatment (Central 3.2, Nyanza 2.3); costs per course are 26.0 shillings (21.2, 21.7); visits per member of the population are 0.44 (0.43, 0.29); time spent per visit is 3.6 hours (2.7, 2.8); cost per head of population is 3.6 shillings (2.8, 2.7); time per head is 1.6 hours (1.2, 0.8).

The principal difference is therefore the increased time per visit, and this is entirely due to raised travel time at 2.3 hours (1.1, 1.2), since waiting time is somewhat reduced at 1.1 hours (1.4, 1.3) and treatment time much the same at 0.2 hours (0.2, 0.3).

Yet again, there appears to be no relation between these patterns and income. As regards type of facility, much the same story holds as in Kenya, though there are no private clinics. In particular, mission hospitals are considerably more expensive, mainly because they charge fees while the public sector institutions broadly do not. One difference is that the top tier in the public system, comprising the regional hospitals, is now relatively expensive, because of high travel costs.

By way of contrast with the foregoing, the inpatient data for Tanzania are more similar to those for Nyanza than Central. Thus total costs per stay are 187.9 shillings (127.0 in Central, 193.6 in Nyanza); there are 3.2 stays per 100 population (1.5, 2.6); the mean length of stay is 20.4 days (12.1, 15.8); this yields 0.65 inpatient days per head (0.19, 0.42) at a cost of 6.0 shillings per head (1.9, 5.1). Once again, there is no relationship with income quintile, and mission hospitals are markedly more expensive than public hospitals.

Thus despite morbidity and outpatient statistics very similar to those for Central, the Tanzanian data suggest a dramatically higher usage of inpatient facilities.

14.4.3. Education

Attainment is markedly lower in our Tanzanian sample than in our Kenyan samples, not only at the secondary level (3–4 per cent as compared to 40 per cent in Central, 11–12 per cent in Nyanza), but also at the primary level where it is 56 per cent as opposed to 75–80 per cent. The picture is rather different as regards adult literacy with this ranging from below 50 per cent in Dodoma (similar to Nyanza) to 76 per cent in Kilimanjaro (well above Central at 67 per cent).

Turning to the costs of education, at 291.7 shillings per student these are intermediate between Central and Nyanza (452.9 and 244.4, respectively). However, the much lower enrollment means there are only 22.8 per cent students per head (36.3 per cent, 33.4 per cent) so costs per head of population are only 66.5 shillings (164.3, 81.6): even so, this is still a sizeable fraction of income. As to the composition of costs, there is no equivalent of the Harambee contribution. The dominant cost is now that for uniforms at 58.5 per cent of the total; fees account for only 21.2 per cent of costs, books for 11.1 per cent.

14.4.4. Ranking of Government Services

The most notable difference is the greatly reduced significance attached to road improvements: only 9.9 per cent highly value those made in the past, and only 7.9 per cent attach a future priority to them. This presumably reflects the fact that Tanzanian peasants are far less integrated into the national economy: they are less dependent on good transport facilities to get their produce to market; the availability problems discussed in earlier chapters also imply a reduced priority on transport facilities to bring in inputs and consumer goods.

Health and water supply are highly rated both retrospectively (25.8 per cent, 15.7 per cent) and prospectively (34.3 per cent, 29.4 per cent). It is true, as for Kenya, that primary schools are highly valued (32.5 per cent) but further provision is not a priority (1.1 per cent). Unlike the situation in Kenya, secondary schools hardly figure in priorities. This is literally true for Dodoma and Ruvuma, whereas in Kilimanjaro 4.6 per cent thought it the most useful thing the government had done, and 13.8 per cent rated it a top priority for the future (this regional breakdown is not given in the appendix tables). This suggests that perceptions of what is desirable are bounded by actual experience; hence prioritization tends to be somewhat incrementalist in nature. A final distinction is that extension services are given a moderate priority (9.4 per cent in each case).

14.5. Tanzania: Urban and Rural Access Compared

Table 14F compares the information obtained in the urban survey with that already reported in the relevant rural tables (14A.3, 14B.1, 14B.3, 14C.3). The comparison is restricted to the overall sample averages, as noted in the Appendix, because of the relatively small size of the urban survey. Hence no breakdowns are provided by per capita income quintile, or type of facility.

Table 14F(a) compares morbidity. Urban occurrences of symptoms are somewhat less frequent (27.7 per cent as opposed to 39.6 per cent), somewhat fewer of the urban population are ill (16.3 per cent as opposed to 18.2 per cent), and they lose somewhat fewer days (1.46 as opposed to 1.65). But overall, the main impression is how very similar morbidity is in the two samples.[10] The only statistic that differs in any marked degree is the incidence of the two cough symptoms, at only 7 per cent in the urban sample, compared to 14 per cent in the rural one (the comparable rural figures for Central and Nyanza are 15 per cent and 14 per cent respectively).

Table 14F(b) compares outpatient costs. Visits per head of population are very similar: 0.41 in the urban sample, 0.44 in the rural one. The pattern of access costs per visit is different: as is to be expected, the urban population spends less time (2.8 hours, as opposed to 3.6) and more money (37.2 shillings, as opposed to 8.1). A great deal of this swing follows from the changed form of travel (0.9 hours, costing 11.5 shillings for the urban visit; 2.3 hours, costing 2.7 shillings, for the rural visit). It also reflects a marked discrepancy in fees (25.1 shillings as opposed to 3.5). Waiting time is increased (1.8 hours as opposed to 1.1) but treatment appears to be more dispatchful in urban facilities (8 minutes, as opposed to 12). Since visits per course are rather similar (2.7 as opposed to 3.2), the per course data show much the same comparative pattern. Time spent per head of population is rather less (1.2 hours, compared to 1.6) and cost per head between four and five times as much (15.2 shillings, compared to 3.6).

Table 14F(c) compares inpatient data. The number of stays per 100 population is similar (2.9 compared to 3.2) and so are costs per stay (205.8 shillings compared to 187.9). As a consequence, costs per head of population are the same at 6.0 shillings. However, the average duration of stay is much shorter, at 9.2 days as compared to 20.4 (it may be recalled that the Kenya rural duration figures were markedly lower than the Tanzanian rural one; Central 12.1, Nyanza 15.8). Hence inpatient days per head are markedly lower in the urban case, at 0.27 instead of 0.65.

Table 14F(d) compares education costs. The composition of costs is somewhat similar, except that uniforms are a less dominant feature, and transport becomes a significant component (13.5 per cent) for the first time. The major difference is in the level of costs, up nearly fourfold at 1146.8 shillings per student (291.7). Since there are also rather more students in the urban population (26.3 per cent as opposed to 22.8 per cent), the discrepancy in cost per head of population is still greater (301.8 shillings, as opposed to 66.5).

[10] A similar finding emerged from the study of childhood illness in the Kenyan IRS4. See CBS, Nairobi (1982, Table 7.7).

There are two main findings of this comparison. First, both need (measured by frequency of symptoms, per cent of population ill, and number of days lost) and access to public services (measured by outpatient visits, inpatient stays, and numbers at school) are remarkably similar. Second, cash costs (of outpatient visits and schooling, though not of inpatient stays) are much higher for the urban population, while time spent (on outpatient visits and inpatient stays) is lower.

14.6. Conclusion

The main conclusions of this chapter can be briefly stated. First, this type of self-reporting survey does appear capable of providing realistic and usable data on the need for public services as well as the extent and costs of access to them. Second, need does appear to be highly variable, and very imperfectly correlated with access, at the regional (provincial) level. Third, the user costs of these services are very high, particularly as a proportion of low rural incomes. Fourth, there does not appear to be any very close relation between income on the one hand and either morbidity or access to various services on the other. Hence the distributional issues raised by public service provision are likely to be between broadly defined groups (rural and urban, or simply regional) rather than being related to the personal intra-rural distribution of incomes.

It remains to consider how these services should be valued, and how productive they are. These questions are examined in the next chapter.

Annex

This annex presents selected tabulations of the survey data. Since the sample size is relatively small for each of the four Tanzanian regions surveyed, the Tanzanian rural data are presented in an aggregated form. While this cannot be interpreted as a national sample, it is probably broadly representative of the country as a whole. The four regions span Tanzania's ecological and economic range; even so the morbidity and access data are relatively uniform between them, and it is noted where there is any marked inter-regional variation.

The Tanzanian urban survey is also rather small, but it would clearly be inappropriate to aggregate this with the rural data. In consequence, these data are presented separately. Because of the small sample size, a more restricted range of disaggregation is feasible than with the rural data. In any case the main purpose of these data is to provide some comparison between mean access in the rural and urban sectors, rather than any distributional analysis within the urban sector.

The Kenyan case is rather different: only two provinces were surveyed, each with a relatively large sample, and there are marked differences between them. It would be less appropriate as well as less necessary to aggregate them: hence data for Central and Nyanza Provinces are presented separately.

For ease of comparison, the rural data for Central, Nyanza, and Tanzania are presented together for each type of tabulation. Tanzania urban data are presented separately (Table 14F). The sample sizes are given in Table 14.1 for easy reference.

Most of the data presented in the tables are in a familiar form; two exceptions are discussed briefly here.

Morbidity is assessed by the frequency with which a variety of symptoms are reported. The symptoms, together with the code appearing in the tables,

TABLE 14.1. *Sample sizes for Kenyan and Tanzanian rural and urban surveys*

	Number of households	Resident household members	Mean household size
Central	342	2,150	6.3
Nyanza	441	3,222	7.3
Kenya sample	783	5,372	6.9
Tanzania rural sample	498	3,516	7.1
Tanzania urban sample	117	817	7.0

are: fever (F); diarrhoea or vomiting (DV); fever and diarrhoea or vomiting (FDV); cough with no blood in sputum (C); cough with blood in sputum (CB).

Tables 14A.1–14A.7 cross-tabulate these morbidity data by a number of household and individual characteristics, such as source of water, per capita income quintile, age, and sex. Here we note only that the data offer a variety of measures of intensity of illness. In particular, we can distinguish between the frequency of occurrences of symptoms, and the number of individual afflicted, since an ill individual may have several recurrences of the same symptom, and may suffer from more than one symptom. Per capita income quintiles is the device chosen for displaying the distributional dimension, as elsewhere in this study. Households are ranked by total income per adult resident member, as a crude indicator of their resources relative to their needs. This ranking is then split into quintiles by numbers of individuals. Since mean household size is not uniform, there is consequently some variation in the number of households in each of these quintiles. As elsewhere, the quintiles are numbered from 1 (lowest) to 5 (highest).

Finally, the quintiles are calculated using current income; lacking consumption data, it is not possible to estimate a reliable permanent income measure from the expenditure side. In view of the implication of the trace data that income is very volatile (see Chapter 2), the discrepancy between rankings based on current income and those based on permanent income would probably be great.

TABLE 14A.1. *Morbidity: frequency and severity by symptom over the preceding three months, when symptoms are so severe as to curtail activity*

	Number of occurrences (% of population)	Number of individuals afflicted (% of population)	Days lost per occurrence	Days lost per sick person	Days lost per head of population
Kenya: Central Province					
F	11.1	7.5	6.1	9.0	0.67
DV	1.2	0.6	4.0	8.8	0.05
FDV	0.9	0.5	5.6	9.7	0.05
C	8.2	3.4	4.5	10.8	0.37
CB	0.5	0.1	3.2	11.7	0.02
All symptoms	21.9	12.1*	5.3	9.5*	1.16
Kenya: Nyanza Province					
F	32.3	14.9	5.0	10.8	1.60
DV	4.9	2.1	4.4	10.2	0.22
FDV	6.2	2.4	5.0	13.0	0.31
C	9.4	4.5	5.1	10.7	0.48
CB	3.1	1.0	4.3	13.2	0.14
All symptoms	56.0	24.9*	4.9	11.0*	2.74
Tanzania: rural					
F	10.8	9.0	8.6	10.3	0.93
DV	3.4	1.7	4.1	8.3	0.14
FDV	4.3	1.4	5.3	16.0	0.23
C	6.5	1.6	4.6	18.3	0.30
CB	1.4	0.3	3.7	18.7	0.05
All symptoms	26.4	14.0*	6.2	11.8*	1.65

* These totals involve an element of double counting, since individuals with two separate symptoms are counted twice.

TABLE 14A.2. *Morbidity: frequency and severity by age and sex over preceding three months, when symptoms are so severe as to curtail activity*

Age range	Number of occurrences (% of population)	Number of individuals afflicted (% of population)	Days lost per occurrence	Days lost per sick person	Days lost per head of population
Kenya: Central Province, males					
0–4	23.16	10.00	4.05	9.37	0.94
5–15	15.59	9.16	5.97	10.16	0.93
16–49	18.69	8.61	4.19	9.10	0.78
50+	33.04	18.26	4.63	8.38	1.53
All males	19.89	10.13	4.78	9.38	0.95
Kenya: Central Province, females					
0–4	21.34	9.15	2.23	5.20	0.48
5–15	16.22	8.35	3.56	6.91	0.58
16–49	26.57	13.78	6.09	11.75	1.62
50+	39.55	19.40	4.87	9.92	1.92
All females	23.55	11.78	4.68	9.36	1.10
Kenya: Nyanza Province, males					
0–4	55.73	22.52	4.21	10.42	2.35
5–15	44.77	18.04	2.79	6.94	1.25
16–49	48.59	16.27	2.84	8.48	1.38
50+	75.42	29.05	5.75	14.92	4.34
All males	51.35	19.49	3.56	9.39	1.83
Kenya: Nyanza Province, females					
0–4	35.65	16.96	5.38	11.31	1.92
5–15	46.40	20.50	3.42	7.75	1.59
16–49	66.62	23.94	4.40	12.25	2.93
50+	117.24	38.62	4.26	12.95	5.00
All females	59.99	23.10	4.20	10.92	2.52
Tanzania: rural, males					
0–4	24.78	13.04	2.65	5.03	0.66
5–15	20.41	9.73	3.83	8.03	0.78
16–49	22.02	10.11	3.70	8.05	0.81
50+	50.92	21.10	9.79	23.63	4.99
All males	25.50	11.78	5.16	11.18	1.32
Tanzania: rural, females					
0–4	38.13	16.73	2.80	6.37	1.07
5–15	18.78	10.54	5.39	9.61	1.01
16–49	26.96	13.74	7.03	13.80	1.90
50+	39.43	17.14	8.96	20.60	3.53
All females	27.01	13.42	6.08	12.23	1.64

TABLE 14A.3. *Morbidity: incidence of illness by per capita income quintile over preceding three months, all cases*

	1	2	3	4	5	Total
Kenya: Central Province, % of population ill						
F	4.32	7.24	10.30	14.12	13.47	10.19
DV	0.86	0.44	0.92	0.57	1.30	0.79
FDV	0.58	0.66	1.14	0.38	1.04	0.74
C	6.92	3.29	10.07	7.44	10.36	7.53
CB	0.00	0.00	0.69	0.00	0.78	0.28
All symptoms	12.10	10.96	21.05	19.47	22.54	17.35
Kenya: Central Province, number of occurrences (% of population)						
F	4.32	9.43	15.56	20.23	19.69	14.33
DV	1.44	0.88	2.97	0.95	1.81	1.58
FDV	1.44	1.54	1.37	0.38	1.04	1.12
C	17.29	9.65	15.79	13.74	17.62	14.56
CB	0.00	0.00	2.52	0.00	1.04	0.70
All symptoms	24.50	21.49	38.22	35.31	41.19	32.28
Kenya: Nyanza Province, % of population ill						
F	15.42	15.05	16.34	19.05	15.55	16.17
DV	2.69	2.08	0.82	2.93	2.99	2.33
FDV	2.57	2.42	1.96	2.93	2.54	2.48
C	5.63	5.19	4.90	5.31	5.08	5.25
CB	0.98	0.35	1.31	1.28	1.35	1.06
All symptoms	22.89	22.32	22.39	28.57	22.72	23.62
Kenya: Nyanza Province, number of occurrence (% of population)						
F	32.80	28.20	29.08	45.97	36.77	34.33
DV	7.96	4.50	1.47	6.04	7.17	5.62
FDV	7.10	7.96	4.74	6.41	6.43	6.55
C	14.44	8.48	8.33	10.62	9.87	10.61
CB	3.55	0.87	2.78	4.58	3.89	3.17
All symptoms	65.85	50.00	46.41	73.63	64.13	60.27
Tanzania: rural, % of population ill						
F	11.68	14.09	14.11	10.75	11.94	12.46
DV	1.24	1.39	1.40	2.15	4.73	2.30
FDV	1.37	1.24	1.55	2.30	2.72	1.88
C	2.61	2.79	1.71	3.84	3.31	2.87
CB	0.27	0.31	0.31	0.77	0.95	0.54
All symptoms	15.80	18.42	18.14	18.28	19.98	18.17
Tanzania: rural, number of occurrences (% of population)						
F	15.80	15.63	15.35	13.52	15.48	15.19
DV	2.47	2.79	2.79	4.30	9.46	4.61
FDV	4.12	3.72	4.65	6.91	8.16	5.63
C	10.44	11.15	6.82	15.36	13.24	11.49
CB	1.37	1.55	1.55	3.84	4.73	2.70
All symptoms	34.20	34.83	31.16	43.93	51.06	39.62

TABLE 14A.4. *Morbidity: action taken by symptom, for most recent illness, % of cases*

Symptom	Nothing	Purchased medicine only	Visited health facility immediately	Visited health facility eventually	
Kenya: Central Province					
F	2.2	19.0	51.4	27.4	100.0
DV	0	15.8	36.8	47.4	100.0
FDV	0	0	52.9	47.1	100.0
C	3.5	20.8	46.5	29.2	100.0
CB	0	0	0	100.0	100.0
All symptoms	2.5	18.6	48.5	30.5	100.0
Kenya: Nyanza Province					
F	5.8	28.4	45.4	20.4	100.0
DV	8.8	16.3	45.0	30.0	100.0
FDV	3.4	11.2	53.9	31.5	100.0
C	7.1	44.7	25.5	22.7	100.0
CB	9.4	15.6	43.8	31.2	100.0
All symptoms	6.2	27.6	42.6	23.6	100.0
Tanzania: rural					
F	4.2	6.6	76.0	13.2	100.0
DV	1.6	6.3	74.6	17.5	100.0
FDV	0	7.4	64.7	27.9	100.0
C	2.3	3.9	82.2	11.6	100.0
CB	4.3	4.3	82.6	8.7	100.0
All symptoms	3.0	6.0	76.1	14.9	100.0

TABLE 14A.5. *Morbidity: percentage of ill persons getting formal treatment by education of eldest wife and distance to health facility (Kenya only)*

Education of eldest wife	Distance to health facility (miles)				% of sample
	0–2	2–4	4+	Total	
Kenya: Central Province					
None	72.9	69.4	75.0	72.5	52.1
Part primary	84.2	60.0	50.0	76.9	14.9
Full primary	85.4	88.2	94.4	87.9	23.8
Secondary	88.9	71.4	—	81.3	9.2
TOTAL	79.9	72.2	78.6	77.7	100.0
% of sample	54.2	25.8	20.1	100.0	
Kenya: Nyanza Province					
None	69.3	60.2	47.1	72.3	73.2
Part primary	78.6	65.6	21.7	60.8	14.0
Full primary	60.0	54.5	60.0	59.0	8.8
Secondary	83.3	100.0	75.0	85.2	3.9
TOTAL	70.3	61.6	45.0	62.7	100.0
% of sample	48.2	33.1	18.7	100.0	

TABLE 14A.6. *Morbidity: percentage of population ill by age, sex, and symptom*

Symptom	% of population afflicted within each age range				
	0–4	5–15	16–49	50+	Total
Kenya: Central Province, males					
F	8.4	8.4	8.6	13.0	9.0
DV	2.6	0.2	0.3	0.9	0.8
FDV	1.6	0.7	0	0	0.6
C	13.2	7.4	6.8	11.3	8.7
CB	0.5	0.5	0	0.9	0.4
% Ill*	23.2	16.6	13.6	25.2	17.8
Kenya: Central Province, females					
F	10.4	7.6	13.5	17.2	11.3
DV	0.6	0.5	1.0	0.7	0.7
FDV	0.6	0.5	1.3	0.7	0.8
C	7.3	4.2	7.5	9.0	6.4
CB	1.2	0	0	0	0.2
% Ill*	17.7	12.0	20.6	27.6	17.8
Kenya: Nyanza Province, males					
F	18.7	13.2	12.4	17.9	14.4
DV	3.8	2.3	0.8	2.2	2.1
FDV	1.1	1.4	1.8	6.1	2.1
C	7.6	4.7	4.2	8.9	5.5
CB	0.6	1.0	1.0	2.8	0.9
% Ill*	27.1	19.0	17.7	33.0	21.5
Kenya: Nyanza Province, females					
F	15.7	16.0	17.5	28.3	17.7
DV	2.6	1.8	3.1	2.8	2.6
FDV	0.9	2.5	3.0	6.9	2.9
C	6.1	5.0	3.4	10.3	4.9
CB	0.4	0.4	2.2	0.7	1.2
% Ill*	23.9	21.9	25.6	42.1	25.6
Tanzania rural, males					
F	14.8	9.6	9.1	20.2	11.5
DV	4.8	1.7	1.3	1.8	2.0
FDV	2.2	1.3	1.1	5.0	1.8
C	4.8	2.7	2.6	4.6	3.2
CB	0.9	0.2	0.3	2.3	0.6
% Ill*	25.7	14.8	13.7	32.1	18.1
Tanzanial: rural, females					
F	16.7	11.9	13.0	15.4	13.4
DV	5.4	2.6	1.9	1.1	2.6
FDV	3.9	1.3	1.5	2.3	1.9
C	3.5	2.1	2.3	4.0	2.6
CB	0.4	0.5	0.4	1.1	0.5
% Ill*	27.2	16.5	18.2	22.9	19.4

* Percentage ill is less than the sum of the corresponding symptom percentages since some individuals suffer more than one symptom.

TABLE 14A.7. *Morbidity: source of water by frequency of illness*

Source of water	% of sample obtaining water from this source	F	DV	FDV	C	CB	Total*
Kenya: Central Province, % of population ill							
Stream	41.7	7.8	0.6	0.4	5.8	0.1	14.7
Spring	5.0	8.3	0.9	1.9	18.5	0.9	30.6
Pond/dam	1.7						
Rainwater	27.8	10.9	0.5	0.5	5.4	0.3	17.6
Well	3.6	14.3	0	0	7.8	0	22.1
Borehole	1.2						
Communal piped water	7.8	15.5	2.4	1.8	14.9	1.2	35.7
Tap in house	11.0	13.9	1.7	0.8	7.6	0	24.1
TOTAL (including uncoded)	100.0	10.2	0.8	0.7	7.5	0.3	19.5
Kenya: Central Province, number of occurrences (% of population)							
Stream	41.7	11.6	1.1	0.4	13.7	0.2	27.1
Spring	5.0	9.3	0.9	4.6	25.9	0.9	41.7
Pond/dam	1.7						
Rainwater	27.8	13.5	1.2	0.8	9.2	1.5	26.3
Well	3.6	27.3	0	0	14.3	0	41.6
Borehole	1.2						
Communal piped water	7.8	21.4	6.0	2.4	27.4	1.8	58.9
Tap in house	11.0	21.5	2.5	0.8	15.6	0	40.5
TOTAL (including uncoded)	100.0	14.3	1.6	1.1	14.6	0.7	32.3
Kenya: Nyanza Province, % of population ill							
Stream	36.2	16.1	2.4	2.5	7.1	1.9	30.0
Spring	17.2	12.2	0.9	1.3	2.9	0.4	17.6
Pond/dam	20.4	16.0	1.5	1.5	2.6	0.3	21.9
Rainwater	4.4	13.3	0.7	4.9	2.8	0.7	22.4
Well	7.7	12.2	0.8	1.2	2.4	1.6	18.2
Borehole	8.7	24.7	9.7	6.5	13.3	0.7	54.8
Communal piped water	3.2	23.3	1.9	4.9	3.9	0	34.0
Tap in house	0.2						
TOTAL (including uncoded)	100.0	16.2	2.3	2.5	5.3	1.1	27.3

*See note to Table 14A.1.

TABLE 14A.7. (cont.)

Source of water	% of sample obtaining water from this source	F	DV	FDV	C	CB	Total*
Kenya: Nyanza Province, number of occurrences (% of population)							
Stream	36.2	33.3	8.0	8.7	13.4	5.8	69.2
Spring	17.2	22.3	1.8	2.9	8.0	1.1	36.1
Pond/dam	20.4	25.7	2.6	2.9	5.0	1.1	37.3
Rainwater	4.4	30.1	1.4	14.0	7.7	0.7	53.8
Well	7.7	57.9	4.0	4.5	8.1	6.1	80.6
Borehole	8.7	51.3	15.4	10.0	24.4	1.1	102.2
Communal piped water	3.2	50.5	5.8	12.6	6.8	0	75.7
Tap in house	0.2						
TOTAL (including uncoded)	100.0	34.3	5.6	6.5	10.6	3.2	60.3
Tanzania: rural, % of population ill							
Stream	22.4	16.4	2.9	3.0	3.7	0.9	26.9
Spring	17.5	14.6	3.1	1.6	1.8	0.5	21.5
Pond/dam	4.5	21.5	0.6	1.3	4.4	0.6	28.5
Rainwater	1.7						
Well	21.7	8.8	1.8	1.2	2.5	0.5	14.8
Borehole	1.1						
Communal piped water	29.7	10.7	2.2	1.8	2.8	0.4	17.8
Tap in house	0.9						
TOTAL (including uncoded)	100.0	12.4	2.3	1.9	2.9	0.5	20.0
Tanzania: rural, number of occurrences (% of population)							
Stream	22.4	20.9	5.8	9.1	14.7	4.4	55.0
Spring	17.5	17.2	6.2	4.9	7.1	2.4	37.7
Pond/dam	4.5	22.2	1.3	3.8	17.7	3.2	48.1
Rainwater	1.7						
Well	21.7	9.6	3.7	3.5	9.9	2.6	29.3
Borehole	1.1						
Communal piped water	29.7	13.9	4.4	5.4	11.1	1.9	36.7
Tap in house	0.9						
TOTAL (including uncoded)	100.0	15.1	4.5	5.6	11.5	2.7	39.4

*See note to Table 14A.1.

TABLE 14B.1. Outpatient costs over the preceding three months by per capita income quintile (PCIQ)

PCIQ	Visits*	Time (h)				Costs (Ksh)				
		Travel	Waiting	Treatment	Total	Fees	Travel	Other	Total
1	2.3	4.0	1.1	0.3	5.5	37.6	14.8	0.1	52.4
2	4.1	4.7	3.4	1.0	9.1	7.5	18.3	3.2	28.9
3	2.7	2.9	3.0	0.6	6.4	1.4	9.3	5.2	15.9
4	3.3	3.5	2.4	0.7	6.5	7.4	9.6	1.5	18.6
5	3.5	3.6	11.6	0.6	15.8	2.8	3.3	5.2	11.2
TOTAL	3.2	3.6	4.6	0.6	8.9	8.1	9.9	3.2	21.2
Kenya: Central Province, costs per visit									
1	0.20	1.7	0.5	0.1	2.4	16.0	6.3	0.0	22.4
2	0.37	1.1	0.8	0.2	2.2	1.8	4.5	0.8	7.1
3	0.40	1.1	1.1	0.2	2.4	0.5	3.4	1.9	5.9
4	0.57	1.0	0.7	0.2	2.0	2.2	2.9	0.5	5.6
5	0.58	1.0	3.3	0.2	4.6	0.8	1.0	1.5	3.2
TOTAL	0.43	1.1	1.4	0.2	2.7	2.5	3.0	1.0	6.5
Kenya: Nyanza Province, costs per course									
1	2.2	2.7	2.6	0.8	6.0	22.0	4.8	0.8	27.6
2	3.0	3.8	6.3	1.0	11.2	3.5	7.3	5.0	15.7
3	2.3	2.8	1.6	0.5	4.9	13.2	14.2	2.5	29.9
4	1.9	1.5	1.8	0.5	3.7	13.1	8.2	4.5	25.8
5	2.2	2.6	2.4	0.6	5.6	3.8	5.4	0.4	9.6
TOTAL	2.3	2.7	3.0	0.7	6.4	11.7	7.5	2.5	21.7

*Visits column gives visits per course in costs per course panels, and gives visits per head of population in costs per visit panels.

TABLE 14B.1. Outpatient costs over the preceding three months by per capita income quintile (PCIQ)

PCIQ	Visits*	Time (h)				Costs (Ksh)			
		Travel	Waiting	Treatment	Total	Fees	Travel	Other	Total
Kenya: Nyanza Province, costs per visit									
1	0.29	1.2	1.2	0.3	2.7	9.8	2.1	0.4	12.3
2	0.42	1.3	2.1	0.3	3.8	1.2	2.5	1.7	5.3
3	0.23	1.2	0.7	0.2	2.1	5.7	6.1	1.1	12.9
4	0.27	0.8	0.9	0.2	2.0	6.9	4.3	2.4	13.5
5	0.26	1.2	1.1	0.3	2.6	1.7	2.5	0.2	4.4
TOTAL	0.29	1.2	1.3	0.3	2.8	5.0	3.2	1.1	9.3
Tanzania: rural, costs per course									
1	2.9	6.8	3.3	0.9	11.0	8.8	5.8	1.7	16.3
2	3.8	9.5	6.3	1.4	17.2	16.0	8.6	3.4	28.0
3	3.1	4.7	2.6	0.7	7.9	8.6	8.3	1.9	18.8
4	2.8	7.2	1.8	0.4	9.4	6.2	7.9	6.6	20.6
5	3.5	8.3	3.4	0.5	12.2	15.2	12.2	12.0	39.4
TOTAL	3.2	7.4	3.5	0.8	11.7	11.3	8.9	5.8	26.0
Tanzania: rural, costs per visit									
1	0.34	2.4	1.2	0.3	3.8	3.1	2.0	0.6	5.7
2	0.54	2.5	1.7	0.4	4.5	4.2	2.2	0.9	7.3
3	0.37	1.5	0.8	0.2	2.6	2.8	2.7	0.6	6.1
4	0.41	2.6	0.7	0.1	3.4	2.2	2.8	2.4	7.4
5	0.54	2.4	1.0	0.1	3.5	4.4	3.5	3.4	11.3
TOTAL	0.44	2.3	1.1	0.2	3.6	3.5	2.7	1.8	8.1

*Visits column gives visits per course in costs per course panels, and gives visits per head of population in costs per visit panels.

TABLE 14B.1a. *Time and cost of outpatient care per member of population over preceding three months by per capita income quantile (PCIQ)*

PCIQ	Kenya Central		Kenya Nyanza		Tanzania rural	
	Time (h)	Cost (Ksh)	Time (h)	Cost (Ksh)	Time (h)	Cost (Tsh)
1	0.46	4.4	0.78	3.6	1.32	2.0
2	0.82	2.6	1.56	2.2	2.42	3.9
3	0.94	2.3	0.49	3.0	0.95	2.3
4	1.12	3.2	0.52	3.6	1.40	3.1
5	2.66	1.9	0.67	1.1	1.87	6.0
TOTAL	1.19	2.8	0.80	2.7	1.60	3.6

TABLE 14B.2. *Outpatient costs over the preceding three months by type of facility*

Kenya: Central Province, costs per course

Facility	Number of courses	Time (h)				Costs (Ksh)				
		Travel	Waiting	Treatment	Total	Fees	Travel	Other	Total	
Dispensary/health centre	189	3.0	5.1	0.5	8.7	0.9	3.6	2.7	7.1	
District hospital	52	3.9	5.3	0.8	9.9	0.4	15.7	3.8	19.9	
Provincial hospital	12	8.0	4.8	1.4	14.1	0.0	22.8	8.6	31.4	
Mission hospital	23	5.5	0.9	0.7	7.1	61.7	20.0	3.3	84.9	
Private clinic	13	3.7	1.3	0.8	5.8	56.2	48.5	3.8	108.5	

Kenya: Central Province, costs per visit

Facility	Visits per course	Time (h)				Costs (Ksh)				
		Travel	Waiting	Treatment	Total	Fees	Travel	Other	Total	
Dispensary/health centre	2.9	1.0	1.7	0.2	3.0	0.3	1.2	0.9	2.4	
District hospital	3.9	1.0	1.4	0.2	2.6	0.1	4.0	1.0	5.1	
Provincial hospital	4.3	1.8	1.1	0.3	3.3	0.0	5.3	2.0	7.3	
Mission hospital	3.6	1.6	0.3	0.2	2.0	17.3	5.6	0.9	23.8	
Private clinic	3.7	1.0	0.4	0.2	1.6	15.2	13.1	1.0	29.4	

Kenya: Nyanza Province, costs per course

Facility	Number of courses	Time (h)			Costs (Ksh)			
		Travel	Waiting	Treatment	Total	Fees	Travel	Other	Total
Dispensary/health centre	221	2.0	2.2	0.5	4.7	5.0	4.2	2.6	11.9
District hospital	114	3.6	4.8	1.0	9.4	8.8	13.0	3.1	25.0
Provincial hospital	21	5.0	4.8	1.3	11.0	4.9	14.8	3.1	22.8
Mission hospital	32	3.2	1.8	0.8	5.8	27.7	6.0	0.3	34.0
Private clinic	14	1.4	0.8	0.4	2.7	114.3	6.1	0.6	121.0

Kenya: Nyanza Province, costs per visit

Facility	Visits per course	Time (h)			Costs (Ksh)			
		Travel	Waiting	Treatment	Total	Fees	Travel	Other	Total
Dispensary/health centre	2.0	1.0	1.1	0.2	2.3	2.5	2.1	1.3	5.8
District hospital	2.7	1.3	1.8	0.4	3.5	3.3	4.9	1.2	9.4
Provincial hospital	3.6	1.4	1.3	0.3	3.0	1.4	4.1	0.9	6.3
Mission hospital	2.3	1.4	0.8	0.4	2.6	12.2	2.6	0.1	14.9
Private clinic	2.0	0.7	0.4	0.2	1.3	57.1	3.0	0.3	60.5

TABLE 14B.2. *(cont.)*

Tanzania: rural, costs per course

Facility	Number of courses	Time (h)			Costs (Tsh)				
		Travel	Waiting	Treatment	Total	Fees	Travel	Other	Total
Dispensary/health centre	336	6.5	2.4	0.7	9.7	3.0	5.4	2.7	11.2
District hospital	41	8.6	8.8	1.0	18.3	0.0	4.0	2.2	6.2
Regional hospital	15	17.1	7.4	1.2	25.7	0.0	50.3	0.0	50.3
Mission hospital	87	8.7	4.3	0.8	13.8	50.7	17.9	20.7	89.2

Tanzania: rural, costs per visit

Facility	Visits per course	Time (h)			Costs (Tsh)				
		Travel	Waiting	Treatment	Total	Fees	Travel	Other	Total
Dispensary/health centre	3.2	2.1	0.8	0.2	3.1	1.0	1.7	0.9	3.5
District hospital	3.1	2.8	2.8	0.3	6.0	0.0	1.3	0.7	2.0
Regional hospital	3.9	4.3	1.9	0.3	6.5	0.0	12.8	0.0	12.8
Mission hospital	3.4	2.6	1.3	0.2	4.0	14.8	5.2	6.1	26.1

TABLE 14B.3. *Annual inpatient frequency and costs per stay by per capita income quintile (PCIQ)*

PCIQ	Length of stay (days)	Costs of stay (sh)				Stays % of population	Days per head of population	Cost per head of population (sh)
		Fees	Travel	Other	Total			
Kenya: Central Province								
1	13.8	252.0	20.4	32.0	304.4	1.4	0.20	4.4
2	12.8	137.2	19.8	8.3	165.3	1.3	0.17	2.2
3	13.8	22.5	22.4	9.0	53.9	2.3	0.32	1.2
4	14.0	101.5	20.3	23.3	145.2	1.1	0.16	1.7
5	5.0	24.2	13.5	6.7	44.3	1.6	0.08	0.7
TOTAL	12.1	92.8	19.6	14.5	127.0	1.5	0.19	1.9
Kenya: Nyanza Province								
1	15.5	175.9	59.6	16.5	252.1	2.0	0.30	4.9
2	13.6	114.9	58.9	11.1	184.8	2.9	0.40	5.4
3	19.7	34.3	37.5	3.0	74.8	3.3	0.64	2.4
4	11.3	150.3	23.8	21.6	195.7	2.6	0.29	5.0
5	17.6	186.2	82.0	12.2	280.3	2.7	0.47	7.5
TOTAL	15.8	128.3	53.1	12.2	193.6	2.6	0.42	5.1
Tanzania: rural								
1	21.6	57.5	17.4	37.5	112.4	4.1	0.89	4.6
2	20.9	81.2	15.4	16.1	112.6	2.0	0.42	2.3
3	20.1	52.3	62.8	96.9	211.9	2.5	0.50	5.3
4	18.8	66.5	52.8	84.0	203.3	4.0	0.75	8.1
5	20.4	80.2	38.7	160.3	279.2	3.2	0.65	8.9
TOTAL	20.4	67.1	37.0	83.9	187.9	3.2	0.65	6.0

TABLE 14B.4. *Annual inpatient frequency and costs per stay by type of facility*
Kenya: Central Province

Facility	Number of stays	Length of stay (days)	Costs of stay (Ksh)			
			Fees	Travel	Other	Total
District hospital	19	13.3	14.9	18.6	4.7	38.2
Provincial hospital	5	10.6	10.0	18.4	20.0	48.4
Mission hospital	6	12.2	256.5	21.8	21.7	300.0
Private clinic	3	6.7	396.7	24.0	53.3	474.0

Kenya: Nyanza Province

Facility	Number of stays	Length of stay (days)	Costs of stay (Ksh)			
			Fees	Travel	Other	Total
Health centre	18	10.2	109.7	27.6	26.7	164.0
District hospital	39	20.4	56.7	53.9	5.4	116.1
Provincial hospital	5	22.2	15.0	11.4	0.0	26.4
Mission hospital	17	13.1	270.6	83.4	18.4	372.4
Private clinic	4	6.8	467.0	22.3	7.5	496.8

Tanzania: rural

Facility	Number of stays	Length of stay (days)	Costs of stay (Tsh)			
			Fees	Travel	Other	Total
Health centre	27	14.0	24.3	7.0	30.0	61.3
District hospital	20	24.5	12.5	85.4	90.0	187.9
Regional hospital	11	25.6	0.0	37.4	100.0	137.4
Mission hospital	54	21.0	122.3	34.0	105.2	261.6

TABLE 14C.1. *Primary and secondary school attainment by sex and per capita income quintile (numbers attaining level of education as % of numbers in specified age cohort)*

PCIQ	Primary school attainment as % of age cohort 5–15		Secondary school attainment as % of age cohort 16–21	
	Males	Females	Males	Females
Kenya: Central Province				
1	80.6	81.2	33.3	47.8
2	81.7	73.5	44.1	42.3
3	74.3	83.9	52.4	36.4
4	81.8	81.2	33.3	31.3
5	70.7	78.8	45.8	36.8
TOTAL	78.2	79.6	41.7	38.5
Kenya: Nyanza Province				
1	75.6	77.4	13.0	11.8
2	86.3	76.4	23.1	16.7
3	79.7	73.6	9.1	6.7
4	83.8	77.3	8.0	8.6
5	86.7	75.9	8.5	12.0
TOTAL	81.6	76.3	11.9	11.5
Tanzania: rural				
1	56.8	60.9	5.2	0.0
2	48.5	64.1	2.8	9.8
3	53.7	49.0	7.4	1.9
4	59.7	61.5	2.2	10.8
5	53.6	55.7	0.0	0.0
TOTAL	54.6	58.3	3.2	4.2

TABLE 14C.2. *Adult literacy by per capita income quintile (%)*

PCIQ	Kenya		Tanzania			
	Central	Nyanza	Ruvuma	Iringa	Dodoma	Kilimanjaro
All adults						
1	69.46	52.43	44.44	63.33	37.38	71.91
2	69.70	54.01	73.77	66.98	47.96	76.92
3	71.05	42.15	58.00	62.16	50.00	78.95
4	60.76	53.64	57.41	74.23	48.86	70.87
5	65.80	47.68	72.00	75.28	44.00	83.95
All adults	67.01	49.77	60.79	67.88	45.49	76.29
Adult males						
1	77.03	71.52	66.67	77.05	50.00	89.19
2	83.33	71.79	83.33	84.31	73.33	90.48
3	80.23	64.75	68.18	78.00	58.93	85.37
4	77.45	70.64	66.67	89.74	62.79	81.13
5	80.85	68.71	85.71	88.10	58.70	91.43
Adult males	79.87	69.42	74.02	82.72	60.78	87.34
Adult females						
1	63.44	37.07	27.78	49.15	29.23	59.62
2	56.86	40.76	64.52	50.91	26.42	61.11
3	63.46	25.27	50.00	49.18	40.00	74.07
4	48.15	41.45	48.15	63.79	35.56	60.00
5	51.52	30.11	62.07	63.83	31.48	78.26
Adult females	56.10	34.59	49.67	55.00	32.21	66.41

TABLE 14C.3. *Annual education costs by per capita income quintile*

Kenya: Central Province

PCIQ	Costs per student % breakdown						Total cost per student (Ksh)	% of students in population	Cost per head of population (Ksh)
	Fees	Harambee cost	Books	Uniform	Transport	Other			
1	29.0	34.4	10.3	21.3	0.5	4.5	555.4	38.3	212.9
2	21.3	42.9	7.2	25.6	0.4	2.7	424.3	37.3	158.2
3	18.4	51.7	6.8	19.6	0.3	3.2	457.7	33.9	155.0
4	25.1	40.1	6.2	22.5	1.1	4.9	366.5	39.3	144.1
5	42.7	26.0	7.1	20.3	1.0	2.9	520.3	31.9	165.8
TOTAL	27.0	39.2	7.5	21.9	0.7	3.7	452.9	36.3	164.3

Kenya: Nyanza Province

PCIQ	Costs per student % breakdown						Total cost per student (Ksh)	% of students in population	Cost per head of population (Ksh)
	Fees	Harambee cost	Books	Uniform	Transport	Other			
1	22.3	30.8	11.2	31.2	0.1	4.3	257.9	34.5	89.0
2	36.3	28.9	8.1	21.6	0.1	5.0	250.6	32.0	80.2
3	27.9	32.2	4.4	32.4	1.9	1.3	176.4	31.4	55.4
4	8.0	39.8	11.9	32.3	5.1	3.0	224.6	35.0	78.6
5	19.9	42.1	7.5	27.8	1.6	1.1	297.1	33.8	100.4
TOTAL	22.6	35.0	9.0	29.0	1.5	3.0	244.4	33.4	81.6

TABLE 14C.3. (cont.)

Tanzania: rural

PCIQ	Costs per student % breakdown					Total cost per student (Tsh)	% of students in population	Cost per head of population (Tsh)
	Fees	Books	Uniform	Transport	Other			
1	13.0	14.8	64.4	1.1	6.7	264.2	24.9	65.7
2	21.1	18.2	51.2	0.7	8.9	218.4	23.4	51.1
3	22.7	11.6	54.3	1.2	10.3	379.7	19.8	75.3
4	32.2	7.8	54.6	0.0	5.4	350.9	21.7	76.0
5	17.6	6.3	65.2	0.2	10.7	273.9	23.8	65.1
TOTAL	21.3	11.1	58.5	0.6	8.4	291.7	22.8	66.5

TABLE 14C.4. Annual education costs by educational level and per capita income quintiles

Educational level	Costs per student % breakdown						Total cost per student (sh)	% of students in population	Cost per head of population (sh)
	Fees	Harambee cost	Books	Uniform	Transport	Other			
Kenya: Central Province									
Primary	4.9	54.9	9.6	27.7	0.1	2.8	324.0	30.6	99.1
Secondary	63.1	15.3	3.2	13.1	1.5	3.7	1,527.2	3.6	55.4
Kenya: Nyanza Province									
Primary	8.3	42.8	9.6	34.8	1.5	3.0	207.0	30.5	63.1
Secondary	77.4	5.7	7.7	5.1	0.6	3.4	1,310.0	1.2	15.5
Tanzania: rural									
Primary	17.1	—	11.9	61.8	0.4	8.8	270.5	21.6	58.5
Secondary	72.9	—	4.0	22.4	0.0	0.7	1,672.7	0.3	4.3

TABLE 14D.1. *Government services: most valued improvements (% of households)*

What was most useful since 1975	What would be most useful in future						
	Roads	Extension service	Health	Water supply	Primary school	Secondary school	Other	Total
Kenya: Central Province								
Roads	1.7	1.0	8.7	25.8	0.3	3.0	2.0	42.5
Extension service	0.7	0	0.3	1.0	0	0	0.3	2.3
Health	7.0	0	1.3	4.0	0.3	0.3	1.0	14.1
Water supply	6.4	1.0	1.0	0.7	0	1.7	1.7	12.4
Primary school	3.7	0.3	3.3	4.0	0	2.7	0.7	14.7
Secondary school	2.3	0	0.7	2.3	0	0	0.7	6.0
Other	3.7	0	2.0	0.7	0.7	0.3	0.7	8.0
TOTAL	25.4	2.3	17.4	38.5	1.3	8.0	7.1	100.0 (299)
Kenya: Nyanza Province								
Roads	2.3	7.5	18.1	14.3	3.3	6.0	3.8	55.1
Extension service	0.3	0.8	0.3	0.5	0	0.3	1.0	3.0
Health	1.5	0.3	0.5	1.5	0	0.5	0.3	4.5
Water supply	1.3	0.3	0.3	0.5	0	0.3	0.8	3.3
Primary school	4.8	0.5	2.8	2.8	0	4.5	1.0	16.3
Secondary school	1.0	0	1.0	1.8	0.8	0.3	0.5	5.3
Other	1.5	0.8	1.8	3.8	0	0.8	4.0	12.5
TOTAL	12.5	10.0	24.6	25.1	4.0	12.5	11.3	100.0 (399)

Tanzania: rural						
Roads	0	0.7	3.1	4.0	0.2	0	1.8	9.9
Extension service	0.2	0.5	1.8	4.5	0	0.7	1.8	9.4
Health	2.7	2.5	4.0	10.5	0.2	2.9	2.9	25.8
Water supply	2.2	2.9	8.7	0	0	0.2	1.6	15.7
Primary school	1.8	2.5	14.4	9.0	0.5	0.2	4.3	32.5
Secondary school	0.5	0	0.2	0	0	0	0.2	1.1
Other	0.5	0.5	2.0	1.1	0.2	0	1.4	5.6
TOTAL	7.9	9.4	34.3	29.4	1.1	4.0	13.9	100.0 (446)

TABLE 14E.1. Allocation of time by age and sex (% of total reported time)

Activity	0–5	6–9	10–15	16–19	20–9	30–49	50+	Total
Central Province, males								
Work on own shamba	0.00	1.64	4.11	25.68	29.23	37.98	62.25	25.89
Off-farm wage employment	0.00	0.00	0.00	0.00	27.37	31.33	9.25	11.94
Own business	0.00	0.00	0.00	0.00	5.81	13.65	9.92	5.35
Work on estates	0.00	0.00	0.00	0.00	1.93	0.03	1.33	0.47
Work on other shambas	0.00	0.00	0.12	3.46	12.87	6.17	5.50	4.28
Fetching water	0.00	2.35	2.93	1.74	3.51	4.99	2.79	3.22
Fetching wood	0.00	1.12	1.97	1.92	2.64	3.51	3.54	2.52
Education	27.80	91.28	88.11	66.48	14.44	0.00	0.00	42.86
Outpatient time	9.49	1.82	0.63	0.05	0.25	0.21	1.94	0.86
Accompanying outpatient	0.00	0.00	0.01	0.00	0.00	0.22	0.17	0.08
Inpatient time	3.34	0.17	0.00	0.00	0.00	0.10	0.23	0.11
Other illness	59.36	1.62	2.11	0.67	1.97	1.80	3.07	2.43
Total people	178	180	224	90	114	133	115	1034
Average hours/year	40	621	1,054	1,003	1,033	1,507	1,254	878
Central Province, females								
Work on own shamba	0.00	2.87	6.54	18.82	36.36	42.09	43.44	29.01
Off-farm wage employment	0.00	0.00	0.83	2.06	5.06	5.11	0.86	2.81
Own business	0.00	0.00	0.00	0.00	1.36	4.00	0.35	1.49
Work on estates	0.00	0.00	0.00	0.00	1.00	0.33	0.00	0.25
Work on other shambas	0.00	0.00	0.28	2.70	8.40	3.86	5.09	3.61
Fetching water	0.00	3.23	7.27	18.96	19.80	20.88	23.88	16.80
Fetching wood	0.00	2.04	5.98	9.97	19.79	20.29	21.24	15.05
Education	44.57	88.97	77.78	44.84	5.40	0.00	0.00	27.68

Outpatient time	15.09	0.48	0.19	0.11	0.36	0.41	0.26	0.36		
Accompanying outpatient	0.00	0.00	0.07	0.12	0.60	0.91	0.15	0.42		
Inpatient time	5.36	0.00	0.00	0.35	0.11	0.10	0.13	0.12		
Other illness	34.98	2.41	1.05	2.07	1.78	2.03	4.59	2.39		
Total people	154	184	223	93	119	187	134	1,094		
Average hours/year	29	566	1,176	1,223	1,710	2,239	1,767	1,245		
Nyanza Province, males										
Work on own shamba	6.18	1.17	11.02	17.08	34.35	40.17	43.07	22.98		
Off-farm wage employment	0.00	0.00	0.00	1.60	14.80	25.15	12.16	8.64		
Own business	0.00	0.00	0.00	0.00	9.17	16.45	13.00	6.17		
Work on estates	0.00	0.00	0.00	0.00	3.12	4.13	2.75	1.57		
Work on other shambas	0.00	0.00	0.05	1.38	5.62	4.39	5.97	2.48		
Fetching water	5.14	4.71	3.52	2.71	4.38	4.54	7.25	4.46		
Fetching wood	2.85	3.03	2.66	2.28	5.10	2.57	4.22	3.13		
Education	34.33	86.91	79.12	70.41	18.55	0.00	0.00	44.62		
Outpatient time	3.43	0.22	0.28	0.20	0.36	0.14	0.41	0.34		
Accompanying outpatient	0.09	0.00	0.01	0.07	0.27	0.32	0.41	0.16		
Inpatient time	3.92	0.20	0.17	0.09	0.06	0.18	0.11	0.24		
Other illness	44.07	3.76	3.18	4.19	4.21	1.96	10.64	5.22		
Total people	256	291	330	130	166	202	179	1,554		
Average hours/year	125	676	1,111	1,049	844	1,379	1,010	857		

TABLE 14E.1. (cont.)

Activity	0–5	6–9	10–15	16–19	20–9	30–49	50+	Total
Nyanza Province: females								
Work on own shamba	8.14	0.76	9.50	22.03	34.50	34.05	34.03	25.16
Off-farm wage employment	0.00	0.00	0.56	0.00	2.11	2.74	1.57	1.56
Own business	0.00	0.00	0.01	0.00	1.93	3.82	4.87	2.16
Work on estates	0.00	0.00	0.00	0.00	0.02	0.00	0.00	0.00
Work on other shambas	0.00	0.00	0.00	0.00	0.03	0.49	1.04	0.29
Fetching water	4.26	9.22	12.54	22.68	32.28	34.89	33.52	26.30
Fetching wood	6.75	4.94	9.21	14.66	20.61	17.40	16.01	14.80
Education	32.89	79.46	64.38	37.30	2.00	0.00	0.00	23.26
Outpatient time	5.28	0.24	0.21	0.08	0.23	0.28	0.44	0.32
Accompanying outpatient	0.00	0.00	0.01	0.12	0.55	0.30	0.10	0.22
Inpatient time	3.13	0.19	0.07	0.08	0.46	0.25	0.43	0.29
Other illness	39.55	5.19	3.50	3.05	5.27	5.76	8.00	5.65
Total people	222	275	281	140	248	343	145	1,654
Average hours/year	110	622	1,288	1,206	1,414	1,799	1,572	1,162

TABLE 14E.2. *Allocation of time by relationship to household head (% of total reported time of those over 5)*

Central Province, males

Activity	Head	Son 6–15	Son 16+	Father	Other relative	Total
Work on own shamba	47.54	2.89	29.81	0.00	12.63	26.12
Off-farm wage employment	21.15	0.00	16.63	0.00	10.65	12.17
Own business	12.46	0.00	2.59	0.00	4.37	5.45
Work on estates	0.76	0.00	0.86	0.00	0.00	0.48
Work on other shambas	6.10	0.09	7.48	0.00	0.00	4.00
Fetching water	4.38	2.23	2.39	0.00	6.25	3.27
Fetching wood	3.98	1.68	1.65	0.00	1.87	2.54
Education	0.00	90.11	36.85	0.00	61.45	43.04
Outpatient time	0.96	1.06	0.18	0.00	0.34	0.79
Accompanying outpatient	0.21	0.01	0.00	0.00	0.00	0.08
Inpatient time	0.16	0.06	0.00	0.00	0.00	0.08
Other illness	2.30	1.86	1.56	0.00	2.44	1.99
Total people	232	342	200	3	44	821
Average hours/year	1,432	915	1,004	0	999	1,084

Central Province, females

Activity	Head	Wife	Daughter 6–15	Daughter 16+	Mother	Other relative	Total
Work on own shamba	39.98	41.68	5.37	27.84	34.23	22.65	29.34
Off-farm wage employment	5.26	2.93	0.00	3.54	0.00	3.07	2.67
Own business	5.07	1.70	0.00	0.00	0.00	0.00	1.51
Work on estates	0.00	0.40	0.00	0.74	0.00	0.00	0.26
Work on other shambas	5.72	4.36	0.22	4.97	16.06	3.23	3.65
Fetching water	19.50	23.57	6.30	19.02	27.21	4.91	16.97
Fetching wood	19.49	21.86	4.70	11.75	15.26	12.17	15.21
Education	0.00	0.00	82.03	30.65	0.00	49.14	27.35
Outpatient time	0.30	0.40	0.22	0.16	1.25	0.24	0.30
Accompanying outpatient	0.20	0.90	0.05	0.18	0.00	0.11	0.42
Inpatient time	0.16	0.11	0.00	0.19	0.00	0.13	0.10
Other illness	4.31	2.09	1.08	0.96	5.99	4.36	2.20
Total people	110	239	333	144	10	65	901
Average hours/year	2,076	2,152	1,007	1,314	718	1,096	1,493

TABLE 14E.2. (cont.)

Nyanza Province, males

Activity	Head	Son 6–15	Son 16+	Father	Other relative	Total
Work on own shamba	40.78	8.76	27.23	35.75	12.21	23.73
Off-farm wage employment	20.01	0.00	9.58	0.00	4.02	8.98
Own business	15.72	0.00	5.75	0.00	0.00	6.42
Work on estates	4.93	0.00	0.00	0.00	0.00	1.63
Work on other shambas	5.61	0.04	1.84	18.09	2.00	2.54
Fetching water	4.41	3.77	5.00	6.62	5.35	4.39
Fetching wood	3.10	2.93	3.53	4.40	3.40	3.16
Education	0.00	80.59	41.90	0.00	69.68	44.30
Outpatient time	0.22	0.23	0.26	2.89	0.21	0.25
Accompanying outpatient	0.32	0.00	0.27	0.00	0.04	0.17
Inpatient time	0.07	0.11	0.22	0.00	0.46	0.15
Other illness	4.82	3.57	4.44	32.23	2.64	4.28
Total people	303	476	308	10	142	1239
Average hours/year	1,397	991	883	829	738	1,033

Nyanza Province, females

Activity	Head	Wife	Daughter 6–15	Daughter 16+	Mother	Other relative	Total
Work on own shamba	28.82	36.61	7.36	29.97	33.71	19.50	25.64
Off-farm wage employment	4.13	1.07	0.00	1.84	0.00	3.05	1.60
Own business	9.87	1.05	0.00	0.00	0.00	3.00	2.21
Work on estates	0.03	0.00	0.00	0.00	0.00	0.00	0.00
Work on other shambas	0.45	0.38	0.00	0.00	0.05	0.58	0.28
Fetching water	29.66	35.29	11.80	20.92	37.01	29.53	26.77
Fetching wood	17.85	18.99	7.97	13.58	16.37	13.81	14.95
Education	0.00	0.58	68.25	28.68	0.00	26.20	22.60
Outpatient time	0.30	0.31	0.19	0.15	0.19	0.22	0.25
Accompanying outpatient	0.25	0.32	0.00	0.25	0.25	0.30	0.23
Inpatient time	0.47	0.33	0.13	0.06	0.00	0.24	0.26
Other illness	8.17	5.07	4.29	4.54	12.42	3.58	5.21
Total people	138	373	405	166	33	251	1,366
Average hours/year	1,957	1,834	1,071	1,197	1,030	1,019	1,374

TABLE 14E.3. *Allocation of time by highest education level attained (% of total reported time excluding that spent in education)*

Activity	None	Primary 1–4	Primary 5–8	Some secondary	Total
Central Province, males					
Work on own shamba	59.51	45.48	40.78	44.18	46.41
Off-farm wage employment	12.61	13.91	22.94	32.22	9.26
Own business	3.63	10.15	12.62	8.43	9.65
Work on estates	0.00	2.19	0.00	4.20	0.85
Work on other shambas	4.61	10.59	8.67	3.20	7.73
Fetching water	4.43	4.54	7.19	4.74	5.75
Fetching wood	6.66	4.85	3.95	0.30	4.48
Outpatient time	0.84	3.73	0.28	0.23	1.20
Accompanying outpatient	0.13	0.00	0.23	0.00	0.14
Inpatient time	0.59	0.08	0.08	0.00	0.19
Other illness	7.00	4.47	3.29	2.51	4.35
Total people	383	295	290	69	1,037
Average hours/year	300	392	796	596	485
Central Province, females					
Work on own shamba	41.44	42.18	37.94	32.40	40.16
Off-farm wage employment	0.48	6.41	5.37	20.61	3.61
Own business	1.56	3.37	2.54	0.00	2.10
Work on estates	0.71	0.00	0.00	0.00	0.35
Work on other shambas	6.04	3.49	3.71	10.54	5.06
Fetching water	23.46	16.88	27.13	16.54	23.35
Fetching wood	21.40	22.54	19.52	19.16	20.92
Outpatient time	0.45	0.47	0.29	0.05	0.39
Accompanying outpatient	0.75	0.29	0.51	0.26	0.59
Inpatient time	0.12	0.31	0.16	0.20	0.16
Other illness	3.60	4.05	2.83	0.24	3.31
Total people	492	272	282	30	1,076
Average hours/year	982	555	1,076	1,085	901
Nyanza Province, males					
Work on own shamba	45.40	35.62	39.97	75.10	41.61
Off-farm wage employment	9.55	15.28	19.18	6.52	14.91
Own business	8.78	12.05	13.66	0.00	11.35
Work on estates	1.01	1.97	5.02	0.00	2.88
Work on other shambas	5.32	5.10	4.04	0.00	4.56
Fetching water	8.21	12.35	5.82	4.08	8.16
Fetching wood	5.52	8.20	4.34	4.83	5.70
Outpatient time	0.60	0.40	0.38	1.29	0.48
Accompanying outpatient	0.28	0.09	0.28	2.19	0.29
Inpatient time	0.84	0.30	0.26	0.11	0.44
Other illness	14.50	8.64	7.04	5.88	9.62
Total people	574	485	450	41	1,350
Average hours/year	373	385	665	584	467

TABLE 14E.3. (cont.)

Activity	None	Primary 1–4	Primary 5–8	Some secondary	Total
Nyanza Province, females					
Work on own shamba	34.01	25.46	35.16	60.59	33.20
Off-farm wage employment	1.77	1.98	2.35	0.00	1.90
Own business	2.86	1.60	3.05	0.00	2.62
Work on estates	0.01	0.00	0.00	0.00	0.01
Work on other shambas	0.45	0.49	0.13	0.00	0.38
Fetching water	33.93	38.23	32.42	17.54	34.08
Fetching wood	18.50	21.96	19.50	20.67	19.37
Outpatient time	0.35	0.33	0.28	0.08	0.33
Accompanying outpatient	0.21	0.42	0.43	0.22	0.29
Inpatient time	0.40	0.52	0.27	0.00	0.39
Other illness	7.52	9.02	6.41	0.90	7.44
Total people	904	398	333	22	1,076
Average hours/year	952	654	927	1,177	901

TABLE 14F. *Tanzania: rural–urban comparison (sample means)*

(a) *Morbidity, three months*

	Number of occurrences % of population					% of population ill	Days lost per head of population
	F	DV	FDV	C	CB	All		
Urban	14.1	1.5	5.1	6.4	0.6	27.7	16.3	1.46
Rural	15.2	4.6	5.6	11.5	2.7	39.6	18.2	1.65

(b.1) *Outpatient costs per course, three months*

	Number of visits per course	Time (h)				Costs (sh)					Time per head of population (h)	Cost per head of population (sh)
		Travel	Waiting	Treatment	Total	Fees	Travel	Other	Total		
Urban	2.7	2.5	4.8	0.4	7.6	67.5	31.0	1.6	100.1	1.2	15.2
Rural	3.2	7.4	3.5	0.8	11.7	11.3	8.9	5.8	26.0	1.6	3.6

(b.2) *Outpatient costs per visit, three months*

	Visits per head of population	Time (h)			Costs (sh)				
		Travel	Waiting	Treatment	Total	Fees	Travel	Other	Total
Urban	0.41	0.9	1.8	0.1	2.8	25.1	11.5	0.6	37.2
Rural	0.44	2.3	1.1	0.2	3.6	3.5	2.7	1.8	8.1

(c) *Inpatient costs, twelve months*

	Lengths of stay (days)	Cost of stay (sh)				Stays % of population	Days per head of population	Cost per head of population (sh)
		Fees	Travel	Other	Total			
Urban	9.2	54.5	76.3	75.0	205.8	2.9	0.27	6.0
Rural	20.4	67.1	37.0	83.9	187.9	3.2	0.65	6.0

(d) *Education costs, twelve months*

	Costs per student % breakdown					Total cost per student (sh)	% of students in population	Total cost per head of population (sh)
	Fees	Books	Uniforms	Transport	Other			
Urban	26.6	17.6	37.9	13.5	4.3	1,146.8	26.3	301.8
Rural	21.3	11.1	58.5	0.6	8.4	291.7	22.8	66.5

15
An Analysis of the Effects of Public Service Provision

15.1. Introduction

There are three ways, broadly, of tracking the impact of public expenditure. The first assumes that there is a rather direct relationship between the costs of providing a service and the effect it has. The second draws inferences from household behaviour as to the valuation users place on the service. The third uses statistical techniques to try to establish some empirical relation between the service and some variable of interest, such as the output of a crop. Investigations in this third category may be more or less successful in establishing the existence and magnitude of effects. It may be possible only to establish that there is (or is not) a relationship, without determining causality. It may be possible to establish a causal relationship and its associated quantitative dimension, without being able to place a value on this. Finally, it may be possible not only to measure the impact, but also to value it. The remainder of this introduction discusses each of these possibilities in turn.

The first procedure is overwhelmingly the most common approach in studies of the incidence of public expenditure; in effect these are attributions of average cost, not of benefit. Since this approach is adopted precisely because benefit information is lacking (which casts considerable doubt on the allocative efficiency of public provision), the need to assume that costs accurately measure benefits is unfortunate. The proper role for this type of cost information is to confront it with independent estimates of benefit, to permit the adequacy of existing levels of provision to be tested.

As noted in Chapter 14, we do not possess the detailed cost breakdowns to make this a feasible exercise. Hence it is not possible to form a view as to what levels of expenditure would be optimal: we have the more limited goal of trying to ascertain what sort of value attaches to existing provision, and what sort of effect a change in provision might have.

The second procedure was discussed in Chapter 13. Section 15.2 of this chapter uses it and the estimate of the shadow wage derived in Chapter 6 to provide very crude estimates of the subjective value households attach to some existing services. These are intended only to offer orders of magnitude, but even so they suggest these services are highly valued.

The third procedure is more familiar, and is reported in Sections 15.3 and 15.4. A number of measures of public service input are developed. In

Section 15.3 these are inserted into a variety of Cobb–Douglas production functions. These functions are fitted to the data, to see what role the public inputs play. The Cobb–Douglas structure is chosen for analytical and computational tractability, because it is relatively stable under this type of piecemeal variation, and also for ease of interpretation of the results.

Let the public service input be measured by m, and let output Q be a function of quantities of the inputs F_i. Then if the public service input enters production multiplicatively in the exponential form,

$$Q = ce^{bm} \Pi_i F_i^{a_i}; c, b, a_i \text{ constant.} \tag{15.1}$$

On logarithmic differentiation,

$$\frac{dQ}{Q} = bdm. \tag{15.2}$$

Hence, for a price-taking household, with the output price p, the value of a change in the input, Δm, is

$$p\Delta Q = pQ \cdot b\Delta m. \tag{15.3}$$

This derivation assumed only one public service input, but provided they all enter multiplicatively equation (15.3) remains the appropriate measure.

Finally, Section 15.4 investigates a number of other statistical relationships, in particular those between health provision and morbidity, and those between public service inputs and labour supply. In each case, some attempt at valuing these quantitative effects can be made using the shadow wage.

15.2. Implicit Household Valuations

As discussed in Chapter 13, these require an estimate of the shadow wage rate. In Chapter 6 we obtained a figure of 2.23 shillings per hour for the mean rural shadow wage in Kenya, using the hybrid maize production function.[1]

We were unable to make a comparable estimate for Tanzania since the (local) maize production function exhibits a high degree of multicollinearity between land area and labour input. This presumably reflects the fact that land is not scarce in Tanzania, so that labour supply is the constraining input.

Table 15.1 summarizes the mean time and cost information reported in Chapter 14, all converted to an annual figure per head of population. It hardly needs to be stressed that the computations are both crude and highly speculative; at best they may suggest orders of magnitude.

---

[1] This is the obvious crop to use in Kenya, since it is grown by over 60% of households; the resulting figure is very similar to the market wage for agricultural labour of 2 shillings per hour.

TABLE 15.1. *Time and cash costs per head per year*

	Days lost through illness	Outpatient visits		Inpatient stays		Education costs (sh)	
		Hours	Shillings	Days	Shillings	All	Secondary
Kenya: Central	4.64	4.8	11.2	0.19	1.9	164.2	55.4
Kenya: Nyanza	10.96	3.2	10.8	0.42	5.1	81.6	15.5
Tanzania: rural	6.60	6.4	14.4	0.65	6.0	66.5	4.3
Tanzania: urban	5.84	4.6	60.8	0.27	6.0	301.8	—

15.2.1. Kenya

We assume that a working day is 6.5 hours, which is consistent with our own data and with farm time studies.[2] Then the shadow cost of illness of Kenyan peasants, making no allowance for the associated distress or cash costs, ranges from 67 shillings (4.1 per cent of income) in Central Province to 159 shillings (10.4 per cent) in Nyanza Province. The valuation placed on outpatient services, using the benchmark case of Chapter 13, is 22 shillings (1.3 per cent of income) in Central and 18 shillings (1.2 per cent) in Nyanza. These figures are underestimates since they take no account of the frequent need for other adults to accompany outpatients. It is less plausible to see inpatient stays in this revealed preference light, but for the sake of comparison, it would value them at 5 shillings and 11 shillings respectively. Overall the costs of accessing health facilities is around 30 shillings or 2 per cent of income.

The cash costs of education, as already noted, amount to 10.0 per cent of income in Central and 5.4 per cent in Nyanza. Making a crude allowance for time costs, say 1,000 hours per year at half the shadow wage, would raise costs per head by 400 shillings in Central (where 36.3 per cent of the population are students) and by 370 shillings in Nyanza (33.4 per cent). This would imply total education costs at 34 per cent of income in Central and 30 per cent in Nyanza.

Another way of looking at education choices would be to consider secondary education only. Cash costs per head are 3.4 per cent of income in Central, 1.0 per cent in Nyanza. Allowing 1,000 hours at the full shadow wage, these rise to 138 shillings, or 8.4 per cent of income in Central, and to 42 shillings, or 2.8 per cent in Nyanza.

Finally, we can compare the implicit valuation of these services across the whole rural sector with the size of the corresponding budgetary items. Lacking urban valuations, this is a most incomplete exercise. Assuming a rural population of 15.5 million in 1982, the total valuation attached to health

[2] See e.g. Cleave (1974).

services by the rural population would, on these figures, be K£25 million, compared to the total health budget of K£70 million. If other sectors of the population also value their access to health services at 2 per cent of income, then the total valuation will closely correspond to the government's expenses of provision. As regards education, the aggregate rural valuation on these figures would range anywhere from K£95 million to K£390 million (if opportunity costs of time are included) compared to a total educational budget (urban and rural) of K£206 million in 1982/3.

15.2.2. Tanzania

If we assume that the shadow wage in Tanzania bears the same relation to per capita income as in rural Kenya, then the mean shadow wage in the rural areas would be 2.1 Tshillings and that for our urban sample would be 5.8 Tshillings. (Recall that the purchasing power of Tanzanian and Kenyan shillings diverges markedly.) On this basis, comparable figures for Tanzania would be: cost of illness, 6.0 per cent of income (5.3 per cent urban); value of outpatient services, 1.8 per cent (2.1 per cent); value of inpatient services, 1.0 per cent (0.4 per cent); cash costs of education, 4.5 per cent (7.3 per cent); total costs of education, 20.5 per cent (25.7 per cent).

What is remarkable about these computations is that they imply rather similar relative valuations, despite the large differences in time/cash cost structure between rural and urban sectors. As compared to Kenya, health services are valued relatively highly (over 2.5 per cent for both rural and urban, compared to 2 per cent) and education rather less so. The latter conclusion is not robust, however; secondary education is heavily rationed in Tanzania, and the costs of access will not be fully captured by these calculations.

In the 1978 census 86.7 per cent of the Tanzanian population was described as rural. Assuming the population in 1983 was 2.6 million urban, 17.1 million rural, these figures may be grossed up to provide estimates of aggregate national valuations. Rural health services would be valued at Tsh 730 million, urban at Tsh 270 million. The total valuation of Tsh 1,000 million compares with government supply costs of probably around Tsh 1,100 million. (Firm figures for 1983 are not available.) As regards education, the rural valuation ranges between Tsh 1,150 million and Tsh 5,200 million; the urban valuation between Tsh 790 million and Tsh 2,800 million. The total valuation in the range Tsh 1,940 million to Tsh 8,000 million compares to government expenses of probably around Tsh 2,400 million.

15.2.3. Summary and Interpretation

What emerges very clearly from these calculations is just how large the user costs associated with the main public services are. They are at least of the same order of magnitude as the government's cost of provision and, in the case of education, probably much higher. Hence any decisions about the level or pattern of public provision which neglect these user costs are likely to be biased and misleading.

However, taking them adequately into account will be a complex undertaking. In particular, it may not be appropriate to conclude that supply should be increased if consumer valuation (as measured here) exceeds public cost of provision, at least until the incremental effect on user cost has been estimated. At one extreme, user costs may be in a relatively fixed complementary relationship to public provision costs. In that case, an expansion of the public service imposes a commensurate cost increase on the private sector. At the other extreme, as argued in Chapter 13, private user costs may be a substitute for public expenditure. In that case, an expansion of public supply may result in an offsetting reduction in private user costs. For example, nearly half of the user costs associated with outpatient services are time costs, principally for travelling and waiting. An increase in supply would normally reduce both these categories. By way of contrast, increasing educational provision will raise the associated time costs, to the extent that the increased supply is utilized.

15.3. Direct Output Effects

Public services may affect output directly, given other factor inputs, or they may operate to alter or enhance these inputs. In this section, we consider the first category, adding a number of public service measures singly to some of the production functions estimated earlier. Of particular interest is the role of information in enhancing performance, as has been extensively argued in Part II. Here we report the results of adding measures of education and of crop extension services to the Kenyan functions. Tables 15.2–15.5 give parameter estimates and absolute t-ratios for the resulting equations, each table reporting the coffee function in the left-hand columns and the hybrid maize function on the right.

The educational measures are cumulative dummy variables for the presence in the household of some primary education (first 4 standards); full primary education; and (at least) some secondary education. The extension service measures are an index of exposure to these services (crop index) and one of exposure specifically in respect of food crops (food index).

The results tabulated are rather weak, with only the food index in the hybrid maize function being significant at the 5 per cent level. On the other hand, only secondary education in hybrid maize has the 'wrong' sign, and that is totally insignificant (t-ratio 0.2). All the other measures have the appropriate sign, and have modest t-ratios in the range 0.8–1.4. It is plausible to conclude that primary education improves productivity in both crops, and

TABLE 15.2. *Impact of some primary education*

	Coffee production	Hybrid maize production
Intercept	2.476 (4.05)	1.602 (2.07)
Area	0.327 (3.00)	0.436 (4.43)
Fertilizer	0.097 (2.32)	0.089 (2.98)
Pesticide	0.049 (1.18)	— —
Hired labour	0.063 (2.04)	— —
Own labour	0.294 (3.76)	0.286 (4.23)
Provincial dummy	0.122 (0.50)	−0.413 (2.63)
Part-primary dummy	0.194 (1.03)	0.246 (1.38)
F-test	16.231	17.681

TABLE 15.3. *Impact of completing primary education*

	Coffee production	Hybrid maize production
Intercept	2.503 (4.14)	1.801 (2.39)
Area	0.324 (2.97)	0.426 (4.32)
Fertilizer	0.096 (2.31)	0.091 (3.03)
Pesticide	0.051 (1.22)	— —
Hired labour	0.062 (2.02)	— —
Own labour	0.289 (3.71)	0.285 (4.19)
Provincial dummy	0.128 (0.53)	−0.433 (2.77)
Full-primary dummy	0.216 (1.30)	0.123 (0.81)
F-test	16.379	17.295

TABLE 15.4. *Impact of some secondary education*

	Coffee production	Hybrid maize production
Intercept	2.676 (4.38)	1.947 (2.61)
Area	0.326 (2.99)	0.419 (4.23)
Fertilizer	0.096 (2.30)	0.093 (3.09)
Pesticide	0.049 (1.17)	— —
Hired labour	0.061 (1.98)	— —
Own labour	0.281 (3.51)	0.287 (4.21)
Provincial dummy	0.120 (0.50)	−0.440 (2.81)
Part-secondary dummy	0.162 (1.12)	−0.028 (0.20)
F-test	16.273	17.101

TABLE 15.5. *Impact of extension advice*

	Coffee production	Hubrid maize production
Intercept	2.571 (4.27)	1.663 (2.26)
Area	0.318 (2.91)	0.432 (4.46)
Fertilizer	0.099 (2.40)	0.088 (2.97)
Pesticide	0.039 (0.93)	— —
Hired labour	0.062 (2.01)	— —
Own labour	0.307 (3.99)	0.302 (4.49)
Provincial dummy	0.152 (0.63)	−0.367 (2.34)
All crop index	0.172 (1.34)	— —
All food index	— —	0.211 (2.35)
F-test	16.403	18.804

secondary education improves it in coffee but not maize production. Extension advice is helpful, particularly in growing maize.

In each case the coefficients are much the same, in the range 0.12–0.25.[3] That on extension advice is difficult to interpret, because this is measured by an index. However, those on education are more straightforward. They measure the proportional increase in output, for given inputs, that would be obtained by moving up into the next educational band. Thus some primary education in the household (as opposed to none) raises coffee output by 19 per cent (or 25 per cent for maize); completing primary education raises it by a further 22 per cent (12 per cent); some secondary schooling then adds a further 16 per cent for coffee, but has no effect on maize production. There are thus some signs of diminishing returns to education, with these being delayed in the case of coffee.

We could go one step further, and make a crude comparison between the costs and benefits of incremental education, as follows. Acquiring complete (as opposed to partial) primary education means, for the average household, purchasing four more years primary education at a cash cost of 1,056 shillings (taking the mean of Central and Nyanza costs from Table 14C.4) and a total opportunity cost (assuming an opportunity cost of time of half the shadow wage as before) of 5,516 shillings. The mean value of coffee output is 3,489 shillings per year, so the mean income gain from completing primary education accruing on coffee production is 22 per cent of this, or 768 shillings. This would represent a 13.9 per cent return to the investment. If the opportunity cost of time were valued at the full shadow wage, the return would be reduced to 7.7 per cent. For comparison, investment in secondary

---

[3] These functions have been re-estimated in each case. An alternative procedure is to regress output on the original estimates of output and the public service measure. This yields virtually identical coefficients and *t*-ratios in every case.

TABLE 15.6. *Impact of adult days ill on production*

	Coffee production	Hybrid maize
Intercept	2.590 (4.27)	1.925 (2.59)
Area	0.327 (2.99)	0.421 (4.26)
Fertilizer	0.0978 (2.32)	0.0926 (3.09)
Pesticide	0.0472 (1.12)	—
Hired labour	0.0646 (2.09)	—
Own labour	0.306 (3.95)	0.286 (4.16)
Provincial dummy	0.105 (0.43)	−0.441 (2.79)
Adult illness rate	−0.0012 (0.39)	0.00016 (0.06)
F-test	16.021	17.090

education (also assuming four years) would cost 5,577 shillings in cash, and 14,497 shillings with time valued at the shadow wage. The incremental income from this investment, accruing from coffee production, would be 558 shillings (16 per cent of 3,489 shillings), yielding a return of only 3.9 per cent.

It should be born in mind that these returns are partial ones; the overall return to education is the sum of the gains accruing in each of the household's manifold activities. However, the coffee component is likely to be a large proportion of the whole. By way of comparison, the mean value of maize output is 815.5 shillings per year. The return on investment from completing primary education is 12 per cent of this, or 98 shillings; a yield (valuing time at half the mean shadow wage) of only 1.8 per cent (compared to 13.9 per cent on coffee).

The upshot of these empirical exercises is that, while the statistical significance of the results is only modest, the potential impact of education in raising agricultural output is rather high. These results are in line with those previously obtained for Tanzania by one of the authors.[4]

Turning from education to health, Table 15.6 presents comparable data with the adult illness rate (number of days lost per adult) as the additional variable. In common with some other studies,[5] no direct effect of illness on output is observed. This is hardly surprising, since the estimation controls for variation in labour supply, and this is the main channel for ill health to affect production. The impact via labour supply is considered in the next section.

15.4. Health Provision, Morbidity, and Labour Supply

This section addresses two questions: how does health provision affect morbidity, and how does morbidity affect labour supply?

---

[4] Collier *et al.* (1986, Table 4.5). [5] See, for example, Pitt and Rosenzweig (1986).

15.4.1. Health Provision and Morbidity

Identifying a causal relationship between health services and ill health is far from straightforward. It might be true that access to health services reduces ill health, but the contrary relationship is also likely to hold, that those suffering from ill health are more likely to use health services. Since all our data were obtained in a single round, that limits the possible avenues through which to explore this relationship. The following procedure resolves the difficulty but involves three stages. First, a predicted ill health variable (ESTIL) is generated, by regressing the number of days ill on the occasion of the most recent illness, against the associated symptom, and the individual's age, age squared, and gender.[6] The results are given in Table 15.7. As can be seen, the Kenyan equation has a far superior fit compared to the Tanzanian one.

The second stage estimates a logit with the probability of an individual using outpatient facilities as a function of predicted illness, a number of individual characteristics, and, in the case of Kenya, distance from the nearest health facility (these data were not available for Tanzania), as well as a provincial dummy. Three household characteristics were also included, household income and the number of male and female adults. The latter were intended to test for difficulties that households with few adults might have in sparing someone to leave the shamba for treatment, or to accompany another. The results are reported in Table 15.8.

Neither logit works spectacularly well, but the Kenyan version is clearly more satisfactory. Leaving aside the symptoms themselves (which are significant in half the cases), nothing is significant at the 5 per cent level for Tanzania, whereas in Kenya full primary education, income, the number of adult females, and the provincial dummy are all significantly positively related to the propensity to use the facility, while distance is significantly negatively related.

TABLE 15.7. *Coefficients of estimated illness equation*

	Kenya	Tanzania
No. of times F	1.472 (4.90)	2.622 (2.82)
No. of times FDV	2.028 (4.19)	1.822 (1.76)
No. of times DV	2.153 (3.74)	1.566 (1.09)
No. of times C	1.810 (4.68)	2.861 (8.96)
No. of times CB	0.640 (0.87)	4.225 (3.75)
Age	0.403 (6.54)	0.114 (1.01)
Age squared	−0.0039 (4.18)	0.0011 (0.70)
Gender	3.485 (3.95)	5.143 (3.01)
F-test	94.762	38.053

[6] Defined as male = 1, female = 0.

TABLE 15.8. *Logit of propensity to use health facility*

	Kenya	Tanzania
Age	−0.012 (1.01)	0.016 (1.03)
Age squared	0.00002 (0.15)	−0.0004 (1.64)
Gender	0.139 (0.97)	0.333 (1.67)
Province	1.124 (6.84)	— —
Distance (miles)	−0.139 (4.81)	— —
Adult males (no.)	0.027 (0.40)	−0.160 (1.82)
Adult females (no.)	0.205 (3.46)	−0.098 (1.38)
Per capita income	0.00007 (3.71)	0.000003 (0.32)
ESTIL	−0.011 (1.01)	0.023 (1.37)
Education dummies		
Partial primary	−0.033 (0.19)	0.185 (0.70)
Full primary	0.655 (3.08)	0.132 (0.41)
Partial secondary	−0.774 (1.72)	5.626 (0.23)
Symptom dummies		
F	0.342 (1.99)	0.719 (2.77)
DV	0.775 (2.65)	0.893 (2.19)
FDV	1.158 (3.54)	0.284 (0.70)
C	−0.039 (0.22)	0.004 (0.01)
CB	0.059 (0.15)	−0.649 (0.82)
Chi squared	135.08	33.55
% Correct prediction	65	61

The third stage is to regress actual days too ill to work or go to school on this fitted propensity to use health facilities and the same list of characteristics, but omitting distance (and numbers of adults). These results are given in Table 15.9.

Once again, neither equation fits particularly well, but there are a number of significant coefficients. These include those on several of the symptoms, unsurprisingly. More interesting is the fact that the propensity to use health facilities is a significant determinant of ill health in each case. The Kenyan equation has the 'right' sign with a high propensity to use health services (conditional on the severity of illness) being associated with a reduction in days lost through illness. The Tanzanian equation, by way of contrast, has a perverse sign, implying that use of health facilities increases illness. This result is quite possible: Tanzanian clinics have notoriously lacked medicines and trained personnel, and it is quite conceivable that visiting them simply exposes patients to infection. However the derivation of the Tanzanian propensity is far from robust, so this inference should be treated with great caution.

To summarize: in Kenya, it appears that distance from a health facility inhibits its use, and that this likely to lead to more days lost through illness. It

TABLE 15.9. *Days ill as a function of the propensity to use health facilities*

	Kenya	Tanzania
Intercept	4.701 (3.49)	10.838 (3.01)
Propensity	−1.265 (2.52)	4.606 (2.97)
Gender	0.715 (1.00)	−1.138 (0.65)
Age	0.083 (1.48)	0.029 (0.24)
Age squared	−0.0003 (0.41)	0.002 (1.32)
F	3.095 (2.94)	−9.661 (2.85)
DV	2.916 (2.02)	−8.627 (2.25)
FDV	6.203 (4.07)	−1.406 (0.38)
C	−0.024 (0.02)	1.880 (0.60)
CB	4,643 (2.28)	−8.784 (1.48)
Income	−0.0001 (1.62)	−0.0001 (1.31)
F-test	6.812	4.101

follows that increased health provision would have positive consequences for the health of Kenyan peasants. In Tanzania, simply increasing the number of clinics may do little good. (We have no way of estimating whether this would increase usage, and some misgivings about what increased usage would entail.) This conclusion has no bearing on the merits of increased provision of drugs or qualified personnel, however.

To obtain a notion of magnitudes, the mean propensity to visit a health facility when ill is, in Kenya, 0.638. Lowering the mean distance to the facility by one mile would raise this about 3 percentage points to 0.669. In turn, this would lower expected days ill per sick person per quarter by 0.176 or around 2 per cent. The effect is therefore small, though it is statistically significant. Since a reduction of mean distance from 2.85 miles to 1.85 miles would involve an enormous duplication of facilities, this does not seem likely to offer a cost-effective means of improving health. By way of contrast, the dummy variable on completing primary education has a highly significant (t-ratio 3.08) coefficient of 0.655: this is nearly five times as large as the coefficient on distance and implies that a policy vigorously promoting primary education is more likely to increase the use of health facilities than is a policy simply providing more of them.

15.4.2. *Labour Supply*

The remaining relationship to be investigated is that between labour supply and a number of public service inputs, or variables related to these. Table 15.10 reports two regressions of total household productive working time (time spent on the shamba, on own business, or in various forms of paid

TABLE 15.10. *Labour supply in Kenya*

	As a function of days actually ill	As a function of predicted days
Intercept	950.0 (13.40)	1,032.3 (12.81)
Time spent fetching water	−0.048 (0.98)	−0.043 (0.88)
Time spent fetching wood	0.005 (0.08)	−0.013 (0.19)
Days actually ill	−2.749 (1.84)	— —
Predicted days ill	— —	−13.510 (2.66)
Outpatient time	0.869 (1.00)	0.355 (0.43)
Inpatient time	−0.154 (0.24)	−0.155 (0.24)
Distance from health facility	−12.59 (0.85)	−12.415 (0.84)
Tap in house (dummy)	285.3 (1.92)	282.1 (1.91)
Communal piped water (dummy)	−9.743 (0.07)	41.09 (0.30)
F-test	1.234	1.703

employment) on these variables, the difference being whether actual illness or predicted illness was used.

It appears from Table 15.10 that predicted illness works better than actual illness, presumably because it is the characteristics which predispose to ill health that also inhibit labour supply, rather than the actual realization of ill health. Predicted days ill is not only highly significant in explaining labour supply, it also has a reasonably high coefficient. Increasing predicted illness by one day lowers labour supply by 13.5 hours or about two days.

The only other item to be verging on significance at the 5 per cent level is the dummy on whether the household has a tap. The coefficient on this is very high indeed; having a tap raises labour supply by around 280 hours per year. The coefficient on time spent fetching water is negligible, and this raises the question of whether the tap-in-house dummy is acting as a proxy for this. Table 15.11 reports a regression of time spent fetching water on the tap and communal piped water dummies. While a tap in the house does indeed reduce

TABLE 15.11. *Time spent fetching water*

Intercept	332.9 (12.52)
Tap	−151.4 (1.35)
Communal	323.1 (3.31)
F-test	6.704

time spent fetching water, the interesting feature of this regression is that communal piped water dramatically (and significantly) raises it. One possible explanation for this result is that households are prepared to travel further for the supposed benefits of piped water; alternatively, they may use more of it. In any event, this aspect of water supply requires further investigation, as do the health aspects already noted.

15.5. Conclusion

The calculations in this chapter have been both piecemeal and speculative and the conclusions must be tentative. Much more needs to be done, both with our own data and in further research, to see how robust these conclusions are. Nevertheless, we have found that those public services of particular interest to rural households are highly valued by them, as evidenced by the considerable user costs they incur. Further, we have found evidence that all these services are productive, in the sense that they raise output or labour supply, or reduce illness. It is not possible to draw any inferences from this as to whether public supply should be expanded or not, that is whether the cost would be justified, but it does appear that an expansion of these services would yield positive benefits.

16
Peasants and Governments

Governments affect peasants by delivering certain services and by altering the prices at which peasants trade, either by regulation or taxation. In this volume we have investigated instances of all three of these interventions. Part IV examined the effects of the provision of rural health, education, and water services, Part III the effects of price regulation, and Part II the effects of indirect taxation designed to stabilize crop prices. Broadly, the normative effects of these three interventions ranged from highly beneficial, in the case of some services, through greatly over-rated, in the case of price-stabilizing taxation, to highly detrimental in the case of price regulation. Perhaps the major overall conclusion to be drawn from our study is that governments are currently implementing policies whose effects span this wide range.

In much of Africa the capacity for policy implementation is severely limited. A common criticism is that governments are attempting to intervene too much and, as a consequence, are doing so badly. However, across-the-board reductions in government intervention are not necessarily desirable. Rather, the task is to identify the relative merits of policies so as to discontinue the less desirable, and concentrate upon improving the implementation of the best. Because of this capacity constraint, even policies which are merely redundant are indirectly detrimental, since they have an opportunity cost in impairing the implementation of other, more desirable policies. Hence, if the domestic stabilization of crop prices is unnecessary, because peasants can handle fluctuations at least as well as the public sector, it represents a complex and expensive diversion of governmental resources. More dramatically, price regulation not only has such an opportunity cost, but its direct consequences are highly damaging. Thus governments have the capacity either substantially to improve or to worsen peasant living standards. The consequences of policy error are therefore high.

Our analysis of various rural public services demonstrated that this dictum continues to hold as policies are disaggregated. The results of Part IV suggest very clearly that expansion of public services in aggregate would have been much appreciated by rural households, and would have had beneficial consequences for production.[1] As regards the relative merits of the different sectors, the major finding is that expenditure on primary education appears to

---

[1] However, as noted in Chapter 13, we do not possess the sort of information to permit any detailed cost–benefit analysis. In particular, we cannot draw any conclusions as to whether increased (productive) public expenditure would have been a more or less beneficial use of income than comparable increases in private expenditures.

have a very high return. This arises from the compounding of three distinct effects. First, the private return to primary education in peasant agriculture is relatively high, as suggested by the production function exercises of Chapter 15. Second, the great bulk of the costs of education are borne in the private sector; hence relatively small amounts of public expenditure are multiplied up into much larger investments. In effect, they act as pump priming expenditures. Third, primary education also brings a number of indirect benefits. For example, it was noted in Chapter 15 that increased primary education appeared to be a more effective way of increasing the use of health facilities than simply building more of them.

In the case of Kenya, primary school enrollments are now so high following the very vigorous policy of the 1970s that there is little scope for further expansion at this level. In contrast, enrollment is much lower in Tanzania, so this looks to have been a significant policy opportunity missed. Indeed, a major aim of the villagization programme was to move households closer to health facilities: it seems all too likely that these resources would have been better devoted to promoting primary education, even if the aim was to improve access to health services. This would certainly be the implication of the Kenyan logit of Chapter 15: as previously noted, the Tanzanian logit is not satisfactory and fails to uncover any systematic influences on the use of health facilities.

The benefits of expanding secondary education are much less clearly demonstrated. Coefficients are often negative and usually not statistically significant. One exception is that on secondary education in coffee production in Kenya. The general shape of these results is familiar; there are few circumstances in which the rural household is likely to obtain real benefit from secondary education, and they are likely to involve innovation and change rather than traditional crops.

Turning to the health sector, the conclusions are more muted. We can say nothing about the benefits of preventive expenditure, except that there is clearly a great deal of ill health to prevent. On the curative side, we have distinct results for the two countries. Kenyan health facilities appear to work in reducing losses from illness though in a modest way; Tanzanian ones do not, or are perverse. This may well constitute a parallel with the case of Tanzanian manufacturing industry, discussed in the companion volume *Controlled Open Economies*. Adding to the capital stock (health facilities) produces no more output, just more spare capacity, because of the lack of complementary inputs (trained personnel and drugs); if this interpretation is correct, there may have been real gains to be had from expansion of health expenditure in Tanzania, always provided it was directed at these complementary inputs.

Expenditure on piped water supplies emerges as highly problematic. It appears all too possible that health effects are perverse, and that, in the communal variety at least, piped water does not reduce time spent obtaining it. Our data do not permit us to investigate potential causes of these adverse effects, and indeed the data may be misleading. However, the results are worrying, and suggest that fuller research into the relation between morbidity and water supply would be worthwhile.

Extension services emerge as beneficial to output, though the effect is hard to quantify in relation to cost. Improved roads are more highly valued than anything else the government does in rural Kenya, but we have no means of quantifying this effect.

Overall, primary education seems to have been the obvious form of increased expenditure during the period: one that the Kenyans were pursuing anyway, and one that the Tanzanians would probably have been well advised to emulate. Otherwise, road improvements and extension services qualify as likely candidates, together with current health service inputs. Building more health centres seems less likely to bring sizeable benefits, and providing piped water seems positively harmful.

Our Kenyan evidence (Part II) is particularly relevant to the debate about the desirability of price stabilization in agricultural economies. In the literature the analysis of price stabilization has largely been confined to the macroeconomy. However, the analysis of the effects on peasants of stabilization measures requires a study of the microeconomic effects of, paradoxically, price volatility, since it is these effects which stabilization policies seek to avoid.

The reaction of Kenyan smallholders to the coffee boom demonstrates, first, that peasants recognized the temporary nature of the increase in their income, saving almost two-thirds of their windfall income, and, secondly, that they allocated these savings sensibly. The recognition of the transient nature of the boom and the very high savings rate indicate that peasants cannot be depicted as myopic,[2] likely to squander a windfall unless prevented from doing so by the government. Hence there appeared to be no custodial reason for shielding peasants from booms (in fact, as we show in *Controlled Open Economies*, the Kenyan government failed to make good use of the windfall income it obtained: the proposed custodian behaved much less responsibly than the peasants allegedly in need of custody).

Two qualifications may be noted. First, given the distorted nature of rural credit markets, the demonstrated ability of peasants to save and hence to respond appropriately to booms does not imply that they respond as well to negative price shocks: their limited capacity to borrow may well introduce an asymmetry.[3]

Secondly, peasant asset formation, while undoubtedly efficient from the private point of view, may well have been socially inefficient, because of

---

[2] Provided, of course, that they can obtain the necessary information on the causes and likely duration of the boom; in Kenya they received such information through the co-operative societies.

[3] See Sen (1981), Ravallion (1987).

restricted asset choices. This qualification, however, is an argument in favour of removing the constraints on peasant asset formation, rather than in favour of price stabilization. Also, while the investment of Kenyan smallholders may have been inefficient compared to the standard of an undistorted economy, it was an improvement compared to the more relevant conterfactual of investment in import substitutes. For coffee and tea planting, and the other agricultural investments, augmented the export capacity of the economy, whereas improvements to housing augmented the flow of non-tradable services. Since investment outside the peasant sector was heavily concentrated in the import-substitute sector (as a result either of government direction or trade and financial controls), peasant investment tended to offset this bias. Hence, a coffee tax would have further skewed the composition of investment towards import substitutes even had the government succeeded in matching the peasant savings rate.

Our Kenyan evidence shows that peasants are employed in activities with very different rates of return, reflecting both barriers to entry and (particularly in the case of coffee growing) economies of scale. This implies that growth is not a process of small continual changes in scale and in the mix of activities, but is characterized by discrete jumps, defined by a hierarchy of activities. We also saw that those who adopt high-return activities such as coffee growing, differ from others not in ability, but in information. This is the basis for the copying effect which we emphasize in Part II. This characterization is likely to apply to many peasant economies. It has two important implications for the response to price shocks. First, a boom may have unusually large benefits if it enables peasants to overcome barriers to entry. Secondly, it implies that a boom may, through the copying of innovations by others, have a strong gearing effect. Thirdly, while (as we argue in *Controlled Open Economies*) the bunching of non-agricultural investment during a boom is likely to be detrimental, the bunching of peasant investment is likely to be beneficial.[4]

While government intervention to stabilize price booms thus appears to have little to commend it, intervention to depress prices appears on the basis of Part III to be highly damaging. Again we should add that our example, while it might generalize to all cases of non-market clearing, does not extend to the effects of subsidies under market-clearing conditions.

The Tanzanian policy of price controls on consumer goods looks like a subsidy to peasants. However, this is true only in a very limited sense. To understand this, price controls must be seen in the broader context of pricing policies. Coffee was subject to a quasi-stabilization tax, which was only gradually taken off so that it became a tax over-and-above the price windfall. This lowered export prices to peasants. Consumer goods were subject to import quota protection which enabled their price to rise above the world price. The combined effect of these two interventions was to lower the price of coffee relative to consumer goods in Tanzania.

[4] Because of the copying effect and also because, as we argued in Chapter 6, bunching tends to lead to relative price increases from which the poor benefit.

Additionally, the exchange rate became increasingly over-valued, foreign exchange being rationed by the Central Bank. This lowered the domestic currency price of tradable goods, and hence the prices of both coffee and consumer goods. The counterpart of the currency over-valuation was an excess supply of money. In the absence of any controls this would have bid up the price of non-tradable goods and sucked in imports of the tradable goods, causing a balance of payments deficit. Price controls alone would have suppressed the increase in the price of non-tradables, thereby diverting expenditure to the tradables and further increasing imports. The other key control was quantity restrictions upon imports. These prevented the excess demand for tradables from being satisfied. In the absence of price controls the price level would therefore have been bid up, since the import controls made the tradable goods non-tradable at the margin. The severe shortages of tradable goods which we have seen were encountered in Tanzania were thus the result of the combination of import controls and price controls.

These shortages generated a new policy instrument for the government, namely the allocation of quantities of consumer goods across the geographic range of markets. Biasing these supplies in favour of urban areas was a quantity extension of the process of peasant taxation: prices were held down nationally, but peasants received disproportionately small allocations. The 'virtual prices' associated with official supplies of consumer goods were thus higher in rural than in urban areas.

This complex double system of peasant taxation, turning the domestic terms of trade against peasants and allocating to them differentially short rations, was inefficient even in terms of government revenue. Goods prices were too high relative to coffee in the sense that under market-clearing conditions the revenue-maximizing tax would probably have been lower (the implicit tax rate was so high that it was probably on the wrong side of the Laffer curve). But goods prices were too low relative to coffee in the sense that given the quantity rationing, a higher price would have generated more coffee sales up to the point at which market-clearing prices were reached (our perverse supply response result). It is in this restricted sense that price controls constituted a subsidy to peasants. Finally, goods prices and coffee prices were both too low relative to money. These interventions were at cross-purposes. The resulting system of surplus extraction was undesirable in three respects. First, by using the appropriate tax rate in a market-clearing regime, it would have been possible both to have improved terms of trade for peasants and to acquire a larger revenue. Secondly, surplus extraction by means of biasing shortages towards the peasant sector is a very short-term ploy. As we have seen, such a strategy causes a subsequent decline in peasant marketings. This in turn reduces goods availability through its effect on foreign exchange earnings. Thirdly, the windfall coffee tax, even had it not persisted beyond the period of high coffee prices, had no custodial justification. As we have seen, in Kenya where peasants received the entire windfall, there is reason to believe that they made good use of it.

Price regulation as adopted in Tanzania was thus both inefficient and unstable. It was also very demanding of government time. Decisions were constantly required between competing claims for goods in excess demand. Even so, the government lacked the administrative capacity to implement household rationing at the village level, thereby generating rent-seeking responses to stochastic shortages. The rent-seeking in turn created government concern over racketeering. The government's energies were therefore consumed in forlorn efforts to allocate shortages and punish rent-seeking. This made it all the more difficult to recognize the need for a regime switch into market-clearing. As we discuss in *Controlled Open Economies*, such a regime switch was not without its own difficulties.

What then can be concluded from the three aspects of government policy towards peasants which have been the focus of our study? What generalizations can be drawn? As regards public expenditure, our comparison of Kenya and Tanzania shows that generalization can be highly precarious. Health services, for example, appeared to be markedly more effective in Kenya than in Tanzania. Further, peasants had significantly different rankings of the benefits of past expenditures and their priorities for future expenditure. Hence, the design of an appropriate public expenditure programme which meets peasants' needs appears to need country-specific data. Public expenditure surveys similar to ours are currently very rare in rural Africa. The conclusion is that they need to be widely replicated in conjunction with data on the public costs of service delivery.

By contrast, our analysis of the consequences of shortages of consumer goods for peasant supply response probably are generalizable. Our results for Tanzania were merely an application of a theoretical model, the assumptions of which are likely to characterize several African economies. For example, Azam and Faucher (1987) provides an interesting application to Mozambique. The presumption must be that regimes which attempt direct control of the price level are highly dangerous in a peasant economy.

Our analysis of peasant behaviour in response to the volatility of crop prices lies between these two bounds of country specificity and wide generality. In Kenya, peasants responded to the coffee boom as predicted by the permanent income theory of how rational, well-informed agents would behave. This suggests the hypothesis that this is indeed how peasants typically respond to temporary price shocks. However, a single consistent observation falls far short of confirming the hypothesis. If found to be correct the implications of the hypothesis are far reaching, for government stabilization schemes would be misconceived. Our study thus establishes that the hypothesis is worth further research (on which the authors are currently engaged).

Four hundred million people live in Sub-Saharan Africa, their average income being only $400 per annum (as of 1985). The population has been growing more rapidly than in any other region. Three-quarters of that population are rural. This large, poor, growing population has been subjected to powerful policy interventions, often well motivated, but usually based on limited understanding. In understanding the peasant sector there is no substitute for survey data, but surveys are costly and laborious and so they are scarce. Even when undertaken, they are commonly subject only to rudimentary tabular analysis. The task set to scholarship before policy makers can operate in an informed environment is formidable. This book is a contribution to that task.

Appendix: The Rural Surveys

The surveys collected information on three topics:
1. The household itself, its farming operations, and its non-farm sources of income.
2. Changes since 1975 in agriculture and assets with special attention to the impact of the coffee boom.
3. Access to government services and health, education, water, wood, and sewage.

1. Survey of Central and Nyanza Provinces, Kenya: October–December 1982

The sampling unit which was enumerated was the household. The enumerator was provided with a map showing the structures to be visited and a list of names of household heads. The structures visited were a subset of those visited in 1977/8 for IRS3. Usually the same household was interviewed, but when this was no longer there the household presently occupying the site was interviewed. We are thus able to distinguish between tracing the same holding and the same household.

PILOT SURVEY

In March 1982 a pilot survey of about thirty households in Kisii was performed. In the light of the experience from this exercise the questionnaire was revised.

SURVEY DESIGN

The sample used was that of the CBS in IRS3 in 1977/8, but only Central and Nyanza Provinces were included. The sample selection procedure is described in CBS: 'The Integrated Rural Survey 1976–79. Basic Report', 1981.

Table A1 gives a list of clusters included in the survey, and there we also report the number of households we were unable to locate.

RESPONSE RATE

In both provinces everybody who was located was willing to respond to the questions. However, some of the households taken from the IRS3 listing could not be found. In Central Province 342 out of 380 were found, that is 90 per

TABLE A1. *Sample clusters, Kenya*

Cluster no.	District	Location	No. of households found	No of households not found
Central province				
011	Nyandarua	N. Kinangop	17	3
012			14	6
021	Kiambu	Gatamaiyo	20	0
022			17	3
031	Kiambu	Ndumberi	19	1
032			19	1
041	Muranga	Kamahuha	16	4
042			16	4
051	Nyeri	Muhito	18	2
052			17	3
061	Kiambu	Ndarugu	19	1
062			19	1
071	Muranga	Ruchu	19	1
072			20	0
081	Kirinyaga	Baragwi	20	0
082			20	0
091	Kirinyaga	Mutithi	19	1
092			17	3
101	Nyeri	Mweiga	16	4
TOTAL			342	38
Nyanza				
311	Siaya	C. Alego	18	2
312			19	1
321	Kisumu	Kajulu	13	6
322			6	14
331	Siaya	E. Alego	19	0
332			(18	1
341	S. Nyanza	W. Kasipul	No list	
342			(18)	0
351	S. Nyanza	Kanyada	(16)	0
352			(20)	0
361	S. Nyanza	Muhuru	17	1
362			10	0
371	Kisii	W. Kitutu	17	0
372			18	2
381	S. Nyanza	Nyabasi	16	4
382			20	0
391	Kisii	E. Kitutu	16	0
392			18	2
401	Kisumu	S. Nyakach	14	0
402			12	8
411	Kisii	Basii	16	3
412			16	2
421	Kisumu	Muhoroni	15	5
422			17	2
431	S. Nyanza	Gem	18	1
432			(17)	0
441	Kisii	Majoge	19	0
442			18	1
TOTAL			441	55

cent. In Nyanza Province there were more problems. Out of the 496 households on the 27 cluster lists 441 were found, that is 89 per cent. However, four of the cluster lists contained households which were not part of the IRS3 (numbers in parentheses). These households have been retained for some purposes.

DATA PROCESSING

Validation of the data was time consuming. Extensive range and consistency checks were performed. The errors were then traced back to the questionnaire unless they could be resolved on the basis of other information on the tape. When the data had been validated a SAS file was created. Finally, a series of tables were run to check for further inconsistencies. Some errors were found at this stage and were corrected.

WEIGHTS

Where we use weights, those from IRS3 adjusted for response rate have been used. The estimates of rural population in both Nyanza and Central were derived from the population censi. The rural population of each province in 1979 is rescaled to get 1982 figures by applying the growth rates for rural population in the two provinces between the 1969 and 1979 censi.

2. Rural Survey of Dodoma, Iringa, Kilimanjaro, and Ruvuma Provinces, Tanzania, September 1983

SAMPLE

In this survey, below referred to as HBS2, we used the same sample as was used by the CBS in HBS1 of 1976/7. We had, however, to restrict our survey to one round in four provinces, which means that the sampling error in our survey would be larger.

Table A2 shows that 7 per cent of the households originally sampled had to be discarded due to incomplete information. The remaining households were thus used to construct the tables for the report on HBS1. We attempted to trace the usable households and managed to find 73 per cent of those. As shown in Chapter 3, our subset of the 498 differs little in income levels from the whole set of 680 in 1976/7.

WEIGHTS

Since we could not find all the households in HBS1, we have adjusted the weights accordingly. In HBS1 the population was divided into wards. Each

TABLE A2. *Number of cases by region, Tanzania*

Province	Number of rural households in HBS1	Usable cases retained for table construction	Number of rural households in HBS2 (and percentage of usable housholds found)
Dodoma	168	145	121 (83%)
Iringa	224	208	152 (73%)
Kilimanjaro	224	217	144 (66%)
Ruvuma	112	110	81 (74%)
TOTAL	728	680	498 (73%)

ward was divided into four strata. The number of sample units then becomes four times the number of wards. We constructed a weight for each sample unit by adjusting the original weights according to response rate. These weights were then normalized so that they sum to 498 (the size of the sample). The estimates of rural populations are extrapolations from the 1978 population census. The tables constructed for the regions are projections on the basis of the weighted sample in the region. An addition of the four regional projections normally differs slightly from the projection made for the total rural sample (see Table A3).

3. Definitions and Concepts used in both Surveys

HOUSEHOLD

A household comprises a person or group of persons generally bound by ties of kinship who normally reside together under a single roof or under several roofs within a single compound and who share a community of life in that they are answerable to the same head and share a common source of food.

Under this definition the polygamous wives within a single compound are included in the same household whatever the cooking arrangements may be. Moreover, if the land is considered by the husband as being his holding, it is assumed that all the wives are reliant on a common source of food even if each wife appears to be cultivating her own plot.

Most of the residents of the household are related to each other but this may not always be the case, e.g. a friend or a servant who is residing and eating with the household is also considered to be a member of the household.

Also included as members of the household are guests who at the time of the interview have been staying with the household for at least two weeks.

TABLE A3. *Sample clusters, Tanzania*

Location	No. of households found	No. of households not found
Dodoma		
1. Hongoro	19	0
2. Mlali	27	1
3. Kimagai	17	4
4. Bahi	18	7
5. Chikola	23	5
6. I. Mvuvi	17	7
TOTAL	121	24
Iringa		
1. Ukumbi	16	8
2. Mahenge	7	18
3. Kasanga	22	6
4. Mapanda	19	7
5. Matola	27	0
6. Lupalilo	24	2
7. Mtwago	23	3
8. Ilembula	14	12
TOTAL	152	56
1. K. M. Magharibi	18	10
2. Mkuu	4	24
3. Benderu	28	0
4. Vunta	12	15
5. Kifula	27	0
6. K. Mashariki	20	6
7. K. V. Magharibi	20	8
8. S. Magharibi	15	10
TOTAL	144	73
Ruvuma		
1. Ligunga	13	14
2. Namsakata	17	10
3. Mptimbi	26	2
4. Lusewa	25	3
TOTAL	81	29

Strictly speaking a husband who has a job in a far off town and sleeps during the working week away from the household which is enumerated is not a member of the household. However, if the husband usually returns at weekends he is included in the household. Children who are away at school in some distant location, living with other relatives or friends and only returning to the household during the holidays, are not included as members of the resident household.

This definition of the household retains the concept of residing together at least within a compound and also of sharing a community of life as revealed by the existence of a common head of household and reliance on the same piece of land or other sources of income.

HOLDING

A holding is defined as all the land and livestock used partly or completely for agricultural purposes and operated by a single holder.

This definition of a holding covers the range of possibilities from a holding solely of nomadic livestock to the situation where the holding is merely the sum of cultivated plots, as is the case with shifting cultivation, or a block of land, parts of which may not be under cultivation at any particular time but which can be easily identified as part of an integrated agricultural operation.

It should be emphasized that what matters is operation, not ownership, and any division of operational control within the household (as defined above) is omitted.

RESIDENT HOUSEHOLD

The persons living on the holding.

NON-RESIDENT HOUSEHOLD

The husband and wives living elsewhere, plus those sons and daughters living elsewhere who are either students, or are expected to return if they lose their job, (or if they have earned enough money), and send money to the household, or receive money from the resident household.

EXTENDED HOUSEHOLD

This consists of the resident household plus the non-resident household.

EXTENDED FAMILY

This consists of the resident household plus wives, husband, and all children living elsewhere.

THE INCOME CONCEPT

Annual household income consists of the following components:
1. Food crops, subsistence, traditional method of cultivation.
2. Food crops, subsistence, modern method of cultivation.

3. Food crops, sale, traditional method of cultivation.
4. Food crops, sale, modern method of cultivation.
5. Cash crops, traditional method of cultivation.
6. Cash crops, modern method of cultivation.

The method of cultivation is determined on the basis of the response to the question about how the farmer learnt the method he uses. However, the use of hybrid maize is always considered to imply a modern method.

Costs of inputs and labour were allocated to cash crops when there was inter-cropping. Costs were split between subsistence and marketed production according to the proportion of crops consumed and sold. Rent was split according to the area used.

7. Small stock, subsistence.
8. Small stock, net cash sales.
9. Small stock, stock valuation change.
10. Large traditional stock, subsistence.
11. Large traditional stock, net cash sales.
12. Large traditional stock, stock valuation change.
13. Large modern stock, subsistence.
14. Large modern stock, net cash sales.
15. Large modern stock, stock valuation change.

Small stock are sheep, goats, pigs, hens, and other livestock. Large stock are bulls, steers, cows, and oxen. They may either be improved (modern) or unimproved (traditional).

Under subsistence are recorded own consumption and gifts given of produce from livestock, including milk. Net cash sales are equal to sales minus purchases of stock plus sale of milk, hides, and eggs. Stock valuation change is equal to births + received gifts − deaths − thefts − own consumption − given to labour − other gifts + purchases − sales.

Costs of purchased inputs are allocated to large modern stock if there is any. Secondly it is allocated to large traditional stock if there is any, and finally, it is allocated to small stock. Costs are then divided among subsistence, cash, and stock valuation change by revenue proportions. Hired labour is distributed over the nine categories pro rata with revenue.

16. Own business, large.
17. Own business, small.

The business is considered to be large if revenue is over 5,000 shs. Profit is equal to revenue less costs.

18. Agricultural wage income.
19. Rural non-farm income, no entry barriers.
20. Rural non-farm income, entry barriers.
21. Urban wage income, no entry barriers.
22. Urban wage income, entry barriers.

Entry barriers are assumed to exist if the person says he needed qualifications, experience, training, or education to get the job.

23. Remittances sent back during the last twelve months by people who have now returned.
24. Remittances brought back by people who have returned during the last twelve months.
25. Remittances from people living elsewhere.
26. Other remittances.

1–26: income of resident household.

27. Retained earnings of non-resident household.

1–27: income of extended household.

Produce not marketed is priced according to average regional price received by those who sell, weighted by sold quantity. If the number of sellers in the region is less than three the national price is computed and used.

Mostly we aggregate incomes into six categories as follows:

1. Food income (categories 1–4).
2. Cash crop income (5–6).
3. Livestock (7–15).
4. Own business income (16–17).
5. Wage income (18–22).
6. Remittances (23–26).

Note that for the extended household we include retained earnings (27) with remittances.

4. The Questionnaire

4.1. HOUSEHOLD COMPOSITION

A. Members who are Resident

List all members of the household who are living in the house at the time of the interview. Include any guests who have been staying for more than 2 weeks and who share meals.

Name of household member)

Relation to household head
   1 = head
   2 = wife
   3 = son
   4 = daughter
   5 = father
   6 = mother

Appendix

    7 = other relative
    8 = a non-relative
Sex
    1 = male
    2 = female
Age (years)
Education
  Type
    0 = none
    1 = primary
    2 = government secondary
    3 = private secondary
    4 = university
    5 = adult literacy
    6 = other (specify)
  Standard or form
    0 = not applicable
    1 = standard/form 1
    2 = standard/form 2
    3 = standard/form 3
    4 = standard/form 4
    5 = standard/form 5
    6 = standard/form 6
    7 = standard 7
    8 = standard 8
Does he/she read and write?
    1 = read and write
    2 = read only
    3 = neither read nor write
Occupation
  Main
    01 = farmer or family farm worker
    02 = labourer on other shambas
    03 = labourer on estate/large farms
    04 = employee working for rural private employer (non-farm)
    05 = employee working for an urban private employer
    06 = employee working for government, or parastatal (rural)
    07 = employee working for government, or parastatal (urban)
    08 = own boss (rural) (non-farm)
    09 = own boss (urban)
    10 = disabled and unable to work
    11 = student (at school)
    12 = looking for work but unable to find any

13 = not in labour force
14 = employee paid by Village Council (Tanzania only)
15 = work on communal shambas (Tanzania only)
16 = work on other communal activities (Tanzania only)

Any other job
As above

B. Past Migration

Have any of these people ever left the household to seek work? (for at least a season?)

If more than one occasion then give details of the most recent.

Where did you go?
1 = another village
2 = agricultural estate
3 = local town
4 = major town (specify)
5 = Dar es Salaam/Nairobi
6 = outside the country

Year of departure

Year of return

Did you get work?
1 = yes
2 = no

Nature of work (as above in Section A)

How much did you send back (shillings/month)? (or value of goods in kind)

How much did you bring back when you returned home (shillings)?

How often did you visit the household whilst working and how long were your visits?
frequency (times per year)
average length of stay (days)

Whilst working away did you take decisions about the shamba?
0 = no
1 = yes, chose crops planted
2 = yes, chose inputs
3 = yes, chose labour hiring
4 = yes, chose more than one of above

Did the household have land allocated away while this person was away? If so how many hectares? (Tanzania only)
0 = no

Did you come back to avoid losing land by reallocation? (Tanzania only)
1 = yes
2 = no

C. Current Migrants

Are there spouses, sons, and daughters of the head of the household who are now living elsewhere?

Relation to household head
    1 = husband
    2 = wife
    3 = son
    4 = daughter

Sex
    1 = male
    2 = female

Age (years)

Education
  Type
    0 = none
    1 = primary
    2 = government secondary
    3 = harambee secondary (Kenya only)
    4 = village polytechnic (Kenya only)
    5 = university
    6 = adult literacy
    7 = other
  Standard
    0 = not applicable
    1 = standard/form 1
    2 = standard/form 2
    3 = standard/form 3
    4 = standard/form 4
    5 = standard/form 5
    6 = standard/form 6
    7 = standard 7
    8 = standard 8

Does he/she read and write? See Section 4.1A.

Occupation
  Main
    As in Section 4.1A
  Any other
    As in Section 4.1A

Where is he/she living now?
    1 = another village
    2 = agricultural estate
    3 = local town

4 = major town (specify)
 5 = Dar es Salaam/Nairobi

When did (s)he leave the household (year)?

Has s(he) been given land by this household? If so, how many hectares?

Why did (s)he go?
 1 = to look for work
 2 = to take up a job offer
 3 = marriage
 4 = land shortage
 5 = other (specify)

About how much does (s)he earn in his present occupation (shillings/month)?

Does (s)he send money back to the household? If so, how much (shillings/month)?

Do you send any money to him/her? If so, how much (shillings/month)?

How often does (s)he visit the household and how long are these visits?
 Times per year
 Average stay (days)

Does (s)he take decisions about the shamba?
 0 = no
 1 = choice of crops planted only
 2 = purchase of inputs only
 3 = both planting and purchases of inputs

Do you expect (s)he will return to live in this household? If so, when and why?
 0 = no
 1 = on retirement
 2 = if lose job
 3 = when they inherit land
 4 = when they have saved enough cash

Do you receive any remittance from anyone other than your spouse or children? If yes, how much (shillings/month)?

4.2. WORK

(Members who are resident only)

A. Did any Household Members Work in Off-farm Wage Employment in the Last 12 Months?

Did (s)he need qualifications/experience/training/education in order to get it?
 1 = experience only
 2 = training only
 3 = qualifications/education only

4 = experience and training
5 = experience and qualifications
6 = training and qualifications
7 = all three
8 = none

For how many years has (s)he worked for this employer (longest)?

How much did (s)he earn per month (shillings) (average)?

How many days per month did (s)he do this work (total)?

How far away was this work (km) (furthest)?

If still doing this work, for how long does (s)he expect to continue in wage employment (years)?

B. Did any Household Member Work on Other People's Shambas in the Last 12 Months?

Typically, how many days per month (total)?

How many hours per day (average)?

How was (s)he paid (main)?
    1 = cash
    2 = payment in kind
    3 = meal
    4 = use of plough

What was the value of this payment per day (shillings) (average)?

How far away is the holding on which (s)he worked (km) (furthest)?

C. Has any Household Member done any Work as his Own Boss in the Last Year, Other than Working on the Shamba? Examples are Handicrafts, Business, Market Stall, Bar, Selling Food.

Typically how many days per month does (s)he work on the business?

How many hours per day?

Type of business
    1 = brewing
    2 = handicrafts
    3 = duka
    4 = bar
    5 = market stall
    6 = other (specify)

What were the sales of the business last year (shillings)?

What were the costs of the business last year (shillings)?
    Hired labour
    All other cash costs

312 Appendix

D. *Has any Household Member Worked on an Estate, Commercial Farm, or State Farm in the Last twelve Months?*

Typically how many days per month?

How many hours per day?

How much did (s)he earn per day (shillings)?

How far away is the estate or farm on which (s)he worked (km)?

E. *Did any Household Member Work on the Communal Shamba in the Last twelve Months? (Tanzania Only)*

Typically how many days per month?

How many hours per day?

How much over the year did (s)he earn from this work (include value of payments in kind) (shillings)?

F. *Did any Household Member Work on any Communal non-Shamba activities in the Last twelve Months? (Tanzania Only)*

Typically how many days per month?

How many hours per day?

How much over the year did (s)he earn form his work (include value of payments in kind) (shillings)?

4.3. CHANGES SINCE 1975

Do you remember that about seven years ago the price of coffee doubled? I want you to tell me a little about your life just before that time. The year I want you to think of is 1975 (refer to age of children then). It was just before the coffee boom and (Tanzania only) just after Operation Sogeza.

When did the household first come here (year)? (Code 01 if a long time ago)

How did the household acquire the holding?
    1 = inherited
    2 = bought
    3 = allocated by Village Council (Tanzania only)
    4 = other (specify)

A. *Changes in Land Area*

Since 1975 has the household bought or sold any land? (Tanzania: changed its land area by buying or selling crops?)
    area (hectares)
    value (shillings)
    year

If bought, how was it financed?
        1 = income from crops
        2 = income from wages

3 = income from business
4 = loan/borrowing
5 = remittances
6 = income from livestock
7 = sale of livestock
8 = other (specify)

If sold why?
1 = need cash for school fees
2 = need cash for business
3 = need cash for livestock
4 = cannot farm land (specify reason)
6 = other

Has the amount of land rented, borrowed, or (Tanzania only) allocated by the Village Council changed? If so, by how many hectares and why?
   change in land let to other households
      increase
      decrease
      why?
         1 = change in the size of household labour force
         2 = change in crops grown
         3 = village rules
   change in land borrowed from other households
      increase
      decrease
      why?
         as above
   change in land allocated to household by Village Council
      increase
      decrease
      why?
         as above

Has the land area changed through sub-division or inheritance? If so, by how much?
   Lost through sub-division
      Area (hectares)
   Acquired through inheritance
      Area (hectares)

B. Cropping Pattern

Since 1975 have you switched hectarage from food crops to cash crops or from cash crops to food crops?
1 = yes
2 = no

If yes, area changed from food crops to cash crops (hectares) Area changed from cash crops to food crops (hectares)

C. Livestock

Can you remember how much livestock you owned in 1975?
  Bulls (number)
  Steers (number)
  Cows (number)
  Oxen (number)
  Sheep (number)
  Goats (number)
  Pigs (number)
  Hens (number)
  Other (specify)

If number of livestock has increased, how did you manage to finance this increase in your livestock?
  1 = income from cash crops
  2 = income from wage employment
  3 = income from own business
  4 = loan/borrowing
  5 = sale of land
  6 = remittances
  7 = income from livestock
  8 = bride price
  9 = natural increase

If the number of livestock has decreased, why have you reduced the herd?
  1 = less communal grazing land available
  2 = needed cash for school fees
  3 = needed cash for other purposes
  4 = deaths
  5 = payment of bride price

D. Other Real Assets

Did you move house in Operation Sogeza? (Tanzania only)
  1 = yes
  2 = no

Since 1975 have you improved any of the buildings on your holding or added any new buildings?
  If yes, what types of change were made?
    0 = no improvement
    1 = new house only
    2 = improved house only
    3 = improved or new farm buildings only

4 = new houses and improved or new farm buildings
5 = improved house and improved or new farm buildings

How much did you spend in total (shillings)?

Since 1975 have you bought any machinery or equipment for your shamba? If yes, how much did you spend in total (shillings)?

Since 1975 have you bought any machinery or equipment for your non-farm business? If yes, how much did you spend in total (shillings)?

Since 1975 have you bought property other than on your holding? If yes, how much did you spend in total (shillings)?

Do you own any of the following? (number owned)
  cart
  plough
  harrow
  hand mill
  wheel barrow
  hand pump
  water tank
  usable bicycle

E. Financial Assets and Liabilities

Do you have an account with one of the following? If so, in which year did you start it?
  commercial bank (year)
  Post Office savings account (year)

Have you contributed to the Village Development Fund during the past year? If so, how much (shillings)? (Tanzania only)

Have you lent any money to other households this year? If so, how much in total did you lend (shillings)?

Was the borrower(s) a relative?
  1 = yes
  2 = no

For how long a period was the loan (months)?

Is interest charged or any gifts made in kind in return for the loan?
  1 = yes, interest charged
  2 = gifts in kind are made
  3 = both interest and gifts in kind are made
  4 = neither interest nor gifts in kind are made

Have you borrowed any money from other households this year? If so, how much in total did you borrow?

Is interest charged or any gifts made in kind in return for the loan?

For how long a period was the loan (months)?

Have you borrowed any money from co-operative societies or banks since 1975?
  1 = yes
  2 = no

F. Labour

Was the head of the household working at the same occupation in 1975 as he is now? If no, what was his main occupation in 1975?
  main
    As in Section 4.1A

If people in this village work for other households on their shambas, typically how much would they be paid for a day's work? Can you remember how much they would have been paid in previous years?
  Shillings per day
  1982
  1981
  1980
  1979
  1978
  1977
  1976
  1975

G. Coffee Boom

How many coffee trees does the household have?

Was the household growing coffee at the time when the price doubled (in 1976)? If not, skip to H. If yes, did you increase the use of fertilizer on your coffee trees when the price was high?
  1 = yes
  2 = no

Did you or other members of your household spend more time working on your coffee when the price was high? If yes, about how much more time?
  man days per year before the boom
  man days per year during the boom

How much of this extra work on coffee was done by doing less work on other crops, and how much by people working longer hours?
  less work on other crops
  worked harder

Did non-household members help you when the coffee price was high? If yes, how many extra man days per year? (yes/no)

What did you do with the extra money?
  spent it on daily needs
  spent more on school fees

spent it on house improvements
bought crops or land
bought livestock
bought farm machinery
saved some of it
invested in non-farm business
bought house
married more wives
other (specify)

H. Coffee Planting

Has the household uprooted any coffee trees since 1975? If so, how many?

Has the household planted any coffee since 1975?
   1 = yes
   2 = no

Was the coffee planted because the price had gone up?
   1 = yes
   2 = no

Do you now regret having done this planting?
   1 = yes
   2 = no

If yes, why
   1 = because the price is now lower
   2 = because of the delay in payment for coffee
   3 = because the coffee has not grown well
   4 = because coffee growing needs too much work
   5 = because of coffee disease

How did you finance planting coffee?
   1 = income from cash crops
   2 = income from wage employment
   3 = income from own business
   4 = loan/borrowing
   5 = sale of land
   6 = remittances
   7 = income from livestock
   8 = sale of livestock
   9 = other (specify)

Is there a delay between your delivery of coffee and the payment for it?
   1 = yes
   2 = no

If yes, how long?
   weeks delay for the first payment
   weeks delay for final payment

4.4. HEALTH

A. In the Last three Months did any Member of the Household have one of the Following Illnesses? If so, How Often was he/she Ill? How Many Days was he/she too Ill to Work or go to School? For the Last Time he/she was Ill, give Details of the Illness and the Actions Taken

In the last three months
    No. of times had illness (F, DV, FDV, C, DB)
        1 = fever (F)
        2 = diarrhoea or vomiting (DV)
        3 = fever and diarrhoea or vomiting (FDV)
        4 = cough but not blood in sputum (C)
        5 = cough with blood in sputum (CB)

Total number of days too ill to work or go to school?

For the most recent of these illnesses
    Type of illness
        1 = fever (F)
        2 = diarrhoea or vomiting (DV)
        3 = fever and diarrhoea or vomiting (FDV)
        4 = cough but no blood in sputum (C)
        5 = cough with blood in sputum (CB)
    When (month)?

How long for (days)?

First action
    01 = none
    02 = went to bed
    03 = traditional medicine
    04 = bought medicine
    05 = went to dispensary
    06 = went to health centre
    07 = went to district hospital
    08 = went to mission hospital
    09 = went to provincial hospital (regional in Tanzania)
    10 = went to referral hospital
    11 = went to private doctor's clinic (Kenya only)
    12 = went to private nursing home or hospital (Kenya only)

Next action
    As above

B. Outpatient Visits During the Last three Months

Has anyone in this household been to a dispensary, hospital, or clinic in the past three months as an outpatient? (If no, skip to C). For each person who was an outpatient, fill in details of each course of visits they made. If they had more than one course of treatment, or if they transferred to a different facility, make a fresh entry for each course and each facility. Give serial number of any accompanying adult.

How many visits were involved?

When was the last visit (month)?

Type of health facility
   1 = dispensary
   2 = health centre
   3 = district hospital
   4 = mission hospital
   5 = provincial hospital (regional in Tanzania)
   6 = referral hospital
   7 = private doctor's clinic (Kenya only)
   8 = private nursing home or hospital (Kenya only)

What led up to the course of visits
   01 = own initiative
   02 = police
   03 = referral from dispensary
   04 = referral from health centre
   05 = referral from district hospital
   06 = referral from mission hospital
   07 = referral from provincial hospital (regional in Tanzania)
   08 = referral from referral hospital
   09 = referral from private doctor's clinic (Kenya only)
   10 = referral from private nursing home or hospital (Kenya only)

What was the highest level of medical staff seen?
   1 = doctor
   2 = clinical officer
   3 = registered nurse
   4 = enrolled nurse
   5 = midwife

What type of treatment did you receive?
   01 = healthy baby care (0–2 years)
   02 = prenatal check
   03 = postnatal check
   04 = inoculation
   05 = tooth extraction
   06 = medicine
   07 = injecting
   08 = wound dressing
   09 = minor operation/stitches
   10 = test
   11 = X-ray

How did you get there?
  1 = walk
  2 = cycle
  3 = bus
  4 = matatu
  5 = other

What was the time spent on a typical visit?
  Travelling to facility (one-way) hours/minutes
  Waiting for treatment (hours/minutes)
  Time being treated (minutes)

What was the cost of the course of visits?
  Fees (shillings)
  Travel costs (shillings)
  Other (shillings)

If you had not used the facility which you did use, what other facility would you have used?
  1 = none
  2 = dispensary
  3 = health centre
  4 = district hospital
  5 = mission hospital
  6 = provincial hospital (regional in Tanzania)
  7 = referral hospital
  8 = private doctor's clinic (Kenya only)
  9 = private nursing home or hospital (Kenya only)

If you paid why did you?
  1 = quicker treatment
  2 = nearer to household
  3 = no drugs at dispensary
  4 = better treatment
  5 = other

Were you referred to another facility? If yes, code facility
  1 = none
  2 = dispensary
  3 = health centre
  4 = district hospital
  5 = mission hospital
  6 = provincial hospital (regional in Tanzania)
  7 = referral hospital
  8 = private doctor's clinic (Kenya only)
  9 = private nursing home or hospital (Kenya only)

Did you go?
   1 = yes
   2 = no
   3 = not yet, but will go

C. *Health: Inpatient Stays During Preceding twelve months*
What was the length of stay (days)?
When was the stay (month)?
Type of hospital
   1 = health centre
   2 = district hospital
   3 = mission hospital
   4 = provincial hospital (regional in Tanzania)
   5 = referral hospital
   6 = private doctor's clinic (Kenya only)
   7 = private nursing home or hospital (Kenya only)
How far is the hospital (miles)?
What led up to the admission as inpatient?
   01 = own initiative
   02 = police
   03 = referral from dispensary
   04 = referral from health centre
   05 = referral from district hospital
   06 = referral from mission hospital
   07 = referral from provincial hospital (regional in Tanzania)
   08 = referral from referral hospital
   09 = referral from private doctor's clinic (Kenya only)
   10 = referral from private nursing home or hospital (Kenya only)
Were you asked to go back or referred to another facility on discharge?
   0 = no
   1 = referral to dispensary
   2 = referral to health centre
   3 = referral to district hospital
   4 = referral to mission hospital
   5 = referral to provincial hospital (regional in Tanzania)
   6 = referral to referral hospital
   7 = referral to private doctor's clinic (Kenya only)
   8 = referral to private nursing home or hospital (Kenya only)
Did you go?
   1 = yes
   2 = no

What payments were made?
    What was the basis for payment
        1 = fixed charge
        2 = daily rate
    Fees (shillings)
    Travel costs (shillings)
    Other (shillings)

D. *Health: Live Births in Household During the Preceding twelve Months*

When was the baby born?

Is infant still alive?
    1 = yes
    2 = no

Place of birth
    1 = at home
    2 = in health facility
    3 = other

Who delivered the baby?
    1 = government doctor
    2 = private doctor
    3 = government nurse or midwife
    4 = private nurse or midwife
    5 = traditional midwife
    6 = relative
    7 = other

Did a nurse visit the mother at home?
    Number of visits during pregnancy
    Number of visits after birth

Were any payments made? If so, how much in total (shillings)?

E. *Health: Other*

For each child under 5

Does the child have a Kadi Ya Kliniki?
    1 = yes
    2 = no

If yes, note from the chart:
    Birth weight (kg)
    Does the growth curve ever fall in the red zone?
        1 = yes
        2 = no
    How many vaccinations has the child had?

For each child at school

Was any medical treatment received at school in the last twelve months?
 1 = yes
 2 = no
Inoculations
Dental examination
Dental treatment
Medical examination
Medical treatment

For all household members
Have there been any deaths in the household in the past 12 months?
If so, give sex and age
 1st death
 2nd death
 3rd death
 4th death

4.5. EDUCATION: HOUSEHOLD MEMBERS ATTENDING SCHOOL

Distance from house to school (miles)

How does member get to school?
 1 = walk
 2 = cycle
 3 = bus
 4 = matatu
 5 = other

How long does it take to get there? (one-way) (hours/minutes)

Is the school a boarding school? If so, how often does the pupil come home (times per year)?

How much are the out of pocket expenses (shillings per year)?
 Fees
 Harambee contributions (Kenya only)
 Books
 Uniforms
 Transport
 Other

Do you receive any money from bursaries to help pay these costs? If so, how much (shillings per year)?

How otherwise do you finance these costs?
 0 = no costs
 1 = income from cash crops
 2 = income from wage employment
 3 = income from own business

    4 = loan/borrowing
    5 = sale of land/trees
    6 = remittances
    7 = income from livestock
    8 = sale of livestock
    9 = other

If those of your children now attending primary school fail to get a place at a government secondary school, will you get them to repeat the exam?
    1 = yes
    2 = no

If your children now in primary school cannot get a government place, will you try to educate them further? If so, how far?
    1 = no
    2 = harambeẹ school up to form 2 in Kenya
      = private school up to form 4 in Tanzania
    3 = harambee school up to form 4 in Kenya
      = private school up to form 6 in Tanzania
    4 = technical school
    5 = commercial course, e.g. driver, typist

4.6. WATER, WOOD, AND SEWAGE

A. Water

Who fetches water (give serial numbers of household members)?

Do you use the same source of water for drinking water and for all other purposes? Do you use the same sources in wet season and dry season? If the answer is yes to both questions, answer the first questions below. Otherwise answer this and other questions as relevant.

Main drinking water supply
  Wet season
    What is the source of water?
      01 = still pond
      02 = small dam
      03 = stream
      04 = spring
      05 = well
      06 = borehole
      07 = sub-surface dam
      08 = rainwater
      09 = piped water: communal tap
      10 = piped water: tap in house
    How long does it take to get there (minutes)?

How many months in the year is the source available?
How much is fetched per day (debes)?
How many hours per day in total do household members spend fetching it?

Dry season (if different from wet season)
What is the source of water?
   01 = still pond
   02 = small dam
   03 = stream
   04 = spring
   05 = well
   06 = borehole
   07 = sub-surface dam
   08 = rainwater
   09 = piped water: communal tap
   10 = piped water: tap in house
How long does it take to get there (minutes)?
How many months in the year is the source available?
How much is fetched per day (debes)?
How many hours per day in total do household members spend fetching it

Other water supply
  Wet season
    What is the source of water?
      As above
    How long does it take to get there (minutes)?
    How many months in the year is the source available?
    How much is fetched per day (debes)?
    How many hours per day in total do household members spend fetching it?

  Dry season (if different from wet season)
    What is the source of water?
      As above
    How long does it take to get there (minutes)?
    How many months in the year is the source available?
    How much is fetched per day (debes)?
    How many hours per day in total do household members spend fetching it?

B. *Wood*

Who collects firewood? (give serial numbers)

How many hours per day in total do household members spend in collecting it?

C. Sewage

How is human waste disposed of?
 1 = in fields
 2 = bucket latrine
 3 = pit latrine
 4 = cesspool
 5 = septic tank
 6 = main sewer

4.7. GENERAL

How far (in miles) is it to the nearest Post Office? Bus route? Matatu route? Market? Dispensary? Health Centre? Primary School? Government Secondary School?
Harambee Secondary School? (All for Kenya only)

How often does a member of the household go to market (times per week)?

How long does it take to get there (hours/minutes)?

How much does it cost (shillings)?

How are inputs usually brought to the holding?
 1 = carried on head or back
 2 = on back of mule or other animal
 3 = cycle
 4 = hand cart
 5 = cart pulled by animal
 6 = motor vehicle

How are outputs usually taken from the holding?
 1 = carried on head or back
 2 = on back of mule or other animal
 3 = cycle
 4 = hand cart
 5 = cart pulled by animal
 6 = motor vehicle

What improvements in government services since 1975 have been most useful to you?
 1 = new or improved roads
 2 = better or more frequent extension services
 3 = better or nearer health facilities
 4 = better or nearer water supplies
 5 = better or nearer primary school
 6 = better or nearer secondary school
 7 = other (specify)

Appendix

What services or things would you like the government to provide that it is not now providing or is providing inadequately?
1 = new or improved roads
2 = better or more frequent extension services
3 = better or nearer health facilities
4 = better or nearer water supplies
5 = better or nearer primary school
6 = better or nearer secondary school
7 = other (specify)

4.8. AVAILABILITY OF GOODS (Tanzania only)

For each of the following goods, if, during the last year, you wanted to buy this good:

Were there times when you wanted to buy this good at the official price but it was not available?
1 = yes
2 = no

How often (days/year) did you manage to buy this good at the official price?

When you did make a purchase at the official price, typically how much did you buy?

Were there times when this good was not available even unofficially?
1 = yes
2 = no

How often (days/year) did you manage to buy this good at unofficial prices?

When you did make a purchase at an unofficial price, typically how much did you buy?

When you did buy this good unofficially typically how much did you pay (price per unit)?

Maize flour (sembe) (kg)
Rice (kg)
Paraffin (bottle)
Cooking oil (bottle)
Soap (bar)
Sugar (kg)
Salt (cup)
Matches (box)
Cigarettes (pkt)
Roofing sheets (no.)
Bicycles (no.)
Bicycle tubes (no.)

Hoes (jembe) (no.)
Panga (no.)
Rake (no.)
Axe (no.)
Bags (no.)
School uniforms (no.)
Khanga/vitenge (piece)
Radios (no.)

During the last season did you get any of the following?
  1 = no
  2 = yes, but too late
  3 = yes and on time
    fertilizer
    seeds
    insecticides

4.9. THE SHAMBA

A. Area and Tenure

How many parcels of land does the household operate?
How big is each parcel?
  Area (hectares)
  Tenure (Kenya)
    1 = owned
    2 = rented
    3 = borrowed
    4 = plough shared
    5 = share cropped

  Tenure (Tanzania)
    1 = allocated by Village Council (not held before Operation Sogeza): block farm
    2 = allocated by Village Council (not held before Operation Sogeza): non-block holding
    3 = held by household before Operation Sogeza
    4 = borrowed from another household
    5 = acquired by exchange for land or goods with another household (bought)

How far is the parcel from the house (km)?
Use
  Used for homestead only (area)
  Crops (area)
  Grazing (area)

Appendix

Unused, suitable for crops (area)
Unused, suitable for grazing only (area)
Not suitable for either (including woodland) (area)

Does the household own any land which it lends to other households?

If yes: give area (hectares)

Do you use a tractor
   1 = no
   2 = yes (owned)
   3 = yes (hired)

Do you use oxen?
   1 = no
   2 = yes (owned)
   3 = yes (hired)

Have you ever been a member of a co-operative society?
   1 = yes
   2 = no

B. What Crops were Produced on the Holding During the Last Year?

First crop
  Crop Number
  Output (kg)
    01 = local maize
    02 = hybrid maize
    03 = beans
    04 = millet
    05 = sorghum
    06 = cassava
    07 = groundnuts
    08 = wheat
    09 = rice
    10 = yams
    11 = sweet potatoes
    12 = peas
    13 = sukuma wiki
    14 = other veg.
    15 = coffee
    16 = bananas
    17 = tea
    18 = tobacco
    19 = cotton
    20 = pyrethrum
    21 = cashew nuts
    22 = coconuts

    23 = sesame
    24 = sunflower
    25 = castor seed
    26 = sugar cane
    27 = onions
    28 = other

Second crop
  Crop No.
  Output (kg)
    As above

Third crop
  Crop no.
  Output (kg)
    As above

Plot area (hectares)

Percentage of farm work time spent on this plot during the year for each person

Hired labour
  Man days
  How paid
    1 = cash only
    2 = payment in kind to take home
    3 = meal, pombe at the place of work
    4 = use of plough
    5 = two of above payments
  Value of payment per man day (shillings)

Knowledge of techniques
  How did you learn about the method which you are using?
    1 = traditional method/from father
    2 = from demonstration
    3 = from extension visit
    4 = from my own trial and error
    5 = from neighbours/relatives
    6 = I read about it
    7 = other
  Have you changed your method in the last five years?
    1 = yes
    2 = no
  If yes why?
    1 = not applicable (no change)
    2 = others were doing it
    3 = more profitable

Appendix

  4 = because the government wanted me to change
  5 = other
Have you ever received any extension advice about the crop or livestock?
  1 = yes
  2 = no
Nature of extension contact?
  0 = no contact
  1 = visit of extension worker to this shamba
  2 = no visit, but I attended demonstration
  3 = both visit(s) and attended demonstration(s)
  4 = attended Farmers Training Centre
Frequency of contact
  1 = no contact
  2 = only once
  3 = once a year
  4 = two or three times a year
  5 = more than three times a year

Inputs
  own produced inputs
    seeds value (shillings)
    other value (shillings)
  purchased inputs
    seeds value (shillings)
    fertilizer
      bags
      total cost (shillings)
  Pesticides, sprays etc. value (shillings)

C. What Crops Were Marketed?

Crop (Kenya only)
    quantity (kg)
    price per kg (shillings)
    revenue (shillings)
  How was the crop sold?
    1 = to marketing board, or board agent, or co-operative
    2 = to middle men
    3 = direct to consumers by household
    4 = multiple channels
Crop (Tanzania only)
  As Section 4.9B
  Official sales
    quantity (kg)
    price per kg (shillings/cents)

    revenue (shillings)
    delay in payment (months)
  Unofficial sales
    quantity (kg)
    price per kg (shillings/cents)
    revenue (shillings)

D. Livestock

Stock now owned
  Type
  Local breed
    no.
    total value (shillings)
  Foreign breed
    no.
    total value (shillings)
Changes during the last year
  Purchases (no.)
  Births (no.)
  Received as gifts (no.)
  Sales (no.)
  Slaughtered (no.)
  Given to labour (no.)
  Death and thefts (no.)
  Given as gifts (including bride price) (no.)
Outputs of milk, eggs, hides, etc. during the last year
Sales
  milk
    value (shillings)
    quantity (litres)
  eggs
    value (shillings)
    quantity (dozens)
  meat
    value (shillings)
    quantity (kg)
  hides etc.
    value (shillings)
Own consumption
  milk
    value (shillings)
    quantity (litres)

eggs
    value (shillings)
    quantity (dozens)
meat
    value (shillings)
    quantity (kg)
hides etc.
    value (shillings)
Outputs used for livestock during the last year
    Purchased feed
        value (shillings)
        quantity (kilos)
    Other cash expenses (e.g. dip fees)
        value (shillings)
    Own produced feed (if stallfed)
        value (shillings)
        quantity (kilos)

References

Aaron, Henry, and McGuire, Martin (1970). 'Public Goods and Income Distribution', *Econometrica*, 38: 907–20.
Azam, J.-P., and Faucher, J.-J, (1987), *Offre de biens manufactures et production agricole: Le Cas du Mozambique*, OECD: Paris.
Bevan, D. L., Collier, P., and Gunning, J. W. (1987). 'Consequences of a Commodity Boom in a Controlled Economy: Accumulation and Redistribution in Kenya, 1975–1983', *World Bank Economic Review*, 1: 489–513.
——, Bigsten, A., Collier, P., and Gunning, J. W. (1988). 'The Decline of Incomes in the United Republic of Tanzania During the "Nyerere Experiment"', in W. van Ginneken (ed.), *Trends in Self-Employment Incomes*, 61–83, ILO: Geneva.
——, Collier, P., and Gunning, J. W., with Bigsten, A., and Horsnell, P. (1989). *Controlled Open Economies: A Neo-Classical Approach to Structuralism*, Oxford University Press: Oxford.
Bigsten, A., (1980). *Regional Inequality and Development. A Case Study of Kenya*, Gower: Aldershot.
——(1984). *Education and Income Determination in Kenya*, Gower: Aldershot.
——(1985). 'What do Smallholders do for a Living', in Mats Lundahl (ed.), *The Primary Sector in Economic Development*, Croom Helm: Beckenham.
Casley, D. J., and Marchant, T. J. (1978). 'Smallholder Marketing in Kenya', Consultant's Report, HIID: Nairobi.
Central Bureau of Statistics, Nairobi (1976). 'Information System for Vital and Health Statistics', *Social Perspectives*, 1 (2), August.
——(1982). *The Integrated Rural Surveys 1976–9:* Basic Report.
Cleave, J. H. (1974). *African Farmers: Labour Use in the Development of Smallholder Agriculture*, Praeger: New York.
Coffee Board Of Kenya, (annual) *Annual Report*.
Coffee Research Foundation, *Annual Report and Accounts*, 1979–80.
Collier, P. (1985). 'The Allocation of Factors in African Peasant Agriculture', mimeo, Development Strategy Division, World Bank: Washington DC.
——, and Lal, D. (1986). *Labour and Poverty in Kenya, 1900–1980*, Oxford University Press: Oxford.
——, Radwan, S., and Wangwe, S. (1986). *Labour and Poverty in Rural Tanzania*, Clarendon Press: Oxford.
Cooksey, B., Fowler, A., and Kwayu, C. (1987a). 'Incentive Goods for Development in Tanzania', Afro-Aid: Dar es Salaam.
——, Kwayu, C., and Lemaa, H. (1987b). 'Incentive Goods in Support of the Netherlands', Tanzania Rural Development Programme, Bumaaco: Moshi.
Coulson, A. (1981). 'Agricultural Policies in Mainland Tanzania', in J. Heyer, P. Roberts, and G. Williams, (eds.), *Rural Development in Tropical Africa*, Macmillan: London.
——(1982). *Tanzania: A Political Economy*, Clarendon Press: Oxford.

David, M., and Wyeth, P. (1978). 'Kenya Commercial Bank Loans in Rural Areas: A Survey', IDS Working Paper no. 342, Nairobi.

Ellis, F. (1982). 'Agricultural Price Policy in Tanzania', *World Development*, 10(6).

——, and Hanak, E. (1980). *An Economic Analysis of the Coffee Industry in Tanzania 1969/70: Toward a Higher and More Stable Producer Price*, Economic Research Bureau: Dar es Salaam.

FAO (1975). 'Raising the Productivity of Small Farmers: Tanzania Case Study', mimeo, Rome.

Flemming, J. S. (1976). *Inflation*, Oxford University Press: London.

Government of Kenya (1937). *Coffee in Kenya*, Department of Agriculture: Nairobi.

——(1963). *A National Cash Crops Policy for Kenya*, Parts I and II.

——(1966–70), (1970–4), (1974–8), (1979–84). *Development Plan*.

——(1968). *Economic Survey of Central Province—1963–4*, Statistics Division, Ministry of Economic Planning and Development: Nairobi.

——(1969a). *National Coffee Policy Plan*, Ministry of Agriculture: Nairobi.

——(1969b). *The Coffee Industry in Kenya in 1969*, Ministry of Agriculture: Nairobi.

——(1971). *An Outline of Coffee Management*, Ministry of Agriculture: Nairobi.

——(1977a). *Coffee Rehabilitation Project*, Loan Application, vol. 2, Nairobi.

——(1977b). *Integrated Rural Survey—1974–5*, Basic Report, CBS.

——(1979). *Labour Requirements/Availability*, Ministry of Agriculture: Nairobi.

——(1980). *Survey of Co-operative Credit, Savings, and Banking Arrangements*, Ministry of Co-operative Development: Nairobi.

——(1981). *The Integrated Rural Surveys 1976–79*, Basic Report, CBS: Nairobi.

——(1982). *Report on a Survey on Coffee Handled by Cooperatives During 1977/8 and 1978/9 Coffee Seasons*, mimeo, Ministry of Co-operative Development: Nairobi.

——(annual) *Statistical Abstract*.

Government of Tanzania (1981) *Statistical Abstract 1973–1979*, Government Printer, Dar es Salaam.

——(1981a). *Price Recommendation for the 1982–83 Agricultural Price Policy Review; Summary*, Government Printer, Dar es Salaam.

——(1983b). *Statistical Abstract 1982*, Government Printer, Dar es Salaam.

——(1984). *Quarterly Statistical Bulletin*, 35(1), Government Printer, Dar es Salaam.

——(1984). *Tanzania: Twenty Years of Independence (1961–1981). A review of Political and Economic Performance*, Bank of Tanzania, Dar es Salaam.

Gsanger, H. G., and Schmidt, G. (1977): *Decontrolling the Maize System in Kenya*, Discussion Paper no. 254, IDS: Nairobi.

Guerreiro, M. (1984). 'The Structure and Performance of Agricultural Marketing in Kenya and Tanzania', M.Litt. thesis, University of Oxford (unpublished).

Hazlewood, A. (1979). *The Economy of Kenya: The Kenyatta Era*, Oxford University Press: Oxford.

Hesselmark, O. (1977). *The Marketing of Maize and Beans in Kenya: A Proposal for Improved Effectiveness*, Working Paper no. 300, IDS: Nairobi.

Heyer, J. (1976). 'The Marketing System', in Heyer, J., et al. (eds.), *Agricultural Development in Kenya*, Oxford University Press: Nairobi, 313–363

——(1981). 'Agricultural Development Policy in Kenya from the Colonial Period to 1975', in Heyer, J., et al. (eds.), *Rural Development in Tropical Africa*, Oxford University Press: Nairobi, 90–120.

——, Maitha, J. K., and Senga, W. M. (eds.) (1976). *Agricultural Development in Kenya*, Oxford University Press: Nairobi.

Heyer, J., Roberts, P., and Williams, G. (eds.) (1981). *Rural Development in Tropical Africa*, Macmillan: London.
Hopcraft, P. (1978). *Milk Pricing in Kenya. The Case of a Bulky, Perishable Commodity with Seasonably Varying Production Costs*, Discussion Paper no. 266, IDS: Nairobi.
——, and Ruigu, G. (1976). *Dairy Marketing and Pricing in Kenya: Are Milk Shortages the Consequence of Drought or Pricing Policies?*, Discussion Paper no. 237, IDS: Nairobi.
Hunt, D. M. (1984). *The Impending Crisis in Kenya*, Gower: Aldershot.
Hyden, G. (1973). *Efficiency Versus Distribution in East African Co-operatives*, East African Literature Bureau: Nairobi.
——(1975). 'Ujamaa, Villagisation and Rural Development in Tanzania', *ODI Review*, 1.
Iliffe, J. (1979). *A Modern History of Tanganyika*, Cambridge University Press: Cambridge.
Judge, G. G., Griffiths, W. E., Carter Hill, R., and Lee, T. C. (1980). *The Theory and Practice of Econometrics*, J. Wiley and Sons: Chichester.
Katona, G. (1975). *Psychological Economics*, Elsevier: New York.
Keeler, A. G., Scobie, G. M., Renkow, M. A., and Franklin, D. L. (1981). 'The Economic Effects of Agricultural Policies in Tanzania', Research Triangle Institute for US AID.
——, Scobie, G., Renkow, M., and Franklin, D. L. (1982). 'The Consumption Effects of Agricultural Policies in Tanzania', Sigma One Corporation, January, Report prepared for US AID: Raleigh, North Carolina.
Kitching, G. (1980). *Class and Economic Change in Kenya*, Yale University Press: New Haven, Connecticut.
Lockheed, M. E., Jamison, D. T., and Lau, L. J. (1980). 'Farmer Education and Farm Efficiency: A Survey', *Economic Development and Cultural Change*, 29: 37–76.
Lundahl, M., and Ndulu, B. J. (1985). 'Market Related Incentives and Food Production in Tanzania: Theory and Experience', mimeo, University of Lund.
Maas, J. van L., and Criel, G. (1982), *Distribution of Primary School Enrollments in Eastern Africa*, World Bank Staff Working Paper no. 511.
Marquardt, D. W. (1963). 'An Algorithm for Least Squares Estimation of Nonlinear Parameters', *Journal of the Society for Industrial and Applied Mathematics*, 11: 431–41.
Meerman, J. (1979). *Public Expenditure in Malaysia: Who Benefits and Why*, Oxford University Press: Oxford.
Mosley, Paul (1983). *The Settler Economies: Studies in the Economic History of Kenya and Southern Rhodesia 1900–63*, African Studies Series no. 35, Cambridge University Press: Cambridge.
Mwenge International (1981). 'Feasibility Study of the Supply and Distribution of Farm Inputs Within the Cooperative Sector', Progress Report, May 1981, Final Report Number 1981, Executive Final Report, February 1982.
——, (1985). Economic Management in Sub–Saharan Africa: 'Key Issues, Experiences and Prospects', mimeo, Boston.
Ndulu, B. J., and Hyuha, M. (1986). 'Inflation and Economic Recovery in Tanzania: Some Empirical Evidence', mimeo, University of Dar es Salaam.
Neary, J. P., and Roberts, K. W. S. (1980). 'The Theory of Household Behaviour Under Rationing', *European Economic Review*, 13: 25–42.

Pitt, M. M., and Rosenzweig, M. R. (1986). 'Agricultural Prices, Food Consumption and the Health and Productivity of Indonesian Farmers', in I. J. Singh, L. Squire, and J. Strauss (eds.), *Agricultural Household Models: extensions, applications and policy*, Johns Hopkins University Press: Baltimore.

Schmidt, G. (1979). *Maize and Beans in Kenya. The Interaction and Effectiveness of the Informal and Formal Marketing Systems*, Occasional Paper no. 31, IDS: Nairobi.

Senga, W. M. (1976). 'Kenya's Agricultural Sector', in Heyer, J., et al. (eds.), *Agricultural Development in Kenya*, Oxford University Press: Nairobi, 69–110.

Shayo, S. A., Edelsten, P., and Tewari, S. C. (1981) 'NMC: Failure in the Post-Siasa ni Kilimo Decade', Tanzania Notes and Records no. 86 and 87 in *The Journal of the Tanzania Society*.

Shepherd, A. (1982). 'The Marketing of Agricultural and other Commodities in the Mbeya Region', RIDEP Report no. 48, Regional Commissioner's Office: Mbeya.

Shiller, R. J. (1984). 'Stock Prices and Social Dynamics', in W. C. Brainard, and G. L. Perry (eds.), *Brookings Papers on Economic Activity*, The Brookings Institution: Washington DC.

Shimwela, N. N. P. (1984). 'Planning, Parastatals, Markets, Prices and What Have You?', mimeo, Workshop on Economic Stabilization Policies in Tanzania, Dar es Salaam.

Singh, I. J., Squire, L., and Strauss, J. (eds.) (1986). *Agricultural Household Models: extensions, applications and policy*, Johns Hopkins University Press, Baltimore.

Smith, L. D. (1976). 'An Overview of Agricultural Development Policy', in Heyer, J., et al. (eds.), *Agricultural Development in Kenya*, Oxford University Press: Nairobi. 111–151.

——(1978). 'Low Income Smallholder Marketing and Consumption Patterns—Analysis and Improvement Policies and Programmes', mimeo, UNDP/FAO: Nairobi.

Tanzania Industrial Studies and Consulting Organisation (1985). *Soap Industry Study*, TISCO: Dar es Salaam.

Tollison, R. D. (1982). 'Rent Seeking: A Survey', *Kyklos*, 35.4: 575–602.

Vandemoortele, J. (1983). 'The Public Sector and Basic Needs Strategy in Kenya: The Experience of the Seventies', World Employment Programme Working Paper WEP 2-32/WP.46, ILO: Geneva.

Van Luijk, J. N. (1984). 'The Utilisation of Modern and Traditional Medical Care', in J. K. van Ginneken, and A. S. Muller (eds.), *Maternal and Child Health in Rural Kenya*, Croom Helm: New York.

——, and King, A. (1975). *An Economic History of Kenya and Uganda 1800–1970*, Macmillan: London.

Whitworth, A. C. (1982). 'Price Control Techniques in Poor Countries: The Tanzania Case', *World Development*, 10(6).

Williams, K. G., and Kabagambe, D. (1982). *The Impact of the Coffee Boom in Meru District Kenya*, Kenya Research Project, Working Paper no. 2, Institute of Planning Studies, University of Nottingham.

Wolff, R. D. (1974). *The Economics of Colonialism. Britain and Kenya 1870–1930*, Yale University Press: New Haven, Connecticut.

World Bank (1982). 'Tanzania: Agricultural Sector Report', Washington D.C.

Index

Note: References to figures are in italic type; references to tables are in bold type.

ability, differences in 81, 106–7
absenteeism from holdings 15
activities
 comparison of returns in 94–105
 hierarchy of 2, 101; sequential movement through 76, 101–4
activity, distribution of between sexes 238
activity mix
 Kenya 26, 27, **28–9**
 Tanzania 55, **56**
activity mobility 104
activity switches 32, 34–6, 83, 84, 94, 102–3, 104–5, 128–9
adopter (proxy) 110–11, 114–15, 117, 133
adoption decisions, bunching of 115
adoption, hypothetical sequence of **115**
adult literacy 236, 241, **262**
Africa, government intervention 291
African farmers
 coffee growing rapidly adopted 10
 excluded from production of coffee, tea, and pyrethrum 9, 10
 and new markets 9
 and tea production 10
African settlement, in Kenya 9
Africans, agricultural activities restricted 9–10
agricultural employment, Kenya, changes in 15–20
agricultural inputs and outputs, Tanzania 45–8
agricultural policy
 pro-peasant stance 10
 shift in in Kenya 10
 Tanzania, based on coercion 44
agricultural supply, elasticity of 204
agricultural value, growth in 27, 142
agricultural wage rates, increase in 74
agricultural wages 111, 132
agriculture, African 10
Arusha Declaration 45
asset accumulation 124
 coffee planting 128
 financial 124–5, 127–8
 improved livestock 128–9
 purchase of buildings and equipment, investment in non-farm businesses and land 129
 tree crops 125

asset expenditure, non-coffee households 129
asset formation 36, 38–9, 42, 134, 143–6
 privately efficient, perhaps socially inefficient 293–4
asset substitution 38–9
assets
 augmentation of 39
 and liabilities, financial 315–16
 liquid 112
 real 314–15
availability 49, 219, 220
 consumer goods, Tanzania 50, **51**
 deterioration of 163, 165
 foodstuffs, Tanzania **50**
 measure of 173
availability constraint 160, 161
availability indices 49, **176**, 177, 216–17

barriers to entry *see* entry barriers
barter economy 157–8
 and a black market 168–9
barter model, spiral of decline 172
Basic Industries Strategy 65
black market 3, 45, 154, 155, 207
 and availability restraints 211
 clearing 170, 218
 and cost of living deflator 61
 determinants of participation 166–7
 illegality of 171
 a market in search activities 165–72
 opportunity cost to seller 171
 subject to quantity restraint 52
 supplies in 52–3
black-market equilibrium *168*
black-market prices 213
black-market purchasing 218
Board of Internal Trade (BIT), Tanzania 177
 allocation of controlled goods 177–9
 goods deliveries to rural areas 50, 52, **53**
British Trusteeship for Tanzania 44
budget line, kinked 153, 166–7
budget shares 175, 204
business income 63

capital 80
capital accumulation, windfall 83

Index

capital stock
  augmentation of 76
  change in 83
capital-to-land endowment ratio 80
cash balances 171
cash crop income, Tanzania 53, **54**
cash crop output 157–8
  and money stock changes 162
cash crop production 166, 167–8, 174
  decline in 215
  elasticity 198
  Tanzania 181–9; real value 184, 189, **190–3**
cash crops 10, 24, 27, 34, 43, 72, 103, 105, 141, 157
  collapse in some outputs, Tanzania 184
  encouraged in Tanzania 44
  estimates of elasticity of 189, 194–8, 219–20
  taxation of 220
cattle offtake 92
Central Province (Kenya) 24
  accumulation of activities and per capita income *102*
  ban on coffee growing by Africans 10
  coffee production 86
  higher education costs 236
  inpatient costs 234, **259–60**
  and loan financing 22
  migration from 121
  outpatient costs 234, **253–8**
  per capita income and land area 27, **30**; real, change in 27, 31, **33**; unchanged 142, 143
  post-coffee boom survey 7, 300–1, 302–33
CES (constant elasticity of substitution) function, nested 88–9, **90**, 91
cheap-labour policies 9
co-operative societies
  disbanded in Tanzania 141
  state-owned 48
Cobb–Douglas function 87–8, **89**, 91, 92, 278
coffee 9, 85, 140
  African growing: banned in Kenya 9–10; successful in Tanganyika and Uganda 10
  capital intensive 80
  determinants of switch to 109–16
  displeasure with labour intensity needed 65
  fixed costs of 107, **108**
  investment in upgrading stock 41
  Kenya, export tax abolished 11
  land, labour, and forgone consumption requirements 107–9
  pure-stand and inter-cropped 85
  scale of operations defined 96
  Tanzania, early growth in 44
  unit cost function 96–7
  world prices high 7
coffee adopters, low rate of regret 150
coffee adoption 106, 109, 132–4
  constrained by lack of information 107
  copying effect 133, 135–6
  desirable or not 149–50
  differing in Kenya and Tanzania 143–4, 146, 148
  divergence in 146
  private consequences, Kenya 150
coffee adoption rate 148–9
coffee berry disease 10
Coffee Board (Kenya) 12
coffee boom 316–17
  as an instrument of change 122–36; secular changes 122–6
  diffusion of via labour markets 148
  direct and indirect benefits/effects 74–6, **82**, 126
  effects of 294
  and favourable climatic conditions 59
  impact of 126–34
  improvement in terms of trade 1
  Kenya: adjustments toward steady state 8; reaction of peasants 293
  peasants' behaviour during 36–42
  presents clearly identifiable reactions 2
  static and dynamic effects 71–2
  Tanzania, behaviour of peasants 65–7
coffee boom money
  use of 39–42; Kilimanjaro **66**
  see also investment; windfall income; windfall investment
coffee co-operative societies (Kenya) 126
  advised investment of coffee boom money 40
  range of activities 12
  recollections of the boom period 39–41
coffee factories, investment in 40
coffee growers
  accumulated assets 127–30
  benefiting from the coffee boom 126
  windfall income to acquire improved livestock 135
coffee growing
  economies of scale 96; entry restricted by 99
  financing of entry or extra planting 38–9
coffee and hybrid maize, comparison of returns in 94–100
coffee marketing 12
coffee planting 7, 38–9, 128, 144, 294, 317
  an income-induced expansion in savings 39
  an investment 36–9
  copying and errors in expectation 136
  input requirements 107–9
  investment in 40–1
  Kilimanjaro (Tanzania) 65
  motivation for 37
  and price expectations 96
  regrets 36–7, 38
  renewal of planting restrictions 11
  social pay-off 135

coffee production 292
  increase in 126, 127; socially beneficial in Kenya 150
  statistics **86**
coffee production function 85–90
  model estimation for 137–9
coffee quotas 150
  Kenya 134–5
coffee rehabilitation programme 11
coffee sales and the black market 169–70
coffee smuggling 126–7
coffee tax 2, 7, 135, 294, 295
  Tanzania 43
coffee and tea trees, gestation periods 75
coffee uprooting 65, 215
commercial banks, access to 22
commodity market
  rationed 161–2
  unrationed 159, 161–2
commodity markets 11–15
commodity price instability 1
complementary activities 214
complementary inputs, lacking in Tanzanian health sector 292
composite index 214
consumer goods
  availability related to future cash crop supply 218
  and the black market 169–70
  non-agricultural, availability of in rural areas 1
  Tanzania: allocation of 295; availability of in rural areas 2, 3, 155–6; supply improved 220
consumer goods availability index 214
consumer goods market, Tanzania 48–53
consumer goods shortages (Tanzania), influence of 214
controlled prices, below market clearing levels 154
controls, relaxation of in Kenya 10–11
convergence criterion 138
copying, an alternative process of decision 149
copying effect 133, 134, 135–6, 147, 149, 294
cost-plus pricing 45–6
credit
  informal 8, 142
  opportunity cost of 38
  to finance coffee planting 38–9
credit constraints, relaxed by boom 2
credit market 23
  formal 22; Tanzania 48
  informal 21–2, 112; Tanzania, more active 48
  rural 293
crop and livestock income, subsistence and marketed 25
crop marketing 164, 165, 207

Kenya 12, **13–14**
Tanzania 46
crop prices
  relative changes in 7
  Tanzania 45–6
crop production 181–9
cropping pattern, changes in 313–14
crops
  drought-resistant, and pricing policy 46
  new 44

demand
  effective 196
  excess 216–17; measure of 173, 177
demand and supply prices, gap between 227
depopulation, Tanzania 44
depression (1930s), and coffee growing 10
diseases, major 231
distribution index 216–17
diversification 103
  of income 25, **26**, 27
drinking water, and illness 232–3, **251–2**
drought 58, 59

earnings
  off-shamba 34
  raised by education, training, and experience 92–4
ecology, an entry barrier 105–6, 109
economic rent, and access to services 225
economies of scale 2, 72, 78, *79*, 80, 83, 88, 96, 294
economy of scale activities, influences on entry to 78–81
education 117, 119, 124, 229, 235–6, 323–4
  attainment in primary and secondary schools 235–6, **262**
  cash costs of 279, 280
  and health 232, **249**
  importance attached to 238
  incremental, costs and benefits compared 283–4
  lower attainment in Tanzania 241
  potential for raising agricultural output high 281–4
  rural valuation of Kenya 280; Tanzania 280
  see also primary education; secondary education
education costs, Tanzania 241, 242, **276**
educational level, and time allocation 239, **273–4**
employment
  Kenya, low in non-agricultural sector 8
  non-agricultural, expansion of due to the boom 148
  urban, income-enhancing effects of expansion in 31–2

endowment ratios **19**, 21, **48**
endowments 110
  differences in 78–81; effect of 207–8
  diversion of 38–9
  increase in total 83
  proxies 111, 112, 115–16, 118
entry barriers 76, 80, 95, 105–22, 294, 306
  access to the labour market 118–22
  adoption of tree crops 109–16
  adoption of improved livestock 116–18
  preserving inequalities 84
  and price increase 38
  to high-return activities 72, 109
  to more profitable activities 2
  to non-agricultural wage labour 76–7
expectations
  rational 206
  specification of 164–5
  and supply response 215–16
expenditure, actual and expected 207
expenditure weights 217
export crop agriculture 9
export crop income 143
export crop marketing system, Kenya 12
export taxation 1–2
extended family 23, 304
  assignment of labour 118–21
  and family credit 22, 23
  and urban wage employment 130–1
extended family social network 124
extended household 23, 304
extension advice, impact of 283
extension services 81, 115, 124, 241
  seen as beneficial 293
  Tanzania 44

factor intensities 78
factor markets 8–9, 94–5, 141–2
  absence of 80
  imperfect 72
  Kenya: changes since Independence 15–23; do not accommodate difference in endowment ratios 21
  structure of 47–53
factor proportions
  as entry barriers 107–9
  maize and coffee 107, **108**
  scale economies and specialization 79
factors
  returns to 78–80, 94–105
  self-employed 95
  shadow price of, differs across holdings 95
factory-gate distribution data 179–80, 217
family labour
  opportunity cost of 98
  shadow price of 98–100
family network (extended family) 147
family social networks 120–1

FAO survey, Tanzania 58, 62
farm income, Tanzania, retreat into subsistence activities 62
farm investment 41
fertilizer, use of increased during the boom 41
financial markets, participation in proxied 112
food cropping 34
food crops 24, 85
  acquisition of cultivation techniques 106
  Tanzania 181, 189, **194**
food growing 102, 157
food markets 141
food, output and marketing data unreliable 215
food prices, Tanzania, variation in 49
food-marketing system, Kenya 12
foodstuffs, availability of, Tanzania 49, **50**
forecasting errors 207
foreign exchange
  allocations of, Tanzania 154
  and import of consumer goods 220
free-rider decision process 133
free-rider opportunities 72–3
free-riding 111, 115, 149
freedom of movement, restricted, Tanzania 45

Gauss–Newton algorithm 137, 138
gearing effect 294
German colonization 44
good health 232, **248**
goods
  access to 160
  availability of 174–7, 178–9, 214; Tanzania 327–8
  distribution of 171–81, 182–4
goods market rationing
  and production of peasant cash crops econometric models 189, 194; effect on current and next period production 194–9, 202, 216
  Tanzania 174–7
government services, ranking of 236–7, **266–7**
governments
  affecting/influencing peasants 1–2, 3, 291
  interventions by 45, 141, 294
grower (proxy) 110–11

health 241, 318–23
health care 229, 233–5, **253–8**
  Tanzania 240
health care data, implications of 235
health facilities 232, 237, **249**
  distance from inhibits use 286–7
  Kenya 292
  Tanzania 239, 240, **249**
  type of 234, **256–8**
  use of 286, 287

health provision, and morbidity 284–7
health services 3, 296
   valuation of: rural Kenya 279–80; Tanzania 280
hired labour 16, 74, 98, 123, 305
   discouraged in Tanzania 47, 62
   expense of 128
   increase in employment and wage rates 82
   increased during coffee boom 41
   peasant holdings 132
   on smallholdings 15–17, 21
hired labour market 141, 148
   small 98, 99
hoe technology 15
holding, defined 304
holdings
   size of, Kenya 122, 123
   sub-division of 122, 123, 124
Household Budget Survey (HBS), Tanzania, weights 175, **176**, **181**, 196, 203, 217
household composition 306–10
household, concepts of 8, 23, 302–4
household heads, allocation of time 238–9, **271–2**
household income, measurement of 23–7
household labour, opportunity costs 98
household size
   increase in and entry barriers 123–4
   Kenya 122–4
households
   coffee-growing 99–100
   differing in endowments 78–81; and preferences 207–10
   hiring labour 98
   income composition of **141**
   land and labour endowment 94
   only in official market 211, 212
   participation in black markets 167
   selling labour 98
   urban, gaining from coffee boom 74
housing improvements 129
housing, investment in 40
hut tax 9, 44
hybrid maize 305
   and family labour 98
   inter-cropped or pure-stand 90
   unit cost function 97
hybrid maize production 84–5
hybrid maize production function (Kenya) 278

ill health
   distribution of 229
   male and female patterns 232, **247**
   Nyanza **246–7**
illness
   by age, sex, and symptom 232, 250
   cost of: Kenya 279; Tanzania 280
ILO–University of Daar es Salaam rural survey 58

imitation 124
import restrictions, Tanzania 295
improved livestock 85, 125, 136, 143
   as an asset 128–9
   barriers to adoption of 116–18
   determinants of adoption 116–18
   returns to 100–1
improved livestock production function 91–2, **93**
incentive effect (consumer goods) 214
incentive goods 197–8, 204
incentive weighting scheme 199
incentive weights 177, **179**, **183**
incentives, measure of 174
income
   actual and planned 209
   analysis of changes in 34–6
   negative 25
   per capita *see* per capita income
   permanent increase in through investment 82
   permanent and transient 146
   real: comparison of changes in 142–3; Tanzania, decline in 62, 63, 143
   sources of 34
   and structure of 24–7
   Tanzania 61–2; changes in composition (1969–1982/3) **62**; structure of 63
   see also peasant income
income changes 81–3
   Kenya (1974–82) 27–36
   Tanzania (1969–83) 43, 55–65
income concept 304–6
income effect 120, 121, 205
   leisure-enhancing 212–13
income effect and labour supply 218
income fluidity 42
income gain 213
income mobility 33–4, 126
income shocks 126
   Kenyan peasants 7
income windfall *see* windfall income
indivisibilities 2, 72
industry (small), investment in 40
information 294
   differential, effects of (proxies) 110–11, 112, 114–15, 118
   full 76
   role of in enhancing performance 281–3
information effect 147
informational barriers 106–7, 109, 110–11
inheritance and mean holding size 20
inpatient costs 234, 235, **259–60**
inpatient data compared 242, **276**
inpatient facilities/services
   higher Tanzanian usage 240
   value of 280
inpatient stays 321–2
   valuation of 279

input availability index 214
inputs 214, 305
   augmented 88
   cash expenditure on (proxied) 111–12
   deterioration in availability of 143
   and expenditure 196–7
   improved livestock 92, 118
   maize 91
   purchased 74, 75, 95, 305
   substitution among 76
inputs index 214
Integrated Agricultural Development Programme, loan programme 22
intercropping 66, 85, 90
International Coffee Agreement 135
   effects of 150
investment 7, 76, 94, 111, 116
   diversion of 75
   increase in 74–5
   intra-activity and activity switching 34–6
   peasant 2
   triggered by windfall income 82–3, 84
investment behaviour, Kenya and Tanzania compared 144–6

job opportunities, intensive and extensive rationing of 76–8
job rationing, changes in extensive and intensive margins 125–6

Kenya
   coffee price increase passed to peasants 2
   high investment rate of coffee growers 144, **145**, 146
   household valuation of health services 279–80
   no windfall coffee tax 7
   peasant response to coffee boom 296
   peasants and price volatility 2
   price change responses 84–136; barriers to entry 105–22; coffee boom as an instrument of change 122–36; comparison of returns in activities 94–105; production functions for major activities 85–94
   rural data 244
   social desirability of coffee adoption 149–50
Kenya, peasant farming in (1974–82) 7–42
   changes in income (1974–82) 27–36
   evolution of peasant economy before the coffee boom 9–11
   peasant behaviour during the coffee boom 36–42
   peasant income, structure of (1982) 23–7
   structure of product and factor markets 11–23
Kenya Tea Development Authority (KTDA) 10, 12
   extension service 115

kin
   and job acquisition 147
   and wage employment 119, 120
Kipande system of labour registration 9
knowledge
   differences in 81; as an entry barrier 106–7, 109, 110–11

labour
   differences in endowments 208
   efforts to reduce supply price of 9
   hired and household 88
   hiring of, effect of ambiguous 17
   own 99; diversion of 75; improved livestock 100; use of during boom 41–2
   reallocation from coffee to food in Tanzania 66
labour hiring
   by peasants 17
   limited (peasants) 21
   restricted, Tanzania 45
labour market
   access to 118–22
   casual 101; effect of coffee boom 41
   non-agricultural, earnings in 118
   rural, peasant participation of little value 20
labour sales 17–18
   non-peasant labour market 17–18
labour supply, Kenya **288**
labour transactions, effect of on farm factor proportions 18–20
labour/leisure substitution 76
Lagrange multipliers 77
land 88
   not widely used as collateral 21–2
   rented out 17
   shadow return to 97
   Tanzania: less important as a differentiating endowment 55; reallocation through rental 46
land abundance 46, 47–8
land area, changes in 312–13
land distribution, stable in Tanzania 46
land exchange 20
land holdings, privatization of in Kenya 15
land law
   and land policy, Kenya, in state of flux 22
   traditional, and land reallocation 15
land purchase 20, 40, 41
land rental market, and equalization of factor proportions **18, 19**, 20–1
land sales, Kenya 15
land transactions, Kenya 8
land-to-labour endowment ratio 78–9, 80
learning 124
leisure 21, 157, 158, 166, 167, 205
   and income, marginal utilities 77
life cycle effects 111, 116, 125
live births 322–3

livestock 24, 34, 53, 72, 102, 103, 314
  as assets 125
  improved *see* improved livestock
  Kenya, African production limited 10
living standards, Tanzania, decline in 58, 65, 143

maize 9, 140
  see also hybrid maize
maize production function
  Kenya 90–1
  Tanzania 278
maize trading, Kenya 12
market failure, sources of in developing countries 153
market imperfections 2, 78
market stability 170
marketing co-operatives
  and peasant finance 22
  Tanzania 44
marketing policies, Tanzania 45–6
markets
  official and black, combined size of 174
  official and unofficial 153
Marquardt–Levenberg algorithm 91, 137, 138
Mau Mau revolt 10
medical attention, need for and health service access 3
migration 10, 23
  current 309–10
  and the extended family 118–19, 121
  Kenya: male, temporary 15; rural–urban 15
  less in Tanzania 55
  past 308
  speculative 147
  work-related 121
milk production 92
monetary accumulation 171, 172
monetary economy, and a black market 169–70
money balances 165
money stock 216
  cost of an increment in 161
  peasant households 158
  rationed and unrationed 161–2
money stock constraint 160, 161
money supply excess 295
money, utility of 160
morbidity 3, 229
  assessment of 244–5
  Kenya 230–3, **246–52**
  and labour supply 287–9
  Tanzania 239–40, 242, **246–52**, 275
myopic peasant hypothesis 1
  rejected 148

National Cereal and Produce Board (NCPB), Kenya 12

national consumer price index, Tanzania, as income deflator 60–1
neighbourhood networks 146–7
neighbours, as channels of information 81
nomadic pastoralism 9
non-coffee growers, boom-induced windfall benefits 129–32
non-farm income sources, Tanzania 58
non-resident household 23–4, 55
  defined 304
Nyanza region (Kenya)
  accumulation of activities and per capita income *103*
  coffee production, lower level of inputs 86–7
  decline in real per capita income 27, 31, **33**
  higher morbidity 235
  inpatient costs 234, **259–60**
  land area and per capita income 27, **30**
  migration from 121
  outpatient care/costs 234, 235, **253–8**
  post-coffee boom survey 7, 300–1, 302–33

official prices, Tanzania 45
oil shock 132
one-way fixed effects model 189
one-way random effects model 189, 194, 198, **199**
Operation Maduka 48–9
out-migration 20–1, 122
outcomes, divergences in (1975–83) 142–6
  explained 146–50
outpatient care, Tanzania vs. Kenya 240
outpatient costs 235
  and per capita income 233–4, **253–4**
  Tanzania 242, **275–6**
outpatient services, valuation of 279
outpatient visits 318–21
output effects, direct, of public services 281–4
output, prices and shortages, Tanzania *200–2*
outputs, relative prices of 95
overproduction, Tanzania 45

parallel markets
  Tanzania 46, **47**
  unreliable 49, 50
peasant agricultural production (Kenya) **31**
peasant economies, Kenya and Tanzania (1975) 140–2
peasant economy
  direct price control dangerous 296
  evolution of 8
  Kenya: evolution of before the coffee boom 9–11; secular trends 8
  Tanzania: changes and collapse in income 66–7; changes during the coffee boom 43; evolution of pre-coffee boom 44–5
peasant finance, sources of 22–3

peasant households
  data on 3
  simple model 158–64
peasant income
  Kenya: changes in (1974–82) 27–36; structure of (1982) 23–7
  Tanzania: changes in (1969–83) 55–65; structure of (1983) 53–5
peasant money demand 170
peasant supply response under shortages, theory of
  basic model 157–64
  rent-seeking 165–72
  specification of expectations 164–5
peasantry, prosperous, commercial, development of 10–11
peasants, and price boom 1, 2
per capita income 24
  real, changes in 27
  Tanzania changes in composition of 58–9; collapse in 150; resident households **57**, 58, 59–60
perception weights 196
perceptions, an accurate guide 218
pesticides 76
piped water 292–3
  communal: a health risk 232–3, **251–2**; Tanzania 240
  effect of 3
  time spent fetching 288–9
planned cash incomes, differences in 208–10
poll tax 9
population growth
  Kenya 8, 122
  Tanzania, and fall in per capita income 184, 189
portfolio adjustment effect 34–6
portfolio composition effect 34–6
preferences, differences in 210
preventive measures 233
price changes
  boom-induced 74–5
  relative, and resource reallocation 74–6
price controls 214, 294, 295
  on consumer goods 153–4
price deflator 61
price effects, role of 202–3
price expectations 38, 95–6, 133
  altered by coffee boom 96
price, perverse response to 157–8
price regulation 291
  effects of inflexibilities 12
  inefficient and stable, Tanzania 295–6
price stabilization 1, 148, 293
prices
  actual and virtual 217
  relative, temporary indirect changes 75–6
  Tanzania: nationally controlled 154; rural, rise in 61

pricing, pan-territorial, problem of 154
pricing policies 45–6
primary education 287, 293
  benefits of expansion 291–2
  impact of **282**, 283
primary schools 237
private goods, cost of waiting for service 225
producer prices 1, 95
  coffee (1976–7) 126
  coffee and tea 7, **37**
  decline in 27, **32**
  increase in 167–8
  Tanzania: depressed 53; real, decline in 46
product markets 8–9
  structure of 11–15, 45–7
product prices, fall in, Tanzania 189
production decisions 215
production functions 84
  coffee growing 85–9, **90**
  improved livestock 91–2
  maize 90–1
  wage employment 92–4
production, inhibited 214
production for sale, Tanzania, stagnation or decline 55, **57**
profitability 97–8
public investment of private income 40
public service input, measures of 277–8
public service provision, analysis of effects of 277–89
  direct output effects 281–4
  health provision, morbidity and labour supply 284–9
  implicit household valuations 278–81
public services 223–8
  access to 243; costly 225–6
  allocation of 224
  costs of related to household payment 227
  distribution of in Kenya and Tanzania 229–43; survey design 229–30
  expansion would be appreciated and beneficial 291–2
  Kenya 230–9
  provision of 1, 3
  Tanzania: compared with Kenya 239–41; urban and rural access compared 241–3
  user costs 243
  valuation of 227–8; with free access to a fixed ration 223–4
  valuation procedure 225–6
purchases, subject to double constraint 160
purchasing patterns (Tanzania), pre-rationing 175, 177

quantity rationing 12
queueing costs 226

racketeering 296
rationing 45, 49–50, 167, 214, 215–16

availability of goods 2, 3, 174–7
consumer goods market 43
crop production 181–9
distribution of goods 177–81
measurement of and peasant response 173–9
on official markets 52
and peasant response, measurement of 173–9
supply responses to 216
rationing problem, solution for 220
rationing system, village level, Tanzania 49
recollection weights **178, 182**, 198, 199
remittances 23, 24, 31, 53, 55, 59–60, 62, 140, 306
increased in Tanzania 63
rent-seeking 165–72, 296
expenditure on 165
rent-seeking activities 225
rents, randomly available, persistence of 171
resident household 23, 24, 55, 304
income structure of (Kenya) 24–5
resource allocation, by unrationed households 77–8
resource reallocation 15, 75–6, 83, 84
Tanzania 150
resources
changes in deployment of 7
substitution of among existing activities 75–6
road improvements 236, 237
Tanzania 241
rural areas, declining availability of goods 50–2, **53**
rural household budget surveys 7–8
IRS1, picture of peasant economy pre-coffee boom 7, 91, 123
IRS3 7–8, 32–3
IRS4 123
rural landlessness 122, 123
rural surveys
definitions and concepts used 302–6
Kenya 85
Tanzania 57–65
rural and urban survey, Tanzania 244
Rybczynski effect 83

savings 2, 38, 41, 72, 143, 293
refused by banks 134
savings rates, Kenya 82
school fees 39, 41
search 165–72
time costs of 165
seasonal labour 15–16
secondary education
benefits of expansion less clear 292
cash costs of (Kenya) 279
impact of **282**, 283
rationed in Tanzania 280

security of tenure (peasants) 10
sembe subsidy 45–6
settler agriculture, Tanzania 44
settler farms, bought out 11
shadow prices 97
shadow wage rate 98, 226, 278
rural, Kenya 278
shadow wages 277
and crop profitability 97–8
own labour 96
Tanzania 280
shamba, the 328–33
area and tenure 328–9
crops marketed 331–2
crops produced 329–31
livestock 332–3
shifting cultivation 44
shops, investment in 40
shortages
consequences of emergence of 164
effect of on marginal utilities, leisure, and consumption *160*
peasant supply response 163–4
rural areas, Tanzania 154–5
sisal 9
slavery 44
smallholders, hiring of labour 16–17
smuggling 170
social network
closed and bounded 120–1
importance of 146–7
social space 147–8
importance in determining activity choice 148
narrowness of for peasant households 149
soil conservation 10, 44
specialization *79*
stabilization policy 1–2
state control, Tanzania 48–9
student costs 236, **263–5**
subsistence 9, 62, 305
replacing cash 63
subsistence agriculture 9
subsistence crops 205
subsistence income 25, 58–9
Tanzania 55
substitution 42, 75
elasticity of 88
substitution effect 167, 168, 205
supply, absolute level of 173
supply measure, based on factory-gate distribution 179–80
supply response 167, 171–2, 173–204
black market and rationing, similarities 170
crop prices and availability, differences in 168, **169**
cross-section tests 205–13; design of a testable hypothesis 205–10; and expectations 215–16

supply response (cont.)
  measurement of rationing and peasant response 173–9
  of peasant economy 168
  and rationing 204
supply–response function 167, 206–10, 213
  black-market component 211–12
  non-black-market component 211
surpluses, Tanzania 45, 46
Swynnerton Plan 10–11
symptom list 230, 244–5
symptoms 231, **246**

Tanzania
  administrative structure of villages 59
  black market 154
  collapse of per capita income 150
  decline in producer price of coffee 144
  decline in real per capita income 142–3
  education costs 241
  effects of government policies 2
  exchange rate over-valued 295
  health facilities poor 286, 292
  household valuation of health services 280
  investment rates of coffee and non-coffee growers 145
  land endowment 141
  less primary schooling 292
  outpatient costs **253–8**
  price control policy on consumer goods 294
  ranking of government services 241
  rationing 173–4; rural 158
  reductions in rural real cash incomes 209
  rural population, relocation of 2
  shift away from commercialized peasant production 45
  urban and rural access compared 241–3, 248, 253–5, **259**, **263**, **275**
Tanzania, peasant farming in (1969–83) 43–67
  evolution of peasant economy prior to the coffee boom 44–5
  income changes (1969–83) 55–65
  peasant behaviour during the coffee boom 65–7
  peasant income, structure of in 1983 53–5
  product and factor markets, structure of 45–53
Tanzania Rural Development Bank (TRDB) 48
Tanzanian peasants, wider opportunities 44
taxation, complex double system of, Tanzania 295
tea 9, 10, 85
  world prices high 7
tea adoption 112, 114, 116, 134
tea marketing, Kenya 12
tea planting 37, 38, 39, 96, 294

techniques
  changes in 76
  new 81
tenancy 20, 141–2
terms of trade, deterioration in for peasants 153
threshold problems 109
  coffee planting 38
time, allocation of (related to public policy) 237–9, **268–74**
time and cash costs, services, Kenya and Tanzania 278, **279**
tradable goods, shortages of, Tanzania 295
trade, long-distance 9, 44
trade shocks, reaction to 1–2
tree crop planting 96
  copying effect 135–6
tree crops 85
  barriers to adoption of 109–16
  effect of investment 75

unit cost function, defined 95
unit cost functions 84, 94–8
unofficial market, supplied by official market 180–1
urban claim on resources, Tanzania 52, **53**, 63–5
urban and rural incomes, Tanzania, comparison of trends in 64
user costs
  of free services 229
  and main public services 280–1

valuation placed by householders on services 277, 278–81
vehicles, investment in 40
villagization programme 46
  health vs. education 292

wage activities, non-agricultural 140
wage employment 22, 104
  agricultural 25, 119
  boom-induced 131
  eases cash constraints 23
  expansion 125–6; effect of 83
  non-agricultural 25, 72, 85, 110, 111, 115, 124; access to 147; determinants of access to 121–2; entry barriers 125; return to labour in 99; rural 120
  off-farm 310–11
  urban 23, 120; increased opportunities for 82, 130, **131**
wage employment production function 92–4
wage income 31, 103–4
  decline in 62
  sources of 25
  Tanzania 143
wage income only 104

wage labour 10, 85
  casual 132
  non-agricultural 98
  on shambas 120
wage labour market 103
  urban, returns higher 101
wage rates 98
  agricultural 74; increase in 75–6
wages 24, 41, 53, 54, 55, 60, 140
  urban, reduction in (Tanzania) 65
waiting times 242
water fetching, time spent on 237, **288**
water source, and morbidity 240
water supply 237, 324–5
  Tanzania 241
weighting schemes 175, 177, 196–9, 217
  negative price effect 203
wheat 9
White Highlands, Kenya 9
white settlement, Kenya 9
windfall income 1, 143, 144
  and asset formation 38–9, 76
  and coffee entry threshold 38
  helping to overcome credit restraints 72
  investment and activity-specific returns 76–83
  investment rate 129–30
  movement from lower to higher return activities 76
  uses of **39**, 40–1, 127–30
windfall investment 143, 143–5
  in new higher return activities 134
  in productive activities 82–3
windfall savings rate, peasant economy (Kenya) 136
women
  bias against 112
  important in tea growing 116, 134
  reduced probability of non-shamba activity 119
  work harder than men 238
wood supply 325–6
work 310–12
world commodity boom, effect of 10